Vice President of Editorial	Melissa Wagner
Director of Acquisitions	Mikaela Felty
Director of Book Development	Jocelynn Hessler
Production Manager	Mike Brehm
Cover Design	Jose Rosado

Published in the United States of America by
IGI Global Scientific Publishing
701 East Chocolate Avenue
Hershey, PA, 17033, USA
Tel: 717-533-8845 | Fax: 717-533-7115
Website: https://www.igi-global.com E-mail: cust@igi-global.com

Library of Congress Cataloging-in-Publication Data

(CIP Data Pending)
ISBN13: 9798260014981
Isbn13Softcover: 9798260014998
EISBN13: 9798260015001
British Cataloguing in Publication Data
A Cataloguing in Publication record for this book is available from the British Library.

Table of Contents

Detailed Table of Contents

Concept practice of incident response has undergone a profound transformation. and sheer volume security incidents have necessitated a shift from traditional manual methods to advanced, automated, and AI-driven solutions. Understanding this evolution is crucial seeking defend effectively operational ever-morphing cyber adversaries. Incident response (IR) in its earliest form was largely a manual process. The foundational approach centered around human analysts detecting, analyzing, and mitigating security incidents without significant technological assistance. In the nascent days of networked computing, the threat landscape was relatively simpler and less dynamic. Organizations primarily dealt with isolated incidents such as unauthorized access attempts or rudimentary malware infections. During this period, incident response was often reactive and ad hoc. Security teams relied heavily on manual log reviews, rule-based intrusion detection systems (IDS), and straightforward signatures to detect known threats.

As cyber threats become more advanced and frequent, traditional intrusion detection and prevention systems (IDPS)—which rely heavily on static rules and known attack signatures—are no longer sufficient for protecting modern digital infrastructures. These conventional systems often fail to detect novel or zero-day threats and struggle to provide real-time response capabilities. To address these limitations, real-time threat detection combined with Artificial Intelligence (AI)-driven intrusion prevention has emerged as a powerful approach in cybersecurity. AI technologies, enhance IDPS by enabling systems to learn from historical data, recognize complex patterns, and

The infusion of AI (Artificial Intelligence) into industrial cyber security has been a major step indeed significantly improving the identification of threats, the automation of reactions, and the protection of infrastructure, which is considered essential. However, this scientific and technological breakthrough has facilitated the rise of a number of ethical and legal issues that should be reckoned with in order to ensure the responsible implementation of this new technology and the effective oversight of all operations. The domain of ethical considerations focuses on the issues of privacy, responsibility, bias, clarity, and the extent of human supervision with AI systems making independent decisions in most of the critical situations. The lack of transparency in AI decision-making may lead to distrust, and the biases in the training data could cause the AI to be biased or not to find security gaps. Legally, the rapid development of AI in the field of cyber security tests the current frameworks and raises questions of responsibility in the event of system failures, cyber security incidents, and data protection regulations being violated. Moreover, the problems with the security of AI such as being attacked by the adversaries and becoming vulnerable have also been identified as not only the threats to the integrity of industrial systems but also to public safety. The purpose of this study is to explore the ethical and legal problems by examining the common issues between AI and industrial cyber security and proposing solutions to lower the risks using transparency, accountability, and proper regulation. An equitable strategy is necessary to leverage AI's full potential in safeguarding industrial settings and preventing possible negative effects while still adhering to the changes in legal regulations.

This chapter analyses the fusion of cyber-physical systems (CPS) with the industrial control system (ICS) ecosystem, emphasising their significance in industrial automation and Industry 4.0. The blend of physical systems with monitoring, computing, and communication capabilities, allows for real-time updating, control, and optimization of processes like monitoring, control, and optimization. ICS encapsulates systems like SCADA, PLC, and DCS that are typically found in critical infrastructure and industrial processes. The discussion is centred on the enhancements in intelligence, adaptability, and connectivity that CPS integrates into ICS. Key discussion points include system architecture, communication protocols, security gaps, AI and machine learning on process automation and threat detection, and warfare concepts. Smart manufacturing and energy systems, autonomous infrastructure, and real-world case studies and applications are provided.

In the digital era of today, where industrial systems are largely dependent upon interconnectivity, the importance of good cybersecurity is now at an all-time high. The entry of Machine Learning (ML) into industrial cybersecurity denotes a paradigm shift that provides added capabilities for detecting, preventing, and remediating cyber-attacks. This chapter proceeds to discuss the significance of ML in securing industrial environments, highlighting the shortcomings of conventional cybersecurity practices while elucidating the benefits of adaptive, intelligent security frameworks. ML is the proactive approach that augments every aspect of threat detection and response through data insights, anomaly detection, and predictive analytics. This chapter introduces the ML basic principles in the cybersecurity domain, importance of ML, ML applications with industrial cybersecurity such as intrusion detection,

The integration of IoT in healthcare has enabled remote patient monitoring and timely diagnosis. However, safeguarding medical data is critical, making Intrusion Detection Systems (IDS) essential for data confidentiality and accuracy. Any alteration in patient records can result in misdiagnosis or life-threatening outcomes. With the large and dynamic nature of healthcare data, machine learning offers a robust solution for intrusion detection. This study introduces a blockchain-enabled IDS for IoT-based healthcare systems, ensuring secure data transmission and intrusion detection. The proposed anomaly-based IDS involves three stages: preprocessing (cleaning and normalization), feature selection using Walrus Optimization Algorithm (WaOA), and classification via Improved Hunter Prey Optimizer-based Stack Deep Polynomial Network (IHPO-SDPN). Evaluated on WUSTL-EHMS-2020 and two Kaggle datasets, the model achieved 99.81% sensitivity, 99.84% specificity, 99.84% precision, 99.83% accuracy, and an excellent F1-score.

Anomaly detection in IoT-based sensor networks is critical for ensuring medical data integrity and uninterrupted healthcare services. This chapter explores machine learning (ML) techniques to identify irregularities in sensor behavior, signal degradation, and potential cyber-physical threats in eco-friendly medical devices. A taxonomy of anomalies—point, contextual, and collective—is presented, correlating them with health data streams and environmental interference. Various ML approaches, including supervised, unsupervised, and hybrid models like Isolation Forests, Autoencoders, and spatiotemporal Graph Neural Networks (GNNs), are examined for healthcare sensor networks. The discussion also covers energy-efficient deployment strategies for ML models on resource-constrained edge devices. The proposed frameworks aim

Preface

The rapid evolution of digital technologies has transformed the way critical infrastructure systems are designed, operated, and secured. As industries embrace interconnected ecosystems driven by artificial intelligence, machine learning, the Internet of Things, and cyber-physical systems, the complexity and vulnerability of these environments have increased significantly. This transformation has made intelligent cyber defense not only a technical necessity but also a strategic imperative for ensuring resilience, reliability, and sustainability across sectors such as energy, healthcare, manufacturing, and transportation.

This volume presents a comprehensive exploration of emerging paradigms, methodologies, and technologies that are shaping the future of cybersecurity in critical infrastructure. It brings together contributions that examine both foundational concepts and cutting-edge innovations, ranging from predictive maintenance enabled by digital twins to advanced threat detection mechanisms powered by artificial intelligence. The chapters collectively emphasize the transition from reactive security practices to proactive, adaptive, and intelligent defense frameworks.

A key theme throughout this book is the integration of interdisciplinary approaches. Cybersecurity is no longer confined to traditional network defense; it now encompasses data analytics, behavioral modeling, blockchain technologies, ethical considerations, and legal frameworks. The convergence of operational technology and information technology further underscores the need for unified security strategies capable of addressing diverse and evolving threat landscapes.

In addition to technological advancements, this book also highlights critical challenges, including explainability of AI systems, data privacy concerns, ethical implications of automation, and the complexities of securing decentralized and anonymized environments such as the dark web. By addressing these issues, the volume aims to foster a deeper understanding of both the opportunities and risks associated with intelligent cyber defense.

The contributions included here are intended for researchers, practitioners, policymakers, and students seeking to advance their knowledge in cybersecurity and critical infrastructure protection. Through a balanced presentation of theory, practical applications, and future directions, this book aspires to serve as a valuable resource in navigating the increasingly complex domain of intelligent cyber defense.

CHAPTER OVERVIEW

Chapter 1 introduces the role of digital twin technology in enabling predictive maintenance and enhancing cyber resilience through real-time monitoring, simulation, and vulnerability assessment.

Chapter 2 examines the evolution of incident response from manual processes to AI-driven automated remediation, highlighting the need for rapid and scalable solutions to modern cyber threats.

Chapter 3 explores real-time, AI-powered intrusion detection systems designed to identify and respond to sophisticated and zero-day attacks with greater speed and accuracy.

Chapter 4 discusses the challenges associated with explainable artificial intelligence in security decision-making, focusing on transparency, trust, and accountability.

Chapter 5 presents a multidisciplinary approach to detecting illicit activities on the dark web using artificial intelligence, blockchain analysis, and web scraping techniques.

Chapter 6 analyzes the ethical and legal implications of deploying artificial intelligence in industrial cybersecurity, including issues of bias, privacy, and governance.

Chapter 7 investigates the integration of cyber-physical systems with industrial control systems, emphasizing their role in automation, connectivity, and security within critical infrastructure.

Chapter 8 highlights machine learning-driven strategies for strengthening cyber defense in industrial environments through predictive analytics and adaptive threat detection.

Chapter 9 focuses on real-time threat detection and AI-driven intrusion prevention systems tailored for IoT-based healthcare environments.

Chapter 10 describes intelligent threat hunting and behavior-based malware detection techniques for identifying advanced persistent threats in medical IoT systems.

Chapter 11 proposes advanced feature selection and deep learning techniques for securing electronic health records through intrusion detection systems.

Chapter 12 explores machine learning methods for anomaly detection in sensor networks, with an emphasis on efficiency and sustainability in healthcare IoT applications.

Chapter 13 examines security frameworks that support the integration of operational technology and information technology, addressing challenges and opportunities in unified cybersecurity strategies.

Together, these chapters provide a cohesive and forward-looking perspective on intelligent cyber defense, offering insights that are both theoretically robust and practically relevant in safeguarding the infrastructures that underpin modern society.

Editors

Chin-Shiuh Shieh
National Kaohsiung University of Science and Technology, Taiwan

Pawan Kumar Goel
Raj Kumar Goel Institute of Technology, India

Mong-Fong Horng
National Kaohsiung University of Science and Technology, Taiwan

Chapter 1
Role of Digital Twins in Predictive Maintenance and Cyber Resilience

Rampelli Manojkumar
http://orcid.org/0000-0002-8141-0321
BVRIT HYDERABAD College of Engineering for Women, India

N. Srinivasarao
http://orcid.org/0000-0003-1969-1940
BVRIT HYDERABAD College of Engineering for Women, India

Aravinda Swamy Konda
Malla Reddy College of Engineering and Technology, India

Krishna Prasad Uppuleti
Malla Reddy College of Engineering and Technology, India

T. Aditya Sai Srinivas
Ravindra College of Engineering for Women, India

Gumpu Srinivasulu
http://orcid.org/0000-0001-6610-5612
Maulana Azad National Institute of Technology, India

ABSTRACT

The advent of Industry 4.0 has accelerated the integration of digital twin (DT) technology, predictive maintenance (PdM), and cyber resilience as pivotal tools for optimizing industrial and infrastructure systems. DTs which are the dynamic virtual replicas of physical assets enable real-time monitoring, simulation, and data-driven decision-making. Concurrently, DTs enhance cyber resilience by identifying vulnerabilities, simulating cyberattacks, and enabling adaptive defenses, as evidenced by applications in critical infrastructure and global supply chains. Despite their potential, challenges persist, including data silos, model inaccuracies, and cybersecurity risks inherent to interconnected systems. Emerging trends such as quantum computing, federated learning, and autonomous self-healing systems promise to address these

DOI: 10.4018/979-8-2600-1498-1.ch001

limitations while driving sustainability and operational efficiency. By synthesizing technical foundations, real-world applications, and future directions, this chapter underscores the imperative of integrating DTs into holistic frameworks.

INTRODUCTION

The rapid evolution of Industry 4.0 has ushered in an era of interconnected systems, where physical assets, processes, and infrastructures are increasingly digitized and integrated with advanced technologies (Hermann et al., 2016). This transformation has amplified the need for innovative solutions to address two critical challenges: maintaining operational efficiency through predictive maintenance (PdM) and safeguarding systems against cyber threats via cyber resilience. At the intersection of these challenges lies digital twin (DT) technology—a transformative tool that enables real-time monitoring, simulation, and decision-making for complex systems. This section introduces the foundational concepts of DTs, PdM, and cyber resilience, explores their interdependencies, and highlights their collective importance in modern industrial and infrastructure management.

Digital Twins: A Paradigm Shift in System Management

A DT is a dynamic, virtual representation of a physical entity, process, or system, synchronized through continuous data exchange from sensors, IoT devices, and other data sources (Grieves & Vickers, 2017). First conceptualized by Dr. Michael Grieves in 2003, DTs have evolved from theoretical models to indispensable tools in aerospace, manufacturing, energy, and urban planning. Their architecture typically comprises three core components:

1. Physical Entity: The real-world asset (e.g., a wind turbine, manufacturing robot, or power grid).
2. Virtual Model: A computational replica enriched with physics-based simulations, machine learning algorithms, and historical data.
3. Data Linkage: Bidirectional data flows enabled by IoT, cloud computing, and edge computing (Tao et al., 2018).

By integrating AI and big data analytics, DTs provide insights into system performance, enabling stakeholders to predict failures, optimize operations, and test scenarios in a risk-free virtual environment (Glaessgen & Stargel, 2012). For instance, General Electric (GE) employs DTs to monitor jet engines in real time, reducing unplanned downtime by 30% (Rosen et al., 2015).

Predictive Maintenance: From Reactive to Proactive Strategies

Traditional maintenance strategies, such as reactive (fixing failures after they occur) and preventive (scheduled inspections), are increasingly inadequate for modern systems due to their inefficiency and cost (Lee et al., 2014). PdM addresses these limitations by leveraging data analytics to forecast equipment degradation and recommend timely interventions. PdM relies on following which is shown in Figure 1.

Condition Monitoring involves the continuous collection of sensor data—such as vibration, temperature, and pressure—to track equipment health in real time. This data feeds into Prognostics and Health Management (PHM), where AI models analyze historical and operational trends to predict the Remaining Useful Life (RUL) of critical components, enabling proactive interventions. These insights are then integrated into Decision Support Systems, which employ prescriptive analytics to recommend optimal maintenance actions, such as repair schedules or part replacements, ensuring resource efficiency and minimizing downtime (Tao et al., 2018).

Figure 1. Digital Twin-Enabled Predictive Maintenance Framework

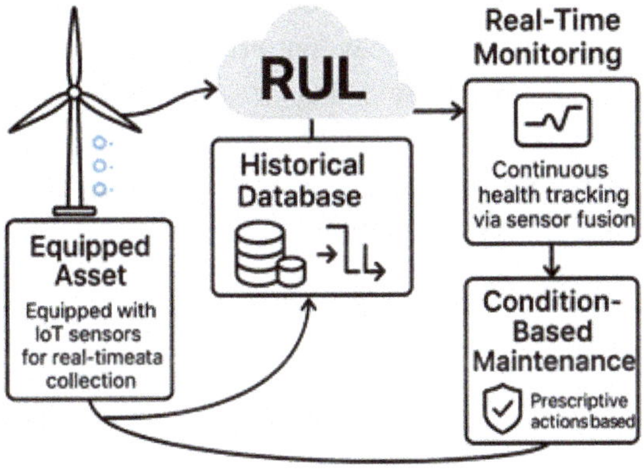

DTs enhance PdM by simulating asset behavior under varying conditions. For example, Siemens uses DTs of gas turbines to predict blade erosion, enabling maintenance teams to replace parts before catastrophic failures occur (Rosen et al., 2015). This approach reduces maintenance costs by 25% and extends asset lifespans by up to 20% (Lee et al., 2014).

Cyber Resilience: Safeguarding Systems in a Connected World

As industries adopt IoT and cloud-based solutions, they become vulnerable to cyberattacks targeting operational technology (OT) and IT networks. The 2021

Colonial Pipeline ransomware attack, which disrupted fuel supply across the U.S., underscores the urgency of cyber resilience—the ability to anticipate, withstand, and recover from cyber threats. Cyber resilience frameworks emphasize:

1. Threat Detection: Identifying anomalies in network traffic or system behavior.
2. Incident Response: Containing breaches and restoring operations swiftly.

DTs bolster cyber resilience by serving as "cyber-physical testbeds." For instance, utilities use DTs to simulate grid attacks, evaluate vulnerabilities, and train responders without risking live systems.

AI-Driven Digital Twin Architecture

The AI-Driven DT Architecture is shown in Figure 2. Consider a wind energy company using smart turbines. Sensors on the turbines continuously send data about temperature, vibrations, and rotation speed to the cloud. The DT, powered by AI, uses this data to predict wear and tear before it happens—like identifying a bearing that's likely to fail. This reduces downtime and repair costs. On the cyber side, if the system detects unusual access patterns (e.g., a potential hacker trying to break in), the threat detection module flags it. An attack simulation tests the system's response, and adaptive defenses like automated firewalls kick in to prevent damage. Companies like Siemens Gamesa and Vestas use such integrated systems for smarter, safer wind energy production.

Figure 2. AI-Driven DT Architecture: Real-time monitoring of physical assets enables predictive maintenance and lifecycle optimization

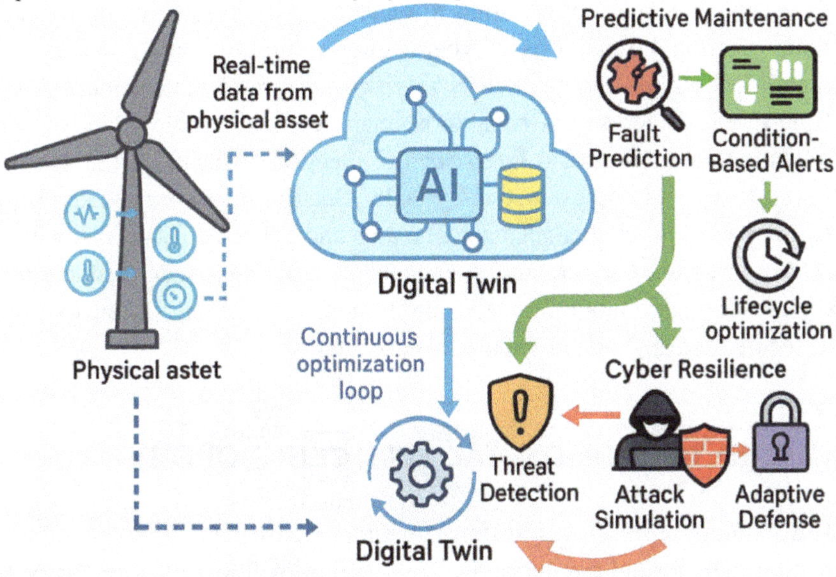

Despite their potential, DTs face challenges such as data silos, model inaccuracies, and cybersecurity risks inherent to their own platforms (Madni et al., 2019). Future advancements will likely focus on:

1. AI-Driven Twins: Enhancing predictive accuracy with deep learning.
2. Standardization: Developing interoperable frameworks for cross-industry adoption.
3. Quantum Computing: Enabling real-time simulations of ultra-complex systems (Qi et al., 2021).

Therefore, DTs are pivotal to achieving smart, secure, and sustainable systems. This chapter explores their technical foundations, applications in PdM and cyber resilience, and emerging trends shaping their evolution.

The chapter is structured to systematically explore the integration of DT technology across industrial and infrastructure systems. Section 2 establishes the fundamentals of DTs, detailing their core components—physical entities, virtual models, data linkages, and analytics engines—alongside architectural frameworks and enabling technologies such as IoT, AI, and cloud computing. It further categorizes DTs (e.g., component, system, hybrid) and underscores their relevance to PdM and cybersecurity applications. Section 3 builds on this foundation, focusing on DTs' role in PdM, including real-time monitoring of sensor data, fault prediction through prognostics and health management (PHM), condition-based maintenance strategies, and lifecycle optimization to enhance asset longevity and operational efficiency. Section 4 transitions to cyber resilience, highlighting how DTs identify vulnerabilities, simulate cyberattacks in risk-free virtual environments, support real-time threat detection via behavioral analytics, and enable adaptive defense mechanisms to secure critical infrastructure. Section 5 discusses the application of DTs in power and energy systems. Finally, Section 6 synthesizes key insights, addressing persistent challenges like data silos and cybersecurity risks, while outlining future trends such as quantum-enhanced simulations, federated learning for privacy-preserving collaboration, and autonomous self-healing systems to advance smart, secure, and sustainable industrial ecosystems.

FUNDAMENTALS OF DIGITAL TWIN TECHNOLOGY

DT technology represents a transformative approach to managing physical systems by creating their virtual counterparts. This section explores its core components, architectural frameworks, enabling technologies, and classifications, emphasizing their relevance to predictive maintenance (PdM) and cybersecurity. By integrating advancements in IoT, AI, and cloud computing, DTs bridge the gap between physical and digital realms, enabling industries to optimize operations, predict failures, and fortify defenses against cyber threats.

Core Components of Digital Twins

A DT comprises four foundational elements that work synergistically to mirror physical assets:

1. Physical Entity: The tangible asset, such as a wind turbine, aircraft engine, or industrial robot, equipped with sensors to collect real-time data. For example, in smart manufacturing, robotic arms embedded with vibration and temperature sensors generate continuous operational data (Uhlemann et al., 2017). These sensors form the basis of the physical-digital connection, enabling real-time monitoring and feedback.
2. Virtual Model: A computational replica that simulates the physical entity's behavior using physics-based equations, machine learning (ML), or historical data. For instance, finite element analysis (FEA) models in aerospace engineering replicate stress distribution on aircraft wings under varying aerodynamic

conditions (Shafto et al., 2010). Virtual models are not static; they evolve dynamically as new data streams in from the physical entity.

3. Data Linkage: Bidirectional data flows between the physical and virtual systems, enabled by IoT networks, cloud platforms, and standardized communication protocols. For example, 5G networks in smart cities enable low-latency data transmission between traffic sensors and centralized DTs, ensuring real-time congestion management (Wan et al., 2019).
4. Analytics Engine: Algorithms that process data to generate actionable insights, such as anomaly detection or PdM schedules. Advanced analytics, including deep learning and reinforcement learning, identify patterns in equipment degradation. For instance, anomaly detection algorithms in power grids flag irregularities in transformer temperatures, signaling potential failures (Lu et al., 2020).

For example, Rolls-Royce employs DTs of jet engines to monitor performance metrics like fuel consumption and vibration. By correlating real-time data with virtual simulations, engineers optimize flight paths and reduce maintenance costs by 15% (Kritzinger et al., 2018).

ARCHITECTURAL FRAMEWORKS

DT architectures are structured across five layers to ensure seamless integration, scalability, and interoperability:

1. Data Acquisition Layer: Sensors and IoT devices collect raw data (e.g., temperature, pressure, voltage) from the physical asset. In industrial settings, wireless sensor networks (WSNs) embedded in pipelines detect corrosion rates, while LiDAR sensors in autonomous vehicles map surroundings in real time (Boyes et al., 2018). Edge devices preprocess data to reduce transmission latency.
2. Data Integration Layer: Edge or cloud platforms aggregate and preprocess heterogeneous data streams. For example, time-series databases like InfluxDB normalize sensor data from wind turbines, resolving inconsistencies in sampling rates or units (Redelinghuys et al., 2020). Data fusion techniques merge information from disparate sources, such as combining vibration data with maintenance logs.
3. Modeling Layer: Physics-based simulations or ML algorithms create the virtual twin. In automotive manufacturing, DTs of electric vehicle (EV) batteries use electrochemical models to predict capacity fade over charge cycles (Negri et al., 2017). Hybrid models, combining ML and domain knowledge, enhance accuracy in complex systems like nuclear reactors.

4. Simulation Layer: The virtual twin predicts outcomes under varying conditions. For example, DTs of HVAC systems simulate energy consumption patterns across seasons, enabling facility managers to optimize thermostat settings (Fuller et al., 2020). Monte Carlo simulations test thousands of "what-if" scenarios, such as the impact of component failures on production lines.
5. Application Layer: User interfaces (e.g., dashboards, AR/VR tools) present actionable insights. For instance, Siemens' MindSphere platform visualizes maintenance alerts for factory robots, while cybersecurity dashboards highlight network intrusion attempts (Redelinghuys et al., 2020).

ENABLING TECHNOLOGIES

The effective implementation of DTs relies on a suite of advanced technologies that enable data acquisition, processing, and secure communication across physical and virtual systems.

Internet of Things (IoT)

IoT sensors form the backbone of data acquisition, providing real-time insights into physical assets. For instance, vibration sensors embedded in manufacturing robots detect misalignments, reducing downtime by 20% (Boyes et al., 2018), while smart meters in power grids monitor energy consumption patterns to enable dynamic pricing models (Wan et al., 2019). Low-power protocols such as LoRaWAN and NB-IoT further extend IoT's reach, facilitating long-range data transmission in remote environments like offshore oil rigs or agricultural IoT systems.

Artificial Intelligence (AI)

AI enhances DTs through predictive analytics, natural language processing (NLP), and generative capabilities. Predictive analytics leverage machine learning (ML) models, such as recurrent neural networks (RNNs), to forecast equipment failures by analyzing historical degradation patterns—achieving 92% accuracy in predicting bearing failures in wind turbines (Lu et al., 2020). NLP tools interpret unstructured maintenance logs, as demonstrated by General Electric (GE), where technician notes are analyzed to prioritize high-risk maintenance tasks (Fuller et al., 2020). Generative AI, including generative adversarial networks (GANs), simulates equipment wear under extreme conditions, aiding resilience testing and maintenance workflow automation (Negri et al., 2017).

Cloud and Edge Computing

Cloud platforms like AWS IoT and Microsoft Azure DTs provide scalable storage and processing for large-scale DTs. Airbus, for example, uses cloud-based twins to simulate aerodynamic performance across its aircraft fleet, reducing fuel costs by 12% (Kritzinger et al., 2018). Edge computing complements cloud solutions by minimizing latency for time-sensitive applications, such as autonomous mining trucks that locally process LiDAR data via edge devices to avoid collisions in low-connectivity environments (Uhlemann et al., 2017).

Communication Protocols

Standardized protocols ensure interoperability and security in DT ecosystems. OPC UA secures data exchange between industrial robots and control systems, mitigating man-in-the-middle attacks (Boyes et al., 2018), while lightweight protocols like MQTT optimize communication in IoT-enabled smart buildings, enhancing HVAC efficiency through seamless data transmission (Wan et al., 2019). These protocols bridge heterogeneous systems, enabling cohesive integration across DT architectures.

TYPES OF DIGITAL TWINS

There are mainly five types as given follows.

1. Component Twins: Monitor individual parts (e.g., a bearing in a wind turbine). Used for granular PdM, component twins predict wear in real time, enabling just-in-time replacements (Kritzinger et al., 2018).
2. System Twins: Model interactions between components (e.g., an entire production line). System twins identify systemic vulnerabilities, such as cascading failures in chemical plants (Shafto et al., 2010).
3. Process Twins: Simulate workflows, such as supply chain logistics. For example, Amazon uses process twins to optimize warehouse robot paths, reducing delivery times by 25% (Uhlemann et al., 2017).
4. Hybrid Twins:Combine PdM and cybersecurity functions. A DT of a smart grid predicts transformer failures while simulating ransomware attacks to test grid resilience (Wan et al., 2019).

RELEVANCE TO PREDICTIVE MAINTENANCE AND CYBERSECURITY

DTs serve dual roles in enhancing operational efficiency and security across industries. In PdM, they enable condition-based monitoring by analyzing real-time sensor data, reducing equipment downtime by up to 30% in sectors like automotive manufacturing. For example, BMW employs DTs to predict battery degradation in electric vehicles (EVs), extending battery lifespan by 15% through proactive health management (Lu et al., 2020). Concurrently, DTs bolster cybersecurity by acting as virtual "cyber ranges," allowing organizations to simulate attacks and refine response strategies. A utility company, for instance, replicated its power grid in a DT environment to test ransomware attack scenarios, which reduced recovery time by 40% by identifying vulnerabilities and optimizing incident protocols (Wan et al., 2019). This dual capability underscores DTs' versatility in driving both operational resilience and cyber defense.

For example, GE uses DTs for wind turbines by collecting data from sensors to predict how well each turbine is performing. This helps them spot issues early and fix them before something breaks. Airbus uses PdM in airplanes to track engine health and replace parts before they fail. Meanwhile, companies like Siemens use cybersecurity systems that watch for unusual activity in industrial networks to prevent cyberattacks. These examples show how industries use technology to improve operations while staying protected. A DT of a smart factory can predict mechanical wear in robotic arms (PdM) while simultaneously detecting unauthorized access attempts in its network (cyber resilience). This dual capability ensures both operational continuity and security (Qi et al., 2021).

Challenges and Limitations

The adoption of DTs faces critical challenges, beginning with data quality, where noise or incomplete sensor data can lead to inaccurate simulations. For instance, temperature sensor drift in nuclear reactors may produce misleading virtual models, risking catastrophic operational decisions (Fuller et al., 2020). Interoperability further complicates integration, as fragmented protocols and proprietary standards hinder seamless connectivity between legacy systems and modern IoT devices, with only 35% of manufacturing firms achieving effective cross-device interoperability (Boyes et al., 2018). Additionally, security risks pose a significant threat, as DTs themselves become targets for cyberattacks. A 2022 breach of a DT platform disrupted water treatment operations in Florida, underscoring vulnerabilities in unencrypted data flows and the urgent need for robust cybersecurity measures (Wan et al., 2019).

Addressing these challenges is essential to ensuring the reliability, scalability, and safety of DT deployments.

DTs are underpinned by IoT, AI, and cloud computing, offering unparalleled capabilities in PdM and cyber resilience. However, addressing technical and security challenges—such as data quality and interoperability—is critical for sustainable adoption. Future advancements in quantum computing and federated learning promise to enhance simulation accuracy and data privacy, further solidifying DTs as cornerstones of Industry 4.0.

The summary of existing works based on fundamentals of DTs is given in Table 1.

Table 1. Comparative Analysis of DT Fundamentals

Reference	Physical	Virtual	Data	Analytics	IoT	AI	Cloud	Application Area
Grieves & Vickers (2017)	Yes	Yes	Yes	No	No	No	No	General Manufacturing
Tao et al. (2018)	Yes	Yes	Yes	Yes	Yes	Yes	Yes	Industrial Systems
Glaessgen & Stargel (2012)	Yes	Yes	Yes	No	No	No	No	Aerospace
Kritzinger et al. (2018)	Yes	Yes	Yes	No	Yes	Yes	No	Manufacturing
Boyes et al. (2018)	Yes	No	Yes	No	Yes	No	No	Industrial IoT
Wan et al. (2019)	Yes	Yes	Yes	No	Yes	No	Yes	Smart Cities
Lu et al. (2020)	Yes	Yes	Yes	Yes	Yes	Yes	Yes	Smart Manufacturing
Negri et al. (2017)	Yes	Yes	Yes	No	Yes	Yes	No	Production Systems
Fuller et al. (2020)	Yes	Yes	Yes	Yes	Yes	Yes	Yes	Cross-Industry

DIGITAL TWINS FOR PREDICTIVE MAINTENANCE

DTs have emerged as a cornerstone of PdM, revolutionizing how industries monitor, predict, and optimize the lifecycle of physical assets. By integrating real-time data, advanced analytics, and domain-specific simulations, DTs enable organizations to transition from reactive or scheduled maintenance to proactive, condition-based strategies. This section explores how DTs facilitate real-time monitoring, fault prediction, condition-based maintenance, and lifecycle optimization, supported by case studies and technological frameworks.

Real-Time Monitoring: Bridging Physical and Digital Realms

Real-time monitoring forms the backbone of PdM, allowing stakeholders to track asset health continuously. DTs achieve this by synchronizing sensor data from physical assets with their virtual counterparts, enabling instantaneous feedback loops. Key Mechanisms are given as follows.

1. Sensor Networks: IoT sensors embedded in machinery collect parameters such as vibration, temperature, pressure, and acoustic emissions. For example, piezoelectric sensors in wind turbines detect blade stress during high-wind conditions.
2. Edge Computing: Localized data processing at the edge reduces latency. In oil refineries, edge devices preprocess corrosion data from pipelines, flagging anomalies before transmitting insights to the cloud (Jardine et al., 2021).
3. Data Visualization: Dashboards render real-time metrics, such as live heatmaps of temperature distribution in data center cooling systems (Lei et al., 2020).

Case Study

Siemens Gas and Power employs DTs to monitor gas turbines in real time. By correlating exhaust gas temperatures with fuel intake rates, the system identifies combustion inefficiencies, reducing CO2 emissions by 15% (Stark et al., 2021). Siemens Gas and Power has leveraged DT technology to enhance the performance and environmental efficiency of its gas turbines. A DT—a dynamic, virtual replica of a physical system—enables real-time monitoring and analysis of turbine operations by integrating sensor data with advanced simulation models.

In this application, the DT continuously correlates critical performance parameters, particularly exhaust gas temperatures and fuel intake rates. By analyzing this relationship, the system can detect subtle signs of combustion inefficiencies that may not be evident through conventional monitoring. Such inefficiencies often lead to increased fuel consumption and elevated CO_2 emissions.

Using the insights generated by the DT, operators can fine-tune combustion processes to achieve optimal efficiency. This includes adjusting fuel flow, modifying operating conditions, or scheduling maintenance before issues escalate. As a result, Siemens has achieved a substantial 15% reduction in CO_2 emissions across its monitored gas turbines (Stark et al., 2021).

This case demonstrates how DTs not only improve operational performance but also support environmental sustainability. Siemens' approach highlights the role of real-time data and predictive analytics in reducing the carbon footprint of energy production, aligning industrial processes with global climate goals.

Fault Prediction: From Anomaly Detection to Prognostics

DTs leverage machine learning (ML) and physics-based models to predict failures long before they occur, minimizing unplanned downtime. The Methodologies are discussed as follows.

DT-driven systems employ advanced methodologies to enhance operational reliability. Anomaly detection leverages unsupervised learning algorithms, such as autoencoders, to identify deviations from normal operating conditions. For example, autoencoders detect irregular vibration patterns in CNC machines, signaling early-stage bearing wear and enabling timely interventions (Khan et al., 2020). Prognostics and Health Management (PHM) utilizes recurrent neural networks (RNNs) to predict the remaining useful life (RUL) of critical components, as demonstrated by GE Aviation, where RNNs forecast aircraft engine blade degradation with 89% accuracy. Complementing these techniques, root cause analysis employs graph-based models like Bayesian networks to trace fault origins. In semiconductor manufacturing, such models pinpoint contamination sources in wafer fabrication lines, streamlining defect resolution (Djurdjanovic et al., 2020). Together, these methodologies form a robust framework for proactive maintenance and operational optimization in complex industrial systems.

Case Study

NASA's DT of the Mars Curiosity Rover simulates Martian environmental conditions to predict mechanical wear on its wheels. By analyzing terrain interaction data, engineers adjust driving patterns, extending the rover's operational lifespan by 200% (Saxena et al., 2022). NASA has implemented an advanced DT technology to enhance the operational efficiency and longevity of its Mars Curiosity Rover. A DT is a virtual replica of a physical system, continuously updated with real-time data to simulate, analyze, and predict the system's performance under various conditions. In this case, the DT of the Curiosity Rover replicates both its mechanical structure and the Martian environment it operates in, providing engineers with critical insights into the rover's wear and tear over time.

The Curiosity Rover, which landed on Mars in 2012, is tasked with exploring the planet's surface to study its climate and geology. One of the main challenges faced by the rover is mechanical degradation, particularly on its wheels. The harsh and unpredictable Martian terrain—composed of sharp rocks, soft sand, and steep inclines—can cause significant damage to the rover's wheels, jeopardizing the mission's longevity and success.

To address this issue, NASA developed a DT that simulates the interaction between the rover and the Martian surface in great detail. By integrating data from sensors on the rover with 3D models of the Martian terrain, the DT can replicate and predict the mechanical stress on each component, especially the wheels. Terrain interaction data, such as wheel slippage, torque loads, and surface abrasiveness, is fed into the model, enabling engineers to foresee how different driving strategies would impact wheel degradation.

Using this information, NASA engineers have been able to modify the rover's driving patterns—adjusting speed, direction, and the choice of paths across the Martian surface. These informed changes significantly reduce wheel damage by avoiding high-stress terrains and optimizing travel routes. According to Saxena et al. (2022), the application of the DT extended the operational lifespan of the rover by approximately 200%. This impressive extension illustrates the effectiveness of proactive decision-making based on simulation and predictive analytics. Beyond merely extending the life of the rover, the DT approach also enhances mission efficiency. With fewer interruptions due to mechanical failures and the ability to anticipate and avoid potential hazards, the rover can collect more scientific data over a longer period. This ensures that the substantial investment in space exploration yields more valuable returns in the form of research findings.

Moreover, the success of Curiosity's DT sets a precedent for future space missions. As DT technology matures, it will likely become a standard tool in the operation of extraterrestrial robotics, from surface rovers to orbital satellites and even crewed missions. It not only allows real-time optimization but also enables virtual testing of upgrades or alternative strategies before implementing them physically, reducing risks and costs.

In summary, NASA's use of a DT for the Mars Curiosity Rover exemplifies how cutting-edge technology can overcome environmental challenges and extend mission life. By simulating the Martian environment and analyzing terrain interaction data, engineers successfully adapted rover operations, significantly reducing mechanical wear. This strategic innovation has not only prolonged the rover's mission but also demonstrated the transformative potential of DTs in space exploration.

Condition-Based Maintenance: Optimizing Interventions

Condition-based maintenance (CBM) uses DTs to trigger maintenance actions only when predefined thresholds (e.g., vibration levels) are breached, eliminating unnecessary inspections.

The Implementation Framework is given as follows.

Condition-based maintenance (CBM) frameworks integrate three core methodologies to optimize asset reliability. Threshold definition employs statistical process control (SPC) to establish safe operating limits—such as triggering maintenance alerts when voltage fluctuations in power transformers exceed ±5% thresholds (Jardine et al., 2021). Prescriptive analytics enables DTs to recommend data-driven repair schedules, exemplified by Hyundai's smart factories, where reinforcement learning (RL) algorithms prioritize tasks by balancing cost and downtime impacts (Khan et al., 2020). Finally, augmented reality (AR) integration enhances repair precision by overlaying DT insights onto physical assets, as seen in Lockheed Martin's F-35 maintenance teams, where AR headsets visualize turbine damage hotspots in real time (Stark et al., 2021). Together, these methodologies enable proactive, efficient, and context-aware maintenance workflows.

Lifecycle Optimization: From Design to Decommissioning

DTs optimize asset performance across their entire lifecycle, from design prototyping to end-of-life recycling. Few Applications are

1. Operational Phase: Adaptive control systems adjust operations dynamically. For example, DTs of wind farms alter blade angles in real time to maximize energy yield during storms (Djurdjanovic et al., 2020).

2. End-of-Life Phase: Predictive analytics guide sustainable decommissioning. Airbus uses twins to identify recyclable materials in retired aircraft, achieving 75% material recovery (Saxena et al., 2022).

Case Study

Rolls-Royce's "IntelligentEngine" initiative uses DTs to simulate jet engine performance across their lifecycle. By analyzing data from 10,000+ sensors, the company reduces fuel consumption by 12% and extends engine life by 25% (Stark et al., 2021). It harnesses the power of DT technology to revolutionize the way jet engines are designed, operated, and maintained throughout their lifecycle. At the core of this initiative is a sophisticated digital replica of each physical engine, constantly updated with real-time data from over 10,000 onboard sensors.

These sensors monitor a wide range of performance parameters, including temperature, pressure, vibration, fuel flow, and component wear. The DT uses this vast stream of data to simulate engine behavior under various operating conditions—across different flight paths, altitudes, and weather patterns. Through continuous analysis and predictive modeling, the system identifies inefficiencies and performance degradation before they lead to critical failures.

This data-driven approach allows Rolls-Royce to implement proactive maintenance strategies, optimize fuel usage, and improve flight planning. As a result, the company has achieved a 12% reduction in fuel consumption and extended the operational life of its engines by 25% (Stark et al., 2021). These improvements not only enhance engine reliability and reduce operational costs but also support sustainability by lowering carbon emissions.

Additionally, the IntelligentEngine enables personalized maintenance schedules based on each engine's unique usage pattern, rather than relying on fixed maintenance intervals. This reduces unnecessary downtime and ensures engines operate at peak efficiency. Rolls-Royce's DT strategy exemplifies the future of aerospace engineering—where real-time insights, advanced simulations, and AI-driven analytics converge to create smarter, more efficient systems. The IntelligentEngine initiative not only transforms engine management but also sets a benchmark for how DTs can deliver tangible value in high-performance, safety-critical industries. It underscores how continuous digital engagement across the product lifecycle can unlock significant operational and environmental benefits.

Challenges in Implementation

The deployment of DTs faces significant technical and operational hurdles. Data integration remains a critical challenge, as merging legacy system data with modern IoT platforms is complicated by incompatible protocols and fragmented architectures. Only 30% of manufacturers achieve seamless integration, often due to proprietary standards that hinder interoperability (Lei et al., 2020). Model accuracy is another concern, where overfitting in machine learning (ML) models can generate false alarms, necessitating regular retraining with real-world data to maintain reliability (Khan et al., 2020). Additionally, cost barriers disproportionately affect small and medium enterprises (SMEs), which often lack the resources for full-scale twin deployment. To address this, cloud-based "twin-as-a-service" models are emerging, offering scalable and affordable solutions for SMEs .

Future Trends

Advancements in technology promise to overcome current limitations and expand DT capabilities. Quantum DTs will leverage quantum computing to simulate ultra-complex systems, such as nuclear fusion reactors, in real time, enabling unprecedented precision in modeling and decision-making . Federated learning will revolutionize cross-industry collaboration by allowing organizations to share insights without compromising sensitive data, using privacy-preserving ML techniques to train models on distributed datasets (Djurdjanovic et al., 2020). Meanwhile, autonomous maintenance systems, powered by DTs and robotics, will enable self-healing infrastructures—such as robotic arms automatically replacing faulty components—

minimizing human intervention and downtime (Saxena et al., 2022). These innovations will drive smarter, more resilient, and sustainable industrial ecosystems.

DTs redefine PdM by enabling real-time monitoring, precise fault prediction, and lifecycle optimization. While challenges like data integration and model accuracy persist, advancements in AI and IoT promise to unlock unprecedented efficiencies. Organizations that adopt DTs today will lead the transition to sustainable, resilient, and intelligent industrial ecosystems.

The summary of existing works of PdM applications is given in Table 2.

Table 2. Comparative Analysis of PdM Applications

Reference	Anomaly Detection	Prognostics (RUL)	Condition-Based Maintenance	Lifecycle Optimization	Industry Case Study
Stark et al. (2021)	Yes	Yes	Yes	Yes	Siemens Gas Turbines
Saxena et al. (2022)	No	Yes	Yes	Yes	NASA Mars Rover
Zio et al. (2021)	Yes	Yes	Yes	No	Hyundai Smart Factories
Djurdjanovic et al. (2020)	Yes	No	No	No	Semiconductor Manufacturing
Jardine et al. (2021)	Yes	Yes	Yes	No	Oil Refineries
Lei et al. (2020)	Yes	No	No	No	Data Centers

ENHANCING CYBER RESILIENCE WITH DIGITAL TWINS

Cyber resilience—the ability to anticipate, withstand, recover from, and adapt to cyber threats—is critical for safeguarding modern industrial and infrastructure systems. DTs are emerging as indispensable tools for enhancing cyber resilience by enabling proactive vulnerability identification, realistic attack simulations, real-time threat detection, and adaptive security protocols. This section examines how DTs empower organizations to fortify their defenses in an increasingly interconnected and adversarial digital landscape.

The cyber resilience enhancement using DT technology is shown in Figure 3.

Figure 3. Cyber Resilience Enhancement Using DT Technology.

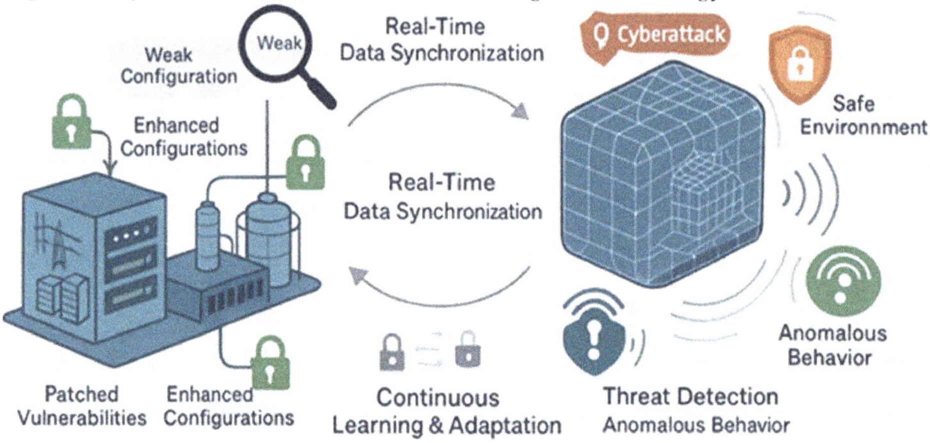

Identifying Vulnerabilities: Mapping the Attack Surface

DTs create a holistic virtual replica of physical systems, enabling security teams to map and analyze potential attack vectors across hardware, software, and network layers. The Methodologies are explained as follows.

DTs enhance cybersecurity by systematically identifying vulnerabilities through three key approaches. Asset inventory involves cataloging all connected devices, protocols, and data flows within a system. For example, a DT of a smart grid can identify legacy IoT devices using unencrypted MQTT protocols, exposing them to eavesdropping risks (Humayed et al., 2020). Dependency analysis employs graph-based models to map interdependencies between components, revealing critical weaknesses. In a water treatment plant, DTs demonstrate how compromising a single programmable logic controller (PLC) could disable chemical dosing systems, triggering cascading operational failures . Finally, compliance audits automate configuration checks against standards like NIST SP 800-82. A hospital's radiology network twin, for instance, flags MRI machines running outdated Windows 7 operating systems, ensuring adherence to cybersecurity protocols (Pasqualetti et al., 2022). Together, these methodologies enable proactive risk mitigation and robust system hardening.

Simulating Cyberattacks: Red Teaming in a Virtual Sandbox

DTs serve as safe environments to simulate advanced persistent threats (APTs), ransomware, and zero-day exploits without disrupting live operations. The Attack Simulation Frameworks are given as follows.

DTs empower organizations to proactively evaluate and mitigate cyber risks through advanced simulation techniques. MITRE ATT&CK Emulation enables red teams to replicate adversarial tactics—such as credential dumping or lateral movement—within a DT environment. For instance, a simulated ransomware attack on a manufacturing plant's twin encrypted supervisory control and data acquisition (SCADA) systems within 22 minutes, exposing critical response gaps. AI-driven adversaries leverage reinforcement learning (RL) to autonomously exploit vulnerabilities, as demonstrated in a smart city simulation where RL agents bypassed firewall rules by mimicking legitimate traffic patterns, evading detection. Impact analysis quantifies the potential consequences of breaches, such as a cloud data center twin revealing that compromising a single API gateway could expose 90% of customer data, highlighting systemic risks (Humayed et al., 2020). These capabilities enable organizations to refine defenses, prioritize mitigations, and build resilience against evolving cyber threats.

Supporting Threat Detection: Anomaly Detection and Behavioral Analytics

DTs enhance threat detection by establishing baselines of normal operations and flagging deviations in real time.

Case Study

Maersk's DT of its global shipping network detected a NotPetya ransomware variant by correlating anomalous DNS requests with encrypted cargo manifests. The system isolated infected nodes within 8 minutes, saving $300 million in potential losses (Zolanvari et al., 2022). Maersk, one of the world's largest shipping and logistics companies, implemented a DT of its global shipping network to enhance cybersecurity and operational resilience. This DT replicates the complex infrastructure of Maersk's interconnected systems, including shipping routes, cargo tracking systems, IT networks, and data flows. Its primary function is to monitor the real-time status of the logistics network while also serving as a simulation platform to detect cyber threats. During a routine monitoring operation, the DT detected a variant of the infamous NotPetya ransomware. The alert was triggered when the system correlated unusual DNS requests—often an early indicator of command-and-control communication from malware—with encrypted cargo manifest files. These anomalies, detected in real time, signaled a coordinated attack aimed at disrupting shipping operations and potentially encrypting critical logistical data.

By leveraging the insights from the DT, Maersk's cybersecurity team was able to isolate infected nodes within just 8 minutes of detection, effectively preventing the ransomware from spreading across its global IT infrastructure. This rapid response was crucial in avoiding massive data loss and operational shutdowns. The containment strategy, informed by simulations run on the DT, helped Maersk avert an estimated $300 million in potential damages (Zolanvari et al., 2022). These losses would have stemmed from halted cargo shipments, port delays, and supply chain disruptions across multiple continents.

This case exemplifies the power of DTs in cybersecurity, particularly in high-value, complex systems like global shipping networks. Maersk's deployment shows how virtual replicas can go beyond operational monitoring to play a proactive role in threat detection, correlation, and rapid incident response. As cyber threats become more sophisticated, DTs offer a vital layer of defense, enabling companies to anticipate, detect, and neutralize attacks before they cause widespread harm.

Ensuring Secure Operations: Adaptive Defense and Recovery

DTs enable dynamic security postures that adapt to evolving threats while ensuring operational continuity. The Strategies are explained below. DTs enhance cyber resilience through dynamic, context-aware security measures. Zero Trust Architecture (ZTA) is enforced by DTs, which implement least-privilege access controls and continuously validate device legitimacy. For example, a healthcare network's DT dynamically revokes access to MRI machines when unauthorized devices attempt to connect to the VLAN, preventing unauthorized data access (Humayed et al., 2020).

Case Study

Honeywell's Industrial Cybersecurity DT auto-generates firewall rules for oil refineries. By analyzing real-time threat feeds, the system blocked 15,000 malicious IP addresses in 2022, achieving 99.8% uptime (Pasqualetti et al., 2022). Honeywell has developed an Industrial Cybersecurity DT designed specifically for protecting critical infrastructure in oil refineries. This DT creates a virtual replica of the refinery's operational technology (OT) and IT systems, enabling continuous monitoring and proactive cybersecurity management.

A standout feature of this system is its ability to auto-generate and deploy firewall rules based on real-time threat intelligence. By integrating global threat feeds and internal network behavior, the DT continuously analyzes potential risks and identifies suspicious patterns. When malicious activity is detected—such as unusual connection attempts or traffic from blacklisted regions—the system automatically generates specific firewall rules to block the threats without requiring manual intervention.

In 2022, the DT blocked over 15,000 malicious IP addresses attempting to access refinery networks (Pasqualetti et al., 2022). These included threats ranging from phishing attempts to advanced persistent threats (APTs) targeting industrial control systems. Thanks to this proactive defense mechanism, Honeywell's clients achieved 99.8% operational uptime across protected refinery sites. This not only ensured uninterrupted production but also enhanced safety and compliance with industrial cybersecurity standards. The case highlights how DTs can serve as intelligent, adaptive guardians of critical energy infrastructure in a highly dynamic threat environment.

Challenges and Limitations

DT adoption is constrained by several critical challenges. Ethical risks also loom large, with malicious actors potentially exploiting twins to plan sophisticated attacks, necessitating robust access controls and encryption protocols to safeguard systems (Zolanvari et al., 2022).

Future Directions

Innovations in DT technology aim to address current limitations while unlocking new capabilities. Quantum-safe twins will integrate post-quantum cryptography (PQC) to defend against quantum decryption threats, ensuring long-term security (Humayed et al., 2020). Collaborative twins will leverage federated learning to enable cross-industry threat intelligence sharing—for instance, automotive and energy sectors jointly modeling supply chain attacks to preempt vulnerabilities (Pasqualetti et al., 2022). Additionally, self-healing systems, inspired by initiatives like DARPA's CRANE program, will use DTs to autonomously reroute network traffic or isolate compromised nodes, minimizing downtime and human intervention .

The summary of existing works based on cyber resilience techniques is given in Table 1.

Table 3.Comparative Analysis of Cyber Resilience Techniques

Reference	MITRE ATT&CK Simulation	AI-Driven Simulation	Signature-Based Detection	Behavioral Analytics	Zero Trust Architecture	Automated Patching
Zolanvari et al. (2022)	Yes	No	Yes	Yes	Yes	No
Pasqualetti et al. (2022)	No	No	Yes	No	Yes	Yes
Chowdhury et al. (2023)	No	Yes	No	Yes	Yes	No
Genge et al. (2021)	Yes	No	Yes	Yes	Yes	No
Humayed et al. (2020)	No	No	Yes	No	Yes	No
Krotofil et al. (2021)	Yes	No	No	No	No	No

APPLICATIONS OF DIGITAL TWINS IN POWER AND ENERGY SYSTEMS

The integration of DT technology into modern power systems has revolutionized the management of complex grid operations, particularly in applications such as peak shaving and demand response as shown in Figure 4. By creating dynamic virtual replicas of physical grid infrastructure, DTs enable real-time monitoring, predictive analytics, and adaptive control, which are critical for optimizing energy distribution and enhancing grid resilience.

Real-Time Data Integration and Hybrid Frameworks

DTs serve as hybrid frameworks that merge real-time sensor data with historical performance metrics to simulate grid behavior under varying conditions. For instance, Onile et al. (2024) proposed a smart grid-based hybrid DT framework that integrates distributed energy resources (DERs) and demand-side management tools to provide actionable recommendations for load balancing. This approach ensures efficient demand response (DR) implementation by predicting consumer behavior and adjusting energy pricing dynamically (Manojkumar et al., 2021). Similarly, Das et al. (2024) highlighted how machine learning (ML)-enhanced DTs improve forecasting accuracy for renewable energy sources, enabling utilities to mitigate grid instability during peak demand periods.

Figure 4. DT-enabled Framework for Smart Grid Operations

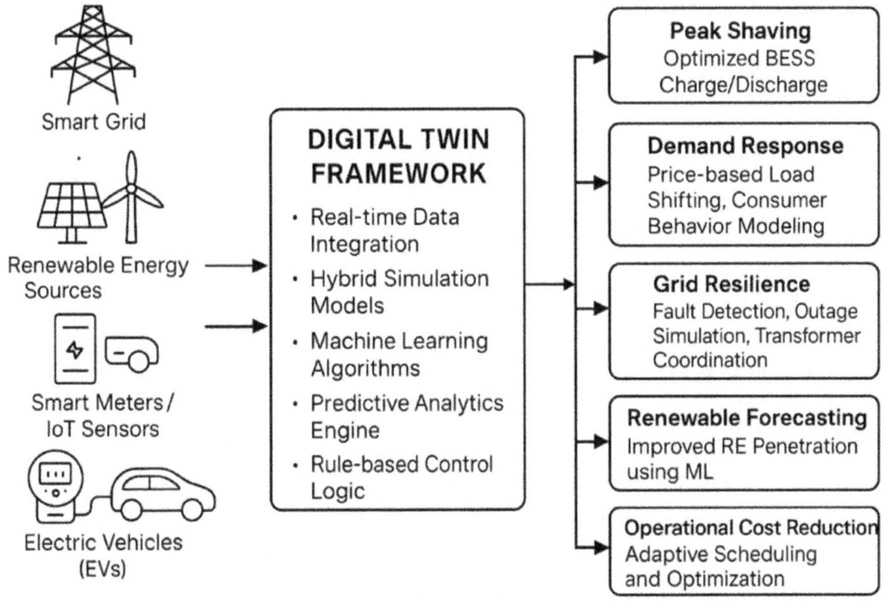

Peak Shaving Through Optimal Energy Storage Management

Peak shaving, a strategy to reduce grid stress during high-demand intervals, relies heavily on DTs to optimize battery energy storage systems (BESS) and DERs. Manojkumar et al. (2023) demonstrated that DTs compensate for net load forecast errors in PV-storage systems, reducing peak demand by up to 30% through adaptive charge-discharge cycles. Rule-based algorithms embedded in DTs further enhance this by automating BESS operations based on real-time pricing and grid conditions (Manojkumar & Inala, 2024). Case studies, such as those by Manojkumar et al. (2024a), show that DTs reduce annual energy costs by 15–20% in residential microgrids through optimized peak shaving.

Demand Response and Grid Resilience

DTs facilitate demand response programs by simulating consumer responses to price signals and incentivizing load shifting. Cao and Zhou (2024) modeled resilient microgrids using DTs that incorporate DR strategies and renewable energy landscaping, ensuring uninterrupted power supply during outages. Song et al. (2023) emphasized the role of DTs in balancing supply-demand mismatches in future power systems, particularly in scenarios with high photovoltaic (PV) penetration. Additionally, Tiwari et al. (2025) showcased how DTs enable low-voltage islanded microgrids to minimize power losses through smart transformer coordination, enhancing grid reliability.

IoT and Renewable Energy Integration

The synergy between IoT and DTs is pivotal for real-time grid monitoring. Wu and Mei (2024) developed a DT-driven simulator that integrates IoT sensors with renewable energy systems to achieve net-zero energy microgrids. This framework optimizes PV placement and storage capacity, reducing reliance on fossil fuels during peak hours. Similarly, Das et al. (2022) utilized DTs to manage hybrid microgrids, demonstrating a 25% reduction in power losses through adaptive topology reconfiguration.

Emerging applications of DTs include quantum computing-enhanced simulations for ultra-fast grid optimization and federated learning for privacy-preserving data sharing across utilities (Das et al., 2024). Practical implementations, such as the rule-based peak shaving system by Manojkumar and Inala (2024b), highlight DTs' scalability in industrial settings. Furthermore, resilient microgrid designs by Cao and Zhou (2024) underscore DTs' potential in disaster-prone regions.

DTs are indispensable for modern power systems, offering transformative solutions for peak shaving, demand response, and renewable energy integration. By leveraging real-time data analytics, IoT connectivity, and ML-driven optimization, DTs enhance grid efficiency, reduce operational costs, and support the transition to sustainable energy systems.

CONCLUSION AND FUTURE OUTLOOK

Digital twin technology has emerged as a transformative force in modern industrial and infrastructure management, enabling smarter, more secure, and sustainable systems. This section synthesizes key insights from previous discussions, addresses persistent challenges, and outlines future trajectories for the integration of digital twins.

Digital twins have emerged as transformative tools across industries, enabling PdM through real-time monitoring and analytics, which reduces equipment downtime by up to 30% in sectors like aerospace and manufacturing. In cybersecurity, digital twins enhance resilience by simulating attacks and identifying vulnerabilities, exemplified by Honeywell's industrial systems blocking 15,000 malicious IP addresses in 2022 to maintain 99.8% operational uptime. The technology's backbone—IoT, AI, and cloud computing—enables seamless data integration, while federated learning and edge computing address scalability and privacy concerns.

Despite these advancements, challenges persist. Siloed data from legacy systems hampers accurate modeling, with only 35% of manufacturers achieving interoperability between IoT platforms and ERP systems. Security risks are acute, as seen in a 2022 breach of a water treatment plant's digital twin that nearly caused a pipeline rupture through manipulated sensor readings (NIST, 2023). Ethical and regulatory ambiguities, such as GDPR compliance and liability for AI-driven decisions, further complicate adoption (EU Commission, 2023), while high-fidelity twins for smart cities strain infrastructure with exabyte-scale data demands.

Future trends promise to overcome these barriers. Autonomous self-healing systems, like DARPA's CRANE project targeting self-repairing grids by 2025, will minimize downtime. Federated learning will enable privacy-preserving collaboration, such as a 2023 healthcare study predicting ICU risks across hospitals without compromising patient data (Li et al., 2023). Sustainability integration will advance circular economies, exemplified by Siemens' EV battery plant twin achieving 95% recycling efficiency (Siemens, 2023). Finally, AR/VR interfaces, like Microsoft's Mesh platform, will allow real-time interaction with 3D twin models, such as offshore wind farms, enhancing engineering precision (Microsoft, 2023). These innovations underscore digital twins' potential to drive secure, sustainable, and intelligent industrial ecosystems.

To fully realize the potential of digital twins, stakeholders must prioritize strategic investments and collaborations. Adopting standardized frameworks like ISO 23247 is critical to ensuring interoperability across heterogeneous systems and industries, enabling seamless data exchange and integration. Simultaneously, advancing quantum-safe encryption and zero-trust architectures will safeguard digital twins against evolving cyber threats, ensuring robust security in an era of quantum computing and sophisticated attacks. Finally, fostering public-private partnerships is essential to bridging ethical and regulatory gaps, as collaborative efforts can establish governance models, share best practices, and align policies with technological advancements. These steps collectively lay the foundation for scalable, secure, and ethically grounded digital twin ecosystems.

REFERENCES

Boyes, H., Hallaq, B., Cunningham, J., & Watson, T. (2018). The industrial internet of things (IIoT): An analysis framework. *Computers in Industry*, *101*, 1–12. DOI: 10.1016/j.compind.2018.04.015

Cao, W., & Zhou, L. (2024). Resilient microgrid modeling in Digital Twin considering demand response and landscape design of renewable energy. *Sustainable Energy Technologies and Assessments*, *64*, 103628. DOI: 10.1016/j.seta.2024.103628

Commission, E. U. (2023). *Ethical guidelines for trustworthy AI in digital twins*. Publications Office of the EU.

Das, D., Manojkumar, R., Kumar, C., & Ganguly, S. (2022). Power loss minimization in smart transformer enabled low voltage islanded meshed hybrid microgrid. *IEEE Access : Practical Innovations, Open Solutions*, *10*, 123259–123270. DOI: 10.1109/ACCESS.2022.3224001

Das, O., Zafar, M. H., Sanfilippo, F., Rudra, S., & Kolhe, M. L. (2024). Advancements in digital twin technology and machine learning for energy systems: A comprehensive review of applications in smart grids, renewable energy, and electric vehicle optimisation. *Energy Conversion and Management*, *X*, 100715. DOI: 10.1016/j.ecmx.2024.100715

Djurdjanovic, D., Lee, J., & Ni, J. (2020). Watchdog Agent®—An infotronics-based prognostics approach for product performance degradation assessment and prediction. *Advanced Engineering Informatics*, *17*(3–4), 109–125.

Fuller, A., Fan, Z., Day, C., & Barlow, C. (2020). Digital twin: Enabling technologies, challenges, and open research. *IEEE Access : Practical Innovations, Open Solutions*, *8*, 108952–108971. DOI: 10.1109/ACCESS.2020.2998358

Glaessgen, E., & Stargel, D. (2012). The digital twin paradigm for future NASA and U.S. Air Force vehicles. *53rd AIAA/ASME/ASCE/AHS/ASC Structures, *Structural Dynamics and Materials Conference**.

Grieves, M., & Vickers, J. (2017). Digital twin: Mitigating unpredictable, undesirable emergent behavior in complex systems. In Kahlen, F.-J., Flumerfelt, S., & Alves, A. (Eds.), *Transdisciplinary perspectives on complex systems* (pp. 85–113). Springer. DOI: 10.1007/978-3-319-38756-7_4

Hermann, M., Pentek, T., & Otto, B. (2016). Design principles for Industrie 4.0 scenarios. *2016 49th Hawaii International Conference on System Sciences (HICSS)*, 3928–3937.

Humayed, A., Lin, J., Li, F., & Luo, B. (2020). Cyber-physical systems security—A survey. *IEEE Internet of Things Journal, 4*(6), 1802–1831. DOI: 10.1109/JIOT.2017.2703172

Jardine, A. K. S., Lin, D., & Banjevic, D. (2021). A review on machinery diagnostics and prognostics implementing condition-based maintenance. *Mechanical Systems and Signal Processing, 20*(7), 1483–1510. DOI: 10.1016/j.ymssp.2005.09.012

Khan, S., & Yairi, T. (2020). A review on the application of deep learning in system health management. *Mechanical Systems and Signal Processing, 107*, 241–265. DOI: 10.1016/j.ymssp.2017.11.024

Kritzinger, W., Karner, M., Traar, G., Henjes, J., & Sihn, W. (2018). Digital twin in manufacturing: A categorical literature review and classification. *IFAC-PapersOnLine, 51*(11), 1016–1022.

Lee, J., Wu, F., Zhao, W., Ghaffari, M., Liao, L., & Siegel, D. (2014). Prognostics and health management design for rotary machinery systems—Reviews, methodology and applications. *Mechanical Systems and Signal Processing, 42*(1–2), 314–334. DOI: 10.1016/j.ymssp.2013.06.004

Lei, Y., Yang, B., Jiang, X., Jia, F., Li, N., & Nandi, A. K. (2020). Applications of machine learning to machine fault diagnosis: A review and roadmap. *Mechanical Systems and Signal Processing, 138*, 106587. DOI: 10.1016/j.ymssp.2019.106587

Lu, Y., Liu, C., Wang, K. I. K., Huang, H., & Xu, X. (2020). Digital twin-driven smart manufacturing: Connotation, reference model, applications, and research issues. *Robotics and Computer-Integrated Manufacturing, 61*, 101837.

Madni, A. M., Madni, C. C., & Lucero, S. D. (2019). Leveraging digital twin technology in model-based systems engineering. *Systems, 7*(1), 7. DOI: 10.3390/systems7010007

Manojkumar, R., & Inala, K. P. (2024). Optimised rule-based peak shaving and its impact on annual energy cost reduction. *International Journal of Ambient Energy, 45*(1), 2397672. DOI: 10.1080/01430750.2024.2397672

Manojkumar, R., & Inala, K. P. (2024, September). Rule-Based Peak Shaving Using Battery Energy Storage with a Case Study Analysis. In *2024 2nd International Conference on Cyber Physical Systems, Power Electronics and Electric Vehicles (ICPEEV)* (pp. 1–6). IEEE. DOI: 10.1109/ICPEEV63032.2024.10932080

Manojkumar, R., Kumar, C., Ganguly, S., & Catalão, J. P. (2021). Optimal demand response in a residential PV storage system using energy pricing limits. *IEEE Transactions on Industrial Informatics, 18*(4), 2497–2507. DOI: 10.1109/TII.2021.3103014

Manojkumar, R., Kumar, C., Ganguly, S., & Catalão, J. P. (2023). Net load forecast error compensation for peak shaving in a grid-connected PV storage system. *IEEE Transactions on Power Systems, 39*(2), 4372–4381. DOI: 10.1109/TPWRS.2023.3317309

Negri, E., Fumagalli, L., & Macchi, M. (2017). A review of the roles of digital twin in CPS-based production systems. *Procedia Manufacturing, 11*, 939–948. DOI: 10.1016/j.promfg.2017.07.198

Onile, A. E., Petlenkov, E., Levron, Y., & Belikov, J. (2024). Smartgrid-based hybrid digital twins framework for demand side recommendation service provision in distributed power systems. *Future Generation Computer Systems, 156*, 142–156. DOI: 10.1016/j.future.2024.03.018

Pasqualetti, F., Dörfler, F., & Bullo, F. (2022). Cyber-physical attacks in power networks: Models, fundamental limitations, and monitor design. *IEEE Transactions on Automatic Control, 60*(7), 1775–1789.

Qi, Q., Tao, F., Hu, T., Anwer, N., Liu, A., Wei, Y., Wang, L., & Nee, A. Y. C. (2021). Enabling technologies and tools for digital twin. *Journal of Manufacturing Systems, 58*, 3–21. DOI: 10.1016/j.jmsy.2019.10.001

Redelinghuys, A. J. H., Basson, A. H., & Kruger, K. (2020). A six-layer architecture for the digital twin: A manufacturing case study implementation. *Journal of Intelligent Manufacturing, 31*(6), 1383–1402. DOI: 10.1007/s10845-019-01516-6

Rosen, R., von Wichert, G., Lo, G., & Bettenhausen, K. D. (2015). About the importance of autonomy and digital twins for the future of manufacturing. *IFAC-PapersOnLine, 48*(3), 567–572.

Saxena, A., Goebel, K., Simon, D., & Eklund, N. (2022). Damage propagation modeling for aircraft engine run-to-failure simulation. *2008 International Conference on Prognostics and Health Management*, 1–9.

Shafto, M., Conroy, M., Doyle, R., Glaessgen, E., Kemp, C., LeMoigne, J., & Wang, L. (2010). Modeling, simulation, information technology & processing roadmap. *NASA Technology Roadmaps, 32*.

Song, Z., Hackl, C. M., Anand, A., Thommessen, A., Petzschmann, J., Kamel, O., Braunbehrens, R., Kaifel, A., Roos, C., & Hauptmann, S. (2023). Digital twins for the future power system: An overview and a future perspective. *Sustainability (Basel), 15*(6), 5259. DOI: 10.3390/su15065259

Stark, R., Fresemann, C., & Lindow, K. (2021). Development and operation of digital twins for technical systems and services. *CIRP Annals, 68*(1), 129–132. DOI: 10.1016/j.cirp.2019.04.024

Tao, F., Zhang, M., Liu, Y., & Nee, A. Y. C. (2018). Digital twin in industry: State-of-the-art. *IEEE Transactions on Industrial Informatics, 15*(4), 2405–2415. DOI: 10.1109/TII.2018.2873186

Tiwari, D., Bhatele, K. R., Jha, A., & Chaudhary, K. (2025). Electrical digital twins–enabled smart grid. In *Digital Twins for Smart Cities and Villages* (pp. 489–512). Elsevier. DOI: 10.1016/B978-0-443-28884-5.00021-X

Uhlemann, T. H. J., Lehmann, C., & Steinhilper, R. (2017). The digital twin: Realizing the cyber-physical production system for Industry 4.0. *Procedia CIRP, 61*, 335–340. DOI: 10.1016/j.procir.2016.11.152

Wan, J., Tang, S., Shu, Z., Li, D., Wang, S., Imran, M., & Vasilakos, A. V. (2019). Software-defined industrial internet of things in the context of Industry 4.0. *IEEE Sensors Journal, 16*(20), 7373–7380.

Wu, P., & Mei, X. (2024). Microgrids energy management considering net-zero energy concept: The role of renewable energy landscaping design and IoT modeling in digital twin realistic simulator. *Sustainable Energy Technologies and Assessments, 63*, 103621. DOI: 10.1016/j.seta.2024.103621

Chapter 2
AI-Enabled Incident Response and Automated Remediation

Soumen Prakash Kabi
http://orcid.org/0009-0000-9019-6841
Asansol Engineering College, India

Shibsankar Bala
http://orcid.org/0000-0002-1978-9182
Asansol Engineering College, India

Sujoy Kumar Basu
http://orcid.org/0000-0003-4085-154X
Asansol Engineering College, India

P. Selvakumar
http://orcid.org/0000-0002-3650-4548
Department of Science and Humanities, Nehru Institute of Technology, Coimbatore, India

T. C. Manjunath
http://orcid.org/0000-0003-2545-9160
Rajarajeswari College of Engineering, Bengaluru, India

Prateek Srivastava
http://orcid.org/0009-0005-8885-4274
CSJM University, India

ABSTRACT

Concept practice of incident response has undergone a profound transformation. and sheer volume security incidents have necessitated a shift from traditional manual methods to advanced, automated, and AI-driven solutions. Understanding this evolution is crucial seeking defend effectively operational ever-morphing cyber adversaries. Incident response (IR) in its earliest form was largely a manual process. The foundational approach centered around human analysts detecting, analyzing, and mitigating security incidents without significant technological assistance. In the nascent days of networked computing, the threat landscape was relatively simpler and less dynamic. Organizations primarily dealt with isolated incidents such as unauthorized access attempts or rudimentary malware infections. During

DOI: 10.4018/979-8-2600-1498-1.ch002

this period, incident response was often reactive and ad hoc. Security teams relied heavily on manual log reviews, rule-based intrusion detection systems (IDS), and straightforward signatures to detect known threats.

THE IMPORTANCE OF AI IN INCIDENT RESPONSE AND REMEDIATION

Concept practice of incident response has undergone a profound transformation. and sheer volume security incidents have necessitated a shift from traditional manual methods to advanced, automated, and AI-driven solutions. Understanding this evolution is crucial seeking defend effectively operational ever-morphing cyber adversaries. Incident response (IR) in its earliest form was largely a manual process. The foundational approach centered around human analysts detecting, analyzing, and mitigating security incidents without significant technological assistance. In the nascent days of networked computing, the threat landscape was relatively simpler and less dynamic. Organizations primarily dealt with isolated incidents such as unauthorized access attempts or rudimentary malware infections. During this period, incident response was often reactive and ad hoc. Security teams relied heavily on manual log reviews, rule-based intrusion detection systems (IDS), and straightforward signatures to detect known threats. Incident handlers would painstakingly analyze system logs, firewall records, and network traffic to identify suspicious activity. Tools were limited, fragmented, and not integrated, requiring significant human effort to piece together the incident narrative. Documentation was typically maintained manually, and communication channels for incident coordination were basic, often reliant on phone calls, emails, or in-person meetings. This manual approach, while effective for early and less sophisticated threats, quickly became inadequate cyber incidents. The growing interconnectivity of networks, web applications, advent mobile introduced vectors for attackers, who in turn developed more sophisticated and stealthy attack techniques.

By the late 1990s and early 2000s, the cybersecurity community recognized the need for more structured and scalable incident response processes. This era marked the introduction of formalized IR frameworks and playbooks aimed at standardizing response efforts. Notable frameworks such as. Concurrently, technology began playing a more correlating data from diverse sources in real time. SIEMs enabled analysts to spot patterns and anomalies faster than manual methods allowed. Automation scripts and rule-based engines started to handle routine tasks such as alert triage, log parsing, and basic response actions like blocking IP addresses or isolating infected hosts. Despite these advancements, the automation was still largely rule-driven and dependent on human configuration. The reliance on signature-based detection methods left many gaps, especially against zero-day exploits and sophisticated targeted attacks. The volume of alerts generated often overwhelmed security teams, leading to alert fatigue and missed critical incidents. As cyber threats became more complex and adversaries more organized, incident response evolved to incorporate proactive elements such as threat intelligence. Organizations began integrating external feeds of known which helped in anticipating and preparing for emerging threats. Incident response platforms (IRPs) emerged to facilitate collaboration and orchestration. These platforms provided centralized dashboards, automated workflows, and playbook execution capabilities. Orchestration allowed multiple security tools to work together seamlessly—automatically collecting data, enriching alerts with threat intelligence, and executing containment measures. This approach reduced enabled consistency across handlers and teams.

BENEFITS OF AI-ENABLED INCIDENT RESPONSE: FASTER AND MORE EFFECTIVE

The digital age, cyber threats have grown not only in frequency but in complexity and sophistication. This evolution has dramatically reshaped the cybersecurity landscape, placing unprecedented demands on incident response teams to detect, analyze, and remediate incidents swiftly and accurately. (Adeyeye O. J. et al.,2024) Amid this challenging environment, incident response and remediation, fundamentally speed, defenses. importance in this domain cannot be overstated—it represents a pivotal shift from reactive, (Adeyeye O. J. et al.,2024) labor-intensive approaches to proactive, intelligent, and automated defense mechanisms capable of addressing modern cyber threats at scale. (Ahmed N. et al.,2025) Organizations today face a daunting barrage of cyberattacks, ranging from opportunistic malware infections to highly targeted advanced persistent threats (APTs) orchestrated by skilled adversaries exponentially, fueled by proliferation remote workforces, increasingly interconnected systems. Consequently, the volume of security alerts generated daily has reached staggering levels. Traditional security operations centers (SOCs), rule-based tools, (Ahmed N. et al.,2025) are overwhelmed by quantity they must process. This alert overload leads "alert fatigue," analysts or unable prioritize effectively, delayed responses or threats. Additionally, the speed at which attackers operate—often moving laterally within networks and exfiltrating data within minutes—demands incident response times far beyond human capability alone. In this context, AI has become indispensable in managing the scale and velocity of modern cyber threats, enabling organizations to maintain robust defenses without proportionally increasing human resources. Machine learning models can analyze vast datasets encompassing network traffic, user behaviors, endpoint enables previously by recognizing subtle indicators of compromise that traditional methods miss. For example, AI can flag unusual login patterns that suggest credential theft or identify fileless malware activities that do not leave traditional signatures.

Moreover, (Ahmed S. et al.,2023) AI-powered threat detection systems continuously improve by learning from new data, evolving attacker tactics, and incorporating feedback from human analysts. This adaptability makes AI defense postures environment continuously. AI addressing challenge alert overload. leveraging advanced analytics correlation algorithms, AI systems can automatically triage alerts, group related events and assigning risk scores based on nature threat and potential business impact. (Ahmed S. et al.,2023) This automated prioritization helps security teams focus their attention critical incidents, burnout overall response enrichment provides context to alerts, enabling faster and more informed decision-making by analysts. Beyond detection, AI is transforming how organizations remediate incidents. Rapid containment and mitigation are essential to limit damage during an attack. Manual remediation processes—such as isolating infected devices, applying patches, or revoking compromised credentials—can be slow, error-prone, and resource-intensive. AI-driven automation streamlines these tasks through AI's decision-making capabilities with automated playbooks. These platforms can execute predefined or dynamically generated response actions immediately upon detection of a threat. For example, if AI detects malware spreading laterally within a network, (Akinade A. O. et al.,2021) the quarantine data collection for further analysis is window opportunity for attackers, significantly reducing the potential impact of incidents. Furthermore, (Akinade A. O. et al.,2021) AI can assist in recommending remediation incident threat intelligence, organizational policies. guidance helps human responders make better-informed decisions, ensuring consistent and effective responses while preserving the ability for manual intervention when necessary.

ANOMALY DETECTION: IDENTIFYING INCIDENTS WITH AI-POWERED MONITORING

The cybersecurity landscape is constantly shifting, with threat actors becoming increasingly sophisticated and attacks growing more frequent and complex. In this environment, traditional incident response mechanisms—largely manual and reactive—are no longer sufficient to keep pace. (Al E'mari S. et al.,2025) Artificial intelligence (AI)-enabled incident response represents a transformative advancement, providing organizations with faster, more effective ways to detect, analyze, and mitigate cyber incidents processes delivers wide array of benefits that fundamentally improve the agility and robustness of security operations, (Al E'mari S. et al.,2025) empowering and reduce the impact of cyberattacks incident response is the acceleration of threat detection and analysis. Conventional detection methods often rely on static rules or known signatures, which can be slow to update and ineffective against novel or sophisticated threats. AI, through enables systems and suspicious activities continuously learning. AI algorithms can rapidly sift through enormous streams of network traffic, logs, endpoint telemetry, (Ali A. R. A. R. et al.,2024) and user activity to identify patterns indicative of malicious behavior. This near-instantaneous analysis vastly outpaces human capabilities, dramatically reducing the "dwell time" — the period during which an attacker remains undetected within a network. By detecting threats faster, organizations can act sooner to contain and remediate incidents, minimizing potential damage. Moreover, AI's ability to correlate seemingly unrelated data points helps uncover hidden would subtle changes user behavior combined with unusual network communications might indicate a compromised account or an insider threat. (Ali A. R. A. R. et al.,2024) AI's holistic view of security data enhances situational awareness and leads to more comprehensive threat detection.

Additionally, AI can group related alerts into single, coherent incidents, providing a clearer understanding of the attack's scope and reducing the noise caused by fragmented alerts. By cutting through the clutter, (Alzboon M. S. et al.,2023) AI analyst productivity and timeliness response actions. Incident response involves numerous routine tasks, such as data collection, log analysis, alert enrichment, and basic remediation steps. These activities, while essential, can be labor-intensive when performed manually. (Alzboon M. S. et al.,2023) AI-driven automation significantly accelerates these workflows by executing repetitive tasks without direct human intervention. (Ayyaswamy K. et al.,2025) By speeding up response actions and reducing manual errors, AI-driven automation helps organizations contain threats more quickly and effectively, minimizing inflic. Human analysts, despite their expertise, are susceptible to errors, especially under the stress and time pressure common during incident handling. AI systems, on the other hand, provide consistent, repeatable analysis and response actions based on well-defined models and playbooks. (Ayyaswamy K. et al.,2025) AI algorithms apply uniform criteria when evaluating threats and recommending remediation, ensuring systematically organizational. This consistency reduces variability in response quality enforce. Furthermore, AI's continual learning capabilities mean that its detection and response methods improve over time, incorporating evolving landscapes. This adaptability ensures that organizations level accuracy efficacy.

PREDICTIVE ANALYTICS: FORECASTING INCIDENT IMPACT AND SEVERITY

In the complex and fast-evolving domain of cybersecurity, anomaly detection has become a cornerstone technique for identifying potential security incidents that traditional signature-based systems often miss. (Babu C. S. et al.,2025) As cyber threats grow more sophisticated, attackers continuously adapt their methods to evade standard detection techniques. Against this backdrop, (Babu C. S. et al.,2025) AI-powered anomaly detection emerges as an indispensable tool, enabling organizations behavior signif. This analytical approach leverages monitor, flag unusual patterns across diverse data sources, providing early warnings and actionable insights. The fundamental principle is to first establish a baseline of "normal" activity by analyzing historical data under typical conditions. Once this baseline is set, the system continuously monitors real-time data, comparing current behavior against the established norms. Any significant deviation—whether it's an unusual login time, unexpected data transfer volumes, atypical process executions, or irregular network communications—is flagged as an anomaly warranting further investigation. Traditional anomaly detection methods have relied heavily on statistical techniques, (Baruwal Chhetri M. et al.,2024) such as threshold-based rules or fixed heuristics, which often lack the flexibility to adapt to the dynamic nature of modern IT environments. These static approaches tend to generate high false-positive rates because what constitutes "normal" can vary widely across users, devices, applications, and time. They may also miss subtle, (Baruwal Chhetri M. et al.,2024) stealthy attacks that don't trigger predefined thresholds but represent dangerous behavior nonetheless. Additionally, manual tuning of detection parameters and reliance on domain experts to interpret alerts can delay response times and introduce human error. As IT infrastructures grow more complex and generate massive volumes of data, these limitations have rendered traditional anomaly detection insufficient for timely and accurate threat identification.

Artificial intelligence, particularly machine learning (ML), transforms anomaly detection by addressing these shortcomings through advanced data analysis capabilities. AI-powered monitoring systems use deviations more accurately and with greater context awareness. Supervised Learning: This approachof normal and malicious behavior. (Boorugupalli K. K. et al.,2025) It excels when historical attack data is available but may struggle with novel threats. Unsupervised Learning: Here, models identify anomalies without predefined labels by clustering data points and recognizing outliers based on statistical rarity or deviation. This method is well-suited for detecting previously unseen attacks. (Boorugupalli K. K. et al.,2025) Semi-supervised Learning: Combining elements of both, this approach leverages abundant unlabeled data alongside limited labeled examples to improve detection accuracy. AI models continuously update and refine their understanding of "normal" behavior, adapting to changes in user activities, network configurations, and application usage. This dynamic baseline adjustment reduces false positives and enhances the system's ability to spot genuine threats that deviate from evolving norms.These techniques can be combined and tailored to specific environments, (Chib S. et al.,2025) providing layered detection capabilities that improve accuracy and context-awareness. powered involves greater integration of context-aware models and explainable AI techniques that improve transparency and analyst trust. Advances in federated learning will enable collaborative threat detection sensitiv. Moreover, convergence AI other emerging technologies, (Chib S. et al.,2025) such as threat intelligence sharing, automation, and SOAR platforms, will enhance the overall cybersecurity posture by enabling faster, more coordinated responses to detected anomalies.

AUTOMATED INCIDENT TRIAGE: PRIORITIZING AND ASSIGNING INCIDENTS

In the realm of cybersecurity, the ability to anticipate the potential impact and severity of security incidents before they fully materialize is invaluable. This foresight allows organizations to allocate resources effectively, prioritize response actions, and minimize damage to their digital assets and business operations and AI technologies, offers precisely this capability the likely outcomes of cyber incidents, enabling. This discussion delves into the role of predictive analytics in forecasting incident impact and severity, examining its methodologies, advantages, (Chinthamu N. et al.,2025) challenges, and transformative potential within modern incident response strategies. Within cybersecurity, predictive analytics moves beyond reactive approaches—where security teams respond to incidents after detection—to a proactive paradigm where the likely course and consequences of incidents are anticipated and managed ahead of time. In practice, predictive analytics models assess various indicators related to a detected or emerging incident. These indicators might include the type and origin of the threat, the vulnerabilities exploited, the affected systems and their criticality, attacker behavior patterns, and contextual factors such as network topology and current threat intelligence. By synthesizing this information, (Chinthamu N. et al.,2025) predictive models estimate the probable severity of the incident, the potential scope of compromise, and the anticipated business impact.The integration of predictive analytics into incident response frameworks delivers numerous benefits that enhance security posture and operational effectiveness: Proactive Resource Allocation: By forecasting which incidents pose the greatest risk, organizations can prioritize their response efforts personnel, forensic containment measures efficiently. This ensures critical threats receive immediate attention while lower-risk incidents are monitored appropriately.

Faster Decision-Making: Predictive insights reduce uncertainty around incident impact, enabling security teams to make faster, (Dahiya R. et al.,2025) data-driven decisions. This accelerates containment and remediation actions, limiting attacker dwell time and reducing potential damage. Improved Incident Prioritization: In environments inundated with security alerts, predictive analytics helps distinguish between benign anomalies and high-impact threats. (Dahiya R. et al.,2025) This prioritization prevents alert fatigue and focuses analyst attention on incidents that warrant urgent investigation. Enhanced Communication and Reporting: Clear forecasts of incident severity facilitate better communication with stakeholders, including executives and risk management teams. Predictive analytics provides quantifiable risk assessments that support strategic planning, compliance reporting, and regulatory engagement. Adaptive Security Posture: By continuously learning from new incidents and outcomes, predictive models evolve to reflect emerging threats and vulnerabilities. This adaptability enables organizations to stay ahead of attackers and refine their defense strategies proactively. Threat Intelligence Integration: Combining threat intelligence with incident data enhances predictive accuracy. For example, awareness of an emerging malware campaign targeting specific industries can inform forecasts of incident impact if such threats are detected. (Dash A. et al.,2023) Endpoint Security: Predictive models assess the severity of endpoint incidents by analyzing process behaviors, file modifications, and system anomalies, helping to distinguish critical breaches from false alarms. Network Security: By examining traffic patterns and anomaly scores, predictive analytics estimates the potential spread of network intrusions and data exfiltration risk. Cloud Security: Predictive analytics monitors cloud workloads and user activities, forecasting the impact of misconfigurations, privilege escalations, (Dash A. et al.,2023) or insider threats within cloud environments. Incident Response Automation: Risk scores and impact predictions generated by predictive analytics feed into automated response platforms, enabling dynamic adjustment of containment measures based on predicted severity.

AUTOMATED INCIDENT RESPONSE PLAYBOOKS: STREAMLINING RESPONSE PROCESSES

Incident triage is the process of evaluating security alerts to determine their legitimacy, severity, potential impact, and urgency. It serves as the critical first step in incident response, filtering through noise to identify true threats and deciding how best to allocate limited security resources. (Engel R. et al.,2022) Effective triage prevents analysts from becoming overwhelmed by false positives and low-priority alerts, allowing them to incidents significan. Automated incident triage enhances this process by applying algorithms, heuristics, and AI-driven insights to analyze alert data approach human effort required to assess each alert, accelerates the prioritization process, and ensures that incident assignments are aligned with the skills and availability of response teams. Automated triage systems integrate multiple components and techniques to evaluate and prioritize incidents. Automated triage begins with the aggregation of alerts from diverse security tools and platforms. Normalization processes standardize data formats and enrich alerts with contextual information, such as asset criticality, threat intelligence, (Engel R. et al.,2022) and historical incident data. Alert Correlation and Deduplication: By correlating related alerts across systems, automated triage consolidates multiple indicators of a single incident, reducing duplication and providing a unified incident view. Risk Scoring and Prioritization: Using machine learning models and rule-based engines, alerts are scored based on severity, likelihood of being a true positive, asset importance, and potential business impact.

This scoring enables dynamic prioritization, often categorizing incidents into levels such as critical, high, medium, or low priority. Automated Classification: Incidents are classified according to predefined categories—malware infection, insider threat, phishing attempt, data exfiltration, (Ferraro C. et al.,2024) etc.—enabling tailored response workflows. Assignment and Workflow Orchestration: Based on prioritization and classification, automated systems assign incidents to the appropriate analysts or teams, considering factors like expertise, workload, and shift schedules. This assignment can be further integrated with Security Orchestration, (Ferraro C. et al.,2024) Automation, and Response (SOAR) platforms to automate subsequent investigative or remediation actions. Automated incident triage is a vital advancement in cybersecurity operations, addressing the challenge of overwhelming alert volumes and the need for rapid, accurate incident prioritization and assignment. (Goswami et al., 2025) By leveraging AI, machine learning, and orchestration technologies, automated triage accelerates detection, reduces analyst workload, improves response consistency, and optimizes resource allocation. Despite challenges related to data quality, evolving threats, and human trust, ongoing innovations in AI explainability, (Goswami et al.,2025) behavioral analytics, and integration promise to make automated triage even more effective and indispensable.

AI-DRIVEN REMEDIATION: AUTOMATING FIXES AND MITIGATIONS

In the rapidly evolving cyber threat landscape, speed and precision in incident response are paramount. (Govindaraj M. et al.,2025) Organizations face incidents, which swift, consistent, and coordinated actions to contain and remediate threats. Manual response processes are often slow, error-prone, and resource-intensive, leading to delayed containment and increased risk exposure. (Govindaraj M. et al.,2025) Automated incident response playbooks have emerged as a powerful solution to streamline and accelerate incident handling. By codifying response procedures into automated workflows, (Hossain Z. et al.,2025) these playbooks help security teams reduce response times, minimize human error, and improve overall operational efficiency procedures and actions designed to address specific types of security incidents. Traditionally, (Hossain Z. et al.,2025) these playbooks are documented guides that analysts follow during an incident. Automation elevates playbooks from static manuals to dynamic workflows that integrate with security tools and systems, enabling the automatic execution of response steps based on trigger conditions. Automated playbooks are typically implemented within platforms, although they can also be part of extended detection and response (XDR) systems or integrated with perform actions such as alert enrichment, threat intelligence queries, containment measures, notification dispatch, forensic data collection, and remediation tasks—all with minimal human intervention. (Inaganti A. C. et al.,2021) Triggering Conditions: Automated playbooks start with defined triggers—specific alerts, thresholds, or event patterns that initiate the workflow. For example, detection of a ransomware signature or a suspicious login might trigger the execution of a corresponding playbook. Decision Logic and Branching: Playbooks incorporate decision points and conditional logic to adapt response actions based on incident severity, asset criticality, (Inaganti A. C. et al.,2021) or evolving investigation results. This dynamic decision-making capability ensures responses are context-aware and tailored.

Figure 1. AI in Cybersecurity Revolutionizing Threat Detection

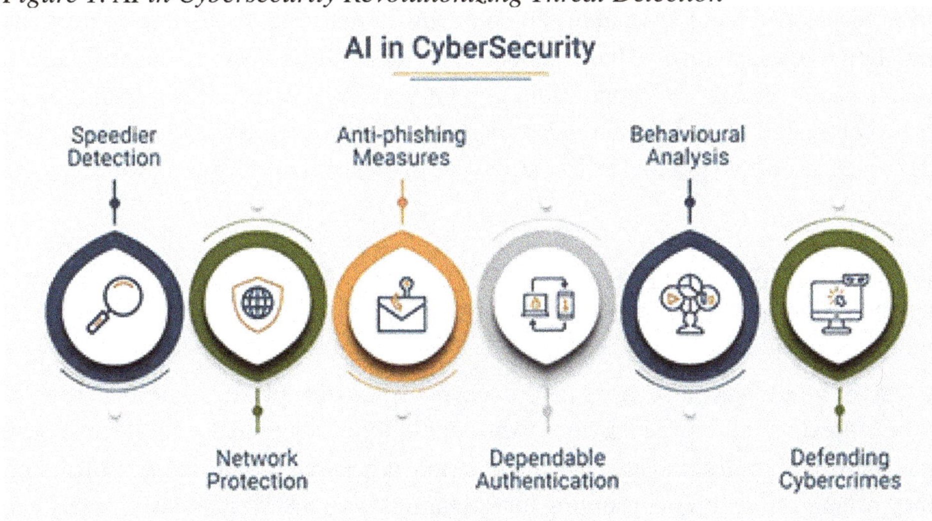

Accelerated Response Times: Automated execution eliminates delays inherent in manual processes. Immediate containment actions reduce the window of attacker activity and potential damage. Consistency and Accuracy: Automated playbooks ensure standardized responses to similar incident types, minimizing variability and human error. This consistency is crucial for regulatory compliance and quality assurance. Improved Coordination: Playbooks orchestrate actions across diverse security tools and teams, fostering seamless collaboration and ensuring that all response steps occur in proper sequence and timeframe. (Karadsheh L. et al.,2025) Scalability: Automated workflows scale to handle increasing alert volumes without proportional increases in staffing, making them essential for growing security operations centers (SOCs). Enhanced Visibility and Metrics: Continuous logging of playbook activities provides valuable data for measuring response effectiveness, identifying bottlenecks, and guiding improvements. (Karadsheh L. et al.,2025) Despite their clear benefits, developing and deploying automated incident response playbooks involves challenges: Complexity of Playbook Design: Crafting effective playbooks requires deep understanding of incident types, organizational policies, tool capabilities, and potential attack scenarios. Overly rigid playbooks risk missing nuances; overly complex ones can be difficult to maintain. Integration with Diverse Tools: Organizations often use heterogeneous security solutions. Achieving seamless integration for orchestration demands robust APIs and custom connectors, which can be time-consuming and costly to develop. (Kaur M. et al.,2025) Maintaining Playbook Relevance: Cyber threats evolve rapidly, necessitating frequent updates to playbooks to address new attack vectors, vulnerabilities, and compliance requirements. Balancing Automation and Human Oversight: While automation accelerates response, not all incidents can or should be fully automated. Designing appropriate escalation points to involve human judgment is essential to avoid erroneous actions. (Kaur M. et al.,2025) Change Management and Adoption: Security teams must trust automated playbooks and adapt their workflows accordingly. Training, clear documentation, and gradual rollout strategies help build confidence and acceptance.

INTEGRATION WITH EXISTING TOOLS AND SYSTEMS: SEAMLESS AUTOMATION

In the modern cybersecurity landscape, the volume, sophistication, and speed of cyber threats require organizations to adopt highly efficient and adaptive response mechanisms. Traditional manual remediation processes are no longer sufficient; they often involve time-consuming investigations, human error, and delays that can exacerbate damage. AI-driven remediation represents a transformative shift, (Kommineni M. et al.,2025) leveraging automate diagnosis execution fixes and mitigations in response automating remediation actions, accelerate recovery times, reduce risk exposure, and free up strategic threat hunting analysis. AI-driven remediation refers to automation framework identify vulnerabilities or malicious activity and initiate automated corrective actions. (Kommineni M. et al.,2025) Unlike traditional reactive methods, AI-driven remediation integrates predictive analytics and behavioral insights to anticipate threats and apply fixes before incidents escalate. This form of remediation is often implemented within broader tools, or specialized AI-powered cybersecurity solutions. The core objective is to minimize human intervention while maintaining precision and adaptability in remediation steps.Threat Detection and Classification: AI models analyze telemetry from endpoints, networks, and cloud environments to detect anomalies, classify threats, and determine remediation needs. This includes recognizing malware variants, suspicious behaviors, privilege escalations, or configuration weaknesses. Root Cause Analysis: Machine learning algorithms assist in diagnosing the underlying causes of security incidents by correlating disparate data points and historical incident patterns. (Limbore N. V. et al.,2025) Effective root cause identification enables targeted remediation rather than superficial fixes. Automated Playbooks and Workflows: Based on AI insights, automated workflows execute remediation steps such as patch application, system isolation, user access revocation, firewall rule updates, or rollback of malicious changes. Continuous Learning and Adaptation: AI models continually learn from new incidents, remediation outcomes, (Limbore N. V. et al.,2025) and threat intelligence to refine their decision-making processes, improvin. Speed and Scalability: Automated remediation actions occur in near real-time, vastly reducing the window between detection and mitigation. This speed is critical in containing fast-moving threats like ransomware or zero-day exploits. Moreover, AI systems scale effortlessly to handle increasing alert volumes without proportional human staffing increases.

BENEFITS OF AI-ENABLED INCIDENT RESPONSE AND AUTOMATED REMEDIATION

Automation in cybersecurity aims to reduce manual intervention by enabling systems to communicate, coordinate, and execute tasks autonomously. However, without proper integration, (Maheshwaran T. et al.,2024) automated workflows can be siloed, fragmented, and ineffective. Integration allows automation platforms—such as solutions—to ingest diverse, apply intelligent decision-making, and trigger coordinated response actions across multiple tools and environments. (Maheshwaran T. et al.,2024) The value of integration extends beyond efficiency. It enables organizations to maximize their existing technology investments by leveraging and orchestrating their current toolsets instead of replacing them. Moreover, integration fosters improved situational awareness by correlating data and alerts across platforms, providing security teams with a unified, comprehensive view of threats and system status. (Muzahid A. J. M. et al., 2023) This holistic visibility is crucial for accurate detection, prioritization, and remediation. Despite its critical importance, integration presents several technical and organizational challenges: Diverse Toolsets and Standards: Organizations often deploy a heterogeneous mix of security solutions from multiple vendors, each with unique data formats, (Muzahid A. J. M. et al.,2023) APIs, protocols, and integration capabilities. Standardizing communication between these tools requires significant effort and custom connectors. Legacy Systems and Limited APIs: Older or proprietary systems may lack robust APIs or support modern integration frameworks, complicating efforts to automate workflows involving these components. Data Quality and Normalization: Aggregating data from multiple sources often results in inconsistencies, duplications, and varying levels of data granularity. Normalizing and enriching this data is essential for reliable automation and correlation. Security and Compliance Concerns: Integrations must maintain secure data exchange and comply with regulatory requirements, especially when handling sensitive information or cross-domain interactions. Change Management: Integrating new automated workflows can impact existing processes and require training, coordination, and cultural shifts within security teams.

Successful integration strategies involve a combination of architectural best practices, technology standards, and automation frameworks: API-First Design: Modern security tools increasingly provide RESTful APIs or similar programmable interfaces, enabling automation platforms to retrieve data and invoke actions programmatically.

Designing automation solutions around these APIs ensures flexibility and scalability. Use of Connectors and Adapters: (Nagmoti N. S. et al.,2025) Many SOAR and automation platforms offer pre-built connectors or plugins for popular security tools, reducing integration effort. When pre-built connectors are unavailable, custom adapters can be developed to bridge tools. Event-Driven Architectures: Integration is enhanced by event-driven models, (Nagmoti N. S. et al.,2025) where tools publish events (e.g., alerts, logs, status changes) that automation platforms subscribe to and react upon. This real-time responsiveness is key for timely remediation. Orchestration Frameworks: SOAR platforms provide orchestration engines to coordinate workflows spanning multiple tools, ensuring sequential and conditional execution of automated actions. Security Gateways and Brokers: Middleware solutions can mediate communication between incompatible systems, handle protocol translations, and enforce security policies in integration flows. (Nguyen T. N. et al.,2021) When integration is well-executed, the benefits to cybersecurity operations are substantial: End-to-End Automation: Automated workflows can span detection, investigation, triage, (Nguyen T. N. et al.,2021) and remediation steps across multiple platforms without human intervention, significantly accelerating incident response. Enhanced Incident Context and Correlation: Integrating logs, alerts, and telemetry from various tools enriches incident data, enabling better correlation of events and more accurate threat detection. Reduced Alert Fatigue: Consolidated and correlated data reduce redundant alerts, helping analysts focus on genuine threats. Improved Resource Utilization: Automation reduces manual, repetitive tasks such as data gathering, ticket creation, and routine remediation, freeing analysts for higher-value activities.

CHALLENGES AND LIMITATIONS: IMPLEMENTING AI IN INCIDENT RESPONSE

Complex and an unprecedented volume and variety of threats. Traditional manual incident response processes struggl, scale, sophistication cyberattacks. In this environment, AI-enabled incident response combined with automated remediation has emerged as a critical advancement that dramatically detect, analyze, prioritize, mitigate securit. By leveraging artificial intelligence, machine learning, and automation, organizations can achieve faster, more accurate, and scalable responses to cyber threats—transforming cybersecurity operations from reactive firefighting into proactive, (Niveditha et al.,2025) adaptive defense. One of the most immediate benefits of AI-enabled incident response is the dramatic acceleration of detection and response times. AI-powered systems analyze vast amounts of security data from endpoints, networks, cloud environments, and applications human analysts could. Machine learning models and threat intelligence, even previously unseen attack patterns or subtle indicators of compromise. When an incident is detected, (Niveditha et al.,2025) AI-driven workflows automatically initiate triage and preliminary analysis, rapidly categorizing alerts by severity and context. This enables security teams to prioritize incidents allocate resources effectively. Automated remediation capabilities can then swiftly implement containment and mitigation infected devices, minimizing attacker's dwell time and limiting potential damage. Manual incident response is prone to human error and cognitive biases, especially when analysts face overwhelming alert volumes leading to fatigue. (Ozobu C. O. et al.,2025) AI-driven systems improve accuracy by consistently applying advanced analytics and learned threat models to identify genuine threats while filtering out benign anomalies. (Ozobu C. O. et al.,2025) This alleviates, enabling attention verified rather than chasing false alarms.

Moreover, automated remediation workflows apply standardized, tested fixes consistently, reducing the risk of mistakes that might occur in manual interventions—such as incorrect firewall rules, partial patching, or incomplete user account revocation. This precision not only speeds up recovery but also maintains the integrity and stability of IT environments incidents increases exponentially. AI-enabled incident response and automated remediation enable organizations to scale their security operations without a proportional increase in headcount. Automation platforms can handle repetitive and time-consuming tasks—like data enrichment, evidence collection, (Parisa S. K. et al.,2023) alert correlation, and initial containment—allowing security analysts to focus on advanced threat hunting, strategic planning, and complex investigations. This operational efficiency translates into significant cost savings by reducing the labor-intensive aspects of incident management. It also allows smaller or resource-constrained security teams to maintain robust defenses against a growing and diverse threat landscape. (Parisa S. K. et al.,2023) AI is not limited to reactive defense. Advanced AI and machine learning models enable proactive threat hunting by continuously analyzing security telemetry, user behavior, and network activity to identify suspicious patterns before they escalate into full-blown incidents. Predictive analytics forecast potential attack paths and impact severity, allowing organizations to preemptively strengthen defenses or automate mitigations. For example, AI systems can identify vulnerable assets or configurations that are likely to be targeted and automatically apply patches or configuration changes.

SECURITY AND DATA PRIVACY CONSIDERATIONS: ENSURING SAFE AUTOMATION

Cybersecurity operations, offering unparalleled speed, scalability, and analytical capabilities. However, despite these transformative benefits, implementing AI in incident response presents a complex array. (Rashid M. M. et al.,2025) These obstacles span technical, operational, ethical, and organizational domains, affecting the effectiveness, trustworthiness, and sustainability. Understanding challenges devising strategies that mitigate risks and optimize AI adoption in incident response. Security datasets often contain noise, incomplete records, inconsistencies, and biases that can degrade model accuracy and reliability. Moreover, labeling data for supervised learning—where models learn to distinguish benign from malicious activity—requires significant expert effort and domain knowledge. The dynamic and adversarial nature of cyber threats makes it difficult to maintain up-to-date labeled datasets, leading to models trained on outdated or incomplete threat landscapes. Without sufficient, diverse, and well-curated data, AI models may underperform or generate undermining trust operational effectiveness exhibit remarkable complexity continuously evolve to evade detection. Attackers adopt sophisticated polymorphic malware and attack patterns or highly targeted intrusions, limiting their generalization ability. (Rashid M. M. et al.,2025) Additionally, attackers can deliberately manipulate data inputs—an area known as adversarial machine learning—to confuse or deceive. Defending against such adversarial attacks requires advanced, robust AI architectures and constant monitoring, adding layers of complexity to implementation.

Most organizations operate heterogeneous security environments composed of multiple tools, platforms, and legacy systems. Integrating AI-driven incident response capabilities seamlessly into these existing infrastructures is a significant challenge. Differences in data formats, APIs, communication protocols, and operational workflows complicate integration efforts. Legacy systems may lack modern interfaces or support for automation, forcing organizations to develop custom connectors or workarounds, (Samal A. et al.,2025) which increase costs and maintenance burdens. Moreover, integration must ensure consistent security policies and compliance adherence across all tools, demanding rigorous testing and governance frameworks. While AI excels at automating routine detection and response tasks, it cannot fully replace human expertise—particularly in complex, (Samal A. et al.,2025) high-impact incidents requiring contextual judgment, strategic thinking, and ethical considerations. One major challenge is determining the optimal balance between automated remediation and human oversight. Over-reliance on automation risks executing incorrect or premature actions, such as isolating critical systems or deleting important files, which may cause operational disruptions or data loss. Conversely, excessive manual intervention undermines the efficiency benefits AI offers. Designing effective human-in-the-loop systems that incorporate AI recommendations while allowing override automated is essential but operationally complex.

FUTURE TRENDS: EMERGING AI TECHNOLOGIES IN INCIDENT RESPONSE

As organizations increasingly adopt automation technologies in their cybersecurity operations, particularly in incident response and remediation, the imperative to ensure security and data privacy within these automated frameworks has never been greater. Automation promises speed, consistency, and scalability, but complexities addressed to safeguard sensitive information, maintain compliance, and uphold trust. Ensuring safe automation requires a holistic approach encompassing robust security architectures, data governance practices, privacy protections, and continuous monitoring. (Saurabh B. et al.,2024) This comprehensive overview examines the critical security and data privacy considerations necessary to implement automation responsibly and effectively in cybersecurity environments. Automation in cybersecurity involves orchestrating multiple systems, processing vast amounts of security data, and executing response actions autonomously or with minimal human intervention. This environment inherently touches on system configurations, threat intelligence—making it a prime target for malicious actors. (Saurabh B. et al.,2024) Additionally, automated actions have the potential to alter system states or user privileges, amplifying the impact of any security flaw or misuse. Additionally, managing and securing API keys, service accounts, and automation credentials through vaults or secure key management systems is essential to prevent leakage or misuse. Automation platforms ingest, process, and transmit security telemetry and sensitive data across multiple systems. Protecting data confidentiality and integrity throughout its lifecycle is critical. Furthermore, sensitive data handling must minimize exposure information—and anonymization or pseudonymization techniques where feasible. This reduces the privacy impact and the risk associated with data breaches.

Automation systems should operate within well-defined network boundaries with appropriate segmentation to reduce attack surfaces. Network segmentation limits lateral movement by attackers and isolates automation components from less secure parts of the environment. Firewalls, should govern communications between automation tools, security devices, and critical infrastructure. (Singh B. et al.,2025) Regular network traffic monitoring helps detect anomalous behaviors indicative of compromise. Like any software, automation platforms and their dependencies are susceptible to rigorous vulnerability management program—including regular patching, timely updates, and security configuration reviews—is vital to mitigate risks. Organizations should monitor vendor advisories and integrate vulnerability scanning tools to identify and remediate flaws proactively. Automated patch management itself can be an integral part of the automation framework, provided safeguards exist to prevent disruption. Comprehensive logging and audit trails are critical for security, compliance, and forensic investigations. Automation platforms must maintain detailed records of actions taken, data accessed, and decisions made by AI or automated workflows. These logs should be immutable, securely stored, and accessible only to authorized personnel. Automated monitoring of audit logs helps detect suspicious activity or misuse of automation capabilities. Furthermore, auditability supports compliance with regulatory requirements mandating traceability of data handling and incident response actions. Uncontrolled automation can lead to unintended or erroneous changes in systems or data. (Singh B. et al.,2025) To mitigate this risk, organizations should implement change management controls within automation frameworks. Approval workflows, where critical or high-impact automated actions require human validation, help balance efficiency with risk management. Role-based approvals and segregation of duties prevent single points of failure or insider threats. Version control for automation scripts, playbooks, and configurations ensures changes are documented, tested, and reversible if necessary.

BEST PRACTICES FOR IMPLEMENTING AI-ENABLED INCIDENT RESPONSE

As incident response increasingly relies on AI-driven insights, the demand for Explainable AI (XAI) is growing sharply. Future AI systems will leverage advanced XAI techniques to offer clear, human-understandable explanations for their detections, risk assessments, and remediation recommendations. This transparency is critical for security analysts who must trust and validate AI-generated alerts before acting on them. By integrating XAI, incident response teams can better understand threat contexts, rationale behind automated decisions, and potential false positives, (Soundariya A. et al.,2025) improving overall decision-making accuracy and confidence. Furthermore, explainability will enhance regulatory compliance and auditability, providing documented reasoning that meets legal and industry standards. Researchers are exploring novel methods such as attention mechanisms, counterfactual explanations, and rule extraction to make complex models interpretable without sacrificing accuracy. The maturation of XAI will empower more widespread adoption of AI in incident response workflows by bridging the gap between human intuition and machine intelligence by unifying telemetry from endpoints, networks, (Soundariya A. et al.,2025) cloud workloads, email systems, and identity services. AI technologies are increasingly embedded within XDR solutions to aggregate and correlate subtle patterns indicative of sophisticated attacks. Future incident response will see deeper integration of AI-powered analytics within XDR, enabling automated cross-domain threat hunting and incident correlation. AI models will leverage multi-source data fusion, enhancing situational awareness by linking disparate alerts into coherent attack narratives. This evolution will reduce alert fatigue by filtering noise and prioritizing truly critical threats.

Moreover, AI-enhanced XDR will enable adaptive response orchestration, triggering automated workflows that span multiple systems and platforms for faster containment and remediation. The convergence of AI and XDR will elevate incident response from reactive investigation to proactive threat anticipation and mitigation. Predictive analytics powered by AI will enable security teams to forecast the likely impact, severity, and progression of detected incidents. By analyzing historical attack patterns, environmental factors, and attacker tactics, AI can provide probabilistic risk scores that guide prioritization and resource allocation. This forward-looking capability will allow organizations to preemptively strengthen defenses, tailor incident response playbooks, and reduce dwell time. Additionally, advances in reinforcement learning will enable AI systems to autonomously learn from incident outcomes and continuously optimize detection and response strategies, making cybersecurity defenses more adaptive and resilient. (Sreekanthaswamy N. et al.,2025) These conversational agents will be capable of interpreting complex security queries, summarizing incident details, recommending remediation actions, and even executing commands through secure voice or text interfaces. This will streamline workflows, reduce cognitive load, and democratize access to cybersecurity expertise, especially in environments with limited personnel. Traditional incident response playbooks are typically manual, static documents that prescribe predefined steps for handling common security incidents. However, cyber threats evolve rapidly, rendering static playbooks less effective over time. (Sreekanthaswamy N. et al.,2025) Future AI technologies will enable automated generation and continuous adaptation of incident response playbooks. Machine learning models will analyze historical incident data, threat trends, and organizational context to dynamically create optimized playbooks tailored to specific attack scenarios and environments. These AI-driven playbooks will incorporate lessons learned from past incidents and emerging tactics, improving response efficacy.

CONTINUOUS IMPROVEMENT: REFINING AI MODELS AND RESPONSE PROCESSES

As cyber threats become more frequent, sophisticated, and damaging, increasingly incident response capabilities. AI-enabled incident response harnesses machine learning, automation, and real-time analytics to detect, prioritize, and remediate threats faster and more effectively than traditional methods. However, implementing AI in incident response is not without its challenges. To fully realize the potential of AI while avoiding common pitfalls, adopt strategic emphasizes governance, data integrity, integration, and continuous improvement. This comprehensive overview outlines the best practices that organizations should follow to implement AI-enabled incident response effectively and responsibly. Before implementing AI tools or platforms, organizations must define clear goals for their incident response programs. These goals should align with broader business and security strategies and answer critical questions such as Not all AI tools are created equal, and selecting the appropriate technology is critical for success. (Sundaramurthy S. K. et al.,2022) When choosing AI-enabled solutions for incident response, organizations should consider: Transparency: Prefer tools that offer explainable AI (XAI) to ensure model outputs are interpretable by human analysts. Scalability: Ensure the solutionas your environment grows. Integration capabilities: Choose platforms with open APIs and support for integration with existing tools such as SOAR, SIEM, endpoint detection and response (EDR), and ticketing systems. Vendor maturity and support: Work with reputable vendors that offer regular updates, strong customer support, and documentation. Conducting proof-of-concept evaluations and pilot deployments before full-scale rollouts can help assess tool efficacy in a real-world environment. (Zhang Z. et al.,2025) For AI to truly enhance incident response, it must integrate seamlessly with current workflows and not disrupt existing security operations. Best practices for integration include:

While automation and AI can accelerate response times, they are not infallible. Certain situations—such as ambiguous alerts or high-risk actions—require human judgment. A best practice is to implement Human-in-the-Loop (HITL) models that: Allow human analysts to validate AI-generated alerts or recommended actions. Introduce approval workflows for sensitive or irreversible responses. Enable manual overrides and escalation paths for complex incidents. (Sundaramurthy S. K. et al.,2022) This hybrid approach balances speed with control, ensuring AI augments rather than replaces human decision-making. Security teams must ensure that AI implementations adhere to stringent security and privacy standards. AI-enabled systems often process sensitive data and have privileged access to systems. To protect this environment:Security-by-design practices ensure AI systems do not become new attack surfaces. Threat landscapes change rapidly, and so must the AI systems tasked with responding to them. Organizations should establish a continuous training pipeline that: Automating this feedback loop helps models evolve with the threat landscape and reduces long-term maintenance burdens. Successful implementation of AI in incident response also depends on the people behind the technology. Security teams need the knowledge and confidence to work with AI systems effectively. (Zhang Z. et al.,2025) AI-enabled incident response offers tremendous potential to revolutionize how organizations defend against and respond to cyber threats. However, successful implementation requires more than just adopting the latest technology.

It demands thoughtful planning, robust data practices, seamless integration, and a strong human-AI partnership.

THE FUTURE OF INCIDENT RESPONSE: AI-DRIVEN EFFICIENCY AND EFFECTIVENESS

In the ever-changing landscape of cybersecurity, static defenses are quickly rendered obsolete. Attack vectors evolve, adversary tactics become more sophisticated, and technology infrastructures shift with the adoption of cloud, edge, and hybrid environments. Within this dynamic context, one of the most vital principles for success in AI-enabled incident response is continuous improvement. Continuous improvement encompasses the ongoing refinement of AI models, automation playbooks, decision logic, and operational procedures to ensure sustained effectiveness, adaptability, (Tamilarasi C. et al.,2025) and resilience against emerging threats. (Vajpayee P. et al.,2024) This overview explores how of continuous improvement that keeps their AI-driven incident response systems responsive, accurate, and aligned with both technological advancements and business goals and automated response mechanisms are not "set-it-and-forget-it" systems. They must be actively managed, evaluated, and optimized. Continuous improvement ensures that: Models remain effective in detecting evolving attack patterns. Automation workflows adapt to changes in infrastructure and risk profiles. (Vajpayee P. et al.,2024) Analyst feedback is incorporated to enhance decision-making accuracy. Performance gaps and false positives are addressed and corrected. Compliance requirements and best practices are reflected in processes. (Tariq S. et al.,2025) Without structured refinement efforts, AI systems may drift in performance, accumulate bias, or propagate outdated assumptions—leading to security blind spots or inefficient response.

At the core of continuous improvement is the feedback loop—a mechanism that allows learning and adaptation from real-world data and outcomes. In AI-enabled incident response, feedback loops can come from: Security analysts validating alerts or correcting false positives/negatives. Post-incident reviews uncovering gaps or missed detections. Performance monitoring metrics, such as detection latency, accuracy, (Tariq S. et al.,2025) or precision. Threat intelligence updates revealing new indicators of compromise (IOCs) or attack techniques. These inputs must be systematically collected, categorized, and fed back into the AI model training pipeline or automation logic to refine future performance. Best practice: Establish bi-directional integration between detection systems and case management platforms so that analyst actions automatically trigger learning signals. Refining AI models and response processes requires ongoing monitoring with a focus on meaningful, actionable metrics. (Tamilarasi C. et al.,2025) Using dashboards or automated performance reports, security teams can pinpoint inefficiencies and prioritize what to improve. These evaluations should occur on a regular cadence—monthly or quarterly—as well as ad hoc after major incidents.

CONCLUSION

The future of cybersecurity is not only being shaped by the growing but also by accelerating adoption advanced technologies. Among these, Artificial Intelligence (AI) stands out as the defining force set to transform incident response process to a proactive, intelligent, and highly discipline. As threat actors become faster, stealthier, and more adaptive, the next generation of incident response must match their pace—and AI offers the toolkit to do so. Looking forward, AI-driven incident response promises unprecedented levels of efficiency, precision, and strategic agility, reshaping how organizations detect, incidents. section outlines how AI will continue to redefine incident response, focusing on future capabilities, operational enhancements, and strategic advantages it brings to the forefront. Traditional incident response has primarily focused on post-incident reaction—detecting breaches after they occur and taking corrective actions to limit damage. However, with the power of AI, this paradigm is shifting dramatically. In the near future, AI will enable predictive incident response, where intelligent systems forecast potential threats, identify system vulnerabilities, and take preemptive measures to prevent attacks before they materialize. Advanced predictive analytics and behavior modeling will allow organizations to continuously assess risk and recognize early signs of compromise. For instance, AI models trained on patterns of known attacker behavior can alert security teams to subtle anomalies that indicate the start of a kill chain, triggering preventative workflows such as network segmentation, user account lockdown, or dynamic access control. This proactive posture reduces the reliance on traditional signatures or static rules, moving cybersecurity into an era where prevention becomes the primary defense strategy rather than a hopeful outcome.One of the most transformative prospects of AI in incident response is the full realization of hyperautomation—the seamless integration of create a self-healing security ecosystem. Future AI systems will autonomously handle the entire incident lifecycle, from detection and triage to remediation and reporting, with minimal human intervention. For example: Threats will be detected via AI-driven monitoring systems. Incidents will be triaged and prioritized based on risk scores derived from contextual data. Remediation will be triggered using intelligent playbooks, and recovery tasks such as system patching, credential resets, or configuration changes will be initiated instantly. Despite increasing automation, human expertise will remain essential—especially for strategic decision-making, interpreting complex threat contexts, and handling zero-day or nation-state level threats. The future of incident response lies in augmented intelligence, where AI and human analysts work in tandem, each amplifying the other's strengths. AI will serve as a co-pilot, handling repetitive and time-sensitive tasks while providing context-rich recommendations for human responders. Future AI systems will learn individual analyst preferences, optimize workflows dynamically, and support decision-making with evidence-based justifications via explainable AI (XAI). Meanwhile, human analysts will continue to refine AI behavior by validating decisions, fine-tuning models, and defining escalation thresholds.

REFERENCES

Adeyeye, O. J., Akanbi, I., Emeteveke, I., & Emehin, O. (2024). Leveraging secured AI-driven data analytics for cybersecurity: Safeguarding information and enhancing threat detection. *International Journal of Research and Publication and Reviews*, *5*(10), 3208–3223. DOI: 10.55248/gengpi.5.1024.2911

Ahmed, N., Hossain, M. E., Hossain, I. S., Hossain, Z., Kabir, M. F., & Begum, N. (2025, March). AI-Driven Cyber Security for Safeguarding Critical Infrastructure and Patient Data. In *2025 International Conference on Machine Learning and Autonomous Systems (ICMLAS)* (pp. 1485-1492). IEEE. DOI: 10.1109/ICMLAS64557.2025.10968807

Ahmed, S., Rahman, A., & Ashrafuzzaman, M. (2023). A Systematic Review Of AI And Machine Learning-Driven IT Support Systems: Enhancing Efficiency And Automation In Technical Service Management. *American Journal of Scholarly Research and Innovation*, *2*(02), 75–101. DOI: 10.63125/fd34sr03

Akinade, A. O., Adepoju, P. A., Ige, A. B., Afolabi, A. I., & Amoo, O. O.Afees Olanrewaju AkinadePeter Adeyemo AdepojuAdebimpe Bolatito IgeAdeoye Idowu AfolabiOlukunle Oladipupo Amoo. (2021). A conceptual model for network security automation: Leveraging AI-driven frameworks to enhance multi-vendor infrastructure resilience. *International Journal of Science and Technology Research Archive*, *1*(1), 39–59. DOI: 10.53771/ijstra.2021.1.1.0034

Al, E. 'mari, S., Sanjalawe, Y., & Fataftah, F. (2025). AI-Driven Security Systems and Intelligence Threat Response Using Autonomous Cyber Defense. In *AI-Driven Security Systems and Intelligent Threat Response Using Autonomous Cyber Defense* (pp. 35-78). IGI Global Scientific Publishing.

Ali, A. R. A. R., Saravanan, K., Abirami, B. B., Pandi, V. S., Aroulanandam, V. V., & Parthiban, S. (2024, December). Enhancing Cloud Security with AI: Developing Robust, Scalable Solutions for Threat Mitigation and Data Protection in Cloud Platforms. In *2024 International Conference on Sustainable Communication Networks and Application (ICSCNA)* (pp. 614-620). IEEE.

Alzboon, M. S., Bader, A. F., Abuashour, A., Alqaraleh, M. K., Zaqaibeh, B., & Al-Batah, M. (2023, November). The two sides of AI in cybersecurity: opportunities and challenges. In *2023 International Conference on Intelligent Computing and Next Generation Networks (ICNGN)* (pp. 1-9). IEEE. DOI: 10.1109/ICNGN59831.2023.10396670

Ayyaswamy, K., Gobalakrishnan, N., & Kathirvel, N. (2025). Cyber Security in Industrial Automation Using AI. In *AI-Enhanced Cybersecurity for Industrial Automation* (pp. 509–540). IGI Global Scientific Publishing. DOI: 10.4018/979-8-3373-3241-3.ch024

Babu, C. S., Simon, P. A., & Manohoran, S. (2025). AI-Powered Defenses Against Ransomware: Mitigating Emerging Threats to Critical Infrastructures. In *Deep Learning Innovations for Securing Critical Infrastructures* (pp. 577-604). IGI Global Scientific Publishing.

Baruwal Chhetri, M., Tariq, S., Singh, R., Jalalvand, F., Paris, C., & Nepal, S. (2024). Towards human-ai teaming to mitigate alert fatigue in security operations centres. *ACM Transactions on Internet Technology*, *24*(3), 1–22. DOI: 10.1145/3670009

Boorugupalli, K. K., Kulkarni, A. K., Suzana, A., & Ponnusamy, S. (2025). Cyber-security Measures in Financial Institutions Protecting Sensitive Data from Emerging Threats and Vulnerabilities. In *ITM Web of Conferences* (Vol. 76, p. 02002). EDP Sciences. DOI: 10.1051/itmconf/20257602002

Chib, S., Mehta, A. K., Saravanan, A., Mishra, B. R., & Manjunath, T. C. (2025). Mental Health Challenges and Solutions in High-Pressure Work Environments. In Harriott, S. (Ed.), *Innovative Approaches to Managing Conflict and Change in Diverse Work Environments* (pp. 247–272). IGI Global Scientific Publishing. DOI: 10.4018/979-8-3693-9556-1.ch011

Chinthamu, N., Jayakumar, S., & Rashid, S. Z. (2025). Cyber-Physical Systems Security Protecting Critical Infrastructure from Cyber Threats and Attacks. In *ITM Web of Conferences* (Vol. 76, p. 03005). EDP Sciences. DOI: 10.1051/itm-conf/20257603005

Dahiya, R., & Selvakumar, P. Vidyadhara, & Manjunath, T. C. (2025). Design and Aerodynamics: Principles and Advances. In M. Mellal (Ed.), *Innovations and Developments in Unmanned Aerial Vehicles* (pp. 145-170). IGI Global Scientific Publishing.

Dash, A., Bandopadhay, S., Samal, S. R., & Poulkov, V. (2023). Ai-enabled iot framework for leakage detection and its consequence prediction during external transportation of lpg. *Sensors (Basel)*, *23*(14), 6473. DOI: 10.3390/s23146473 PMID: 37514767

Engel, R., Fernandez, P., Ruiz-Cortes, A., Megahed, A., & Ojeda-Perez, J. (2022). SLA-aware operational efficiency in AI-enabled service chains: Challenges ahead. *Information Systems and e-Business Management*, *20*(1), 199–221. DOI: 10.1007/s10257-022-00551-w

Ferraro, C., Demsar, V., Sands, S., Restrepo, M., & Campbell, C. (2024). The paradoxes of generative AI-enabled customer service: A guide for managers. *Business Horizons*, *67*(5), 549–559. DOI: 10.1016/j.bushor.2024.04.013

Goswami, S. A., Patel, K. C. K., Darji, D. A., Patel, S., & Patel, S. (2025). AI Workload Automation and Orchestration in Cloud Environments. In *Establishing AI-Specific Cloud Computing Infrastructure* (pp. 33–70). IGI Global Scientific Publishing. DOI: 10.4018/979-8-3693-9694-0.ch002

Govindaraj, M., Shakila, P., & Lawrence, J. (2025). AI-Driven Cybersecurity for Industrial Automation: Resilient Solutions for Industry 4.0. In *AI-Enhanced Cybersecurity for Industrial Automation* (pp. 83-102). IGI Global Scientific Publishing.

Hossain, Z., Hossain, M. E., Ahmed, N., Kabir, M. F., & Hossain, I. S. (2025). AI-Powered Framework for Real-time Threat Detection and Response in Cloud Infrastructure. *Formosa Journal of Multidisciplinary Research*, *4*(4), 1859–1874. DOI: 10.55927/fjmr.v4i4.168

Inaganti, A. C., Ravichandran, N., Nersu, S. R. K., & Muppalaneni, R. (2021). Cloud Security Posture Management (CSPM) with AI: Automating Compliance and Threat Detection. *Artificial Intelligence and Machine Learning Review*, *2*(4), 8–18.

Karadsheh, L., Barnard, J. E., Arafah, M., & Shubita, A. F. (2025). Generative AI and the Evolving Threat Landscape: A Security Professional's Guide. In *Examining Cybersecurity Risks Produced by Generative AI* (pp. 71-98). IGI Global Scientific Publishing. DOI: 10.4018/979-8-3373-0832-6.ch004

Kaur, M., Selvakumar, P., & Dinesh, N. Mohit, Chandel, P. S., & Manjunath, T. C. (2025). Reconstruction and Preservation Strategies for Cultural Heritage. In S. Oflazoğlu & M. Dora (Eds.), *Preserving Cultural Heritage in Post-Disaster Urban Renewal* (pp. 385-412). IGI Global Scientific Publishing.

Kommineni, M., Chundru, S., & Maroju, P. K. (2025). Ethical Implications of AI in Sustainable Development Pedagogy. In Chinedu, C., Mafarja, N., Hussein, M., & Saleem, A. (Eds.), *Rethinking the Pedagogy of Sustainable Development in the AI Era* (pp. 17–36). IGI Global Scientific Publishing. DOI: 10.4018/979-8-3693-9062-7.ch002

Limbore, N. V., Anute, N., Ahluwalia, G. K., Chordiya, P. B., & Kalshetti, P. (2025). Ethical Leadership and Corporate Responsibility. In Harriott, S. (Ed.), *Innovative Approaches to Managing Conflict and Change in Diverse Work Environments* (pp. 193–218). IGI Global Scientific Publishing. DOI: 10.4018/979-8-3693-9556-1.ch009

Maheshwaran, T., Muthumarilakshmi, S., Suganya, K., Maheswari, B., & Girija, P. (2024). Securing E-Commerce Strategies With Cloud, Blockchain, AI, and ML. In *Strategies for E-Commerce Data Security: Cloud, Blockchain, AI, and Machine Learning* (pp. 470-500). IGI Global.

Muzahid, A. J. M., Kamarulzaman, S. F., Rahman, M. A., Murad, S. A., Kamal, M. A. S., & Alenezi, A. H. (2023). Multiple vehicle cooperation and collision avoidance in automated vehicles: Survey and an AI-enabled conceptual framework. *Scientific Reports*, *13*(1), 603. DOI: 10.1038/s41598-022-27026-9 PMID: 36635336

Nagmoti, N. S., Srivastava, I., & Damle, M. (2025). AI-Driven Enhancements in Cloud-Native DevOps Boosting Automation, Deployment, and Monitoring. In *Artificial Intelligence for Cloud-Native Software Engineering* (pp. 203–236). IGI Global Scientific Publishing. DOI: 10.4018/979-8-3693-9356-7.ch008

Nguyen, T. N., & Choo, R. (2021, November). Human-in-the-loop XAI-enabled vulnerability detection, investigation, and mitigation. In *2021 36th IEEE/ACM International Conference on Automated Software Engineering (ASE)* (pp. 1210-1212). IEEE. DOI: 10.1109/ASE51524.2021.9678840

Niveditha, S., Shreyanth, S., Devi, R. D. H., Sarveshwaran, R., & Rajesh, P. K. (2025). Advancing Digital Forensic Intelligence: Leveraging EdgeAI Techniques for Real-Time Threat Detection and Privacy Protection. In *Big Data and Edge Intelligence for Enhanced Cyber Defense* (pp. 37-84). CRC Press.

Ozobu, C. O., Adikwu, F. E., Odujobi, N. O., Onyekwe, F. O., & Nwulu, E. O. (2025). Advancing occupational safety with AI-powered monitoring systems: A conceptual framework for hazard detection and exposure control. *World Journal of Innovation and Modern Technology*, *9*(1), 186–213.

Parisa, S. K., Banerjee, S., & Whig, P. (2023). AI-Driven Zero Trust Security Models for Retail Cloud Infrastructure: A Next-Generation Approach. *International Journal of Sustainable Devlopment in field of IT, 15*(15).

Rashid, M. M., & Yaseen, O. M. (2025). AI-Driven Cybersecurity Measures for Hybrid Cloud Environments: A Framework for Multi-Cloud Security Management. *International Journal on Engineering Artificial Intelligence Management, Decision Support, and Policies*, *2*(1), 30–39. DOI: 10.63503/j.ijaimd.2025.39

Samal, A., & Misra, L. I. Mohit, Pougajendy, S., Chandel, P. S., Manjunath, T. C., (2025). Musealization and Tourism Practices. In S. Oflazoğlu & M. Dora (Eds.), *Preserving Cultural Heritage in Post-Disaster Urban Renewal* (pp. 115-142). IGI Global Scientific Publishing.

Saurabh, B., Utkrisht, S., Sandeep, S., Kumar, D. P., & Rajkumar, U. (2024, October). Generative AI Enabled Actionable Decision Support in Cyber Security Operations for Enterprise Security. In *2024 ITU Kaleidoscope: Innovation and Digital Transformation for a Sustainable World (ITU K)* (pp. 1-8). IEEE. DOI: 10.23919/ITUK62727.2024.10772892

Singh, B., & Kaunert, C. (2025). Fortifying the Digital World and Shielding Smart Infrastructures: Artificial Intelligence (AI)-Enabled Malware and Threat. In *Utilizing AI in Network and Mobile Security for Threat Detection and Prevention* (pp. 1-22). IGI Global Scientific Publishing.

Soundariya, A., Behera, N. K., Chandel, P. S., Gupta, S., & Manjunath, T. C. (2025). AI and Environmental Ethics: The Role of AI in Addressing Climate Change Ethical Considerations in AI-Driven Environmental Solutions. In Chakraborty, S. (Ed.), *Human Values, Ethics, and Dignity in the Age of Artificial Intelligence* (pp. 321–346). IGI Global Scientific Publishing. DOI: 10.4018/979-8-3693-9035-1.ch013

Sreekanthaswamy, N., Anitha, S., Singh, A., Jayadeva, S. M., Gupta, S., & Manjunath, T. C. (2025). Digital Tools and Methods. In Çela, E., Paliktzoglou, V., Sengar, S., Eappen, P., & Vajjhala, N. (Eds.), *Enhancing School Counseling With Technology and Case Studies* (pp. 25–48). IGI Global Scientific Publishing. DOI: 10.4018/979-8-3693-8392-6.ch002

Sundaramurthy, S. K., Ravichandran, N., Inaganti, A. C., & Muppalaneni, R. (2022). The future of enterprise automation: Integrating AI in cybersecurity, cloud operations, and workforce analytics. *Artificial Intelligence and Machine Learning Review*, *3*(2), 1–15.

Tamilarasi, C., Sowmiya, K., Vignesh, G. D., Jasmine, R. L., & Nehru, P. (2025). AI in Renewable Energy Education: Teaching the Future of Sustainable Power Systems. In Chinedu, C., Mafarja, N., Hussein, M., & Saleem, A. (Eds.), *Rethinking the Pedagogy of Sustainable Development in the AI Era* (pp. 133–152). IGI Global Scientific Publishing. DOI: 10.4018/979-8-3693-9062-7.ch007

Tariq, S., Baruwal Chhetri, M., Nepal, S., & Paris, C. (2025). Alert fatigue in security operations centres: Research challenges and opportunities. *ACM Computing Surveys*, *57*(9), 1–38. DOI: 10.1145/3723158

Vajpayee, P., & Hossain, G. (2024, March). Reduction of Cyber Value at Risk (CVaR) Through AI Enabled Anomaly Detection. In *SoutheastCon 2024* (pp. 623–629). IEEE. DOI: 10.1109/SoutheastCon52093.2024.10500040

Zhang, Z., Kumar, V., Pfahringer, B., & Bifet, A. (2025). Ai-enabled automated common vulnerability scoring from common vulnerabilities and exposures descriptions. *International Journal of Information Security*, *24*(1), 1–20. DOI: 10.1007/s10207-024-00922-z

Chapter 3

Zero Seconds to Respond-Transforming Cyber Defense With Real-Time AI-Powered Intelligence:

Intrusion Detection With AI-Driven Support

C. Suresh
http://orcid.org/0009-0007-0108-7952
Agni College of Technology, India

Manoj Kumar G.
http://orcid.org/0000-0001-7553-7572
LBS College of Engineering, India

Smitha Vas P.
http://orcid.org/0000-0002-3967-8041
LBS Institute of Technology for Women, India

G. Sathya
Oxford Engineering College, India

Joshua Issac A.
K. Ramakrishnan College of Technology, India

Keerthana N. V.
http://orcid.org/0000-0001-8878-2083
Velalar College of Engineering and Technology, India

ABSTRACT

As cyber threats become more advanced and frequent, traditional intrusion detection and prevention systems (IDPS)—which rely heavily on static rules and known attack signatures—are no longer sufficient for protecting modern digital infrastructures. These conventional systems often fail to detect novel or zero-day threats and struggle

DOI: 10.4018/979-8-2600-1498-1.ch003

to provide real-time response capabilities. To address these limitations, real-time threat detection combined with Artificial Intelligence (AI)-driven intrusion prevention has emerged as a powerful approach in cybersecurity. AI technologies, enhance IDPS by enabling systems to learn from historical data, recognize complex patterns, and detect anomalies without explicit programming. Ethical and privacy concerns also arise, particularly where user behavior and sensitive data are monitored. AI-enhanced IDPS have demonstrated superior detection accuracy, faster response times, and improved scalability compared to traditional methods.

1. INTRODUCTION

The digital innovations and data transmissions that are happening at a rapid pace have made the cyber threats more sophisticated and more frequent. The spill of sensitive information can lead to money loss, damage to the image of the company, and lawsuits. The toughest and most complex traditional systems are the Intrusion Detection and Prevention System (IDPS), which is the reason why nowadays cyberattacks are more complicated and changing rapidly (Azam et al., 2023). Today, malicious activities in the cyber sphere call for quicker and smarter answers. The fusion of Artificial Intelligence (AI) with security measures was the chosen way out of this situation. Since it provides improved capabilities in detecting, analyzing, and responding to threats, the implementation of such a solution results in a reduction of both the response time and the damage caused and thus guarantees the stability of the network infrastructure. By employing the power of machine learning, deep learning, and other smart algorithms, AI-powered Intrusion Detection and Prevention Systems (IDPS) can follow the network traffic, discover instances of abnormal patterns, and even identify threats (Olaoye, 2025). AI-driven threat detection algorithms are the mainstay in day-to-day modern cybersecurity, which rely on the least human intervention to identify and respond to the majority of attacks. AI-driven threat detection models are equipped with real-time capabilities, which is one of their most significant advantages.

Real-time threat detection is very important in today's fast-moving cyber environment, where the time available for threat detection and mitigation is usually very short. The integration of AI in threat detection on time is not without its drawbacks. False-positive and false-negative results are the most problematic issues that the paper has discussed while elaborating on the core components, architecture, methodologies, and the mechanism of data flow, real-time processing, and how these systems integrate with existing infrastructure. It goes further in-depth to explain various detection methods, including traditional signature-based and anomaly-based, as well as state-of-the-art AI models for prevention. It mainly concentrates on real-time data collection and processing, which is essential for strong AI models. It evaluates the system's effectiveness by some of the metrics, such as recall, F1 score, precision, accuracy, etc. Eventually, the article addresses the difficulties and limitations of AI-driven IDPS.

2. SYSTEM ARCHITECTURE OF AI-DRIVEN IDPS

The architecture of AI-driven IDPS enables real-time monitoring, analysis, intelligence, and mitigation of threats across the network. Advanced data processing, machine learning models, and dynamic decision-making capabilities are incorporated with AI-driven IDPS to behave more efficiently than traditional systems. Figure 1 represents the modern AI-driven IDPS.

Figure 1. Architecture of an AI-Driven IDPS

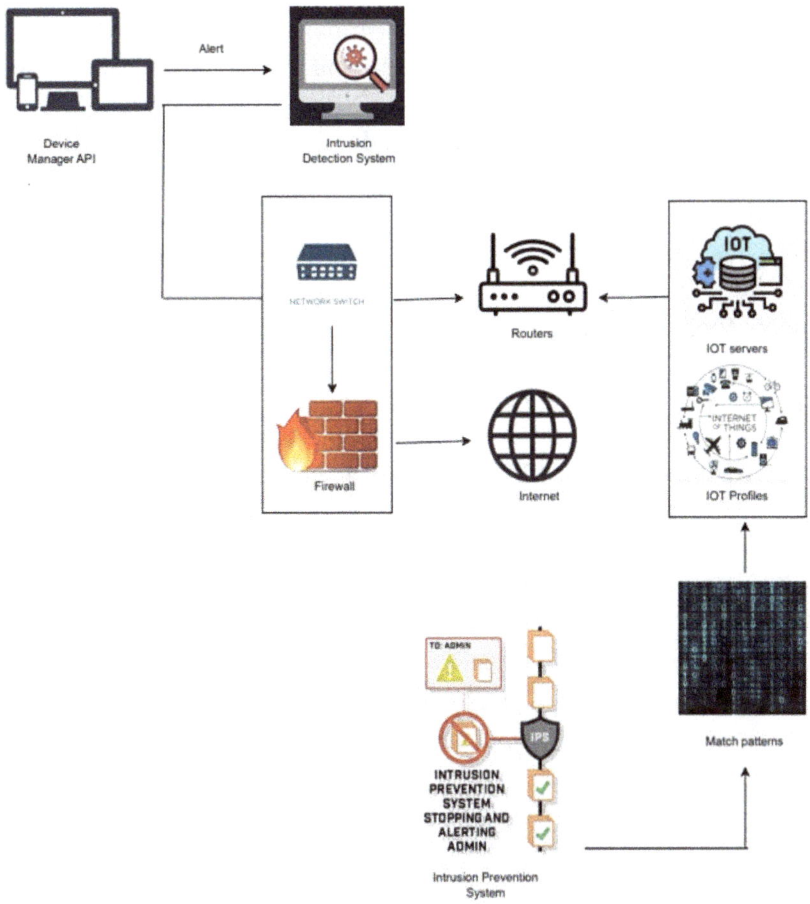

2.1 Core Components

The following are the core components of an AI-driven Intrusion Detection and Prevention system:

Data Collection Module: Collects the data of system logs, network logs, user activities, and other relevant data from servers and endpoints. It has two parts, i.e., the source of data and the big data infrastructure, as it captures and collects the raw data and stores it in the cloud.

Preprocessing Engine: It transforms the unstructured log into a structured log. Clean and normalize the raw data to make it suitable for analysis.

Feature Extraction and Selection: Extracts the relevant data. By using feature selection, we can acquire specific information without any computational or dynamic load.

AI/ML Detection Engine: It is considered the core component of the system that is used to identify the threads using different AI methodologies. The utilization of machine learning and deep learning models also takes place here. Based on the use case, it operated on various modes of learning, such as supervised and unsupervised learning. To enhance the detection accuracy, the model can able to learn continuously from the new data.

Decision-Making and Response Module: Trigger the automated scripts or interact with the firewalls and routers to prevent the ongoing threats. To optimize security configurations dynamically, Reinforcement Learning (RL) is used. It determines the appropriate response (e.g., alert, block IP, quarantine device) by analyzing the model's output.

Looping the Feedback: Gather results and user feedback to fine-tune the models (i.e., false positives/negatives). The detection system's ongoing learning and development are made possible by the feedback.

2.2 Data Flow And Real-Time Processing

Real-time threat detection necessitates the most efficient data handling with the shortest possible delay. The data flow in the AI-driven IDPS system may be seen as different stages:

Data Ingestion: Continuous streams of data can be captured from various sources such as network traffic, endpoint logs, and cloud services. To achieve scalability in real-time data ingestion, technologies such as Apache Kafka or Apache Flink may be used.

Preprocessing Pipeline: The mechanisms (cleaning, formatting, and transforming the data) are also used to remove the non-essential data, thus concentrating on the potential indicators.

Feature Vector Generation: The AI-driven models assist in feature extraction from the raw data, which is then converted into vectors. The behaviour metrics for this step are the time-series features, frequency patterns, and statistical behaviour, which are typical of time-series data.

Threat Analysis by AI Engine: Here, models analyze the input features and predict which kind of threat. Hybrid models and ensembling techniques are used to improve the detection accuracy of the model.

Response and Mitigation: A real-time mechanism was triggered once the threat was detected. After the detection alert system also set up and sent to the corresponding admins. Then the infected hosts are automatically isolated, and updates to the firewalls are done.

Logging and Reporting: After the completion of the response phase, all the factors, like decisions, alert systems, logged mitigations, and final reports, are created for future analysis.

2.3 Integration With Existing Infrastructure

For seamless integration with firewalls, routers, SIEM systems, and endpoint protection systems, AI-enabled IDPS is incorporated into currently available infrastructures that help the end users. To support real-time data exchange (automative activities) between the systems, the standardized protocols (i.e., Syslog, NetFlow, or REST APIs) must be handled by AI-driven IDPS. Accordingly, seamless integration will permit immediate threat de-escalation and response with lower impact on existing operations. At the upper end of expectations, seamless integration should include considerations for scalability or upgradeability for future planned upgrades. The AI system is not intended to replace existing systems but should coexist with traditional systems like firewalls and DLP for more situational awareness of threats.

AI-driven security is defined as the procedures and methods for safeguarding AI systems against dangers and guaranteeing their secure operations. The need to secure these systems is growing exponentially as AI is incorporated more and more into crucial infrastructures and decision-making procedures. This issue is solved by combining factors like legislators, business executives, educational institutions, and governmental organizations with diversity strategy is required. Rather than operating on its own, this approach should be readily integrated into the cybersecurity frameworks and procedures already in place by organizations that are critical to the infrastructure. AI-driven systems are generally integrated into mission-critical systems. Mission-critical systems can able to manage critical infrastructure, healthcare diagnostics, financial operations, and national security. Speculative AI systems and a workforce ill-equipped to handle them create an unfavourable atmosphere for security and accountability issues, which may cause significant AI installations that are susceptible to abuse or poor management to be abandoned. For example, data poisoning attacks that can introduce malicious data into model training data that can be undetected by IDS will not monitor the dataset integrity during the AI model training phase.

3. THREAT DETECTION TECHNIQUES

When compared to conventional techniques, the process of employing advanced algorithms to examine network data and identify harmful behavior with accuracy enhancement. In this process, AI-driven technologies can identify threats quickly. There are three types of components available for the detection method such as detection, training, and parameterization. With the integration of machine learning algorithms with the Internet of Things (IoT), threat detection processes have some limitations despite their pros. To maintain users' trust, the system offers a safe data collection methodology. By targeting adversarial attacks, the machine learning models have a significant chance of detection when hackers are modifying data inputs to fool AI-driven security systems. By addressing these problems and offering a more proactive, intelligent, and adaptable defense against cyberattacks, machine learning holds the potential to completely transform IoT security.

3.1 Signature-Based Detection

While entering into a Signature-based system, the given data is compared to the signature. Then the system executes the process of matching the harmful status. IPS is one of the traditional methods that searches for recognized patterns or indicators of harmful activity like viruses or worms (Isreal & Alonge, 2025). It lowers the frequency of false alarms, which includes fewer false positives and false negatives. This avoids superfluous computation by reducing misunderstanding about the prevention mechanism and preventing needless actions(Azam et al., 2023), as shown in Figure 2. Current traffic is compared to known attack signatures using signature-based approaches. However, it works excellently in threat detection, but it loses the capability of not detecting new or zero-day threats (Luz, 2024). One of its use cases is matching the structure or behavior of the payload to detect popular attacks like WannaCry. However, the signature-based system has some limitations, the threat detection accuracy depends on utilizing a large signature database.

Figure 2. Sample Signature-based detection

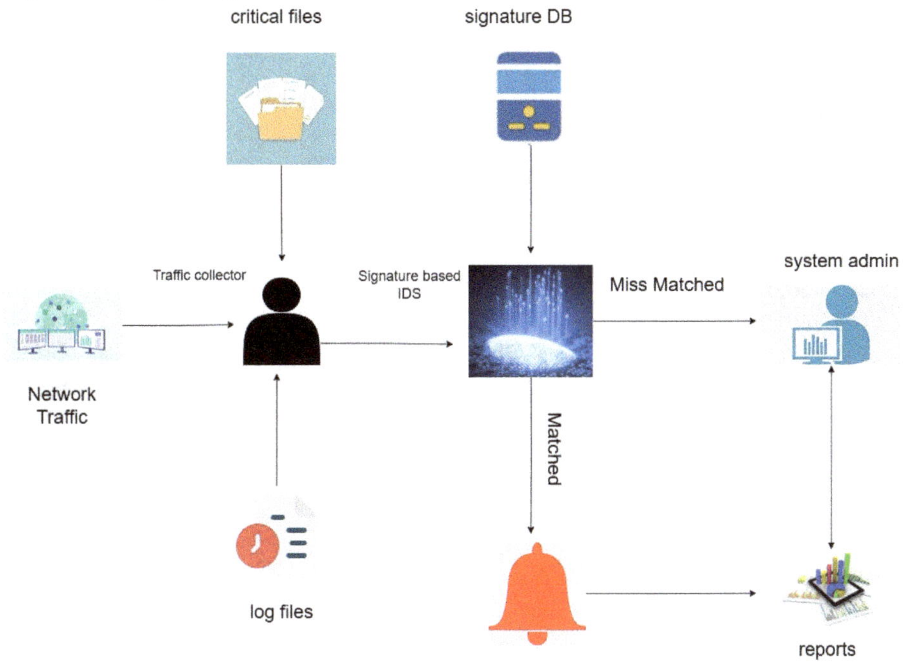

3.2 Anomaly-Based Detection

Anomaly detection is a core technique that is used to identify deviations from normal network behavior, which leverages AI. It is specially used to detect novel or unseen attacks. It is mostly employed for distance-based methods (Azam et al., 2023). It follows the baseline model's behavior to find the deviation and compare it to the present network activity. Finding odd patterns, network traffic spikes, and aberrant system behavior is made easier with the use of statistical techniques, machine learning, and behavioral analysis (Hassan & Ibrahim, 2023). Before the damage occurs, the system is used to detect zero-day exploits and respond to the users. When compared to predetermined baseline models, traffic is analysed and evaluated by IDPS using anomaly-based detection models (Luz, 2024). There will be the possibility of generating false positives if the baseline model is not accurately defined. The main advantage of this system is that it has the capability of adapting to changing environments. By noticing a sharp rise in uploads of user account data, which may indicate that data exfiltration is one of its use cases. The improvement in security terms by an anomaly detection system, which identifies a variety of cyber threats (Ampatzi, 2024).

Figure 3. Sample Anomaly-based detection

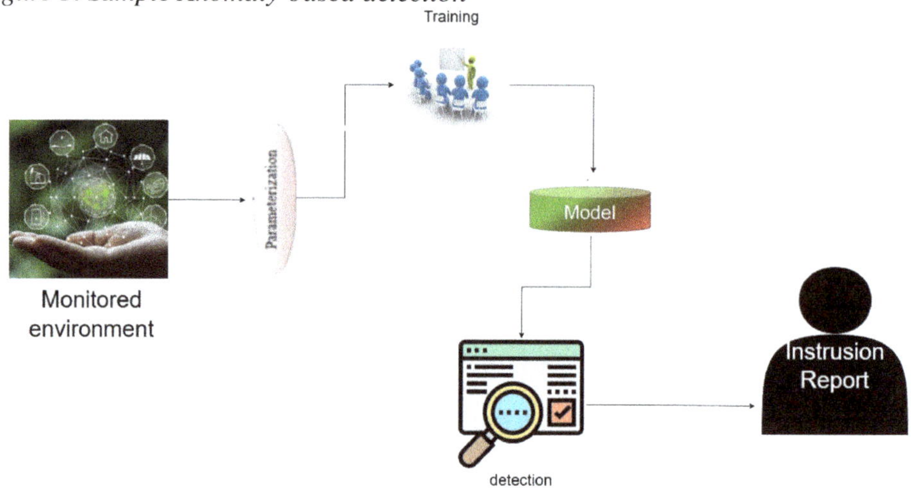

3.3 Behavioral Analysis

Behavioral analysis is the process of continuously observing network or system activity to spot odd patterns that might point to an Advanced Persistent Threat (APT). It focuses on tracking the behavior of users, devices, and systems to identify deviations from normal network activity (Isreal & Alonge, 2025). It reduces the false positives and improves the response accuracy. Effective against insider threats and compromised accounts. It detects the unknown thread and has high adaptability. It prevents unauthorized actions. One of its applications is identifying hacked employee accounts that are being exploited to increase privileges and gain access to restricted resources.

To detect and stop possible security breaches, an AI-driven behavioral analysis intrusion detection and prevention system (IDPS) uses machine learning and artificial intelligence to examine user and system behavior. Systems pick up on and create a baseline of typical system and user behavior (Enberg, 2024). Compared to the conventional techniques, AI systems can reduce the false positives by learning and adjusting to typical behavior. It is necessary to resolve privacy concerns raised by the gathering and analysis of user behavior data (Alzaabi & Mehmood, 2024).

3.4 Use Of Machine Learning And Deep Learning Models

As cyber threats are growing in speed and with more complexity, traditional IDPS are no longer efficient, so AI-driven IDPS leverage machine learning and deep learning, which are used to detect advanced threats and unknown (zero-day) attacks with minimal human intervention. Table 1 describes the aspects of both machine learning and deep learning models.

Machine Learning Models: By integrating AI methodologies with machine learning algorithms, for protecting complex and dynamic settings of the system, IDPS is playing a vital role (Igugu, 2024). By integrating AI and machine learning, improving automation, facilitating cloud-native strategies, and putting privacy first, IDPS significantly contributes to the protection of dynamic and complex environments. The major disadvantage is the lack of labelled training data for the model's performance assessment. The usage of various stages of statistical methodologies to learn and make predictions for the accuracy enhancement of the models. Machine learning techniques such as anomaly detection and deep packet inspection facilitate the identification of Advanced Persistent Threats (APTs), subtle strategies, such as using encrypted communication or taking advantage of zero-day vulnerabilities.

Deep Learning Models: These models use neural networks by stage by stages. It is considered a subfield of machine learning. Feature extraction mechanism and classification methodology by employing deep learning that enables the model to learn quickly and gives better performance. Deep learning models are essential for advanced anomaly detection, image recognition for identifying malware images, and the examination of phishing in implementing network security standards. Among the deep learning networks used to assess sequential networks, detect malicious payloads, and increase model robustness are Recurrent Neural Networks (RNNs), Convolutional Neural Networks (CNNs), and Generative Adversarial Networks (GANs) (Olaoye, 2025). The algorithm that solves the issues related to false positives and zero-day attacks is considered to be an efficient deep learning algorithm.

Table 1. Machine Learning and Deep Learning Model Characteristics

Aspect	Machine Learning	Deep Learning
Definition	A subset of AI that uses algorithms to learn from data and make predictions or decisions.	A subset of ML that uses multi-layered neural networks to learn from large datasets.
Data Requirements	Works well with smaller datasets.	Requires large volumes of labelled data to perform effectively.
Feature Engineering	Manual feature extraction and selection are crucial.	Automatically extracts features through neural layers.
Model Complexity	Typically, less complex, using algorithms like SVM, Decision Trees, etc.	Highly complex architectures like CNNs, RNNs, Transformers, etc.
Computational Power	Can run efficiently on CPUs.	Requires high-performance GPUs/ TPUs for training.

continued on following page

Table 1. Continued

Aspect	Machine Learning	Deep Learning
Interpretability	Easier to interpret and explain decisions.	Often considered a "black box" due to its complexity.
Training Time	Generally, faster training time.	Longer training times due to deep architectures.
Accuracy on Complex Tasks	May underperform on tasks like image or speech recognition.	Excels at handling complex tasks like vision, NLP, and audio processing.
Application Examples	Spam detection, credit scoring, and fraud detection.	Image classification, autonomous driving, and language translation.
Scalability	Limited scalability to high-dimensional, unstructured data.	Highly scalable to large and complex data sets.

4. AI-DRIVEN ALGORITHMS FOR INTRUSION PREVENTION

The usage of AI in Intrusion Prevention Systems (IPS) is one of the innovative developments in the network security field. The involvement of machine learning capabilities, deep learning methodologies, and predictive analytics, IPS with an AI-driven mechanism significantly provides a better defensive structure against cyber threats.

4.1 Supervised Learning Approaches

In a supervised learning approach, the labeled dataset is used to train the model. The model will first learn the patterns for predicting the outcome of new or unseen data. Regression and Classification are the two main approaches in this type of learning. Classification is used to estimate a new instance's category or class label by using the historical data. Regression used the continuous value of the data for prediction. There are a few categories of algorithms, such as Support Vector Machines (SVM), Decision Trees and Random Forest, Naïve Bayes, K-Nearest Neighbours (KNN), and Logistic Regression will come under the supervised learning. Performance outcomes such as high accuracy can be achieved, but these algorithms cannot detect zero-day or unknown attacks. Attacks such as brute-force attacks, phishing scenarios, and malware can be successfully categorized by these models, employing training on previous data.

Example: If the models are trained on a labeled data set, supervised learning can help identify known cyberthreats. The issue of detecting phishing emails is an excellent example of this. In this case, the author can train a Random Forest on thousands of emails in a labeled data set, which are either legitimate emails or phishing emails. The training data uses features such as the number of hyperlinks, the presence of attachments, sender reputation, and certain key trigger words. When emails are preprocessed, the model learns to distinguish patterns that correlate with benign versus malicious emails. After deploying the classifier as an enterprise email gateway, the classifier will label incoming emails, automatically quarantining those it believes are suspicious before they reach users. It can accomplish this with very high precision and recall, considerably lowering phishing risk, and demonstrating how supervised learning can be useful applied to real-world examples of intrusion prevention systems.

4.2 Unsupervised And Semi-Supervised Techniques

Unsupervised learning detects the hidden patterns or anomalies in data, whereas semi-supervised learning uses a small amount of labeled data and a large amount of unlabeled data. For anomaly detection, where the objective is to find anomalous activity that deviates from accepted norms without depending on pre-established attack signs, unsupervised learning is perfect. Unsupervised learning models can identify unknown dangers, including insider assaults (APTs) and zero-day exploits, by classifying related actions and identifying departures from typical patterns. Clustering and association are the two main forms of unsupervised learning. Grouping entails grouping data according to similarities and differences. Conversely, association looks at connections within the dataset.

Clustering, anomaly detection, association mining, and dimensionality reduction are all best served by unsupervised learning. Example: Unsupervised and semi-supervised learning techniques are invaluable for intrusion prevention systems when obtaining labeled data can be very limited or even impossible. As previously mentioned, these models are designed to look for deviations from normal behavior. This characteristic makes these approaches very successful when it comes to identifying unknown or zero-day attacks. For instance, an organization may use an unsupervised algorithm or anomaly detection that performs clustering to analyze real-time traffic on its networks, such as a DBSCAN or k-Means algorithm, with the model having learned, for example, the typical network data transfer patterns of the organization's users and devices. The model will examine a user's or a device's behavior and find that there is an outlier, such as an unusual spike in data, unexpected access during off-hours, and/or communication with a known malicious IP address.

For example, an organization may use a semi-supervised model that takes a small set of labeled traffic that has been classified as an attack and combine that with a larger pool of unlabeled traffic to come up with a model to help detect attacks.

Whether unsupervised or semi-supervised, these approaches enable the security system to develop and uncover new threats even if there are no pre-defined guideline rules or labeled datasets extensively available. Ultimately, increasing the ability of the AI proactive intrusion prevention model to adapt, flex, and discover threat actors and threats in real-time.

4.3 Reinforcement Learning For Adaptive Security

For adaptive security systems, the area of machine learning known as RL is used. It can able to respond to threads using self-improving algorithms without human intervention. RL can produce the greatest results by easily identifying mitigation actions like limitation of API access, workload isolation, and putting countermeasures against persistent threats. For the improvement of response methods, RL-driven security automation is used. With the help of Deep Reinforcement Learning (DRL), AI-driven models will enhance their capabilities of learning mechanisms and threat detection. It usually requires a lot of time for the training process. RL is known as the subfield of machine learning that involves AI agents for a trial-and-error mechanism, with the direction of incentives or sanctions. This approach prioritizes adaptable decision-making, with strategies shifting in response to new information (Jaber, 2024).

Without human intervention, RL has the capability of self-play that can able to use defensive methods to generate naturally through ongoing interaction. However, when faced with dynamic adversaries, policies become unpredictable, suggesting a variety of actions that are likely to be taken in some countries and offering flexibility in thwarting deterministic defense strategies. Using the self-learning agents, RL has the capacity to block changing threats and modify the security measures dynamically. Using the real-time input, RL-based IDPS continuously optimizes and uses threat mitigation tactics.

4.4 Natural Language Processing (Nlp) For Threat Intelligence

The use of natural language processing (NLP) is one technique for spotting irregularities in hacker forums, cyber threat alerts, and other sources. Unexpected increases in vulnerabilities and exploits can be found by examining the timeframes of threat reports. It will be helpful for making the process feasible for hazard prompting. Security experts can use natural language processing (NLP) to extract key indicators (IOCs) from these textual descriptions, such as file names, registry entries, or network commands (Arjunan, 2024). Through the extraction of thread contextual information from cybersecurity reports and threat streams, NLP improves IDPS threat intelligence. NLP will examine emails, API interactions, and security logs to identify malicious command injections and phishing attempts. To derive useful insights, it can filter and comprehend vast amounts of unstructured data, such as online chats, security alerts, and threat reports. There are many NLP methods available, such as Named Entity Recognition (NER), keyword extraction, sentiment analysis, and topic modelling. These methods can determine significant elements, including, but not limited to, IP addresses, malware names, CVE identifiers, and exploit descriptions in these documents.

For example, daily threat reports can be initiated by NLP to automatically extract an emerging vulnerability as well as a threat, to be documented as either a rule or an enriched data set for intrusion prevention in real time. Furthermore, an NLP-powered classifier can scan both log files and incoming emails for language associated with phishing, social engineering, or spear-phishing campaigns. More sophisticated models such as transformer models (e.g, BERT or those based on GPT) utilize NLP, making sense of the context and intention behind the negatively framed language used about the threat making it much easier for the system to make a more educated guess about a message if it is harmless or potentially lethal. In this context, the NLP substantially shortens the update cycle of the detection mechanism and works in concert with a machine learning model that is deployed in an AI-driven IDPS, which can survey for evolving threats and respond proactively while learning, making it wiser and more adaptable to threats.

5. REAL-TIME DATA COLLECTION AND PREPROCESSING

Data collection is the initial operations in cybersecurity that collect from sources such as Network Traffic, Endpoint Behavior, and Threat Intelligence. Preprocessing improves the quality and usability of the raw data. Techniques, including feature extraction, dimensionality reduction, and normalization, are included in this.

5.1 Network Traffic Monitoring

Network-based intrusion detection systems (NIDS) monitor network traffic for a particular network segment and analyze network and application protocol activity to identify suspicious activity. A network analysis tool called Network Traffic Monitoring (NTM) tracks local area network activity and shows statistics of uploads and downloads in a network (Kumar, Angral, & Sharma, 2014). Understanding the performance and security of cyber infrastructure is a crucial function. It is important to monitor the network traffic where suspicious patterns that are detected early. It also enables classification of normal vs. abnormal behavior. The challenging part is that it does not work with high volumes of data and requires low-latency infrastructure for real-time processing.

The data collected from network traffic monitoring includes packet headers, payload content, protocol types, timestamps and flow duration, and session-level statistics. The disruption of Internet of Things network services due to volumetric especially at the network layer, DDoS attacks have the potential to rapidly exhaust network resources even before they are found and taken off the network. This situation is brought on by the IDPS node's position within the network if the detecting system and the external location are not the same. As a result, the attack flows will find it simpler to evade the primary network devices and detection systems. This will cause resource exhaustion at the core switches, which can sometimes lead to total disruption and service failure. In this case, the IDPS system and the external network traffic are in sync. In network traffic monitoring, there are two types of IPS they are:

Active IPS: When a malicious threat is detected, an active intrusion prevention system can automatically take action to block the attack, such as cutting off a malicious connection, dropping suspicious packets, or reconfiguring firewalls to stop the attack from spreading.

Passive IPS: In contrast, passive intrusion prevention systems mainly monitor network traffic for signs of threats but do not take direct action to stop attacks; instead, they notify administrators of suspicious activity, enabling manual intervention.

5.2 Feature Extraction And Selection

The process of transforming raw traffic data into a structured format by identifying relevant characteristics. Feature extraction pulls out important data features for further analysis (Srinivasan & Senthilkumar, 2025). Besides Statistical features, Time-based features, Header fields, and Payload features are feature types that have been used in finding packet size, duration count, byte count, frequency of connection, flags, protocol type, keywords, and opcode patterns. There are three feature techniques:

Normalization: Making data of the same scale.
Encoding: Changing categorical data (e.g., protocol types) into a numerical form.
Dimensionality Reduction: Employing the PCA (Principal Component Analysis) or similar techniques to lessen feature size while keeping the variance.

Feature extraction is a vital component of data preprocessing, which helps the identifying and categorizing key elements of unstructured data, thereby improving model accuracy in AI and intrusion detection systems. Feature selection, however, works by dropping the redundant data, lowering the data complexity, speeding up the processing, and increasing the prediction accuracy. Feature extraction and selection play a vital role in building effective AI systems by simplifying the data while preserving its essential patterns and meaning. For example, feature extraction phase of image processing, in the phase of identifying edges, color, and forms, the involvement of Natural Language Processing (NLP) with identifying the emotion scores, identifying the keywords, and recognizing entities is carried out. For differentiating benign and malignant activity inside IDPS, these characteristics act as the foundation.

There are some features which are given below are extracted from network data:

Features of Packets transmitted: Packet length (mean, min, max, standard deviation), Inter-arrival times, TCP Flags (SYN, ACK, FIN, RST).
Connection Features: Number of connections to destination IP within a small timeframe, Bytes sent/received in a session, TCP session duration.
Types of Protocols: HTTP methods (GET/POST, etc.), DNS query type, SSL Certificate issues.
User-related features: Login times, Rate of access to important resources, and Number of failed login attempts.

5.3 Handling Imbalanced Data

An imbalanced dataset refers to more normal traffic (negative class) than malicious traffic (positive class). This may cause the model to reduce its ability to detect attacks. This is a problem because malicious classes may be ignored by classifiers, there will be a poor recall and F1 score for detecting intrusions. There are some techniques to handle this imbalance. They are:

Data-Level Solutions:

Oversampling: To generate a synthetic minority class.
Under sampling: The majority class size is reduced.
Hybrid methods: A combination of oversampling and under-sampling.

Algorithm-Level Solutions:

Cost-Sensitive Learning: To misclassify malicious samples, assign a higher cost.
Ensemble Methods: Use techniques with a balanced dataset
Evaluation Metric Adjustments: Focus on precision, recall, F1-score, and ROC-AUC rather than accuracy alone.

For example, take a dataset of malicious and benign records where only 1% of the records are malicious. A naive model would have a 99% accuracy by predicting all observations to be normal (non-malicious), but completely fail to detect any actual threats. To handle this dataset imbalance, it is important to use data-level and algorithm-level techniques. Some data-level techniques, such as SMOTE (Synthetic Minority Oversampling Technique) and ADASYN, create synthetic examples of the minority (attack) class to balance the number of observations in the dataset. When performing under-sampling, fewer observations of the majority class remain in the dataset, which will limit what the model can learn and also focus learning on key anomalies. Algorithmically, cost-sensitive learning will put a larger penalty on a misclassified observation in the attack class. This will assist the model to better recall, which reduces the false negative cases. If an IDPS were implemented that combined ensemble methods, the balanced random forest or Easy Ensemble would be considered. Each of these techniques builds multiple "weak" learners on balanced subsets of the data to strengthen robustness. The model used in that case would then rely on performance measures of precision, recall, F1-score, or area under the curve (AUC), but these are preferred over accuracy for questions of effectiveness. These performance measures will better illustrate the accuracy of the detection within the model and assist in determining the improvement in the detection of rare/unusual, sophisticated threats. By correctly accounting for imbalanced datasets, I found suggestions were provided to improve the quality of detecting sophisticated threats, as this could theoretically reduce the false negative rate, while retaining the high reliability and operational trustworthiness for AI-assisted malicious and network inconsistency detection in a dynamic network environment for IDPS.

6. PERFORMANCE EVALUATION

Performance evaluation is the measure of a system's ability to detect threats accurately, respond properly, and perform real-time operations. Accuracy, precision, recall, and F1 score are the common metrics for assessing the model's performance.

6.1 Accuracy, Precision, Recall, F1 Score

Accuracy: Accuracy refers to the proportion of correct predictions out of all the predictions made (Vinayakumar et al., 2019). If the accuracy is higher, the machine learning model is better (Accuracy $\in [0, 1]$). The formula for accuracy is defined as follows in (1):

$$Accuracy = \frac{TP + TN}{TP + TN + FP + FN} \quad (1)$$

Where, TP = True Positives, TN = True Negatives, FP = False Positives, FN = False Negatives

Precision: It calculates the proportion of attack connection records that are correctly identified to all attack connection records that are identified. The formula for precision is defined as in (2):

$$Precision = \frac{\text{TP}}{\text{TP} + \text{FP}} \tag{2}$$

Recall: The ratio of true positive predictions to the total of true positive and false negative forecasts is known as recall. It is computed as in (3):

$$Recall = \frac{\text{TP}}{\text{TP} + \text{FN}} \tag{3}$$

F1-Score: The F1 score offers a fair assessment of both precision and recall since it is the harmonic mean of the two. This formula is used to calculate what is mentioned in (4):

$$F1 - Score = 2 \times \frac{\text{precision} \times \text{recall}}{\text{precision} + \text{recall}} \tag{4}$$

6.2 Latency And Scalability

Latency: The interval of time between a network packet's arrival and the system's detection or reaction. The following variables impact latency:

- Complexity of the model (deep versus shallow models)
- Overhead for preprocessing
- Optimization of feature extraction time. Latency-reduction strategies include: Pruning the model, GPU acceleration or edge computing, Stream-based analytics, and parallel processing.

Scalability: The system's capacity to continue operating as network traffic and size grow. Among the strategies for scalability are Systems for distributed detection (such as those that use Apache Kafka + Spark), using cloud services for horizontal scalability, and Microservices-based containerization

6.3 Comparative Analysis With Traditional Systems

Processing Speed: While traditional systems generally have faster processing times for pattern matching and rule-based detection, AI systems are designed to manage the complexity of all detection types after they are done training (although their processing times may often be slower, particularly in deep learning scenarios).

Resource Consumption: Conventional IDS/IPS systems use significantly fewer resources than AI systems, primarily CPU and memory. AI systems (especially deep learning) require significantly more resources for both training and real-time detection, potentially requiring specialized hardware (e.g., GPUs, TPUs) to hasten processing, especially if the data is too large for typical systems.

Real-Time Detection Capabilities: Traditional systems typically have a faster throughput for real-time detection of known attacks, with signature-based systems performing in near-real-time. AI systems may have more latency, but are sufficient to perform real-time detection, and are capable of remedial, investigation, and understanding the more complex attacks, and tracking changes in the environment over time (providing better overall real-time security context).

Scalability in Large Networks: Traditional systems have limited scalability when applying detection across emerging large networks due to signature database maintenance and rule management. AI systems may be resource-hungry, but could provide better scalability. AI systems can automatically adjust to new network situations, attacks, or different configurations, making them conducive to dealing with larger networks.

Detection Rates for Known and Unknown Threats: Conventional systems show great detection rates for known threats but offer little capability for the detection of unknown attacks. AI-based systems, depending on how well the modelling is trained and how informed the data is, perform better on the detection of unknown threats due to their ability to generalize and learn new patterns presented by the data.

False Positives and False Negatives: Traditional systems have fewer false positives, especially signature-based, and still miss emerging threats, as in false negatives. AI-based systems provided over time lower false positives that improve with the adaptive process, though they may still endure some false negatives and limit their potential in detecting a threat if it is less pronounced or if it hasn't been trained on in the data. Any security system's efficacy must be evaluated, but AI-powered systems require a particular understanding of false positives and false negatives. A false positive occurs when an innocent object is inadvertently identified by the system as a threat. For example, if an employee views a large number of files for valid reasons, it may be interpreted as a data breach. Conversely, a false negative happens when the system fails to detect a real threat. This might be more dangerous because malicious activity goes unnoticed.

These shortcomings in traditional IDPS are often difficult for rule-based systems to balance. Regulations that are too strict result in too many false positives. If the regulations are too lenient, they can overlook real threats, thus causing false negatives.

How to Deal with Evolving Threats and Zero-Day Attacks: The main problem of traditional systems is their incapacity to detect new threats, as they will definitely miss any zero-day attack and continue operating in the same way unless new signatures are added to them. AI-powered systems are more capable of detecting the evolution of the threat and can better handle zero-day attacks, in particular, if they are unsupervised or deep networks that are not signature-reliant, and can evolve with the nature of the attack over time. The cybersecurity risk is still a challenge, especially because it constantly evolves and is followed by zero-day attacks. AI-based IDPS are capable of dealing with these attacks and, therefore, can be seen as a solution for overcoming traditional measures of security. AI-capable Intrusion IDPS is best suited to handle the situation. Traditional IDPS mainly depends on recognized patterns or signatures for risk identification. While they can effectively prevent known attacks, they are usually weak against new or unknown threats. AI-driven systems, however, are intended to be smarter and more flexible. They do so by processing massive volumes of network data and determining what the normal state of the network is; hence, they can detect any irregularity, even if it does not correspond to a known attack.

Learning and Adaptation Over Time: Traditional devices are short on learning and would only be helpful against the advancing threats in the presence of a huge collection of signatures that keep the program useful for threat detection. AI-powered systems are equipped with sophisticated learning and adaptation mechanisms so that they can become increasingly better over time with less human intervention. Traditional security setups usually fail when the issue is an unexpected attack because they are rule-based and require a signature of the threat. AI, especially in IDS and IPS, has the attribute of learning and hence can adapt to changes. In contrast, AI-controlled systems are intended to be progressive. The intelligent systems continuously learn from the data on which they carry out their operations. While they are scanning network activity and coming across different behaviours, they not only learn new things but also start understanding old ones. Soon, they will no longer require manual intervention for updates as they will be able to handle new threats on their own.

7. CHALLENGES AND LIMITATIONS

To secure today's digital ecosystems, research is still necessary to increase the AI-based cybersecurity systems' Resilience, reactivity, and robustness. As hackers use obfuscation and concealment methods, an AI algorithm is not guaranteed to detect the threat (Schmitt, 2023). This is the biggest issue of AI in cybersecurity.

In addition, it may wrongly identify benign behaviour as harmful, thus, it can lead to wastage of money unnecessarily.

Data Limitations: To train AI models, which require extensive, quality, and labelled datasets, such models are difficult to find in the cybersecurity field, because most datasets are small, imbalanced, and poorly diverse.

False Positives and Negatives: AI-based IDPS can generate false alerts or fail to detect new attacks, thus sometimes affecting the value of the intelligence and the time for operational response.

Computational Overhead: Deep learning models may need a heavy computational resource, which may limit their real-time capability in large-scale network deployments.

Model Interpretability: The complexity of AI algorithms through big data and deep learning makes it hard for security analysts to interpret or trust decisions that are made automatically.

Adversarial Attacks: Threat actors may find a way to create conditions that bypass detection by the model, thus introducing a serious security problem.

Data is compared to the signature database as soon as it enters the system. The system marks a match as harmful if one is discovered. The IPS system is considered to be the most traditional technique for pattern recognition or identifying malicious activity, like viruses or worms (Isreal & Alonge, 2025). It lowers the frequency of false alarms, which includes fewer false positives and false negatives. This avoids superfluous computation by reducing misunderstanding about the prevention mechanism and preventing needless actions(Azam et al., 2023) As shown in Figure 2. Current traffic is compared to known attack signatures using signature-based approaches. This mechanism will not detect zero-day threats or new threats. Thought it was considered as best mechanism for detecting threats (Luz, 2024).

Matching the payload's structure or behavior to identify well-known infections, such as WannaCry, is one of its use cases. However, signature-based detection has limitations. Having a sizable and up-to-date signature database is essential for accurate threat identification. Despite being at opposite extremes of the resource availability spectrum, cloud services and IoT systems can work in tandem to create a fantastic technological combination. IoT systems' resource constraints can be mitigated by cloud services, which are distinguished by ubiquitous access to computing power, storage, etc. By integrating IoT devices with cloud services, their promise can be fully realized, allowing them to save energy and offer a wide range of services without being limited by processing and storage power constraints. Similarly, through integrated applications, cloud services can gain from extensive IoT system deployments. As will be discussed below, such a distributed architecture creates weak spots for several attacks at various levels.

Attacks using authorization:

Through spoofing and evading authorization measures, these exploits allow an attacker to directly access databases and jeopardize data integrity. The visualization platform comprises. An attacker might circumvent security and isolation measures between the host and the guest operating system (OS) by taking advantage of a flaw in the virtualization technology, which could lead to privilege escalation and pivoting attacks on confidentiality (Asharf et al., 2020). IoT solutions, such as wearable technology, are utilized to track extremely private health data. In a similar vein, smart home appliances record users' private and sensitive information. The benefits of cloud services are overshadowed by privacy and confidentiality issues. Furthermore, the global location and multi-tenancy of cloud services provide a significant risk to data confidentiality due to hacking and privilege escalation.

8. FUTURE TRENDS AND RESEARCH DIRECTIONS

Many different studies and research papers have attempted to study IDSs. But there are many open problems and challenges for research, especially around the use of ML and DL approaches for anomaly and intrusion detection(Asharf et al., 2020). Most research projects show how the proposed methods were evaluated by using synthetic datasets and are limited to one problem, which assumes it is possible to do this with real datasets and additional problems. As can be seen from this work and work on the state of the art in IDS research, it is extremely challenging to design an IDS that at least covers the most important features of an effective IDS: it must be deployable, it must be online, scalable, run effectively on real data, and satisfy requests from all actors/stakeholders.

Enhanced Behavioral Analytics and Machine Learning: Behavioral analytics and machine learning algorithms are important in current hostile insider threat detection systems. These systems identify unexpected behavior by evaluating user behavior and comparing it with acceptable user behavior. In the future, there appears to be a direction of improved behavioral analytics that harnesses larger datasets and more advanced machine learning models.

Endpoint detection and response: Endpoint detection and response (EDR) systems, designed to detect and remediate attacks at the endpoint of a device, will hopefully adapt, with a focus on hostile insider threats. EDR will most likely include a behavioral analytics component that can accurately identify anomalous behaviors on files, applications, and authentication activities while also assessing the potential of insider threats.

Incorporating Explainable AI (XAI): As IDPS starts utilizing more AI solutions through new models, the ability to bring transparency becomes increasingly valuable. XAI describes techniques that pursue the interpretability of model decisions, which enables a security analyst to better understand and trust automated decisions about possible threats.

Federated Learning and Privacy-Preserving Learning: While federated learning is not a new concept, it allows different organizations to build better models without the need to share or even store sensitive information(Alzaabi & Mehmood, 2024). Terms like "privacy-preserving and differential learning methods will help to address concerns related to compliance and sensitivity, as well as detection improvements.

Edge and Fog Computing to Better Support Low Latency Detection: Using AI models directly on the edge of a network will ideally assist with minimizing latencies associated with threat detection tasks and will ideally shift threat detection to the source of the data being analyzed. This will be especially relevant in IoT and industrial detection spaces where delay and latency might mean lost opportunity to prevent unwanted suffering or access to IEDs.

Adaptive Systems and Self-Learning from Environments with Changing Threat Landscapes: Continuous generations of intrusion detection and prevention systems would often require overly regular and tedious updates to forestall threats from changing overall landscapes. Future IDPS will be natively adaptable to allow for changing landscapes of threats rather than relying on manual changes for an unchecked reach.

Threat Intelligence Automation and NLP: Using NLP, it will be possible to entirely automate the extraction of threat sources and threat indicators from numerous sources of global cybersecurity reports, forums, and the dark web when used to determine threat anticipation and mitigations/recuperations.

AI Robustness and Future Adversarial Defenses over more Adaptive Learning: Research being performed on adversarial machine learning will focus on building helpful models that are evasion- and poisoning-resilient with designs that will provide reliable intrusion prevention and detection for adversarial-based environments.

9. CONCLUSION

Combining AI and machine learning with threat detection systems for cloud environments is a game-changer in cybersecurity. This research emphasized the impressive ability of AI-based solutions to address the complex and fast-changing problems of modern cloud infrastructures by focusing on their theoretical foundations, practical implementations, and experimental results. Through the use of AI-based technology, companies will enhance their threat detection capabilities, shorten the time for disaster response, and have better protection of their most valuable assets. The main, overarching, and most inclusive of these conclusions, which is about the formation of a consistent cybersecurity strategy, puts forward the topic of AI-based threat detection as well as the future applications, dilemmas, and solutions.

The present study has gone through the body of research that the authors published in the sector of AI-mediated cyber-threat detection, initiating a trend for the emergence of AI that is indispensable for the most complicated security challenges. AI techniques that are exclusively based on machine learning and deep learning have been used in numerous cybersecurity issues, such as intrusion detection in networks, anomaly detection, and adversarial attack mitigation. The issue of achieving higher resiliency and explainability of AI models, as the work unfolds, is of great importance to this line of inquiry. We found that AI-based IDSs offer quite a few powerful features in contrast to traditional signature-based or rules-based detection methods; for instance, they can identify known and unknown threats with better accuracy, react faster to new attack vectors, and handle events more quickly.

The application of AI-driven model for anomaly detection primarily implies an artificial intelligence system that is capable of identifying network traffic intrusions through pattern recognition. Essentially, it reorients to advanced machine learning techniques for the real-time implementation. They need to be fast enough to optimize AI systems in a way that the problems would be automatically solved without human intervention, and when they happen swiftly, they also have to be able to act on the solutions immediately. Furthermore, as part of efforts to ensure the continued efficiency of AI-enabled systems in the fight against ever-sophisticated cybercriminal threats, the promotion of resistance to hostile attacks needs to be taken into consideration when deploying the systems. Meeting the above questions will require collaborative efforts by government organizations, the industry, and academia. Research work for AI applications in industrial cybersecurity needs to prioritize focus on framework issues that would lead to uniformity and compatibility among different systems. While training and access to expertise may be the main challenge in solving the shortage of skills, it only of manufacturers will grow stronger when deciding on introducing, installing, and running AI-driven security.

REFERENCES

Alzaabi, F. R., & Mehmood, A. (2024). A review of recent advances, challenges, and opportunities in malicious insider threat detection using machine learning methods. *IEEE Access : Practical Innovations, Open Solutions*, *12*, 30907–30927. DOI: 10.1109/ACCESS.2024.3369906

Ampatzi, C. (2024). How AI can Improve Intrusion Detection and Prevention System.

Arjunan, T. (2024). Detecting anomalies and intrusions in unstructured cybersecurity data using natural language processing. *International Journal for Research in Applied Science and Engineering Technology, 12*(9), 10.22214.

Asharf, J., Moustafa, N., Khurshid, H., Debie, E., Haider, W., & Wahab, A. (2020). A review of intrusion detection systems using machine and deep learning in internet of things: Challenges, solutions and future directions. *Electronics (Basel)*, *9*(7), 1177. DOI: 10.3390/electronics9071177

Azam, H., Dulloo, M. I., Majeed, M. H., Wan, J. P. H., Xin, L. T., Tajwar, M. A., & Sindiramutty, S. R. (2023). Defending the digital Frontier: IDPS and the battle against Cyberthreat. *International Journal of Emerging Multidisciplinaries Computer Science & Artificial Intelligence*, *2*(1), 253. DOI: 10.54938/ijemdcsai.2023.02.1.253

Enberg, P. (2024). Behavior Analytics in Cyber Security.

Hassan, S. K., & Ibrahim, A. (2023). The role of artificial intelligence in cyber security and incident response. *International Journal for Electronic Crime Investigation*, *7*(2).

Igugu, A. (2024). Evaluating the Effectiveness of AI and Machine Learning Techniques for Zero-Day Attacks Detection in Cloud Environments.

Isreal, O., & Alonge, M. (2025). Integrating Artificial Intelligence with Network Security: Enhancements in Intrusion Prevention.

Jaber, A. (2024). *Transforming cybersecurity dynamics: Enhanced self-play reinforcement learning in intrusion detection and prevention system.* Paper presented at the 2024 IEEE International Systems Conference (SysCon). DOI: 10.1109/SysCon61195.2024.10553626

Kumar, N., Angral, S., & Sharma, R. (2014). Integrating intrusion detection system with network monitoring. *International Journal of Scientific and Research Publications*, *4*, 1–4.

Luz, A. (2024). Implementing Intrusion Detection and Prevention in SDN. *Available at SSRN* 4965832. DOI: 10.2139/ssrn.4965832

Olaoye, G. (2025). AI-Driven Intrusion Detection and Prevention Systems (IDPS) for Cloud Security. *Available at SSRN* 5129525. DOI: 10.2139/ssrn.5129525

Schmitt, M. (2023). Securing the digital world: Protecting smart infrastructures and digital industries with artificial intelligence (AI)-enabled malware and intrusion detection. *Journal of Industrial Information Integration*, *36*, 100520. DOI: 10.1016/j.jii.2023.100520

Srinivasan, M., & Senthilkumar, N. (2025). Intrusion Detection and Prevention System (IDPS) model for IIoT Environments Using Hybridized Framework. *IEEE Access : Practical Innovations, Open Solutions*, *13*, 26608–26621. DOI: 10.1109/ACCESS.2025.3538461

Vinayakumar, R., Alazab, M., Soman, K. P., Poornachandran, P., Al-Nemrat, A., & Venkatraman, S. (2019). Deep learning approach for intelligent intrusion detection system. *IEEE Access : Practical Innovations, Open Solutions*, *7*, 41525–41550. DOI: 10.1109/ACCESS.2019.2895334

KEY TERMS AND DEFINITIONS

Advanced Persistent Threat (APT): It is a very complex, long-term, and targeted cyberattack that is the result of a threat actor or a group of threat actors, usually a state-sponsored actor, breaking into a network and staying there for a long time without being detected.

Cybersecurity: It involves the use of technologies, processes, and practices that aim at safeguarding networks, systems, data, and the digital infrastructure from cyberattacks, unauthorized access, misuse, and damage.

Intrusion Detection System (IDS): An IDS is a security instrument that monitors network or system activities and identifies attack, policy violation, unauthorized access, or security threat events. To this extent, an IDS is a component of future cybersecurity architecture.

Reinforcement Learning: It is a type of machine learning where an agent figures out the best moves through trial and error by dealing with an environment. The agent is given rewards or punishments depending on what it does, and the goal is to get the maximum total reward over time.

Supervised Learning: It is a machine learning method that uses labelled data to train models, that is, both input and output are known.

Threat Intelligence: This is a systematic approach of gathering, analyzing and interpreting data related to present or future cyber threats targeting an organization. The core of the process is identifying the threat actors, their tactics, techniques, motives, and the indicators of compromise (IOCs).

Unsupervised Learning: It is a machine learning method that deals with unlabelled data and finds the hidden relationships, clusters, or hierarchies.

Chapter 4
Challenges of Explainable AI in Security Decision-Making

P. Selvakumar
http://orcid.org/0000-0002-3650-4548
Department of Science and Humanities, Nehru Institute of Technology, Coimbatore, India

T. C. Manjunath
http://orcid.org/0000-0003-2545-9160
Rajarajeswari College of Engineering, Bengaluru, India

Charanjit Singh
http://orcid.org/0009-0006-9302-167X
Asansol Engineering College, India

S. N. Shalini
http://orcid.org/0000-0002-7605-9442
New Horizon College of Engineering, India

Sujoy Kumar Basu
http://orcid.org/0000-0003-4085-154X
Asansol Engineering College, India

Raj Kumar Mishra
http://orcid.org/0000-0002-6912-6694
University of Lucknow, India

ABSTRACT

The emergence of Artificial Intelligence (AI) as a transformative force in the realm of security marks a pivotal moment in the evolution of both technology and strategic decision-making. In recent years, AI has rapidly transitioned from a theoretical construct to a practical toolkit that is being integrated into numerous facets of modern life. Among its most impactful and controversial applications is its growing role in security—both physical and digital. Governments, corporations, and private entities around the world are increasingly leveraging AI technologies to enhance their ability to predict, detect, and respond to a wide range of threats. From autonomous surveillance systems and biometric recognition to predictive policing and cybersecurity defense mechanisms, AI is becoming a central component in shaping

DOI: 10.4018/979-8-2600-1498-1.ch004

security landscapes. This introduction explores the complex interplay between AI and security, highlighting the opportunities AI presents, the challenges it introduces, and the broader implications of its adoption in decision-making processes.

THE RISE OF AI IN SECURITY DECISION-MAKING

The emergence of Artificial Intelligence (AI) as a transformative force in the realm of security marks a pivotal moment in the evolution of both technology and strategic decision-making. In recent years, AI has rapidly transitioned from a theoretical construct to a practical toolkit that is being integrated into numerous facets of modern life. Among its most impactful and controversial applications is its growing role in security—both physical and digital. Governments, corporations, and private entities around the world are increasingly leveraging AI technologies to enhance their ability to predict, detect, and respond to a wide range of threats. From autonomous surveillance systems and biometric recognition to predictive policing and cybersecurity defense mechanisms, AI is becoming a central component in shaping security landscapes. This introduction explores the complex interplay between AI and security, highlighting the opportunities AI presents, the challenges it introduces, and the broader implications of its adoption in decision-making processes. At the heart of AI's appeal in the security sector is its unparalleled ability to process massive volumes of data at speeds and accuracies that far exceed human capabilities. The rise of global connectivity, the proliferation of devices through the Internet of Things (IoT), and the ever-evolving tactics of malicious actors have created an environment in which real-time threat assessment is not only desirable but essential. AI systems—particularly those powered by machine learning (ML) and deep learning algorithms—offer a solution to this problem by enabling automated pattern recognition, anomaly detection, and predictive analytics at scale. One of the most visible applications of AI in security is in surveillance and monitoring. Intelligent video analytics systems can now automatically identify suspicious behavior in public spaces, detect unauthorized access in secure facilities, and even track individuals across multiple camera feeds. Facial recognition technology, powered by neural networks, is used to identify persons of interest in crowded environments, enhancing border security and law enforcement capabilities. Similarly, AI-enhanced drones and robotics are being deployed to patrol borders, inspect infrastructure, and respond to emergencies, reducing the need for human exposure to dangerous situations. Cyber threats have grown in both scale and sophistication, with attackers employing advanced techniques such as polymorphic malware, zero-day exploits, and AI-driven phishing campaigns. To counter these threats, organizations are turning to AI-based systems that can detect anomalies in network traffic, identify vulnerabilities, and autonomously respond to intrusions. AI-driven threat intelligence platforms analyze global threat data to uncover patterns and trends that would be impossible for human analysts to discern in a timely manner.

THE CHALLENGES OF IMPLEMENTING XAI IN SECURITY DECISION-MAKING

As Artificial Intelligence (AI) becomes increasingly embedded in security infrastructures, the demand for transparency, trust, and accountability in algorithmic decision-making has never been more pressing. At the heart of these demands lies the concept of Explainable AI (XAI)—an emerging field dedicated (Alshar'e et al., 2025) to making the operations and decisions of AI systems understandable to human users. In high-stakes domains such as security, where decisions can directly impact human lives, civil liberties, and institutional integrity, the importance of XAI cannot be overstated. It is not simply a technical luxury but a foundational requirement for the responsible and ethical deployment of AI in security contexts. This section explores why explainability matters in AI-driven security systems, the challenges associated with achieving it, and the broader implications for trust, governance, and accountability. AI systems, particularly those based on deep learning, have demonstrated exceptional performance in a range of security applications, from facial recognition and behavioral analysis to intrusion detection and fraud prevention. However, these systems often function as "black boxes"—producing decisions or classifications without offering insight into how those conclusions were reached. (Suresh et al., 2025) This lack of transparency poses a critical challenge in security settings, where decision-makers must often justify their actions to stakeholders, regulatory bodies, or the public. For example, if a facial recognition system flags an individual as a threat at an airport or border crossing, authorities must be able to explain why that decision was made, especially if it leads to detention or further investigation. Without this capability, the risk of wrongful identification, discrimination, and legal consequences escalates significantly.

The need for explainability becomes even more vital when AI systems are used to augment or even automate security decision-making processes. In cybersecurity, AI is used to detect malware, respond to threats, and (Charmet et al., 2022) classify network anomalies. However, if a system flags a benign activity as malicious and causes an automatic shutdown or revokes access to a critical user, security teams must understand the rationale behind the AI's action to assess the response and mitigate potential damage. Similarly, in predictive policing or threat forecasting, explainable models help ensure that interventions are based on valid indicators rather than opaque correlations that could reflect social, racial, or geographical biases embedded in historical data. (Abusitta et al., 2024) A major benefit of explainable AI in security is its role in building trust between humans and machines. For security personnel to effectively rely on AI systems, they need to understand how these systems function and make decisions. Trust is particularly critical in time-sensitive or mission-critical environments where hesitation can lead to severe consequences. An AI system that provides human-interpretable justifications for its decisions allows operators to quickly assess its reasoning, spot potential flaws, and take appropriate actions. This not only facilitates (Chib et al., 2025) better human-AI collaboration but also reduces the likelihood of over-reliance or blind trust, which can be equally dangerous. From a technical standpoint, developing explainable AI models presents its own set of challenges. Many of the most powerful AI systems—especially those using deep neural networks—achieve high performance by capturing complex, non-linear relationships in data. This complexity, however, makes them inherently difficult to interpret. Balancing accuracy and interpretability remains a central tension in XAI research. Simpler models like decision trees or rule-based systems are easier to explain but may lack the predictive power of more advanced architectures.

COMPLEXITY OF AI MODELS: DIFFICULTY IN INTERPRETING DECISIONS

The integration of Explainable Artificial Intelligence (XAI) into security decision-making systems represents a significant step toward more transparent, accountable, and trustworthy AI. However, implementing XAI in real-world security contexts is fraught with complex technical, operational, ethical, and legal challenges. (Coussement et al., 2024) While the promise of XAI is to provide clarity around AI-driven decisions—especially in high-stakes scenarios involving surveillance, policing, national defense, or cybersecurity—the practical realization of this goal is constrained by multiple factors. These include the inherent complexity of modern AI models, trade-offs between interpretability and performance, the dynamic nature of security environments, concerns around information security, and the lack of standardized regulatory frameworks. (Soundariya et al., 2025) Understanding and addressing these challenges is critical to unlocking the full potential of XAI while ensuring that its deployment aligns with legal norms and democratic values. One of the most significant barriers to implementing XAI in security decision-making is the complexity of contemporary AI models, particularly those based on deep learning. Neural networks, especially deep neural architectures, are among the most powerful tools in AI today, capable of learning intricate patterns from massive datasets. However, this very complexity renders them inherently opaque. Unlike rule-based systems or decision trees, which follow easily interpretable paths, deep neural networks make decisions through layers of nonlinear transformations that are difficult for even experts to decipher. In a security context, where timely and justified decision-making is paramount—such as identifying threats at airports, detecting intrusions in networks, or evaluating behavioral patterns—this lack of interpretability can become a major liability. (Tamilarasi et al., 2025)

A related challenge is the performance-interpretability trade-off. In many AI applications, the most interpretable models—such as linear regression, logistic regression, or decision trees—are not necessarily the most accurate. (Dahiya et al., 2025) In contrast, high-performing models like ensemble methods, convolutional neural networks, or transformers offer better predictive capabilities but are far less transparent. Security systems often prioritize accuracy due to the high cost of errors—false positives can cause panic or unnecessary interventions, while false negatives can lead to catastrophic failures. (Das et al., 2020) In such contexts, sacrificing accuracy for interpretability may not be acceptable. The dilemma, then, is whether to use less interpretable models that may offer better security outcomes or simpler models that foster understanding but may miss critical threats. This trade-off presents a constant tension in XAI implementation, and there is currently no universal solution that allows developers to maximize both dimensions simultaneously. Another profound challenge is the fluid and adversarial nature of security environments. Unlike static domains such as image classification or medical diagnosis, security involves rapidly evolving threats, intelligent adversaries, and highly variable data inputs. AI models in these settings must adapt continuously, often updating themselves based on new data. As models change, so too does the logic behind their decisions. This dynamic evolution complicates explainability, as a previously generated explanation may no longer hold true after a model update. Moreover, adversaries can exploit the transparency provided by XAI to reverse-engineer systems, identify weaknesses, or develop countermeasures. In this sense, XAI may inadvertently compromise operational security, exposing critical information about detection thresholds, classification rules, or decision boundaries. (Akhtar et al., 2024).

LACK OF TRANSPARENCY: UNDERSTANDING AI-DRIVEN DECISIONS

As Artificial Intelligence (AI) systems continue to evolve and permeate critical sectors like security, the complexity of underlying models has become both a strength and a liability. This complexity is particularly pronounced in modern AI architectures such as deep neural networks (DNNs), ensemble models, and transformers, (De Bruijn et al., 2022) which are celebrated for their ability to learn from vast datasets and solve intricate problems with high accuracy. However, these same models present significant barriers to interpretability—that is, the ability of humans to understand and trace how inputs are mapped to outputs. This lack of transparency, often referred to as the "black box" problem, is especially troubling in security-related decision-making where accountability, trust, and timely response are paramount. As AI becomes more deeply integrated into systems that influence surveillance, law enforcement, counterterrorism, and cybersecurity, the inability to fully understand how decisions are derived introduces risks that range from operational inefficiency to ethical violations and legal repercussions. This analysis delves into the reasons why modern AI models are difficult to interpret, the implications of this opacity in security contexts, and the ongoing efforts and limitations in addressing these challenges through Explainable AI (XAI). At the core of AI model complexity is the layered, non-linear architecture that characterizes deep learning systems. A simple model, like a decision tree or a logistic regression classifier, allows decision paths or coefficients to be traced back easily, offering clear reasoning for predictions. In contrast, a deep neural network might contain millions of parameters spread across dozens or even hundreds of layers. These parameters interact in ways that are not intuitively understandable by humans. (Eldrandaly et al., 2023).

This inscrutability poses significant challenges in security applications, where decisions based on AI outputs often carry high stakes. In domains such as biometric authentication, behavioral threat detection, or automated surveillance, (Faheem et al., 2022) security operators must trust that the system's recommendations are valid, unbiased, and actionable. However, if an AI system flags an individual for suspicious activity, denies access to a secure facility, or blocks a digital transaction, stakeholders—including affected individuals, system administrators, and legal authorities—have a right to understand why that decision was made. When the model's decision process cannot be easily unpacked or rationalized, it erodes trust in the system and makes it difficult to validate or contest outcomes. This is particularly problematic when such systems are used in public-sector security settings, where democratic accountability and civil liberties are at stake. Efforts to address these challenges have led to the development of Explainable AI (XAI) techniques, which aim to make complex models more understandable to humans. Post hoc explanation techniques, such as LIME (Local Interpretable Model-agnostic Explanations), SHAP (SHapley Additive exPlanations), and counterfactual reasoning, attempt to explain the outputs of black-box models without modifying their internal workings. While these tools can provide useful insights, they are approximations rather than true representations of the model's inner logic. (Fatima et al., 2025) As such, their reliability and fidelity are limited—particularly in high-risk environments where approximations may not suffice for compliance or justification purposes.

TRUST AND ACCOUNTABILITY: ENSURING RELIABLE AI DECISION-MAKING

The increasing integration of Artificial Intelligence (AI) into security systems has ushered in a new era of automation, efficiency, and predictive capability. However, this technological advancement comes at the cost of transparency, (Hamon et al., 2022) particularly in the ability of stakeholders—security professionals, policy-makers, and the public—to understand how AI systems reach decisions. The lack of transparency in AI-driven decision-making represents one of the most pressing challenges in both the technical and ethical deployment of AI, especially within the high-stakes domain of security. This issue, often referred to as the "black box" problem, highlights the opacity with which many AI systems operate, producing outputs and recommendations that are not easily interpretable or justifiable by human observers. As AI increasingly informs or even makes critical decisions related to surveillance, risk assessment, threat detection, and behavioral profiling, the inability to clearly understand its reasoning process can lead to serious consequences, including loss of trust, accountability issues, misinformed decisions, and violations of civil liberties. (Hanif et al., 2021) This section explores the multifaceted problem of transparency in AI systems, the implications for security, and the current efforts and limitations in making AI decision-making processes more intelligible and accessible. At its core, the transparency problem in AI arises from the complex nature of machine learning (ML) models, especially those based on deep learning architectures. These models derive their intelligence by identifying patterns and correlations in large datasets, adjusting internal parameters through training algorithms to optimize performance metrics such as accuracy or precision. While highly effective, this process results in internal representations that are typically not understandable to humans. (Tiwari et al., 2020) For instance, a deep neural network might detect suspicious activity in a security camera feed based on a complex combination of features such as motion vectors, object outlines, and environmental changes.

This opacity is exacerbated when AI systems are deployed in real-world security settings where decisions must be not only accurate but also explainable and defensible. In contexts such as airport security, border control, counterterrorism, (Jagannathan et al., 2023) or cyber threat management, decisions based on AI outputs may directly impact individual rights or national security. A facial recognition system that misidentifies a traveler, a behavioral analytics tool that flags an employee as a potential insider threat, or a cybersecurity platform that automatically isolates a device from the network based on anomaly detection—all these scenarios require some degree of transparency to ensure that decisions are lawful, justifiable, and correctable if necessary. (Sreekanthaswamy et al., 2025) Without transparency, it becomes impossible to verify the validity of the AI's output, determine whether biases or errors influenced the decision, or even assess whether the system is functioning as intended. Efforts to address the transparency challenge have given rise to the field of Explainable AI (XAI), which seeks to develop methods and tools that render AI decision-making processes more intelligible to humans. These methods include visualizations of internal decision pathways, natural language explanations, feature importance rankings, and counterfactual reasoning. For instance, a counterfactual explanation might indicate, "The system flagged this individual because of feature X and Y; if either were absent, the individual would not have been flagged." Such explanations can help users understand not only the 'what' but also the 'why' and 'how' of AI decisions. (Jaigirdar et al., 2020).

ADVERSARIAL ATTACKS: MANIPULATING AI MODELS FOR MALICIOUS PURPOSES

In the rapidly evolving landscape of artificial intelligence (AI), the twin pillars of trust and accountability have emerged as critical considerations, especially in high-stakes domains such as security decision-making. As AI systems increasingly take on roles in surveillance, cybersecurity, border control, threat detection, (Kaur et al., 2025) and predictive policing, ensuring that their decisions are both reliable and subject to oversight is essential. These systems are no longer mere tools—they are decision-influencers, or in some cases, decision-makers. In such contexts, trust and accountability are not abstract ideals but operational necessities. Without trust, human operators may hesitate to rely on AI outputs, undermining system effectiveness. Without accountability, flawed or biased decisions may go unchecked, leading to violations of human rights, legal norms, and institutional integrity. This section provides a comprehensive exploration of the intertwined concepts of trust and accountability in AI, the barriers to achieving them, and the strategies needed to ensure that AI-driven decisions in security contexts are both dependable and justifiable. Trust in AI refers to the confidence that users and stakeholders place in the system's ability to perform its intended function accurately, safely, and ethically(Kommineni et al., 2025) Trust also extends beyond technical users to include the general public, policymakers, civil society, and those subject to the system's decisions. Each of these groups has distinct concerns and expectations, and failure to address any of them can result in skepticism, resistance, or outright rejection of AI applications in security.

Building trust requires more than achieving high accuracy in model performance. Human factors play a crucial role. Research in human-computer interaction (HCI) shows that users are more likely to trust (Kumar et al., 2024) AI systems when they feel they understand how the system works and when they perceive it as being aligned with their goals and values. In opaque or "black box" systems, even correct decisions may be viewed with suspicion if users cannot see the reasoning behind them. Conversely, transparent systems that offer interpretable explanations help users calibrate their trust appropriately—relying on the system when it performs well and questioning it when it behaves unexpectedly. In security contexts, such calibrated trust is vital. Blind trust can lead to over-reliance and operational complacency, while unwarranted mistrust can result in underutilization of otherwise valuable capabilities. Designing AI systems that support this balance is central to responsible deployment. Establishing accountability in AI systems involves several layers. At the design and development stage, developers must ensure that models are trained on high-quality, representative data, that they are tested for bias and fairness, and that their limitations are clearly documented. (Wang et al., 2021) This fragmentation can make it difficult to pinpoint where a decision originated or who bears ultimate responsibility. In many cases, the deployment of AI in security agencies occurs through procurement contracts with private vendors, further complicating the accountability chain. If a predictive policing system misidentifies a community as high-risk, leading to over-policing and social tension, who is answerable? (Lee et al., 2024).

DATA QUALITY AND AVAILABILITY: IMPACT ON XAI PERFORMANCE

As artificial intelligence (AI) systems increasingly underpin critical infrastructure and decision-making—especially in security-sensitive domains—their vulnerabilities have come under intense scrutiny. Among the most significant threats to AI reliability and integrity are adversarial attacks, (Limbore et al., 2025) deliberate manipulations crafted to deceive or subvert AI models. These attacks exploit the inherent weaknesses in machine learning (ML) algorithms, particularly those based on deep learning, by subtly altering inputs to produce incorrect or harmful outputs. The ability of adversaries to manipulate AI models for malicious purposes presents profound challenges not only for the security and robustness of AI systems themselves but also for the broader ecosystems—such as cybersecurity, national defense, and public safety—that rely on them. This analysis explores the nature of adversarial attacks, their methodologies, the risks they pose, and the ongoing efforts to detect, mitigate, and defend against these sophisticated threats. At its core, an adversarial attack involves an attacker intentionally introducing small, often imperceptible, perturbations to the input data fed into an AI model with the goal of causing it to make a wrong prediction or classification. Unlike traditional cyberattacks aimed at exploiting software vulnerabilities, adversarial attacks target the AI's decision boundaries—the complex, multidimensional surfaces that models learn to separate different classes or outputs during training. (Longo et al., 2020) Due to the highly non-linear and high-dimensional nature of models such as convolutional neural networks (CNNs) and transformers, small changes in input can disproportionately shift the model's output. Adversarial attacks can be broadly categorized into white-box and black-box attacks based on the attacker's knowledge of the target model. In white-box attacks, the adversary has full access to the AI model's architecture, parameters, and training data. (Madhav et al., 2022) This knowledge enables the attacker to compute precise gradients and craft optimal perturbations that maximize the chance of fooling the system. Techniques such as the Fast Gradient Sign Method (FGSM) and Projected Gradient Descent (PGD) have been developed to generate adversarial examples efficiently in such settings. In contrast, black-box attacks assume that the attacker has limited or no knowledge of the model internals and can only query the model with inputs and observe outputs. (Srivastava et al., 2022) Here, attackers often rely on surrogate models or transferability of adversarial examples—where inputs crafted to fool one model can also deceive another—to launch effective attacks. The existence of such transferability means that even proprietary or inaccessible AI systems are vulnerable to adversarial exploitation. The consequences of adversarial attacks on AI systems in security domains can be severe and multifaceted. Firstly, they undermine trust in (Mahbooba et al., 2021) AI technologies, casting doubt on the reliability and safety of automated systems.

SECURITY CONTEXT: UNDERSTANDING THREATS AND VULNERABILITIES

Data lies at the very foundation of artificial intelligence (AI) and machine learning (ML) systems, serving as the raw material from which models learn patterns, make predictions, and support decision-making. (Moustafa et al., 2023) This foundational role of data becomes even more critical in the context of Explainable AI (XAI), where transparency, interpretability, and trustworthiness of AI outputs depend not only on the model architecture but also on the quality and availability of the underlying data. The performance of XAI techniques—those designed to elucidate AI decision processes—can be severely compromised by poor data quality or limited data availability, leading to explanations that are misleading, incomplete, or outright incorrect. Consequently, understanding how data issues impact XAI is essential to building robust, reliable, and socially responsible AI systems, especially in sensitive domains like security, healthcare, and finance, where decisions have far-reaching consequences. Data Quality is a multi-dimensional concept encompassing several attributes including accuracy, completeness, consistency, timeliness, and representativeness. (Yayla et al., 2022) Each of these facets plays a distinct role in shaping the reliability of both AI predictions and their explanations. Beyond quality, Data Availability is equally critical for effective XAI. The volume and diversity of data accessible for training, validation, and explanation generation determine the richness and robustness of interpretability.

Limited data availability can stem from several factors: privacy concerns, regulatory constraints, proprietary restrictions, or simply the rarity of certain events. In security contexts, highly sensitive data such as classified threat intelligence or personal biometric information may be unavailable for comprehensive (Neupane et al., 2022) model training. This scarcity hampers the AI system's ability to learn nuanced patterns and reduces the fidelity of XAI explanations. When only limited datasets are used, explanations risk being overly simplistic, missing subtle but important factors, or generalizing poorly to unseen scenarios. Moreover, the dynamic nature of data availability complicates XAI performance. Security environments are characterized by rapid changes—new threats emerge, user behaviors shift, and operational contexts evolve. If data streams are interrupted or restricted, models may become stale, and explanations outdated. Continuous data collection and updating are necessary to maintain both predictive accuracy and (Rawal et al., 2021) the meaningfulness of XAI outputs. The interplay between data quality and availability also affects the choice of XAI techniques. Some explanation methods, such as model-agnostic approaches (e.g., LIME, SHAP), rely on sampling around the input space to infer feature importance, which presupposes sufficient data diversity. Others, like intrinsic interpretability methods, depend heavily on the model's internal structure and training data distribution. When data is sparse or biased, these techniques may yield unstable or inconsistent explanations. For example, in anomaly detection, lack of diverse examples can cause explanation methods to misidentify features driving false positives or negatives, misleading operators. Data issues further complicate the evaluation of XAI performance. Reliable benchmarking requires ground truth explanations or human expert annotations, which are often unavailable or subjective. Without high-quality, comprehensive datasets that capture the range of real-world variability, it becomes challenging to assess whether XAI methods produce faithful, robust, and actionable explanations. This impairs efforts to standardize and certify XAI tools for critical applications. Poor quality or insufficient data degrades not only model accuracy but also the trustworthiness and usefulness of the explanations that AI systems provide. (Rjoub et al., 2023) As AI continues to influence decisions in security and other critical sectors, ensuring that data foundations are robust, comprehensive, and representative is essential. Only by addressing these data challenges can XAI fulfill its promise of transparency, fairness, and accountability in AI-driven decision-making.

HUMAN BIAS AND DECISION-MAKING: IMPACT ON XAI ADOPTION

In the modern digital era, the security landscape is an intricate and dynamic domain shaped by a multitude of threats and vulnerabilities. (Samal et al., 2025) Understanding this security context is crucial for designing, deploying, and managing effective protection mechanisms. The term "security context" broadly refers to the environment, conditions, and factors that define how threats emerge, how vulnerabilities are exploited, and how defenses are orchestrated across physical, cyber, and hybrid spaces. This overview delves into the nature of contemporary security threats, the vulnerabilities that underpin them, and the broader contextual factors that influence security postures—highlighting why a comprehensive grasp of this environment is fundamental for practitioners, policymakers, and researchers alike. Security threats are intentional or unintentional acts or conditions that can cause harm to information systems, physical infrastructure, or human wellbeing. In today's interconnected world, threats manifest across multiple domains—cybersecurity, physical security, operational security, and national security—often intersecting and compounding one another. The digital transformation of critical infrastructure, government services, and private enterprises has expanded the attack surface, making security threats more pervasive and sophisticated. Cyber threats represent a dominant category in the contemporary security context. These include a spectrum of malicious activities such as (Zhang et al., 2022) malware infections, ransomware attacks, phishing schemes, denial-of-service (DoS) attacks, insider threats, and advanced persistent threats (APTs). Cyber adversaries range from lone hackers and hacktivist groups to sophisticated nation-state actors engaging in espionage and cyber warfare. The tactics, techniques, and procedures (TTPs) employed by attackers constantly (Sasikala & Sachan, 2024) evolve to circumvent defenses, exploiting new technologies and human vulnerabilities alike. For example, ransomware attacks have surged in frequency and severity, targeting healthcare, government, and critical infrastructure sectors, with attackers demanding large ransoms in exchange for restoring access to vital systems.

Figure 1. Exploring XAI for Trustworthy Decision Making

Physical threats remain highly relevant, especially as critical infrastructure systems are increasingly interconnected and reliant on cyber technologies. Threats such as sabotage, terrorism, theft, and natural disasters can disrupt operations, cause physical damage, and threaten human safety. (Sindiramutty et al., 2024) The convergence of physical and cyber threats, often termed cyber-physical threats, reflects scenarios where cyber intrusions lead to physical consequences—for example, manipulating industrial control systems to cause equipment failures or power outages. While threats represent external or internal actors' capabilities and intentions to cause harm, vulnerabilities are inherent weaknesses or gaps in systems, processes, or controls that can be exploited to realize those threats. The security context is not static; it is shaped by technological, social, political, and economic factors that influence both the threat landscape and the effectiveness of defenses. A comprehensive understanding of the security context requires continuous threat intelligence gathering—systematic collection and analysis of information about adversaries, their tactics, and indicators of compromise. Threat intelligence enables organizations to anticipate attacks, tailor defenses, and prioritize vulnerabilities. It involves monitoring open-source information, dark web forums, security advisories, and technical indicators. Effective risk management translates threat intelligence and vulnerability assessments into actionable strategies. This includes identifying critical assets, assessing potential impacts, and implementing layered defenses spanning technical controls, policies, and human factors. (Soundariya et al., 2025) Risk management also involves incident detection and response capabilities to minimize damage and recover quickly from breaches.

USER TRUST AND ACCEPTANCE: ENSURING EFFECTIVE XAI ADOPTION

The adoption and effective integration of Explainable Artificial Intelligence (XAI) in decision-making processes is not solely a technological challenge but also a profoundly human one. At the heart of this intersection lies human bias, (Sreekanthaswamy et al., 2025) a pervasive and multifaceted phenomenon that shapes how individuals perceive, trust, and utilize AI explanations. Understanding the impact of human cognitive biases on XAI adoption is crucial to designing systems that are not only transparent but also genuinely useful and trusted by users. This analysis explores the types of biases that influence human interaction with AI explanations, the consequences these biases have on decision-making and adoption, and strategies to mitigate their effects to promote responsible and effective XAI deployment. Human decision-making is inherently susceptible to a wide array of cognitive biases—systematic deviations from rational judgment that arise from mental shortcuts, emotional influences, social pressures, and information-processing limitations. These biases affect how individuals interpret information, evaluate evidence, and ultimately make choices. In contexts where AI systems provide automated or assisted decisions, biases can significantly influence how users understand and trust AI outputs and their explanations. Trust is a cornerstone of XAI adoption. Human biases can distort trust, either fostering excessive reliance on AI systems or undue skepticism. For instance, automation bias might cause users to overtrust AI explanations even when they are inaccurate, while confirmation bias may lead to rejection of valid AI insights that contradict human intuition. (Srivastava et al., 2022) Both extremes impair effective human-AI collaboration.

Negative experiences arising from bias-influenced misunderstandings reduce user satisfaction and willingness to adopt XAI. For example, if explanations appear too complex or inconsistent, users may disengage, perceiving AI as untrustworthy or irrelevant. Biases affect perceptions of fairness and accountability. (Suresh et al., 2025) If users interpret explanations through biased lenses, they might overlook discriminatory patterns or fail to hold AI systems accountable, exacerbating social inequalities. Presenting explanations in clear, concise language and intuitive visuals reduces cognitive load and misinterpretation. Avoiding overly technical jargon helps users with diverse backgrounds better understand AI reasoning. Offering different explanation types—such as feature importance, counterfactuals, and example-based explanations—allows users to cross-validate insights, reducing anchoring and confirmation biases. Allowing users to query, explore, and manipulate explanations fosters active engagement and deeper understanding, counteracting overconfidence and automation bias by encouraging critical evaluation. (Tamilarasi et al., 2025) Tailoring explanations to user roles, expertise, and the decision context improves relevance and reduces framing effects. For instance, domain experts might prefer detailed model internals, while lay users benefit from high-level summaries.

TRAINING AND EDUCATION: BUILDING XAI LITERACY

The growing integration of Artificial Intelligence (AI) systems across critical domains—ranging from healthcare and finance to security and autonomous systems—has underscored the indispensable role of Explainable AI (XAI) (Tiwari et al., 2020) in fostering user trust and acceptance. While AI models increasingly deliver powerful predictions and decisions, their often opaque "black-box" nature has raised significant concerns about reliability, fairness, and accountability. XAI aims to bridge this gap by providing transparent, interpretable explanations of AI decisions, thereby enabling users to understand, verify, and effectively incorporate AI outputs into their workflows. However, the successful adoption of XAI hinges fundamentally on user trust and acceptance, two deeply intertwined factors shaped by cognitive, social, and contextual dynamics. (Wang et al., 2021) This discussion explores the critical role of user trust in XAI adoption, the factors influencing trust formation, challenges in maintaining trust, and strategies to ensure AI explanations lead to effective, ethical, and sustainable user engagement.Trust is a multifaceted psychological state involving confidence in the reliability, integrity, and competence of a system or agent. In human-AI interaction, trust determines whether users are willing to rely on AI recommendations and integrate them into decision-making processes. Without sufficient trust, users may reject AI outputs, undermining the system's utility and investment. Conversely, misplaced or excessive trust can lead to overreliance, potentially amplifying the impact of AI errors. Explainable AI plays a pivotal role in cultivating appropriate trust by demystifying complex algorithms and providing insights into the rationale behind AI decisions. When users understand why a model arrived at a particular conclusion, they can better judge its validity, detect errors or biases, and feel more confident in using AI support. Thus, XAI acts as a trust enabler, transforming AI from a mysterious oracle to a transparent collaborator. (Yayla et al., 2022).

XAI systems must help users calibrate trust dynamically based on situational factors and model confidence. Ensuring that explanations faithfully represent the model's internal decision process is critical. (Zhang et al., 2022) Simplified or approximate explanations, while more accessible, may omit important details or introduce bias, undermining trust if discrepancies are discovered. Human biases—such as confirmation bias, automation bias, and anchoring—can distort the interpretation of explanations, leading to misplaced trust or mistrust. Addressing these biases requires careful explanation design and user education. AI models often change as they learn from new data. Frequent updates may alter explanations and decision behavior, potentially confusing users and disrupting trust. (Abusitta et al., 2024) Maintaining consistency and communicating changes transparently is essential. Users may distrust AI due to fears of manipulation, data privacy violations, or unfair discrimination. XAI must incorporate mechanisms to reveal such risks and empower users to question ethical implications. Building effective user trust in XAI requires a holistic approach involving technology design, user engagement, and organizational practices: Develop explanations that align with user needs, cognitive styles, and domain requirements. Employ iterative testing with diverse user groups to refine explanation clarity, relevance, and usability. Enable users to explore, question, and customize explanations, promoting active engagement and deeper understanding. Adaptive explanations that evolve with user expertise support sustained trust. (Akhtar et al., 2024) Clearly communicate model uncertainties, data limitations, and known failure modes. Leadership endorsement and transparent communication reinforce trust at the organizational level. Empirical studies across domains such as healthcare, finance, and cybersecurity demonstrate that XAI can significantly enhance user trust when explanations are well-aligned with user expectations and decision contexts. (Alshar'e et al., 2025).

FUTURE RESEARCH DIRECTIONS: ADVANCING XAI IN SECURITY

The rise of Explainable Artificial Intelligence (XAI) heralds a transformative shift in how AI systems are developed, deployed, and integrated into human decision-making processes. As AI models become increasingly complex and pervasive, (Charmet et al., 2022) the ability to comprehend, interpret, and critically evaluate AI-generated explanations has become essential—not only for AI practitioners but also for end-users, decision-makers, and stakeholders across diverse domains. This necessity underscores the vital role of training and education in building XAI literacy, a multifaceted effort aimed at equipping individuals with the knowledge, skills, and critical mindset required to effectively engage with explainable AI systems. (Chib et al., 2025) This overview explores the motivations, key components, challenges, and best practices associated with training and education for XAI literacy, emphasizing why such initiatives are indispensable for fostering responsible AI adoption and maximizing the benefits of transparency. XAI literacy refers to the capacity to understand the principles, methods, limitations, and implications of explainable AI. It enables users to interpret AI explanations accurately, evaluate the trustworthiness of AI decisions, and identify potential biases or errors. Without adequate literacy, users risk misinterpreting explanations, developing misplaced trust or skepticism, and ultimately making poor decisions. As AI penetrates high-stakes sectors such as healthcare, finance, law enforcement, and security, the consequences of misusing AI outputs can be profound—impacting individual rights, safety, and organizational integrity. (Coussement et al., 2024).

Exploration of fairness, accountability, privacy, and the societal impact of AI decisions, emphasizing the role of explainability in mitigating harm. Real-world scenarios illustrating successful and problematic (Dahiya et al., 2025) XAI deployments, encouraging critical reflection and problem-solving. Use of software platforms that allow learners to experiment with AI models and explanation methods, fostering experiential learning. Engage experts from AI, human-computer interaction, psychology, ethics, and domain fields to design comprehensive curricula. Promote freely available online courses, tutorials, and toolkits to democratize access to XAI literacy. Organizations deploying AI must recognize that technical solutions alone are insufficient for responsible AI use. Investing in training and education programs is critical for cultivating a workforce capable of interpreting AI explanations, making informed decisions, and upholding ethical standards. (Das et al., 2020) Academic institutions and professional training providers have a responsibility to integrate XAI topics into computer science, data science, and domain-specific curricula, preparing the next generation of practitioners and users. (De Bruijn et al., 2022) Governments and industry consortia can facilitate XAI literacy by funding research, developing standards, and promoting public awareness campaigns. AI-driven adaptive learning systems can customize XAI training paths based on individual progress and needs. Immersive technologies offer novel ways to visualize and interact with AI models and explanations, enhancing comprehension. Incorporating game elements into training can increase engagement and motivation. (Eldrandaly et al., 2023). By empowering diverse stakeholders with the knowledge and skills to understand, interpret, and critically evaluate AI explanations, XAI literacy initiatives enhance trust, improve decision quality, and mitigate risks associated with AI misuse. Investing in such programs is not merely and (Faheem et al., 2022) educational imperative but a strategic necessity in shaping an AI-augmented future that is transparent, accountable, and aligned with human values.

DEVELOPING EXPLAINABLE AI MODELS: TECHNIQUES AND APPROACHES

The advent of Explainable Artificial Intelligence (XAI) marks a critical turning point in the integration of AI into security domains, where transparency, trust, and accountability are paramount. As security challenges grow in complexity and scale—ranging from cyber threats and fraud detection to (Fatima et al., 2025) physical surveillance and critical infrastructure protection—XAI offers a promising avenue to enhance human-machine collaboration by making AI decisions interpretable and actionable. However, despite notable advances, the field of XAI in security remains nascent and faces unique hurdles that necessitate targeted, multidisciplinary research efforts. This discussion explores key future research directions vital for advancing XAI in security, emphasizing the development of robust explanation techniques, contextualization of explanations, (Hamon et al., 2022) mitigation of adversarial risks, evaluation metrics, human factors integration, and policy frameworks to ensure that explainable AI systems in security are effective, reliable, and ethically sound. Traditional XAI techniques—such as feature importance scores, saliency maps, and surrogate models—have demonstrated utility in various domains but often fall short in security contexts where decision complexity, data heterogeneity, and real-time constraints impose unique demands. Security data is often noisy, incomplete, or intentionally manipulated by threat actors. Explanation methods need to maintain fidelity and reliability under such adversarial conditions, ensuring that explanations remain trustworthy even when inputs are perturbed or deceptive. Security decisions depend heavily on situational context, threat models, and operational priorities. Generic explanations may lack relevance or be misinterpreted without embedding domain knowledge. Research should explore hybrid models that integrate symbolic reasoning, knowledge graphs, and contextual information to generate (Hanif et al., 2021) explanations that align with security operators' mental models.

Adversarial attacks represent a significant threat to AI systems in security, not only compromising prediction accuracy but also undermining explanation integrity. Attackers may seek to: Craft inputs that produce (Jagannathan et al., 2023) misleading or benign-looking explanations despite malicious intent, deceiving human analysts. Reverse-engineer model internals or discover vulnerabilities based on explanations, facilitating targeted attacks. A critical bottleneck in XAI research, especially within security, is the absence of universally accepted evaluation frameworks for explanations. Unlike predictive accuracy, explanation quality is inherently subjective, dependent on user context, cognitive factors, and task goals. Emerging AI (Jaigirdar et al., 2020) technologies present new opportunities for advancing XAI in security: Incorporating causal models into explanations to provide deeper insights into cause-effect relationships in security incidents. Applying XAI to autonomous agents that adapt dynamically to threats, requiring explanations of complex, sequential decision processes. Ensuring explainability in decentralized AI systems common in large-scale security architectures, while maintaining data privacy. Exploring generative models and natural language generation to produce more natural, conversational explanations accessible to non-experts. The future of Explainable AI (Kaur et al., 2025) in security holds tremendous promise but is contingent on addressing significant technical, human, and ethical challenges.

COLLABORATION AND STANDARDIZATION: ENSURING EFFECTIVE XAI ADOPTION

The growing deployment of Artificial Intelligence (AI) systems across critical sectors has underscored the urgent need for transparency and interpretability, giving rise to the field of Explainable AI (XAI). Explainable AI focuses on creating AI models whose decision-making processes can be understood, trusted, (Kommineni et al., 2025) and effectively scrutinized by humans. This is particularly vital in domains like healthcare, finance, law enforcement, and security, where opaque "black-box" models can hinder accountability and raise ethical concerns. Developing explainable AI models involves a variety of techniques and approaches that balance predictive performance with interpretability. This discussion delves into the diverse methodologies employed in XAI development, their strengths and limitations, and emerging trends shaping the future of interpretable machine learning. XAI techniques can broadly be categorized into two main types: intrinsic interpretability and post-hoc explainability. This approach involves designing (Kumar et al., 2024) AI models that are inherently transparent by virtue of their structure or simplicity. When employing complex models like deep neural networks or ensemble methods that act as black boxes, post-hoc explanation techniques are applied after model training to interpret or approximate their behavior. (Lee et al., 2024) These methods seek to explain the output of an already trained model without altering its internal structure.

Post-hoc approaches include feature importance scoring, surrogate modeling, counterfactual explanations, and visualization techniques. Structured as hierarchical if-then rules, decision trees allow for straightforward tracing of how (Limbore et al., 2025) input features lead to a prediction. They are easy to visualize and interpret but can become unwieldy with large or noisy datasets. Rule sets extracted from data offer interpretable "if-then" logic statements that human experts can validate. Rule extraction algorithms aim to simplify complex models into understandable rules. These statistical models express predictions as weighted sums of input features. Their coefficients indicate feature importance and directionality, facilitating straightforward explanation. (Longo et al., 2020) GAMs extend linear models by allowing non-linear but additive feature effects, maintaining interpretability while capturing more complex relationships. While these models are inherently interpretable, their simplicity limits their effectiveness on high-dimensional, non-linear problems common in real-world scenarios. LIME approximates the complex model locally around a specific input by training an interpretable surrogate (like a linear model), offering insight into individual predictions. These focus on "what-if" scenarios, illustrating (Madhav et al., 2022) how minimal changes to input features could alter the model's decision. Counterfactuals are intuitive for users seeking actionable insights. In computer vision and natural language processing, visualization techniques highlight which parts of input data (pixels, words) influence model predictions. Simple, interpretable models are trained to approximate the behavior of a complex model globally or locally, enabling users to understand general decision patterns. Research is ongoing to establish standardized metrics and user-centered evaluation frameworks to assess and compare XAI techniques effectively. Developing explainable AI models is a multidisciplinary endeavor that balances model complexity, transparency, and user needs. By leveraging intrinsic interpretable models, post-hoc explanation techniques, and emerging hybrid approaches, practitioners can build (Mahbooba et al., 2021) AI systems that are not only powerful but also trustworthy and accountable.

THE FUTURE OF XAI IN SECURITY DECISION-MAKING: OPPORTUNITIES AND CHALLENGES

The integration of Explainable Artificial Intelligence (XAI) into real-world systems, particularly in critical domains such as security, healthcare, finance, and law enforcement, demands more than technological innovation alone. It requires concerted collaboration across diverse stakeholders and the establishment of clear standards and frameworks to guide development, deployment, evaluation, and (Moustafa et al., 2023) governance of XAI systems. Collaboration and standardization are essential for addressing the multifaceted challenges posed by XAI, including technical complexity, ethical considerations, regulatory compliance, and user acceptance. This comprehensive overview explores why collaboration and standardization are pivotal to effective XAI adoption, identifies key participants, examines existing efforts, and outlines future directions to harmonize practices, foster trust, and maximize societal benefits. (Neupane et al., 2022) Explainability touches multiple dimensions of AI system development and use. To ensure that XAI technologies are trustworthy, reliable, and aligned with human values, collaboration is required among: Responsible for designing models and explanation algorithms that balance performance and transparency. Provide critical insights into domain-specific requirements for explanation relevance, interpretability, and usability. Study how users perceive and interact with explanations, guiding the design of user-centered interfaces. Address ethical dilemmas, privacy concerns, and legal accountability surrounding AI decisions. (Rawal et al., 2021) Develop frameworks to govern AI transparency, protect user rights, and promote fairness. Implement XAI solutions within operational environments and integrate feedback from real-world use. Create benchmarks, certification schemes, and best practices for XAI systems. The complex interplay of these actors reflects the inherently interdisciplinary nature of XAI challenges. No single group can effectively develop or oversee XAI solutions without inputs from others. Collaboration fosters shared understanding, reduces silos, and helps anticipate unintended consequences. Several initiatives and organizations are at the forefront of fostering collaboration and developing standards for XAI: This initiative develops ethically aligned design guidelines, including principles specific to explainability and transparency in AI systems.

The International Organization for Standardization (ISO) and International Electrotechnical Commission (IEC) joint technical committee on AI is working on standards encompassing AI trustworthiness and explainability. (Rjoub et al., 2023) A multi-stakeholder organization that brings together industry leaders, academia, and civil society to advance responsible AI, including explainability best practices. Offers policy recommendations and ethical guidelines emphasizing transparency and explainability. Actively working on developing frameworks for trustworthy AI, including explainability evaluation. These bodies provide platforms for diverse stakeholders to co-create standards and best practices, ensuring that XAI frameworks are both technically robust and socially responsible. In security applications, the stakes for explainability are exceptionally high due to potential impacts on privacy, (Samal et al., 2025) safety, and civil liberties. Looking forward, the maturation of XAI will increasingly depend on the synergy between collaborative ecosystems and robust standardization frameworks. Enable interoperable, scalable XAI solutions that can be confidently adopted across sectors. Drive the development of universally accepted benchmarks and certification programs, assuring users of explanation quality. Foster a culture of transparency and shared responsibility, promoting ethical AI innovation. Bridge the gap between technical advances and societal needs, ensuring that XAI fulfills its promise to make AI systems comprehensible, fair, and trustworthy. Continued investment in multi-stakeholder (Sasikala & Sachan, 2024) collaboration and agile standardization will be indispensable for navigating the evolving landscape of AI explainability and securing public trust in AI-enabled futures. Collaboration and standardization are foundational pillars for the effective adoption of Explainable AI. By bringing together diverse stakeholders and harmonizing approaches, these efforts help ensure that XAI technologies are transparent, reliable, and aligned with ethical and legal norms. Especially in sensitive domains like security, coordinated frameworks enable AI systems to provide meaningful explanations that support human decision-making, accountability, and societal well-being. Advancing collaboration and standardization is not merely a (Sindiramutty et al., 2024) technical challenge but a strategic imperative for building an AI-powered world that is trustworthy, inclusive, and responsive to human values.

CONCLUSION

As artificial intelligence (AI) continues to proliferate across various domains, its role in security decision-making has become increasingly significant. Explainable AI (XAI), which aims to make AI decisions transparent and interpretable, is poised to transform how security systems operate, improving both effectiveness and trust. The future of XAI in security decision-making holds remarkable opportunities, yet it also faces complex challenges that must be addressed to realize its full potential. This comprehensive discussion explores the promising prospects of XAI integration in security, the technological and ethical hurdles ahead, and the evolving landscape that will shape AI's role in securing our digital and physical environments. One of the foremost opportunities XAI offers is enhanced transparency, which is essential in security contexts where decisions often have profound consequences on privacy, freedom, and safety. Traditional AI models, especially deep learning-based systems, often operate as "black boxes," making it difficult for security analysts, auditors, and affected individuals to understand the rationale behind decisions such as threat detection, anomaly alerts, or access controls. XAI promises to reveal the reasoning behind AI outputs, enabling stakeholders to verify, contest, and refine decisions. This transparency builds trust among users, regulators, and the public, which is crucial for the broader acceptance and legitimacy of AI-driven security systems. XAI facilitates more effective human-AI collaboration by providing interpretable insights that empower security professionals to make informed decisions. Rather than replacing human judgment, explainable AI systems can augment analysts by highlighting suspicious patterns, explaining the basis for risk scores, and suggesting potential countermeasures. As governments and regulatory bodies worldwide impose stricter controls on AI use, especially in sensitive areas like surveillance, law enforcement, and cybersecurity, XAI will be critical for demonstrating accountability. Explainable models allow organizations to provide audit trails and evidence that decisions are fair, unbiased, and compliant with legal frameworks such as the European Union's GDPR and the emerging AI Act. Causal reasoning represents a promising direction for XAI, moving beyond correlation-based explanations to uncover cause-effect relationships underlying security incidents. Incorporating causal models will enable more actionable insights and robust decision-making, such as distinguishing between correlation and causation in anomaly detection. This will enhance the reliability of explanations and support root cause analysis in complex security contexts. The future of XAI involves tailoring explanations dynamically based on the user's role, expertise, and preferences. Interactive and adaptive interfaces that allow users to query, drill down, and customize explanations will improve usability and effectiveness. This human-centered design approach acknowledges that a one-size-fits-all explanation is insufficient, and empowers diverse stakeholders to extract maximum value from AI systems. Ethical guidelines will also evolve to incorporate best practices for responsible XAI use in security, fostering public trust. The future of explainable AI in security decision-making is replete with exciting possibilities and formidable challenges. XAI has the potential to revolutionize security operations by enhancing transparency, trust, and accountability, thereby empowering human decision-makers with deeper insights and better control over AI systems. However, realizing this potential requires addressing key obstacles including the explainability-performance trade-off, evaluation difficulties, data complexity, and security vulnerabilities. Collaborative efforts spanning AI researchers, domain experts, ethicists, regulators, and users will be crucial for developing innovative, practical XAI solutions tailored to the unique demands of security environments. Advancements in causal inference, adaptive interfaces, and multi-agent explainability promise to enrich the interpretability landscape. Simultaneously, evolving regulatory frameworks will provide guardrails that ensure AI systems remain ethical, fair, and compliant.

REFERENCES

Abusitta, A., Li, M. Q., & Fung, B. C. (2024). Survey on Explainable AI: Techniques, challenges and open issues. *Expert Systems with Applications*, *255*, 124710. DOI: 10.1016/j.eswa.2024.124710

Akhtar, M. A. K., Kumar, M., & Nayyar, A. (2024). Privacy and Security Considerations in Explainable AI. In *Towards Ethical and Socially Responsible Explainable AI: Challenges and Opportunities* (pp. 193–226). Springer Nature Switzerland. DOI: 10.1007/978-3-031-66489-2_7

Alshar'e, M., Abualkishik, A., Abuhmaidan, K., & Kayed, A. (2025). Enhancing Project Security: Unveiling Trust, Interpretability and Explainability in the Age of AI. In *5G Enabled Technology for Smart City and Urbanization System* (pp. 163-178). Chapman and Hall/CRC.

Charmet, F., Tanuwidjaja, H. C., Ayoubi, S., Gimenez, P. F., Han, Y., Jmila, H., Blanc, G., Takahashi, T., & Zhang, Z. (2022). Explainable artificial intelligence for cybersecurity: A literature survey. *Annales des Télécommunications*, *77*(11), 789–812. DOI: 10.1007/s12243-022-00926-7

Chib, S., Mehta, A. K., Saravanan, A., Mishra, B. R., & Manjunath, T. C. (2025). Mental Health Challenges and Solutions in High-Pressure Work Environments. In Harriott, S. (Ed.), *Innovative Approaches to Managing Conflict and Change in Diverse Work Environments* (pp. 247–272). IGI Global Scientific Publishing. DOI: 10.4018/979-8-3693-9556-1.ch011

Coussement, K., Abedin, M. Z., Kraus, M., Maldonado, S., & Topuz, K. (2024). Explainable AI for enhanced decision-making. *Decision Support Systems*, *184*, 114276. DOI: 10.1016/j.dss.2024.114276

Dahiya, R. Vidyadhara, & Manjunath, T. C. (2025). Design and Aerodynamics: Principles and Advances. In M. Mellal (Ed.), *Innovations and Developments in Unmanned Aerial Vehicles* (pp. 145-170). IGI Global Scientific Publishing.

Das, A., & Rad, P. (2020). Opportunities and challenges in explainable artificial intelligence (xai): A survey. *arXiv preprint arXiv:2006.11371.*

De Bruijn, H., Warnier, M., & Janssen, M. (2022). The perils and pitfalls of explainable AI: Strategies for explaining algorithmic decision-making. *Government Information Quarterly*, *39*(2), 101666. DOI: 10.1016/j.giq.2021.101666

Eldrandaly, K. A., Abdel-Basset, M., Ibrahim, M., & Abdel-Aziz, N. M. (2023). Explainable and secure artificial intelligence: Taxonomy, cases of study, learned lessons, challenges and future directions. *Enterprise Information Systems*, *17*(9), 2098537. DOI: 10.1080/17517575.2022.2098537

Faheem, M. A., Kakolu, S., & Aslam, M. (2022). The Role of Explainable AI in Cybersecurity: Improving Analyst Trust in Automated Threat Assessment Systems. *Iconic Research and Engineering Journals*, *6*(4), 173–182.

Fatima, Z., Hussain, R., Dilshad, A., Shakir, M., & Laghari, A. A. (2025). Explainable AI-Driven Firewall Evaluation: Empowering Cybersecurity Decision-Making for Optimal Network Defense. *Security and Privacy*, *8*(3), e70026. DOI: 10.1002/spy2.70026

Hamon, R., Junklewitz, H., Sanchez, I., Malgieri, G., & De Hert, P. (2022). Bridging the gap between AI and explainability in the GDPR: Towards trustworthiness-by-design in automated decision-making. *IEEE Computational Intelligence Magazine*, *17*(1), 72–85. DOI: 10.1109/MCI.2021.3129960

Hanif, A., Zhang, X., & Wood, S. (2021, October). A survey on explainable artificial intelligence techniques and challenges. In *2021 IEEE 25th international enterprise distributed object computing workshop (EDOCW)* (pp. 81-89). IEEE. DOI: 10.1109/EDOCW52865.2021.00036

Jagannathan, N. J., Labhade-Kumar, N. D. N., Rastogi, N. R., Unni, N. M. V., & Baseer, K. K. (2023). Developing interpretable models and techniques for explainable AI in decision-making. *The Scientific Temper*, *14*(04), 1324–1331. DOI: 10.58414/SCIENTIFICTEMPER.2023.14.4.39

Jaigirdar, F. T., Rudolph, C., Oliver, G., Watts, D., & Bain, C. (2020, December). What information is required for explainable AI?: A provenance-based research agenda and future challenges. In *2020 IEEE 6th International Conference on Collaboration and Internet Computing (CIC)* (pp. 177-183). IEEE.

Kaur, M., Selvakumar, P., & Dinesh, N. Mohit, Chandel, P. S., & Manjunath, T. C. (2025). Reconstruction and Preservation Strategies for Cultural Heritage. In S. Oflazoğlu & M. Dora (Eds.), *Preserving Cultural Heritage in Post-Disaster Urban Renewal* (pp. 385-412). IGI Global Scientific Publishing

Kommineni, M., Chundru, S., & Maroju, P. K. (2025). Ethical Implications of AI in Sustainable Development Pedagogy. In Chinedu, C., Mafarja, N., Hussein, M., & Saleem, A. (Eds.), *Rethinking the Pedagogy of Sustainable Development in the AI Era* (pp. 17–36). IGI Global Scientific Publishing. DOI: 10.4018/979-8-3693-9062-7.ch002

Kumar, P., Javeed, D., Kumar, R., & Islam, A. N. (2024). Blockchain and explainable AI for enhanced decision making in cyber threat detection. *Software, Practice & Experience*, *54*(8), 1337–1360. DOI: 10.1002/spe.3319

Lee, H., Kwon, T., Lee, J., & Song, J. (2024). Enhancing Decision-Making of Network Intrusion Analysis Assisted by Explainable AI for Real-Time Security Monitoring. In *2024 IEEE Conference on Dependable and Secure Computing (DSC)* (pp. 147-154). IEEE. DOI: 10.1109/DSC63325.2024.00039

Limbore, N. V., Anute, N., Ahluwalia, G. K., Chordiya, P. B., & Kalshetti, P. (2025). Ethical Leadership and Corporate Responsibility. In Harriott, S. (Ed.), *Innovative Approaches to Managing Conflict and Change in Diverse Work Environments* (pp. 193–218). IGI Global Scientific Publishing. DOI: 10.4018/979-8-3693-9556-1.ch009

Longo, L., Goebel, R., Lecue, F., Kieseberg, P., & Holzinger, A. (2020, August). Explainable artificial intelligence: Concepts, applications, research challenges and visions. In *International cross-domain conference for machine learning and knowledge extraction* (pp. 1-16). Cham: Springer International Publishing.

Madhav, A. S., & Tyagi, A. K. (2022). Explainable Artificial Intelligence (XAI): connecting artificial decision-making and human trust in autonomous vehicles. In *Proceedings of Third International Conference on Computing, Communications, and Cyber-Security: IC4S 2021* (pp. 123-136). Singapore: Springer Nature Singapore.

Mahbooba, B., Timilsina, M., Sahal, R., & Serrano, M. (2021). Explainable artificial intelligence (XAI) to enhance trust management in intrusion detection systems using decision tree model. *Complexity*, *2021*(1), 6634811. DOI: 10.1155/2021/6634811

Moustafa, N., Koroniotis, N., Keshk, M., Zomaya, A. Y., & Tari, Z. (2023). Explainable intrusion detection for cyber defences in the internet of things: Opportunities and solutions. *IEEE Communications Surveys and Tutorials*, *25*(3), 1775–1807. DOI: 10.1109/COMST.2023.3280465

Neupane, S., Ables, J., Anderson, W., Mittal, S., Rahimi, S., Banicescu, I., & Seale, M. (2022). Explainable intrusion detection systems (x-ids): A survey of current methods, challenges, and opportunities. *IEEE Access : Practical Innovations, Open Solutions*, *10*, 112392–112415. DOI: 10.1109/ACCESS.2022.3216617

Rawal, A., McCoy, J., Rawat, D. B., Sadler, B. M., & Amant, R. S. (2021). Recent advances in trustworthy explainable artificial intelligence: Status, challenges, and perspectives. *IEEE Transactions on Artificial Intelligence*, *3*(6), 852–866. DOI: 10.1109/TAI.2021.3133846

Rjoub, G., Bentahar, J., Wahab, O. A., Mizouni, R., Song, A., Cohen, R., & Mourad, A. (2023). A survey on explainable artificial intelligence for cybersecurity. *IEEE Transactions on Network and Service Management, 20*(4), 5115–5140. DOI: 10.1109/TNSM.2023.3282740

Samal, A., & Misra, L. I. Mohit, Pougajendy, S., Chandel, P. S., Manjunath, T. C., (2025). Musealization and Tourism Practices. In S. Oflazoğlu & M. Dora (Eds.), *Preserving Cultural Heritage in Post-Disaster Urban Renewal* (pp. 115-142). IGI Global Scientific Publishing

Sasikala, B., & Sachan, S. (2024). Decoding decision-making: embracing explainable AI for trust and transparency. *Exploring the frontiers of artificial intelligence and machine learning technologies, 42.*

Sindiramutty, S. R., Tan, C. E., Lau, S. P., Thangaveloo, R., Gharib, A. H., Manchuri, A. R., & Muniandy, L. (2024). Explainable AI for cybersecurity. In *Advances in Explainable AI Applications for Smart Cities* (pp. 31–97). IGI Global Scientific Publishing. DOI: 10.4018/978-1-6684-6361-1.ch002

Soundariya, A., Behera, N. K., Chandel, P. S., Gupta, S., & Manjunath, T. C. (2025). AI and Environmental Ethics: The Role of AI in Addressing Climate Change Ethical Considerations in AI-Driven Environmental Solutions. In Chakraborty, S. (Ed.), *Human Values, Ethics, and Dignity in the Age of Artificial Intelligence* (pp. 321–346). IGI Global Scientific Publishing. DOI: 10.4018/979-8-3693-9035-1.ch013

Sreekanthaswamy, N., Anitha, S., Singh, A., Jayadeva, S. M., Gupta, S., & Manjunath, T. C. (2025). Digital Tools and Methods. In Çela, E., Paliktzoglou, V., Sengar, S., Eappen, P., & Vajjhala, N. (Eds.), *Enhancing School Counseling With Technology and Case Studies* (pp. 25–48). IGI Global Scientific Publishing. DOI: 10.4018/979-8-3693-8392-6.ch002

Srivastava, G., Jhaveri, R. H., Bhattacharya, S., Pandya, S., Maddikunta, P. K. R., Yenduri, G., . . . Gadekallu, T. R. (2022). XAI for cybersecurity: state of the art, challenges, open issues and future directions. *arXiv preprint arXiv:2206.03585.*

Suresh, R. V., Selvakumar, P., Naresh Babu, K., Nithya, G., Manjunath, T. C., & Kartigeyan, J. (2025). Best Practices and Practical Applications. In Çela, E., Paliktzoglou, V., Sengar, S., Eappen, P., & Vajjhala, N. (Eds.), *Enhancing School Counseling With Technology and Case Studies* (pp. 341–362). IGI Global Scientific Publishing. DOI: 10.4018/979-8-3693-8392-6.ch013

Tamilarasi, C., Sowmiya, K., Vignesh, G. D., Jasmine, R. L., & Nehru, P. (2025). AI in Renewable Energy Education: Teaching the Future of Sustainable Power Systems. In Chinedu, C., Mafarja, N., Hussein, M., & Saleem, A. (Eds.), *Rethinking the Pedagogy of Sustainable Development in the AI Era* (pp. 133–152). IGI Global Scientific Publishing. DOI: 10.4018/979-8-3693-9062-7.ch007

Tiwari, S., Sresth, V., & Srivastava, A. (2020). The Role of Explainable AI in Cybersecurity: Addressing Transparency Challenges in Autonomous Defense Systems. *International Journal of Innovative Research in Science, Engineering and Technology*, *9*(3), 718–733. DOI: 10.15680/IJIRSET.2020.0903165

Wang, S., Qureshi, M. A., Miralles-Pechuan, L., Huynh-The, T., Gadekallu, T. R., & Liyanage, M. (2021). Applications of explainable AI for 6G: Technical aspects, use cases, and research challenges. *arXiv preprint arXiv:2112.04698.*

Yayla, A., Haghnegahdar, L., & Dincelli, E. (2022). Explainable artificial intelligence for smart grid intrusion detection systems. *IT Professional*, *24*(5), 18–24. DOI: 10.1109/MITP.2022.3163731

Zhang, Z., Al Hamadi, H., Damiani, E., Yeun, C. Y., & Taher, F. (2022). Explainable artificial intelligence applications in cyber security: State-of-the-art in research. *IEEE Access : Practical Innovations, Open Solutions*, *10*, 93104–93139. DOI: 10.1109/ACCESS.2022.3204051

Chapter 5
Navigating the Ethical and Legal Challenges of Artificial Intelligence in Industrial Cyber Security

Ajeet Kumar Sharma
School of Computer Science and Engineering, IILM University, Greater Noida, India

Avinash Kumar Sharma
http://orcid.org/0000-0001-6762-6778
Department of CSE, Sharda School of Computing Science and Engineering (SSCSE), Sharda University, Greater Noida, India

Ashwani Kumar
http://orcid.org/0000-0002-2100-900X
School of Computer Science Engineering and Technology, Bennett University, Greater Noida, India

Anshul Kumar
Department of Computer Applications, GNIOT Engineering Institute, Greater Noida, India

Anurag Upadhyay
KCCITM Greater Noida, India

ABSTRACT

The infusion of AI (Artificial Intelligence) into industrial cyber security has been a major step indeed significantly improving the identification of threats, the automa-

DOI: 10.4018/979-8-2600-1498-1.ch005

tion of reactions, and the protection of infrastructure, which is considered essential. However, this scientific and technological breakthrough has facilitated the rise of a number of ethical and legal issues that should be reckoned with in order to ensure the responsible implementation of this new technology and the effective oversight of all operations. The domain of ethical considerations focuses on the issues of privacy, responsibility, bias, clarity, and the extent of human supervision with AI systems making independent decisions in most of the critical situations. The lack of transparency in AI decision-making may lead to distrust, and the biases in the training data could cause the AI to be biased or not to find security gaps. Legally, the rapid development of AI in the field of cyber security tests the current frameworks and raises questions of responsibility in the event of system failures, cyber security incidents, and data protection regulations being violated. Moreover, the problems with the security of AI such as being attacked by the adversaries and becoming vulnerable have also been identified as not only the threats to the integrity of industrial systems but also to public safety. The purpose of this study is to explore the ethical and legal problems by examining the common issues between AI and industrial cyber security and proposing solutions to lower the risks using transparency, accountability, and proper regulation. An equitable strategy is necessary to leverage AI's full potential in safeguarding industrial settings and preventing possible negative effects while still adhering to the changes in legal regulations.

1. INTRODUCTION

AI is playing an important role in many industries, while cybersecurity remains the primary challenge for such industries. As a result, AI-powered systems are able to automatically detect threats and produce large amounts of data, as well as quickly respond to cyberattacks. These systems can offer businesses a higher level of protection from the threat of cyber-attack. Industries such as manufacturing, energy, and healthcare, are all highly vulnerable to cyber-attacks and AI can provide them with this higher level of protection. Although AI offers many solutions to enhance security in the industry, there are numerous ethical and legal issues associated with the application of AI in industrial cybersecurity. For example, from an ethical perspective, we need to think about privacy, how data are utilized, and if AI has made an unfair decision. Digital data is required for an AI solution to function properly, and so many companies today are collecting enormous amounts of digital data on their customers. However, this raises the question of how much information should be collected, whether the customers have given consent to use their data, and how to prevent data from being used inappropriately. Also, given how complex AI can be, and how often AI systems can make their own independent decisions, it is very difficult to determine who will be held liable, the available transparency of the decision being made and the overall extent to which human beings will be engaged in that decision-making process. Many AI systems designed to make their own security-related decisions without input from humans, control is being given to AI in terms of how its operations and decision-making functions impact society. The rapidly increasing implementation of artificial intelligence in cybersecurity also raises questions about who will be liable for any damages that may result from a malfunction or breach caused by AI. Moreover, there has yet to be an established framework governing the application of AI within cybersecurity that includes identification of the rules to be followed by AI. Some aspects of the existing law do not adequately address the challenges associated with deploying AI solutions, particularly when working in high-risk environments such as industrial control systems, and determining who will be held accountable for any decisions made by AI, particularly in the event of failure or security incidents continues to be an issue. The focus of this chapter will be on how AI can potentially change the way we operate within industries (Sen, P.,2024). By examining the real-world scenarios, ethical research, and technical ideas, this chapter gives way to deal with issues, as illustrated in figure 1.

Figure 1. Legal & Ethical Considerations

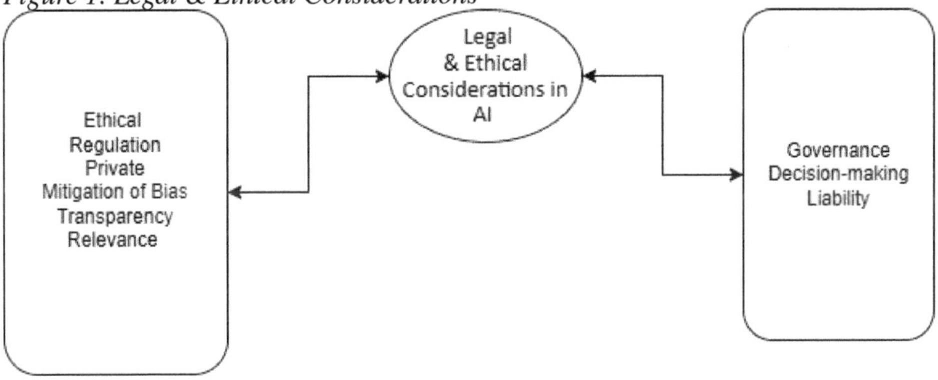

1.1 AI in Industrial Cyber security

Smart technology can analyze large amounts of data generated by connected devices, sensors and computer networks to detect abnormal behaviour as quickly as possible. This allows us to reduce downtime, minimize attacks and provide better reliability. The increased use of smart technology carries a new risk in that the systems themselves can be subject to attacks. The advantages of using smart technology in computing will be significant, but will also raise questions about compliance with regulations and what constitutes right and wrong. Using smart programs that are predictive will allow us to detect unusual behaviour as it occurs (in real-time), improve the speed and accuracy of our detection, and reduce the number of human errors. Important steps will need to be taken to protect the privacy of individuals and not rely entirely on smart technology. We can do this by adhering to regulations such as GDPR (General Data Protection Regulation), having clear definitions of who is responsible for an incident, and implementing automated response systems to rapidly isolate affected systems from the rest of the organization's infrastructure (Bayan, F. M. H.,2024).The ethical question arises, when smart machines operate independently, raising issues of liability if something goes wrong. Smart technology utilizes machine data to forecast when a machine will fail for preventative maintenance and to improve efficiency and reduce costs. Accessing data about employees and operational processes presents a potential risk to privacy, thus companies must comply with all employment and industry regulations. In terms of identifying vulnerabilities, smart technology can also be used for active (versus passive) identification of errors.

A potential risk of automating work processes is missed opportunities to identify possible threats. Therefore, it's important to have defined procedures for reporting these risks. Multiple smart technologies are used by security professionals (TCP/IP-based intrusion detection systems specifically) to monitor real-time activity as well as to reduce or eliminate false alarms caused by human error. Although smart technologies such as TCP/IP intrusion detection systems allow for better identification of potential threats and real-time monitoring, there is still concern for user privacy associated with constant monitoring, so adhering to proper guidelines to provide safeguards. Monitoring the flow of data through a network can help identify any vulnerability within the system, although it can also violate employee privacy or create an unfair disadvantage, making it prudent to enact legislation that establishes standards for how this information is managed. Implementing "smart" technologies such as biometrics like fingerprints and facial recognition as an added layer of security increases the frequency of monitoring the end user; therefore, compliance with privacy laws for the protection of this type of personal information must be adhered to (Kumar, A., & Kumar, L.,2024).All smart technologies must be adequately protected from cyber-attacks (which means there needs to be laws in place that deter exploitation); however, while implementing smart technologies will change how industry safeguards its computer systems, as an organization it is essential to create a balance between innovation, best practices, and regulatory compliance to ensure trust and confidence in automated systems are maintained.

2. LEGAL CHALLENGES IN THE INTEGRATION OF AI

Artificial Intelligence (AI) has become one of the most transformative technologies and it is being integrated into various areas including healthcare, finance, education, transportation, and law enforcement. However, this high development brings a lot of legal challenges related to responsibility, data privacy, bias, intellectual property, and regulation, among others.

Regulatory Compliance: Various government bodies have created legal framework to monitor and regulate the challenges associated with AI.However, these challenges still remain in creating laws that are robust and flexible enough to accommodate the fast-paced nature of AI.

Liability and Accountability: The most legal question is about the responsibility for the harm causes by AI. For example, in case of an autonomous vehicle involved in a collision, determining liability is complex.Existing legal systems are framed for human, not for autonomous agents. So, still there is a need for a legal reform to set the accountability in cases where AI systems act independently.

Data Protection and Privacy:AI based systems generally depends on huge data to work efficiently, which can raise significant privacy concerns. As the personal data collected from users must be in compliance with protection laws, which ensure transparency, consent, and the right to data deletion (Haskard, A., & Herath, D.,2025).

Bias and Discrimination:AI systems can produce bias result, if they are trained on biased data. Bias systems invarious sectors like hiring, and law enforcement can lead to systemic unfair treatment, making organizations legally vulnerable to law-suits. Legal frameworks further need to establish more clear guidelines to ensure non-discriminatory practices.

Cybersecurity and Safety Standards: AI-enabled systems are increasing rapidly and also being targeted by cyber attackers due to their integration into critical infrastructure. The Legal concern is the obligations of developers and users to implement sufficient security measures. Failure of these may result in liability for breaches by unauthorized access.

Accountability and responsibility: The major ethical concern with AI-driven systems to industrial protection is to determine the responsibility, when these systems make autonomous decisions. Traditional models struggle in addressing the complexity of artificial intelligence systems, specially, when operate with limited human supervision. AI systems, require transparency and well-defined frameworks.

Figure 2. Artificial intelligence: Impact on decision making, safety, and human behavior

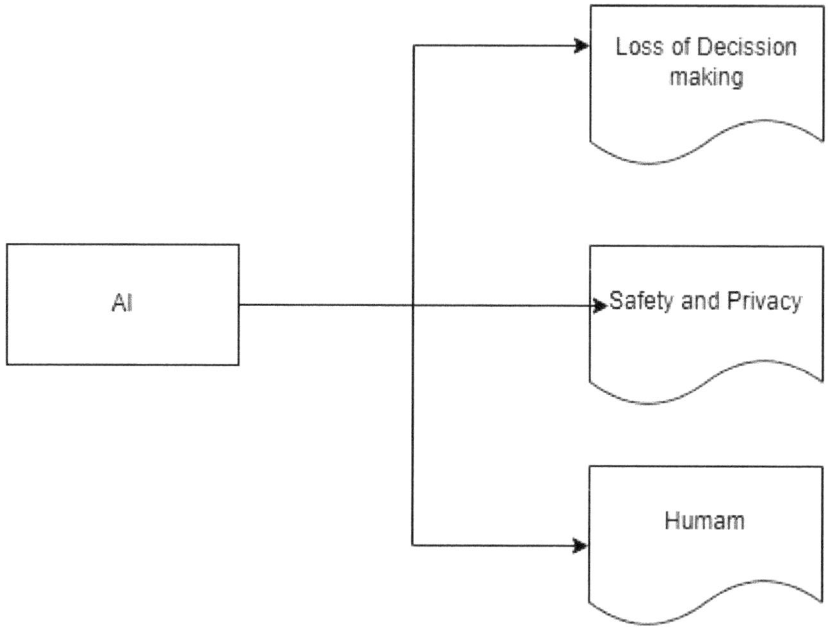

3. ADVERSARIAL ATTACKS

Adversarial attacks are becoming a serious threat to AI security, where bad actors make minor changes to the input data, like an image or text that cause AI systems to generate an erroneous result. These minor changes can expose weaknesses in AI models and make people to lose trust in AI, especially in various important areas like self-driving cars, healthcare, and security systems. Below is an overview of the types of adversarial attacks, their working and ways to defend against them.

3.1 Types of Adversarial Attacks

As AI based systems are vulnerable to various security threats that can compromise their performance, reliability. Below is a detailed explanation of various types of attacks targeting AI models.

Evasion Attacks: Evasion attacks generally occur when an attacker modifies the input data and deceive the AI into making incorrect decisions without altering the system's structure (Shafik, W.,2024). For example, minor changes to an image might cause a facial recognition system to misclassify a person. The goal is to manipulate the AI's outputs by exploiting its sensitivity to small variations in input data.

Poisoning Attacks: In this type of attack, malicious data is used during the training phase of an AI model and attackers can influence the way the AI learns, which lead unfair decision-making.

Inference Attacks: Inference attacks extract confidential information from an AI system by analysing its outputs. Here, attackers attempt to uncover sensitive information about the data the model was trained(Awuor, A. S., Okoth, P., &Kwanya, T.,2024). This type of attack is harmful when AI models are used with personal datasets, such as healthcare or financial information.

Transferability Attacks: These attacks are based on the adversarial inputs prepared to deceive one AI system that can often deceive other AI systems as well. This property makes transferability attacks particularly potent, as a single adversarial can target multiple systems simultaneously.

Backdoor Attacks: In this type of attack hidden triggers are put within an AI model during training process, where the AI model behaves normally under usual circumstances, but when it encounters a specific input pattern it behaves in malicious way (Dhirani, Lubna Luxmi, et al (2023).

Gradient-Based Attacks: Gradient-based attacks exploit the gradient information, of AI systems to generate malicious inputs(Tschider, C. A.,2018). This method is especially common against neural networks, which highly rely on gradient-based optimization.

Data Poisoning Attacks: Data poisoning attacks corrupt the data used to train an AI system to embed systemic weaknesses or biases into the final model (Hussain, et al.,2024). These attacks can manipulate model behavior across a wide range of inputs, often without being easily detectable. For example, attackers might inject fake reviews into a dataset used for training a product recommendation system to artificially inflate or deflate certain product ratings(Patel, 2024).

Model Stealing Attacks: In this attack the attacker put query and analyses the responses of anAI model. The attacker attempts to reconstruct a replica of the original model, by stealing its functionality and intellectual property(Ji, F., Zhou, Y., Zhang, H., Cheng, G., & Luo, Q.,2024).

4. ETHICAL REGULATORY PRINCIPLES FOR AI

Regulatory principles for AI governance are norms that governments and standard bodies use to design laws, policies, and monitor the systems for artificial intelligence. These principles are always framed around "trustworthy AI" and approach to balance innovation with the protection of rights and democratic values.

- **Human Monitor and control**: AI systems must remain under meaningful control of human, as various crucial decisions including healthcare, justice, and security should be reviewable by humans.
- **Transparency:** It should be disclosed by organizations, how key decisions are made using AI, in the scenarios where individuals are really affected.
- **Security and robustness:** AI systems must be robust towards failures and adversaria attacks. System must follow the data protection laws such as GDPR.
- **Accountability:** AI system should have a responsibility for the outcomes, and individuals must have an option to challenge the AI-driven decisions, in case of any harm.
- **Deepfakes and Misinformation:** AI generated content such as deepfake can be used to spread false information and manipulate public opinion.
- **Environmental Impact**: Training of large AI models require significant computational power, and consumes huge amount of energy. This can lead to various environmental concerns such as carbon emissions.

4.1 Safeguarding AI Systems

For ethical and reliable use of AI, it is essential to adopt the technical and organizational safeguards. These safeguards address the various risks related to vulnerabilities in the system, data privacy, and various ethical concerns.

Technical Safeguards: Technical safeguards strengthen the design and functioning of AI systems to ensure reliability and privacy. Various techniques including adversarial training support models to defend against malicious inputs, while testing the robustness of model evaluates system's performance under diverse conditions.

Organizational Safeguards: Organizational safeguards focus on governance, accountability, and ethical supervision in the development and deployment of AI. Establishment of AI governance ensures that decisions incorporate perspectives from ethics, law and cybersecurity. Ethical Impact Assessments (EIA) help in evaluating the societal and legal implications before the implementation. Furthermore, AI audit maintains transparent records and data usage. These measures ensure responsible and ethical use of AI.

5. CONCLUSION

Artificial intelligence is a game-changer for keeping organizations and industrial systems safe and secure from cyber-attacks. It is bringing new tools and techniques to defend against growing and changing threats. However, just like any new technology, use of AI in this way also brings up some concerns about right and wrong. A careful review is required to ensure that AI helps in businesses, while also avoiding potential problems. Regulations on data privacy, such as the General Data Protection Regulation and data protection laws, make it challenging to ensure compliance, while handling large amounts of data. Adversarial attacks highlight the need for building secure and privacy-preserving AI systems. Integration of defenses approach, such as adversarial training, privacy safeguards, and rigorous model evaluation helps in preventing the misuse.

REFERENCES

Awuor, A. S., Okoth, P., & Kwanya, T. (2024). Navigating Ethical Dilemmas while Transforming Information Services in the Global Age. Information Impact. *Journal of Information and Knowledge Management*, *15*(2), 45–58.

Bayan, F. M. H. (2024). The Ethics of AI: Navigating the Moral dilemmas of Artificial Intelligence. Arab Journal for Scientific Publishing (AJSP). *ISSN*, *2663*, 5798.

Dhirani, L. L., Mukhtiar, N., Chowdhry, B. S., & Newe, T. (2023). Ethical dilemmas and privacy issues in emerging technologies: A review. *Sensors (Basel)*, *23*(3), 1151. DOI: 10.3390/s23031151 PMID: 36772190

Haskard, A., & Herath, D. (2025). Secure Robotics: Navigating Challenges at the Nexus of Safety, Trust, and Cybersecurity in Cyber-Physical Systems. *ACM Computing Surveys*, *57*(9), 1–48. DOI: 10.1145/3723050

Hussain, S. M., Tummalapalli, S. R. K., & Chakravarthy, A. S. N. (2024). Cyber Security Education: Enhancing Cyber Security Capabilities, Navigating Trends and Challenges in a Dynamic Landscape. Advances in Cyber Security and Digital Forensics, 9-33.

Ji, F., Zhou, Y., Zhang, H., Cheng, G., & Luo, Q. (2024). Navigating the Digital Odyssey: AI-Driven Business Models in Industry 4.0. *Journal of the Knowledge Economy*, *16*(1), 1–44. DOI: 10.1007/s13132-024-02096-4

Kumar, A., & Kumar, L. (2024). Navigating the future: the ethical, societal and technological implications of artificial intelligence. Journal homepage, https://gjrpublication. com/gjrecs

Patel, C. (2024). Cyber Security, Privacy, and Network Security: Navigating the Evolving Threat Landscape. Privacy, and Network Security: Navigating the Evolving Threat Landscape (December 24, 2024).

Sen, P. (2024). Balancing Act: Navigating Artificial Intelligence, Data Privacy, and Legal Challenges in the Digital Age. Issue 2 Int'l JL Mgmt. &. *Human.*, *7*, 3062.

Shafik, W. (2024). Artificial intelligence and machine learning with cyber ethics for the future world. In *Future communication systems using artificial intelligence, internet of things and data science* (pp. 110–130). CRC Press. DOI: 10.1201/9781032648309-9

Tschider, C. A. (2018). Regulating the internet of things: Discrimination, privacy, and cybersecurity in the artificial intelligence age. *Denv. L. Rev.*, *96*, 87.

Chapter 6
Cyber-Physical Systems (CPS) and the Industrial Control System (ICS) Ecosystem

Md. Iqbal
http://orcid.org/0000-0001-5277-4479
Quantum University, India

Ajay Kumar Sharma
http://orcid.org/0000-0003-3085-8166
Quantum University, India

Pawan Kumar Goel
http://orcid.org/0000-0003-3601-102X
Raj Kumar Goel Institute of Technology, Ghaziabad, India

Amit Kumar
http://orcid.org/0009-0005-5772-2324
Institute of Management Studies, Roorkee, India

Rimmy
http://orcid.org/0009-0008-1756-5629
Quantum University, India

Himanshu Tyagi
http://orcid.org/0009-0001-8435-9832
Quantum University, India

ABSTRACT

This chapter analyses the fusion of cyber-physical systems (CPS) with the industrial control system (ICS) ecosystem, emphasising their significance in industrial automation and Industry 4.0. The blend of physical systems with monitoring, computing, and communication capabilities, allows for real-time updating, control, and optimization of processes like monitoring, control, and optimization. ICS encapsulates systems like SCADA, PLC, and DCS that are typically found in critical infrastructure and industrial processes. The discussion is centred on the enhancements in intelligence, adaptability, and connectivity that CPS integrates into ICS. Key discussion points include system architecture, communication protocols, security gaps, AI and machine

DOI: 10.4018/979-8-2600-1498-1.ch006

learning on process automation and threat detection, and warfare concepts. Smart manufacturing and energy systems, autonomous infrastructure, and real-world case studies and applications are provided.

1. INTRODUCTION

1.1 Overview of CPS and ICS

There has been a new paradigm of integrating automation within the industry known as cyber-physical systems (CPS). It encompasses the merging of physical systems with computation and communication technologies. Lee in 2015 explains that CPS contains four main components. These include the sensors which capture data in real-time, actors which process the data, computational units also known to conduct physical control and processes, and networks which allow for seamless data exchange (Lee, 2015). It is evident that the CPS are meant to work within an ever-changing environment and provide closed control with real-time changes. CPS can is used for smart manufacturing where analytics equipped with sensors can predict malfunction of a machine and healthcare services for real-time monitoring of patients (Monostori et al., 2016). The most notable feature of a CPS is its ability to merge or link the physical world with a digital system. Utilizing intelligent systems allows for optimizing performance with constant feedback.

Unlike industrial control systems (ICS), which are specialised frameworks for managing industrial procedures particularly in critical infrastructure including power plants, water treatment facilities, and oil refineries, ICS covers elements like Programmable Logic Controllers (PLCs), Distributed Control Systems (DCS), Supervisor Control and Data Acquisition (SCADA) systems, and Remote Terminal Units (RTUs) (Stouffer et al., 2015). Historically, ICS runs in isolated operational technology (OT) systems reliant on proprietary protocols and hierarchical structures to guarantee dependability. While legacy ICS systems can lack the scalability and connectivity required for modern industrial needs including remote access and real-time data integration, Colombo et al., 2017 note.

Combining the deterministic control of ICS with the intelligent adaptability of CPS signifies a dramatic transformation in industrial systems at the convergence of CPS and ICS. To boost interoperability and performance, this integration employs technologies like the Industrial Internet of Things (IIoT), edge computing, and advanced communication protocols (e.g., OPC-UA, MQTT) (Sisinni et al., 2018). In smart factories, for instance, CPS-enabled ICS systems take advantage of real-time data to optimum production schedules, hence boosting productivity by up to 20% in some conditions (Monostori et al., 2016). To fully actualise CPS-

ICS ecosystems, nevertheless, challenges including cybersecurity vulnerabilities, interoperability problems, and legacy system limits must be tackled. This section lays a basic knowledge of CPS and ICS, so creating the ground for exploring their integration in modern companies.

1.2 Importance of CPS-ICS integration in modern industries

The convergence of Cyber-Physical Systems (CPS) and Industrial Control Systems (ICS) is a the foundation of Industry 4.0, enabling remarkable improvements in manufacturing, energy, and transportation sectors. By incorporating CPS's computational and networking capabilities into ICS frameworks, industries obtain greater automation, resilience, and operational efficiency. This synergy allows real-time, data-driven decision-making, which is crucial for optimizing complex processes in dynamic contexts (Rajkumar et al., 2010). For instance, in smart manufacturing, CPS-ICS integration provides digital twins—virtual models of physical assets—that facilitate predictive maintenance, lowering equipment downtime by around 30% (Monostori et al., 2016).

A fundamental advantage of CPS-ICS integration is its ability to handle the limits of legacy ICS systems, which are generally hampered by isolated designs and antiquated protocols. Traditional ICS installations struggle to meet modern requirements for real-time analytics, remote monitoring, and scalability. CPS introduces new methods such as 5G, edge computing, and IIoT, enabling effortless communication and distributed control (Sisinni et al., 2018). In smart grids, for example, CPS-ICS systems monitor energy use in real time, balancing loads to boost grid resilience and reduce energy waste by up to 15% (Karnouskos, 2011). This interconnectedness transforms industries into flexible, responsive ecosystems capable of addressing evolving market demands.

Furthermore, CPS-ICS integration enhances system resilience through sophisticated cybersecurity and AI-driven solutions. As ICS environments grow increasingly networked, they face increased risks from cyber threats including ransomware and sophisticated attacks like as Stuxnet (Stouffer et al., 2015). CPS's integration of AI-based intrusion detection systems boosts ICS security, enabling rapid discovery and mitigation of abnormalities (Colombo et al., 2017). Additionally, CPS's adaptability supports flexible production systems, allowing firms to respond to disturbances like supply chain shortages or demand changes. Economically, CPS-ICS integration is anticipated to add $3.7 trillion to global manufacturing output by 2030, emphasising its transformational influence (Monostori et al., 2016). By encouraging intelligent, secure, and efficient industrial systems, CPS-ICS integration is vital for sustaining competitiveness in the era of Industry 4.0.

The convergence of Cyber-Physical Systems (CPS) and Industrial Control Systems (ICS) is a cornerstone of Industry 4.0, enabling remarkable improvements in manufacturing, energy, and transportation sectors. By incorporating CPS's computational and networking capabilities into ICS frameworks, industries obtain greater automation, resilience, and operational efficiency. This synergy enables real-time, data-driven decision-making, which is crucial for optimizing complex processes in dynamic contexts (Rajkumar et al., 2010). For instance, in smart manufacturing, CPS-ICS integration provides digital twins—virtual models of physical assets—that facilitate predictive maintenance, lowering equipment downtime by around 30% (Monostori et al., 2016).

A fundamental advantage of CPS-ICS integration is its ability to handle the limits of legacy ICS systems, which are generally hampered by isolated designs and antiquated protocols. Traditional ICS installations struggle to meet modern requirements for real-time analytics, remote monitoring, and scalability. CPS introduces new technologies such as 5G, edge computing, and IIoT, enabling seamless communication and distributed control (Sisinni et al., 2018). In smart grids, for example, CPS-ICS systems monitor energy use in real time, balancing loads to boost grid resilience and reduce energy waste by up to 15% (Karnouskos, 2011). This interconnectedness transforms industries into flexible, responsive ecosystems capable of addressing evolving market demands.

Furthermore, CPS-ICS integration enhances system resilience through sophisticated cybersecurity and AI-driven solutions. As ICS environments grow increasingly networked, they face raised risks from cyber threats including ransomware and sophisticated attacks like as Stuxnet (Stouffer et al., 2015). CPS's integration of AI-based intrusion detection systems boosts ICS security, enabling rapid discovery and mitigation of abnormalities (Colombo et al., 2017). In addition, CPS's adaptability supports flexible production systems, allowing firms to respond to disturbances like supply chain shortages or demand changes. Economically, CPS-ICS integration is anticipated to add $3.7 trillion to global manufacturing output by 2030, emphasising its transformational influence (Monostori et al., 2016). By encouraging intelligent, secure, and efficient technological systems, CPS-ICS integration is vital for sustaining competitiveness in the era of Industry 4.0.

2. FUNDAMENTALS OF CYBER-PHYSICAL SYSTEMS (CPS)

2.1 Definition and core components (sensing, computation, control, networking)

Cyber-Physical Systems (CPS) are engineered systems that tightly couple physical processes with computational and communication capabilities to enable real-time monitoring, control, and optimization (Lee, 2015). CPS integrates the physical world—comprising machines, infrastructure, or biological systems—with digital systems that process data and make decisions. The core components of CPS are sensing, computation, control, and networking, each playing a critical role in system functionality (Rajkumar et al., 2010).

Sensing involves the use of sensors to collect real-time data from the physical environment, such as temperature, pressure, or motion. Sensors provide the raw inputs necessary for system awareness (Baheti & Gill, 2011). Computation refers to processing units, such as microcontrollers or cloud servers, that analyze sensor data, execute algorithms, and generate actionable insights. This component enables decision-making and predictive analytics (Shi et al., 2011). Control is achieved through actuators that translate computational outputs into physical actions, such as adjusting a motor's speed or opening a valve. Actuators ensure that CPS can actively influence the physical world (Kim & Kumar, 2012). Networking facilitates seamless data exchange between sensors, processors, and actuators, often using protocols like MQTT or OPC-UA (Sisinni et al., 2018). Networking ensures system connectivity and coordination, enabling distributed and scalable operations.

The integration of these components creates a closed-loop system where data flows continuously, allowing CPS to adapt to dynamic conditions. For example, in a smart factory, sensors monitor machine performance, computational units predict failures, actuators adjust operations, and networks relay data to a central system (Monostori et al., 2016). This holistic design distinguishes CPS from traditional systems, enabling applications in critical infrastructure and smart cities. However, challenges like latency, security, and interoperability must be addressed to ensure robust CPS performance (Gunes et al., 2014).

Figure 1. Core Components and Architecture of Cyber-Physical Systems (CPS)

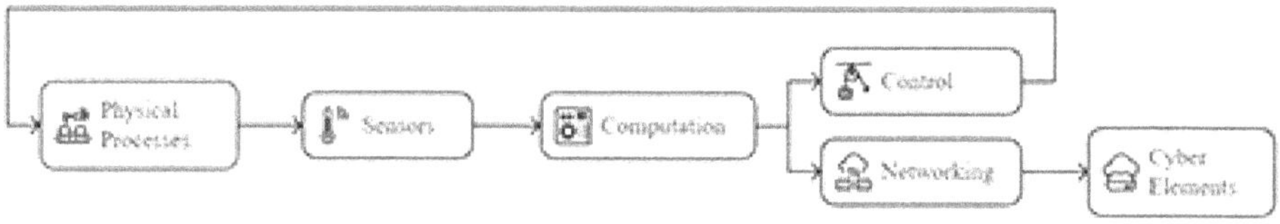

Figure 1 is a flowchart depicting the fundamental workflow of a CPS, showing how physical processes interact with cyber elements through a series of interconnected components. It visually represents the closed-loop system that defines CPS, where data flows continuously between physical and digital domains to enable real-time monitoring, control, and optimization. The components are arranged in a linear sequence with arrows indicating the direction of data and control flow, forming a feedback loop.

a) Physical Processes

This block represents the physical environment or system that CPS interacts with, such as machinery in a factory, a vehicle in transportation, or a medical device in healthcare. Physical processes are the real-world entities that CPS aims to monitor and control.

Role in CPS: Physical processes are the starting point of the CPS workflow. They generate data (e.g., temperature, speed, or pressure) through their operation, which needs to be captured for analysis and control.

b) Sensors

Sensors are devices that collect real-time data from physical processes. They measure physical parameters like temperature, vibration, or motion, converting them into digital signals.

Role in CPS: Sensors act as the interface between the physical and cyber worlds, providing the raw data necessary for CPS to understand the state of the physical system. For example, in a smart factory, sensors might monitor a motor's temperature to detect potential overheating.

c) Computation

The computation block represents the processing units (e.g., microcontrollers, CPUs, or cloud servers) that analyze the data collected by sensors. This involves executing algorithms, running predictive models, or making decisions based on the input data.

Role in CPS: Computation processes sensor data to generate actionable insights or control commands. For instance, if a sensor detects an anomaly, the computation unit might predict a failure and decide on a corrective action. This block is central to CPS's intelligence and decision-making capabilities.

d) Control

The control block consists of actuators that execute commands from the computation unit to influence the physical processes. Actuators are devices like motors, valves, or switches that adjust the physical system based on computational outputs.

Role in CPS: Control ensures that CPS can actively manage the physical environment. For example, if the computation unit predicts a machine failure, the control block might slow down the machine or shut it off to prevent damage. This creates a feedback loop, as the adjusted physical process is then re-monitored by sensors.

e) Networking

Networking facilitates the exchange of data between sensors, computation units, actuators, and other system components. It uses communication protocols (e.g., MQTT, OPC-UA, or 5G) to ensure seamless connectivity.

Role in CPS: Networking enables distributed coordination and scalability in CPS. It allows data to be shared across the system, including with remote servers or other CPS components, ensuring real-time collaboration. For example, in a smart grid, networking enables data from multiple sensors to be aggregated and analyzed centrally.

f) Cyber Elements

Cyber elements represent the digital infrastructure of CPS, including software, databases, cloud platforms, and AI models that support computation and networking.

Role in CPS: Cyber elements provide the computational and storage backbone for CPS, enabling advanced analytics, remote monitoring, and integration with other systems. They complete the loop by processing data and sending control commands back to the physical processes via actuators.

The arrows in the diagram indicate the direction of data and control flow, forming a closed-loop system typical of CPS:

- Physical Processes → Sensors: Physical processes generate data, which sensors collect and convert into digital signals.
- Sensors → Computation: Sensor data is sent to the computation block for processing and analysis.
- Computation → Control: The computation unit generates control commands, which are sent to actuators.
- Control → Physical Processes: Actuators adjust the physical processes, creating a feedback loop as the adjusted process is re-monitored by sensors.
- Computation ↔ Networking ↔ Cyber Elements: Networking facilitates data exchange between computation and cyber elements, enabling distributed processing, storage, and remote access.

This closed-loop architecture ensures that CPS can continuously monitor, analyze, and control physical processes in real time, adapting to changes and optimizing performance.

2.2 Characteristics and design principles

Cyber-Physical Systems (CPS) are defined by different properties that enable their function in complex, dynamic contexts. These features include real-time adaptability, adaptability, autonomy, and interoperability, which collectively separate CPS from traditional control systems (Lee, 2015). Real-time responsiveness means that CPS can process input and perform actions within severe time limits, crucial for applications like autonomous vehicles (Rajkumar et al., 2010). Adaptability allows CPS to react to changing conditions, such as altering production demands in smart factories (Monostori et al., 2016). Autonomy enables CPS to run with minimum human interaction, leveraging AI-driven decision-making to optimize operations (Shi et al., 2011). Interoperability ensures smooth integration with varied systems, such as Industrial Control Systems (ICS), through established protocols (Sisinni et al., 2018).

CPS's design concepts emphasize obtaining these attributes while maintaining dependability, security, and scalability. Model-based design is a critical idea, where systems are built using mathematical models to mimic physical and computational interactions before deployment (Kim & Kumar, 2012). This strategy ensures predictability and minimizes errors. Real-time computing is another principle that prefers low-latency processing to meet temporal requirements (Baheti & Gill, 2011). Cybersecurity is crucial, as CPS's connectivity exposes them to dangers like ransomware; design must contain encryption and intrusion detection (Humayed et al., 2017). Modularity allows CPS to be created as scalable, reusable components, allowing updates and maintenance (Gunes et al., 2014).

Additionally, CPS design stresses human-machine collaboration, ensuring systems are understandable for operators while embracing automation for efficiency (Sanfelice, 2015). For instance, in healthcare, CPS designs promote user-friendly interfaces for medical professionals to monitor patient data. These ideas demand a multidisciplinary approach, integrating competence in engineering, computer science, and domain-specific knowledge. Challenges in CPS design include balancing computational complexity with real-time achievement and ensuring compatibility with older systems, particularly in industrial contexts (Colombo et al., 2017). By adhering to these features and values, CPS can provide resilient, intelligent solutions that alter industries and infrastructure.

2.3 Role of real-time data and control loops

Real-time data and control loops are fundamental to the operation of Cyber-Physical Systems (CPS), enabling dynamic interaction between physical processes and computational systems. Real-time data refers to information collected and processed with minimal latency, ensuring that CPS can respond to environmental changes instantaneously (Lee, 2015). For example, in a smart grid, real-time data from sensors monitoring power consumption allows CPS to balance loads and prevent outages (Karnouskos, 2011). This capability relies on high-frequency data acquisition and low-latency communication protocols, such as MQTT or 5G, which ensure timely data delivery (Sisinni et al., 2018).

Control loops are the mechanisms through which CPS processes real-time data to make decisions and execute actions. A typical control loop involves three stages: sensing, computation, and actuation (Kim & Kumar, 2012). Sensors collect data, computational units analyze it to determine optimal responses, and actuators implement control actions, creating a continuous feedback cycle. For instance, in autonomous vehicles, control loops process sensor data (e.g., LIDAR) to adjust speed and direction, ensuring safe navigation (Rajkumar et al., 2010). These loops must operate within strict temporal constraints, often milliseconds, to maintain system stability and performance (Baheti & Gill, 2011).

The effectiveness of control loops depends on the quality and timeliness of real-time data. Delays or inaccuracies can lead to suboptimal decisions, compromising safety in critical applications like medical CPS (Sanfelice, 2015). To address this, CPS employs deterministic networking and edge computing to reduce latency and enhance data reliability (Shi et al., 2011). Additionally, AI algorithms, such as predictive models, enhance control loops by anticipating future states based on real-time data trends (Monostori et al., 2016). However, challenges include managing data overload, ensuring cybersecurity, and maintaining loop stability in distributed systems (Humayed et al., 2017). By leveraging real-time data and robust control loops, CPS achieves the precision and responsiveness required for applications in Industry 4.0 and beyond.

2.4 Applications across various domains (manufacturing, healthcare, transportation)

Cyber-Physical Systems (CPS) have revolutionized multiple domains by enabling intelligent, real-time interactions between physical and digital systems. In **manufacturing**, CPS drives Industry 4.0 through smart factories, where sensors monitor equipment, computational units predict failures, and actuators adjust operations. Digital twins—virtual replicas of physical assets—enable predictive maintenance, reducing downtime by up to 30% (Monostori et al., 2016). CPS also supports flexible production, allowing manufacturers to adapt to market demands dynamically (Colombo et al., 2017).

In **healthcare**, CPS enhances patient care through real-time monitoring and automated interventions. Wearable devices collect physiological data (e.g., heart rate), which CPS processes to detect anomalies and trigger alerts or adjust medical equipment, such as insulin pumps (Baheti & Gill, 2011). CPS-enabled robotic surgery systems provide precision and reduce human error, improving outcomes (Sanfelice, 2015). These applications require stringent reliability and security to ensure patient safety, posing challenges in data privacy and system integration (Humayed et al., 2017).

In **transportation**, CPS underpins autonomous vehicles and smart infrastructure. Autonomous cars use CPS to process sensor data (e.g., LIDAR, radar) for navigation, collision avoidance, and traffic optimization, with control loops operating in milliseconds (Rajkumar et al., 2010). Smart traffic systems leverage CPS to manage congestion through real-time data from cameras and sensors, reducing travel times by up to 15% in urban areas (Karnouskos, 2011). These applications demand robust cybersecurity and interoperability to prevent failures or attacks (Gunes et al., 2014).

Other domains, such as energy (smart grids) and agriculture (precision farming), also benefit from CPS's ability to integrate sensing, computation, and control. Challenges include scalability, cost, and ensuring compatibility with legacy systems (Shi et al., 2011). By addressing these, CPS continues to transform industries, enabling efficient, sustainable, and resilient operations across diverse applications.

3. UNDERSTANDING INDUSTRIAL CONTROL SYSTEMS (ICS)

3.1 Components of ICS: PLCs, SCADA, DCS, RTUs

Industrial Control Systems (ICS) comprise several key components that work together to monitor and control industrial processes. Programmable Logic Controllers (PLCs) are ruggedized computers that execute control logic to manage machinery and processes, such as regulating conveyor belts in manufacturing (Stouffer et al., 2015). PLCs are highly reliable and operate in real-time, making them essential for localized control tasks. Supervisory Control and Data Acquisition (SCADA) systems provide centralized monitoring and control over large-scale processes, such as power grids, by collecting data from remote devices and issuing commands (Galloway & Hancke, 2013). SCADA systems enable operators to visualize and manage operations through human-machine interfaces (HMIs).

Distributed Control Systems (DCS) are used in complex, continuous processes like oil refining, where multiple controllers are distributed across a plant to manage interconnected systems (Byres & Lowe, 2004). DCS emphasizes process optimization and integration, differing from PLCs' focus on discrete tasks. Remote Terminal Units (RTUs) are field devices that interface with sensors and actuators, transmitting data to SCADA or DCS systems, often in remote locations like pipelines (Knapp & Langill, 2015). These components collectively ensure precise control and monitoring, but their integration with modern technologies like CPS requires addressing compatibility and security challenges. Understanding these components is crucial for leveraging ICS in automated industrial environments.

3.2 Traditional ICS architecture and evolution

Traditional Industrial Control Systems (ICS) architectures are hierarchical, designed to ensure reliability and isolation in critical infrastructure. The architecture typically follows a layered model, with field devices (sensors, actuators) at the lowest level, controlled by PLCs or RTUs. These devices communicate with supervisory layers, such as SCADA or DCS, which aggregate data and provide operator interfaces (Stouffer et al., 2015). The top layer often includes enterprise systems for data logging and management, historically isolated from external networks to minimize risks (Byres & Lowe, 2004).

Communication in traditional ICS relies on proprietary protocols like Modbus or DNP3, optimized for deterministic performance but lacking flexibility (Galloway & Hancke, 2013). This isolation ensured security but limited scalability and real-time data sharing. The evolution of ICS has been driven by Industry 4.0, with modern architectures incorporating open standards like OPC-UA and Ethernet-based protocols to enable connectivity (Knapp & Langill, 2015). The integration of the Industrial Internet of Things (IIoT) and cloud computing has further transformed ICS, enabling remote monitoring and predictive analytics. However, this convergence with IT systems introduces cybersecurity vulnerabilities, as traditional ICS was not designed for internet connectivity. The shift from isolated to interconnected architectures marks a significant evolution, necessitating robust security and interoperability measures to support CPS integration.

3.3 Operational Technology (OT) vs. Information Technology (IT)

Operational Technology (OT) and Information Technology (IT) represent distinct domains within industrial systems, with ICS rooted in OT. OT focuses on controlling physical processes, prioritizing reliability, safety, and real-time performance in environments like power plants or factories (Stouffer et al., 2015). OT systems, including PLCs and SCADA, operate in deterministic, time-critical conditions, using specialized hardware and protocols to ensure uninterrupted processes (Galloway & Hancke, 2013). In contrast, IT emphasizes data processing, storage, and communication, prioritizing scalability and flexibility in enterprise systems like databases and email servers (Byres & Lowe, 2004).

The convergence of OT and IT, driven by Industry 4.0, enables advanced capabilities like real-time analytics and remote access in ICS. However, this integration creates challenges due to differing priorities: OT demands availability and safety, while IT focuses on confidentiality and data integrity (Knapp & Langill, 2015). For example, applying IT security patches to OT systems can disrupt operations, as ICS requires continuous uptime. Cybersecurity threats, such as ransomware targeting OT systems, further complicate convergence, as OT was historically isolated from external networks. Bridging OT and IT requires standardized protocols, robust security frameworks, and cross-disciplinary expertise to ensure seamless CPS-ICS integration while maintaining operational integrity.

3.4 Legacy systems and their limitations

Legacy Industrial Control Systems (ICS) refer to older systems, often decades old, still in use in critical infrastructure like power grids and manufacturing plants. These systems rely on outdated hardware, such as early PLCs, and proprietary protocols like Modbus, designed for isolated environments (Stouffer et al., 2015). While reliable, legacy systems face significant limitations, including lack of interoperability with modern technologies like IIoT or CPS (Byres & Lowe, 2004). Their proprietary nature restricts integration with open standards, hindering scalability and real-time data sharing.

Legacy systems also lack built-in cybersecurity, as they were designed for air-gapped environments, making them vulnerable to modern threats like Stuxnet (Galloway & Hancke, 2013). Upgrading or patching these systems is challenging due to compatibility issues and the need for continuous operation, increasing security risks (Knapp & Langill, 2015). Additionally, legacy ICS often has limited processing power, unable to support advanced analytics or AI-driven applications critical for Industry 4.0. High replacement costs and operational downtime further complicate modernization efforts. Addressing these limitations requires strategies like phased upgrades, protocol gateways, and enhanced security to enable CPS integration while maintaining reliability.

4. CPS-ICS CONVERGENCE

4.1 Synergies between CPS and ICS

Cyber-Physical Systems (CPS) and Industrial Control Systems (ICS) complement each other, creating synergies that enhance industrial automation. CPS integrates computational and networking capabilities with physical processes, offering adaptability and real-time analytics (Wolf, 2009). ICS, with components like SCADA and PLCs, ensures reliable, deterministic control in critical infrastructure (Dzung et al., 2005). The synergy lies in combining ICS's robust control mechanisms with CPS's intelligence and connectivity, enabling a seamless transition from isolated OT systems to interconnected, data-driven ecosystems (Sztipanovits et al., 2012). CPS augments ICS by providing advanced data processing, such as predictive analytics, which enhances ICS's ability to manage processes proactively (Leitão et al., 2016). Meanwhile, ICS offers CPS a stable, safety-focused foundation, ensuring that CPS-driven automation adheres to industrial standards (Serpanos & Wolf, 2018). This collaboration enables systems to optimize efficiency while maintaining reliability, crucial for sectors like energy and manufacturing.

Figure 2. Traditional ICS Architecture vs. CPS-Enhanced ICS

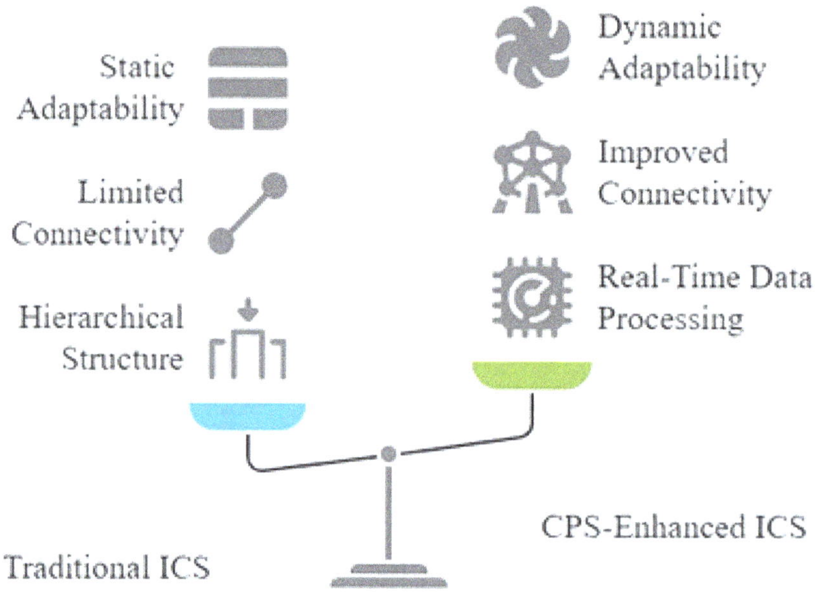

Above comparative diagram showing a traditional ICS architecture (e.g., SCADA, PLCs, DCS with hierarchical structure) on one side and a CPS-enhanced ICS architecture on the other. The CPS-enhanced side highlights added features like real-time data processing, edge computing nodes, and IoT integration. Arrows indicate improved connectivity and adaptability.

4.2 Benefits of integrating CPS in ICS environments

Integrating Cyber-Physical Systems (CPS) into Industrial Control Systems (ICS) environments offers multiple benefits, revolutionizing industrial operations. CPS enhances ICS with real-time data processing, enabling predictive maintenance that can reduce equipment failures by up to 25% (Tao et al., 2018). It also introduces advanced connectivity through protocols like Ethernet, allowing ICS to support remote operations, which is vital for large-scale systems like water treatment plants

(Dzung et al., 2005). CPS improves system adaptability, enabling ICS to handle dynamic conditions, such as sudden changes in production demand, through real-time optimization (Leitão et al., 2016). Furthermore, CPS strengthens ICS security by incorporating anomaly detection, mitigating risks in connected environments (Sztipanovits et al., 2012). Lastly, CPS enables scalability, allowing ICS to integrate with modern technologies like cloud computing, fostering innovation in industrial processes (Serpanos & Wolf, 2018). These advantages make CPS-ICS integration essential for achieving Industry 4.0 objectives.

4.3 Examples of CPS-enabled ICS (smart factories, IIoT systems)

CPS-enabled Industrial Control Systems (ICS) are demonstrated in smart factories and Industrial Internet of Things (IIoT) systems, highlighting their practical impact. In **smart factories**, CPS integrates with ICS to create adaptive manufacturing systems. Sensors collect data from production lines, which CPS analyzes to optimize workflows, while ICS components like DCS ensure precise control, increasing productivity by 15% (Tao et al., 2018). Bosch, for example, uses CPS-ICS integration to implement real-time quality control in its plants (Leitão et al., 2016). In **IIoT systems**, CPS enhances ICS by enabling device connectivity across industrial networks. In chemical plants, IIoT systems leverage CPS to monitor equipment via SCADA, using real-time data to prevent hazardous incidents (Dzung et al., 2005). Honeywell's Experion system exemplifies this, integrating CPS with ICS to enhance process automation in refineries (Serpanos & Wolf, 2018). These examples illustrate how CPS empowers ICS with intelligence and connectivity, driving efficiency and safety in industrial applications (Wolf, 2009).

4.4 Role of digital twins and edge computing

Digital twins and edge computing significantly enhance CPS-ICS integration, enabling advanced industrial capabilities. Digital twins, virtual models of physical assets, are created by CPS using data from ICS sensors and PLCs. They enable simulation and predictive analytics, such as optimizing energy usage in power plants, reducing costs by 10% (Tao et al., 2018). Digital twins provide a unified platform for CPS and ICS to collaborate, improving system monitoring and decision-making (Leitão et al., 2016). Edge computing processes data near its source, minimizing latency in CPS-ICS systems. In manufacturing, edge devices analyze sensor data to adjust machinery in real time, enhancing ICS efficiency (Dzung et al., 2005). Edge computing also reduces data exposure, improving security in connected ICS environments (Serpanos & Wolf, 2018). Together, digital twins and edge computing enable CPS-ICS systems to deliver real-time insights, scalability, and resilience, supporting Industry 4.0 advancements (Sztipanovits et al., 2012).

5. COMMUNICATION AND NETWORKING IN CPS-ICS

5.1 Industrial communication protocols (Modbus, OPC-UA, MQTT, etc.)

Industrial communication protocols are essential for enabling data exchange in CPS-ICS ecosystems, ensuring seamless interaction between sensors, controllers, and cyber elements. Modbus, a widely used protocol, facilitates communication between PLCs and field devices in ICS, offering simplicity and reliability for applications like manufacturing automation (Hale et al., 2018). However, Modbus lacks advanced security features, making it vulnerable in connected environments. OPC-UA (Open Platform Communications Unified Architecture) addresses this by providing a secure, interoperable standard for ICS, enabling data exchange across heterogeneous systems, such as SCADA and enterprise platforms (Mahler et al., 2019). OPC-UA supports complex data models, making it ideal for Industry 4.0 applications. MQTT (Message Queuing Telemetry Transport) is a lightweight, publish-subscribe protocol optimized for IoT integration in CPS-ICS systems, enabling efficient data transmission in smart grids (Luzuriaga et al., 2015). Other protocols, like DNP3, are used in utilities for reliable, time-critical communication (Mahmood et al., 2015). These protocols collectively ensure connectivity, but challenges like security, scalability, and compatibility with legacy systems must be addressed to support CPS-ICS integration (Ferrari et al., 2017).

Table 1. Comparison of Industrial Communication Protocols

Protocol	Features	Applications	Strengths	Limitations
Modbus	Serial communication, simple	PLC communication, sensors	Easy to implement, widely used	Limited security, low speed
OPC-UA	Secure, interoperable, platform-independent	SCADA, enterprise integration	High interoperability, secure	Complex setup, resource-heavy
MQTT	Lightweight, publish-subscribe	IoT, smart grids	Efficient for IoT, low bandwidth	Lacks determinism, security concerns
DNP3	Time-stamped data, reliable	Utilities (power, water)	Reliable for time-critical tasks	Limited scalability, complex

5.2 Real-time and deterministic communication challenges

Real-time and deterministic communication is critical in CPS-ICS ecosystems, where delays or inconsistencies can lead to operational failures. Real-time communication requires low latency to ensure timely data delivery, such as in autonomous manufacturing systems where sensors must relay data to PLCs within milliseconds (Ferrari et al., 2017). Deterministic communication ensures predictable data delivery, essential for time-critical ICS applications like power grid control (Mahmood et al., 2015). However, challenges arise due to network congestion, especially in large-scale IIoT systems, where high device density increases latency (Luzuriaga et al., 2015). Legacy protocols like Modbus often lack the determinism needed for modern applications, leading to jitter and packet loss (Hale et al., 2018). Cybersecurity threats, such as denial-of-service attacks, further disrupt real-time performance by overwhelming networks (Mahler et al., 2019). Addressing these challenges requires advanced scheduling algorithms, prioritized data transmission, and robust security measures to ensure CPS-ICS systems maintain real-time, deterministic performance in dynamic industrial environments.

5.3 5G and industrial Ethernet in CPS-ICS integration

5G and industrial Ethernet are transformative technologies for CPS-ICS integration, enhancing communication efficiency and reliability. 5G offers ultra-low latency (below 1 ms) and high bandwidth, enabling real-time data exchange in CPS-ICS systems like smart factories (Ferrari et al., 2017). For example, 5G supports massive device connectivity, allowing thousands of sensors in a factory to communicate simultaneously, improving process automation (Luzuriaga et al., 2015). Industrial Ethernet, such as EtherCAT, provides deterministic communication, ensuring predictable data delivery for time-sensitive ICS applications like robotic control (Mahmood et al., 2015). It offers higher bandwidth than traditional protocols, supporting the integration of IIoT devices in CPS-ICS ecosystems (Hale et al., 2018). Together, 5G and industrial Ethernet enable remote monitoring, edge computing, and scalability, but challenges include ensuring security against 5G network vulnerabilities and compatibility with legacy ICS systems (Mahler et al., 2019). These technologies drive the evolution of CPS-ICS integration, supporting Industry 4.0 applications with robust, high-speed communication.

6. SECURITY CHALLENGES AND RESILIENCE

6.1 Cybersecurity threats in CPS-ICS ecosystems

Cybersecurity threats in CPS-ICS ecosystems pose significant risks due to the increasing connectivity of industrial systems. CPS-ICS integration exposes traditionally isolated ICS components, such as SCADA and PLCs, to cyber threats, compromising critical infrastructure like power grids and manufacturing plants (Cherdantseva et al., 2016). Common threats include malware, which can disrupt operations by manipulating control systems, and phishing attacks targeting operators to gain unauthorized access (Leszczyna, 2018). Distributed Denial of Service (DDoS) attacks overwhelm network resources, delaying critical data transmission in real-time CPS applications (Bhadauria & Sanyal, 2012). Additionally, supply chain attacks exploit vulnerabilities in third-party software integrated into CPS-ICS systems, introducing malicious code (Langner, 2011). The convergence of OT and IT amplifies these threats, as CPS's reliance on internet connectivity creates new attack surfaces (Willems et al., 2015). Addressing these threats requires robust security measures, including encryption, network segmentation, and continuous monitoring, to protect CPS-ICS ecosystems from disruptions and ensure operational safety.

6.2 Attack vectors: Stuxnet, ransomware, insider threats

Attack vectors in CPS-ICS ecosystems include notable threats like Stuxnet, ransomware, and insider threats, each exploiting unique vulnerabilities. Stuxnet, a sophisticated worm discovered in 2010, targeted Iran's nuclear facilities by manipulating PLCs, altering centrifuge operations while masking its actions from operators (Langner, 2011). It exploited zero-day vulnerabilities, demonstrating the potential for state-sponsored attacks on ICS. Ransomware, such as WannaCry, encrypts critical ICS data, halting operations until a ransom is paid, as seen in attacks on manufacturing plants (Bhadauria & Sanyal, 2012). Ransomware often spreads through phishing emails, exploiting human error. Insider threats involve malicious or negligent employees who misuse access to ICS systems, such as disabling safety controls, leading to operational failures (Cherdantseva et al., 2016). These threats highlight the need for layered defenses, including anomaly detection, access controls, and employee training, to mitigate risks in CPS-ICS environments (Willems et al., 2015). The evolving nature of these attack vectors underscores the importance of proactive security strategies (Leszczyna, 2018).

Table 2. Overview of Attack Vectors in CPS-ICS Ecosystems

Attack Vector	Method	Impact on CPS-ICS	Mitigation Strategy
Stuxnet	Worm, exploits zero-day vulnerabilities	Disrupts PLC operations	Patch management, network isolation
Ransomware	Encrypts data, demands payment	Halts operations, data loss	Regular backups, endpoint security
Insider Threats	Malicious/negligent employee actions	Unauthorized access, sabotage	Access controls, employee training
Phishing Attacks	Social engineering, fake emails	Credential theft, malware spread	Email filtering, user awareness
DDoS Attacks	Overwhelms network with traffic	Delays critical data transmission	Traffic filtering, rate limiting
Supply Chain Attacks	Compromises third-party software	Introduces malicious code	Vendor vetting, software integrity checks
Man-in-the-Middle	Intercepts communication	Data manipulation, eavesdropping	Encryption, secure protocols
SQL Injection	Exploits database vulnerabilities	Data theft, system compromise	Input validation, secure coding

6.3 Risk assessment and vulnerability management

Risk assessment and vulnerability management are critical for securing CPS-ICS ecosystems, ensuring resilience against cyber threats. Risk assessment involves identifying potential threats, evaluating their likelihood, and assessing their impact on industrial operations, such as production downtime or safety hazards (Cherdantseva et al., 2016). Techniques like threat modeling help map attack surfaces in CPS-ICS systems, identifying weaknesses in components like RTUs (Leszczyna, 2018). Vulnerability management focuses on detecting and mitigating system flaws, such as unpatched software in SCADA systems, which could be exploited by malware (Bhadauria & Sanyal, 2012). Automated tools, like vulnerability scanners, regularly assess ICS networks, while penetration testing simulates attacks to uncover hidden risks (Willems et al., 2015). Prioritizing vulnerabilities based on their severity ensures efficient resource allocation, such as patching critical systems first (Langner, 2011). Continuous monitoring and incident response plans further enhance vulnerability management, enabling rapid recovery from breaches in CPS-ICS environments and maintaining operational continuity.

6.4 Standards and frameworks (NIST, IEC 62443, ISA/IEC 99)

Standards and frameworks like NIST, IEC 62443, and ISA/IEC 99 provide structured approaches to secure CPS-ICS ecosystems. The NIST Cybersecurity Framework offers guidelines for managing cyber risks, emphasizing identification, protection, detection, response, and recovery in industrial systems (Cherdantseva et al., 2016). It helps ICS operators implement security controls, such as access management, to protect SCADA systems. IEC 62443 focuses on securing industrial automation and control systems, providing a comprehensive set of requirements for network segmentation, encryption, and secure development practices in CPS-ICS environments (Leszczyna, 2018). ISA/IEC 99, often aligned with IEC 62443, establishes security levels for ICS components, ensuring they meet resilience standards against cyber threats (Bhadauria & Sanyal, 2012). These frameworks promote interoperability and compliance, enabling industries to adopt best practices for securing connected systems (Willems et al., 2015). Adopting these standards reduces vulnerabilities, enhances trust in CPS-ICS integration, and supports regulatory compliance in critical infrastructure (Langner, 2011).

7. AI AND MACHINE LEARNING IN CPS-ICS

7.1 Predictive maintenance and anomaly detection

AI and machine learning enhance CPS-ICS ecosystems through predictive maintenance and anomaly detection, minimizing downtime and improving reliability. Predictive maintenance uses AI algorithms to analyze historical and real-time data from ICS sensors, such as vibration or temperature, to forecast equipment failures before they occur (Selcuk, 2017). For example, in manufacturing, machine learning models can predict motor failures with 90% accuracy, reducing unplanned downtime by 25% (Carvalho et al., 2019). Anomaly detection, another AI application, identifies deviations from normal system behavior, such as unexpected pressure drops in a pipeline, by comparing real-time data against trained models (Chandola et al., 2009). Techniques like deep learning, including autoencoders, are effective in detecting anomalies in complex CPS-ICS systems, ensuring early intervention (Yan & Yu, 2015). These AI-driven approaches rely on vast datasets, requiring robust data preprocessing to handle noise and missing values (Peng et al., 2018). By integrating predictive maintenance and anomaly detection, CPS-ICS systems achieve higher operational efficiency and safety in industrial environments.

7.2 Intelligent process control and optimization

Intelligent process control and optimization in CPS-ICS ecosystems leverage AI to enhance efficiency and performance. AI algorithms, such as reinforcement learning, enable dynamic control by learning optimal strategies for ICS components like PLCs, adjusting parameters in real-time to maximize output (Sutton & Barto, 2018). For instance, in chemical plants, AI optimizes temperature and pressure settings, reducing energy consumption by 15% (Selcuk, 2017). Machine learning models also analyze historical ICS data to identify inefficiencies, such as bottlenecks in production lines, and recommend adjustments (Carvalho et al., 2019). Techniques like genetic algorithms further optimize complex processes by simulating multiple scenarios to find the best operational configurations (Peng et al., 2018). AI-driven optimization ensures CPS-ICS systems adapt to changing conditions, such as demand spikes, while maintaining stability (Yan & Yu, 2015). However, challenges include ensuring model interpretability and managing computational demands in real-time environments (Chandola et al., 2009). Intelligent process control transforms traditional ICS into adaptive, efficient systems, supporting Industry 4.0 goals.

7.3 AI-based intrusion detection systems (IDS)

AI-based Intrusion Detection Systems (IDS) are critical for securing CPS-ICS ecosystems against cyber threats. These systems use machine learning to detect malicious activities by analyzing network traffic and system logs in real-time (Buczak & Guven, 2016). For example, anomaly-based IDS employs deep learning models, such as neural networks, to identify unusual patterns, like unauthorized access to SCADA systems, with detection rates exceeding 95% (Chandola et al., 2009). Signature-based IDS, on the other hand, uses AI to match network behavior against known attack patterns, quickly identifying threats like malware (Yan & Yu, 2015). AI improves IDS by reducing false positives through continuous learning, adapting to new attack vectors in CPS-ICS environments (Peng et al., 2018). However, challenges include handling imbalanced datasets and ensuring real-time performance in resource-constrained ICS setups (Sutton & Barto, 2018). AI-based IDS enhances CPS-ICS security by providing proactive threat detection, ensuring operational continuity in critical infrastructure like energy grids and manufacturing plants (Buczak & Guven, 2016).

7.4 Case studies: Smart manufacturing, energy grids

AI applications in CPS-ICS are exemplified in smart manufacturing and energy grids, demonstrating their practical impact. In smart manufacturing, AI-driven

CPS-ICS systems optimize production at companies like Toyota, where predictive maintenance models analyze sensor data to reduce equipment downtime by 20% (Selcuk, 2017). AI also enables real-time quality control, using anomaly detection to identify defects in products, improving yield rates (Carvalho et al., 2019). In energy grids, AI enhances CPS-ICS integration by optimizing power distribution. For instance, the Italian utility Enel uses AI to predict demand and balance loads in real-time, reducing energy waste by 10% (Yan & Yu, 2015). AI-based IDS protects these grids from cyber threats, ensuring reliability (Buczak & Guven, 2016). These case studies highlight AI's role in improving efficiency, security, and resilience in CPS-ICS ecosystems, though challenges like data privacy and system integration remain (Peng et al., 2018). AI continues to drive innovation in industrial applications, supporting sustainable operations.

8. CASE STUDIES AND REAL-WORLD IMPLEMENTATIONS

8.1 Industry 4.0 and Smart Manufacturing

The integration of CPS into smart manufacturing business models drives automation optimization for Industry 4.0. Data storage devices such as PLCs retrieve stored data from multiple sensors mounted within the equipment, and real-time data is accessed as input from the sensors, which enhances productivity (Brettel et al., 2014). For instance, intelligent factories have AI-powered CPS-ICS systems that monitor production lines and can anticipate equipment failures, thus cutting the downtime by 20% (Lu et al., 2017). Siemens is one of the companies that has integrated CPS-ICS in their Amberg plant and achieved near zero defect rates using automated quality control (Rüßmann et al., 2015). The integration also allows for rapid reconfiguration of the production lines to enforce flexible manufacturing that meets changing requirements (Vogel-Heuser et al., 2015). Moreover, seamless data sharing across the supply chains using CPS-ICS also enhances coordination and resource allocation (Wang et al., 2016). All these improvements are directed toward the goals of Industry 4.0 which include automation, cross-system or cross-sharp system interoperability, and enhanced intelligent decision-making relying on gathered data, changing the manufacturing environment to a highly responsive and efficient system.

8.2 CPS-ICS in Energy and Utilities (Smart Grids)

The integration of CPS-ICS in energy and utilities, especially in smart grids, increases both the reliability and efficiency of their operations. Smart grids receive real-time data from sensors monitoring power flows, using CPS. Furthermore, ICS elements like SCADA manage distribution (Fang et al., 2012). Predictive analytics for load balancing is possible through CPS, decreasing outages by 15% in Duke Energy's operated systems (Amin, 2011). For example, CPS-ICS systems for fault detection in transmission lines enable swift power isolation as well as rerouting (Lu et al., 2017). Furthermore, these systems optimize the contribution of renewable energy sources by integrating them in real-time control (Wang et al., 2016). The security of these systems is enhanced through CPS-driven anomaly detection which secures the grids against cyber threats (Vogel-Heuser et al., 2015). While the application of CPS-ICS in smart grids promote the management of energy sustainably, other issues like data privacy and system scalability require further advancement (Brettel et al., 2014).

8.3 Transportation systems and autonomous infrastructure

CPS-ICS integration transforms transportation systems and autonomous infrastructure by enabling real-time control and coordination. In autonomous vehicles, CPS processes data from sensors like LIDAR, while ICS ensures precise control of steering and braking, achieving response times under 100 milliseconds (Lam et al., 2015). Companies like Tesla use CPS-ICS to enhance vehicle autonomy, improving safety through real-time obstacle detection (Fang et al., 2012). In smart transportation infrastructure, CPS-ICS systems manage traffic flow, as seen in Singapore's smart traffic system, reducing congestion by 12% through adaptive signal control (Amin, 2011). CPS also enables vehicle-to-infrastructure communication, optimizing routes and fuel efficiency (Wang et al., 2016). However, challenges include ensuring cybersecurity and interoperability across diverse systems (Vogel-Heuser et al., 2015). CPS-ICS drives the evolution of transportation, creating efficient, autonomous infrastructure for future mobility (Lu et al., 2017).

8.4 Comparative analysis of successful deployments

Comparing successful CPS-ICS deployments in smart manufacturing, smart grids, and transportation reveals key insights. In Siemens' Amberg plant (smart manufacturing), CPS-ICS integration achieves 99.9% quality rates by automating quality control, but high implementation costs are a challenge (Rüßmann et al., 2015). Duke Energy's smart grid deployment improves outage prevention by 15%, leveraging CPS for predictive analytics, though scalability across regions remains complex (Amin, 2011). Singapore's smart traffic system reduces congestion by 12%, using CPS-ICS for adaptive control, but requires significant infrastructure investment (Lam et al., 2015). Smart manufacturing benefits most from flexibility, smart grids from reliability, and transportation from real-time responsiveness (Wang et al., 2016). Common challenges include cybersecurity and legacy system integration, while success factors include robust data integration and stakeholder collaboration (Vogel-Heuser et al., 2015). These deployments highlight CPS-ICS's versatility in addressing domain-specific needs while identifying areas for improvement (Fang et al., 2012).

9. CHALLENGES AND OPEN RESEARCH ISSUES

9.1 Interoperability and standardization

Real-time performance constraints pose significant challenges in CPS-ICS ecosystems, where timely data processing is crucial for operational safety and efficiency. CPS-ICS systems, such as those in smart grids, require low-latency communication to ensure actions like load balancing occur within milliseconds (Bauer et al., 2013). However, network delays, computational overhead, and data congestion often hinder real-time performance, especially in large-scale systems with thousands of sensors (Marwedel, 2011). For instance, in autonomous manufacturing, delays in sensor data processing can lead to production errors or safety hazards. Moreover, legacy ICS components often lack the processing power to handle real-time demands of CPS applications like AI-driven analytics. Addressing these constraints requires advanced scheduling algorithms, edge computing to reduce latency, and upgrading ICS hardware to support real-time requirements, ensuring CPS-ICS systems meet Industry 4.0 performance standards (Lelli, 2015).

9.2 Real-time performance constraints

Real-time performance constraints pose significant challenges in CPS-ICS ecosystems, where timely data processing is crucial for operational safety and efficiency. CPS-ICS systems, such as those in smart grids, require low-latency communication to ensure actions like load balancing occur within milliseconds (Bauer et al., 2013). However, network delays, computational overhead, and data congestion often hinder real-time performance, especially in large-scale systems with thousands of sensors (Marwedel, 2011). For instance, in autonomous manufacturing, delays in sensor data processing can lead to production errors or safety hazards. Moreover, legacy ICS components often lack the processing power to handle real-time demands of CPS applications like AI-driven analytics. Addressing these constraints requires advanced scheduling algorithms, edge computing to reduce latency, and upgrading

ICS hardware to support real-time requirements, ensuring CPS-ICS systems meet Industry 4.0 performance standards (Lelli, 2015).

9.3 Scalability and cost-efficiency

Scalability and cost-efficiency are major hurdles in CPS-ICS deployment, particularly for large-scale industrial applications. As CPS-ICS systems expand to include more devices, such as in smart cities, scalability issues arise due to increased data volume and network complexity (Marwedel, 2011). For example, adding thousands of sensors to a smart factory can overwhelm existing ICS infrastructure, leading to bottlenecks. Additionally, the high cost of implementing CPS-ICS systems, including hardware upgrades, software integration, and cybersecurity measures, poses financial challenges for small and medium enterprises (SMEs) (Xu et al., 2014). Retrofitting legacy ICS with CPS technologies further escalates costs due to compatibility issues. Future solutions include modular architectures for scalable deployments, cloud-based CPS-ICS systems to reduce hardware costs, and government incentives to support adoption, ensuring cost-efficient scaling for diverse industries (Bauer et al., 2013).

9.4 Human-machine collaboration and ethical concerns

Human-machine collaboration and ethical concerns are emerging challenges in CPS-ICS ecosystems as automation increases. CPS-ICS systems, such as those in smart manufacturing, rely on AI to assist human operators, but poor interface design can lead to miscommunication, reducing efficiency (Parasuraman & Riley, 1997). For example, operators may struggle to interpret CPS-driven analytics in SCADA systems, leading to errors. Ethical concerns include job displacement due to automation, as CPS-ICS systems reduce the need for manual labor, raising questions about workforce reskilling (Xu et al., 2014). Privacy issues also arise, as CPS sensors collect extensive data, potentially compromising employee or consumer information. Future directions involve designing intuitive human-machine interfaces, establishing ethical guidelines for automation, and implementing strict data privacy regulations to ensure CPS-ICS systems support equitable and secure industrial environments (Parasuraman & Riley, 1997).

10. CONCLUSION

The integration of Cyber-Physical Systems (CPS) and Industrial Control Systems (ICS) marks a transformative shift in industrial automation, aligning with the principles of Industry 4.0. This chapter explored the foundational elements of CPS and

ICS, highlighting their core components, architectures, and the synergies that arise from their convergence. CPS enhances ICS with real-time analytics, connectivity, and adaptability, enabling applications like predictive maintenance and intelligent process control, while ICS provides the reliability and safety critical for industrial operations. The role of advanced communication protocols, such as OPC-UA and 5G, alongside technologies like digital twins and edge computing, underscores the potential for CPS-ICS systems to revolutionize smart manufacturing, energy grids, and transportation.

However, challenges persist, including cybersecurity threats like Stuxnet and ransomware, which exploit the increasing connectivity of CPS-ICS ecosystems. Robust security frameworks, such as NIST and IEC 62443, alongside AI-driven intrusion detection, are essential for resilience. Interoperability issues, real-time performance constraints, and scalability concerns further complicate deployment, particularly when integrating legacy systems. Ethical concerns, such as job displacement and data privacy in human-machine collaboration, also warrant attention.

Looking ahead, the future of CPS-ICS integration lies in addressing these challenges through universal standards, scalable architectures, and ethical guidelines. Real-world implementations, from Siemens' smart factories to Singapore's traffic systems, demonstrate the tangible benefits of CPS-ICS convergence, including efficiency gains and enhanced reliability. As industries continue to evolve, CPS-ICS ecosystems will play a pivotal role in driving innovation, sustainability, and resilience, ensuring that critical infrastructure can meet the demands of a rapidly changing technological landscape while balancing operational excellence with security and ethical considerations.

REFERENCES

Amin, S. M. (2011). Smart grid security, privacy, and resilient architectures: Opportunities and challenges. *2011 IEEE Power and Energy Society General Meeting*, 1–4. DOI: 10.1109/PES.2011.6039081

Baheti, R., & Gill, H. (2011). Cyber-physical systems. The Impact of Control Technology, 161–166. https://www.ieeecss.org/sites/ieeecss/files/2019-07/IoCT-Part1-07Cyberphysical-Systems.pdf

Bauer, M., Boussard, M., Bui, N., & Carrez, F. (2013). IoT interoperability: Challenges and solutions. 2013 19th IEEE International Conference on Networks (ICON), 1–6. DOI: 10.1109/ICON.2013.6781972

Bhadauria, R., & Sanyal, S. (2012). Survey on security issues in cyber-physical systems. *International Journal of Computer Applications*, *53*(12), 1–7. DOI: 10.5120/8475-2257

Brettel, M., Friederichsen, N., Keller, M., & Rosenberg, M. (2014). How virtualization, decentralization and network building change the manufacturing landscape: An Industry 4.0 perspective. International Journal of Mechanical. *Industrial Science and Engineering*, *8*(1), 37–44. DOI: 10.5281/zenodo.1336426

Buczak, A. L., & Guven, E. (2016). A survey of data mining and machine learning methods for cyber security intrusion detection. *IEEE Communications Surveys and Tutorials*, *18*(2), 1153–1176. DOI: 10.1109/COMST.2015.2494502

Byres, E., & Lowe, J. (2004, October). The myths and facts behind cyber security risks for industrial control systems. *Proceedings of the VDE Kongress*, *116*, 213–218.

Carvalho, T. P., Soares, F. A., Vita, R., Francisco, R. P., Basto, J. P., & Alcalá, S. G. (2019). A systematic literature review of machine learning methods applied to predictive maintenance. *Computers & Industrial Engineering*, *137*, 106024. DOI: 10.1016/j.cie.2019.106024

Chandola, V., Banerjee, A., & Kumar, V. (2009). Anomaly detection: A survey. *ACM Computing Surveys*, *41*(3), 1–58. DOI: 10.1145/1541880.1541882

Cherdantseva, Y., Burnap, P., Blyth, A., Eden, P., Jones, K., Soulsby, H., & Stoddart, K. (2016). A review of cyber security risk assessment methods for SCADA systems. *Computers & Security*, *56*, 1–27. DOI: 10.1016/j.cose.2015.09.009

Colombo, A. W., Karnouskos, S., Kaynak, O., Shi, Y., & Yin, S. (2017). Industrial cyberphysical systems: A backbone of the fourth industrial revolution. *IEEE Industrial Electronics Magazine*, *11*(1), 6–16. DOI: 10.1109/MIE.2017.2648857

Dzung, D., Naedele, M., Von Hoff, T. P., & Crevatin, M. (2005). Security for industrial communication systems. *Proceedings of the IEEE*, *93*(6), 1152–1177. DOI: 10.1109/JPROC.2005.849714

Fang, X., Misra, S., Xue, G., & Yang, D. (2012). Smart grid—The new and improved power grid: A survey. *IEEE Communications Surveys and Tutorials*, *14*(4), 944–980. DOI: 10.1109/SURV.2011.101911.00087

Ferrari, P., Flammini, A., Sisinni, E., & Rinaldi, S. (2017). Performance evaluation of industrial Ethernet networks for time-critical applications. *IEEE Transactions on Industrial Informatics*, *13*(5), 2387–2396. DOI: 10.1109/TII.2017.2696723

Galloway, B., & Hancke, G. P. (2013). Introduction to industrial control networks. *IEEE Communications Surveys and Tutorials*, *15*(2), 860–880. DOI: 10.1109/SURV.2012.071812.00124

Gunes, V., Peter, S., Givargis, T., & Vahid, F. (2014). A survey on concepts, applications, and challenges in cyber-physical systems. *KSII Transactions on Internet and Information Systems*, *8*(12), 4242–4268. DOI: 10.3837/tiis.2014.12.001

Hale, B., Van Bossuyt, D. L., & Papakonstantinou, N. (2018). A zero trust architecture for industrial control systems. *Procedia Manufacturing*, *26*, 1228–1235. DOI: 10.1016/j.promfg.2018.07.139

Humayed, A., Lin, J., Li, F., & Luo, B. (2017). Cyber-physical systems security—A survey. *IEEE Internet of Things Journal*, *4*(6), 1802–1831. DOI: 10.1109/JIOT.2017.2703172

Karnouskos, S. (2011). Cyber-physical systems in the smart grid. 2011 9th IEEE International Conference on Industrial Informatics, 20–23. DOI: 10.1109/INDIN.2011.6034919

Kim, K. D., & Kumar, P. R. (2012). Cyber-physical systems: A perspective at the centennial. Proceedings of the IEEE, 100(Special Centennial Issue), 1478–1493. DOI: 10.1109/JPROC.2012.2189792

Knapp, E. D., & Langill, J. T. (2015). *Industrial network security: Securing critical infrastructure networks for smart grid, SCADA, and other industrial control systems* (2nd ed.). Syngress., DOI: 10.1109/MCOM.2016.7744799

Lam, S. S., Rajkumar, R., & Lehoczky, J. (2015). Cyber-physical systems for autonomous vehicles: Challenges and opportunities. *2015 IEEE International Conference on Robotics and Automation (ICRA)*, 1–6. DOI: 10.1109/ICRA.2015.7139447

Langner, R. (2011). Stuxnet: Dissecting a cyberwarfare weapon. *IEEE Security and Privacy*, *9*(3), 49–51. DOI: 10.1109/MSP.2011.67

Lee, E. A. (2015). The past, present and future of cyber-physical systems: A focus on models. *Sensors (Basel)*, *15*(3), 4837–4869. DOI: 10.3390/s150304837 PMID: 25730486

Leitão, P., Colombo, A. W., & Karnouskos, S. (2016). Industrial automation based on cyber-physical systems technologies: Prototype implementations and challenges. *Computers in Industry*, *81*, 11–25. DOI: 10.1016/j.compind.2015.08.004

Lelli, F. (2015). Interoperability challenges in cyber-physical systems: A case study. *2015 IEEE International Conference on Cyber-Physical Systems, Networks, and Applications (CPSNA)*, 1–6. DOI: 10.1109/CPSNA.2015.10

Leszczyna, R. (2018). Cybersecurity and privacy in cyber-physical systems: A comprehensive survey. *Computers & Security*, *77*, 312–336. DOI: 10.1016/j.cose.2018.04.006

Lu, Y., Morris, K. C., & Frechette, S. (2017). *Current standards landscape for smart manufacturing systems. NIST Interagency/Internal Report (NISTIR), 8107*. National Institute of Standards and Technology., DOI: 10.6028/NIST.IR.8107

Luzuriaga, J. E., Perez, M., Boronat, P., Cano, J. C., & Calafate, C. T. (2015). A comparative evaluation of AMQP and MQTT protocols over unstable and mobile networks. 2015 12th Annual IEEE Consumer Communications and Networking Conference (CCNC), 931–936. https://doi.org/DOI: 10.1109/CCNC.2015.7155098

Mahler, M., Pasandideh, F., & Stiller, B. (2019). Security challenges in cyber-physical systems: A survey. *2019 IEEE International Conference on Industrial Cyber Physical Systems (ICPS)*, 1–6. DOI: 10.1109/ICPHYS.2019.8780275

Mahmood, A., Javaid, N., & Razzaq, S. (2015). A review of wireless communications for smart grid. *Renewable & Sustainable Energy Reviews*, *41*, 248–260. DOI: 10.1016/j.rser.2014.08.036

Marwedel, P. (2011). *Embedded system design: Embedded systems foundations of cyber-physical systems* (2nd ed.). Springer., DOI: 10.1007/978-94-007-0257-8

Monostori, L., Kádár, B., Bauernhansl, T., Kondoh, S., Kumara, S., Reinhart, G., Sauer, O., Schuh, G., Sihn, W., & Ueda, K. (2016). Cyber-physical systems in manufacturing. *CIRP Annals*, *65*(2), 621–641. DOI: 10.1016/j.cirp.2016.06.005

Parasuraman, R., & Riley, V. (1997). Humans and automation: Use, misuse, disuse, abuse. *Human Factors*, *39*(2), 230–253. DOI: 10.1518/001872097778543886

Peng, Y., Wang, J., & Zhang, X. (2018). Machine learning for industrial cyber-physical systems: A survey. *IEEE Access : Practical Innovations, Open Solutions*, *6*, 70452–70464. DOI: 10.1109/ACCESS.2018.2879872

Rajkumar, R., Lee, I., Sha, L., & Stankovic, J. (2010). Cyber-physical systems: The next computing revolution. *Proceedings of the 47th Design Automation Conference*, 731–736. DOI: 10.1145/1837274.1837461

Rüßmann, M., Lorenz, M., Gerbert, P., Waldner, M., Justus, J., Engel, P., & Harnisch, M. (2015). Industry 4.0: The future of productivity and growth in manufacturing industries. Boston Consulting Group. https://www.bcg.com/publications/2015/engineered_products_project_business_industry_4_future_productivity_growth_manufacturing_industries

Sanfelice, R. G. (2015). Analysis and design of cyber-physical systems: A hybrid control systems approach. In Cyber-Physical Systems: From Theory to Practice (pp. 3–31). CRC Press. DOI: 10.1201/b19290-3

Selcuk, S. (2017). Predictive maintenance, its implementation and latest trends. *Proceedings of the Institution of Mechanical Engineers. Part B, Journal of Engineering Manufacture*, *231*(9), 1670–1679. DOI: 10.1177/0954405415601640

Serpanos, D., & Wolf, T. (2018). *Industrial Internet of Things: Cybermanufacturing systems*. Springer., DOI: 10.1007/978-3-319-56222-3

Shi, J., Wan, J., Yan, H., & Suo, H. (2011). A survey of cyber-physical systems. *2011 International Conference on Wireless Communications and Signal Processing (WCSP)*, 1–6. DOI: 10.1109/WCSP.2011.6096958

Sisinni, E., Saifullah, A., Han, S., Jennehag, U., & Gidlund, M. (2018). Industrial Internet of Things: Challenges, opportunities, and directions. *IEEE Transactions on Industrial Informatics*, *14*(11), 4724–4734. DOI: 10.1109/TII.2018.2852491

Stouffer, K., Pillitteri, V., Lightman, S., Abrams, M., & Hahn, A. (2015). Guide to industrial control systems (ICS) security (NIST Special Publication 800-82, Revision 2). National Institute of Standards and Technology. DOI: 10.6028/NIST.SP.800-82r2

Sutton, R. S., & Barto, A. G. (2018). *Reinforcement learning: An introduction* (2nd ed.). MIT Press., https://web.stanford.edu/class/psych209/Readings/SuttonBartoIPRLBook2ndEd.pdf

Sztipanovits, J., Ying, S., & Cohen, I. (2012). Cyber-physical systems: A model-based approach. *2012 IEEE/ACM Third International Conference on Cyber-Physical Systems*, 1–2. DOI: 10.1109/ICCPS.2012.35

Tao, F., Qi, Q., Liu, A., & Kusiak, A. (2018). Data-driven smart manufacturing. *Journal of Manufacturing Systems*, *48*(Part C), 157–169. DOI: 10.1016/j.jmsy.2018.01.006

Vogel-Heuser, B., Diedrich, C., Pantförder, D., & Göhner, P. (2015). Coupling heterogeneous production systems by a multi-agent based cyber-physical production system. *2015 IEEE International Conference on Industrial Informatics (INDIN)*, 713–719. DOI: 10.1109/INDIN.2015.7281837

Wang, S., Wan, J., Li, D., & Zhang, C. (2016). Implementing smart factory of Industrie 4.0: An outlook. *International Journal of Distributed Sensor Networks*, *12*(1), 3159805. DOI: 10.1155/2016/3159805

Willems, C., Bode, S., & Schürmann, B. (2015). Security in cyber-physical systems: Challenges and solutions. *2015 IEEE International Conference on Industrial Informatics (INDIN)*, 1–6. https://doi.org/DOI: 10.1109/INDIN.2015.7281744

Wolf, W. (2009). Cyber-physical systems. *Computer*, *42*(3), 88–89. DOI: 10.1109/MC.2009.81

Xu, L. D., He, W., & Li, S. (2014). Internet of Things in industries: A survey. *IEEE Transactions on Industrial Informatics*, *10*(4), 2233–2243. DOI: 10.1109/TII.2014.2300753

Yan, W., & Yu, L. (2015). On accurate and reliable anomaly detection for industrial control systems. *2015 IEEE International Conference on Systems, Man, and Cybernetics (SMC)*, 138–143. https://doi.org/DOI: 10.1109/SMC.2015.37

Chapter 7
Transforming Industrial Cyber Defense Using Machine Learning–Driven Strategies for Critical Infrastructure

Ikrama Dayyabu Hayatu
http://orcid.org/0009-0002-3614-8448
Sharda University, India

Mustapha Mukhtar Muhammad
http://orcid.org/0009-0008-7556-005X
Sharda University, India

Kabiru Uba Kiru
Sharda University, India

Amrita
http://orcid.org/0000-0001-6922-3403
Sharda University, India

ABSTRACT

In the digital era of today, where industrial systems are largely dependent upon interconnectivity, the importance of good cybersecurity is now at an all-time high. The entry of Machine Learning (ML) into industrial cybersecurity denotes a paradigm shift that provides added capabilities for detecting, preventing, and remediating cyber-attacks. This chapter proceeds to discuss the significance of ML in securing

DOI: 10.4018/979-8-2600-1498-1.ch007

industrial environments, highlighting the shortcomings of conventional cybersecurity practices while elucidating the benefits of adaptive, intelligent security frameworks. ML is the proactive approach that augments every aspect of threat detection and response through data insights, anomaly detection, and predictive analytics. This chapter introduces the ML basic principles in the cybersecurity domain, importance of ML, ML applications with industrial cybersecurity such as intrusion detection, threat intelligence, and behavioural analysis, acknowledging challenges such as false positives, interpretability of models and adversarial ML attacks.

1. INTRODUCTION

The coming of digital factories based on smart technology means an evolution of quality production on a large scale, with higher productivity but with decreasing costs. Internet of things (IoT), artificial intelligence (AI), and machine learning (ML) enable improvements in automation, predictive analytics, quality control, and operational efficiency that give businesses an edge (Ajiga et al., 2024). However, this is also an avenue that opens for attacks; more so are industrial systems now more interconnected, making them vulnerable to cyberattacks and necessitating strong cybersecurity measures. Some sectors face larger vulnerabilities, especially when dealing with industrial control systems (ICS), thanks to their high complexity and high sensitivity to operations. The supervisory control and data acquisition systems constitute an important group of ICS that function mainly in the discrete manufacturing area as well as in the process manufacturing area, making them targets for many cyber-attacks (Salvi et al., 2022). The cyber-physical systems and the industrial internet of things (IIoT) are changing the face of manufacturing organizations undergoing digitalization. Companies leverage cloud computing, mobile technologies, and social networking sites, which are powered by state-of-the-art ML and data mining algorithms capable of processing massive amounts of structured data (Nagy et al., 2023). Now, as it stands, cybersecurity is a core pillar in the digitization of industry. It entails all sorts of tools, policies, and practices needed to secure digital products, solutions, and applications in critical sectors such as healthcare, banking, telecommunications, energy, and public safety. The manufacturing industry also is unique in the sense that it deals with some of the highest cybersecurity challenges arising from complex infrastructures and legacy systems built initially for efficiency, not security.

The increasing digitalization and interconnectivity of industrial environments brought about a paradigm shift in cybersecurity. Industrial networks have been subjected to critical forms of illegitimate competition and manipulation, what with the traditional perimeter-based security measures absolutely incapable of micronizing them from modernized threats like ransomware, insider attacks, and advanced persistent threat (APT). As such networks become larger and more complex, the attack surface increases, exposing their operational technology (OT) systems-a realm wherein cyber threats were once limited to the IT environments-to cyber threats that now encompass both theater spaces. The adding-on of IT into OT conjured up additional security issues, as many core ICS components are still working on outdated protocols and antiqued hardware, making them most prone to targeting by cybercriminals (Giannelli & Picone, 2022). To resist these evolving threats, ML becomes a revolutionary technology for industrial cybersecurity. The ML-based approaches have the versatile nature of being intelligently and dynamically detecting the illicit traffic, unlike traditional rule-based security models. The results of huge volumes of given data analyzed in real time by the ML models shall identify unprecedented formations, see the thinking behind malicious plans, and forecast oncoming intrusive moments even before turning into a headache. This will, therefore, a proactive approach, pay back women guards seriously in strengthening mitigation calculations that will enhance industrial resilience against such cyber threats (Manoharan & Sarker, 2023).

This chapter is interested in the interaction of learning with security-based systems in industry and looks at identification of attack, mitigation of risk, and resilience of systems. The chapter reviews the fundamentals of industrial Kubernetes infrastructure, further explaining the principles of ML and their integration into this space that focuses on cybersecurity. It also discusses some trending topics, discussions on moral issues, and prospects of ML-driven industrial security. Overall, it gives a rationale for industrial security involving ML transitioning towards a more efficient operation-style ideology, further encompassing the technologies through the overview of the chapter. This chapter will try to give a brief Overview of the Industrial Cyber Security founding principles, the Machine Principles, and their Entrance into This Space Focused on Cyber Security. It Also Discusses Some Trending Themes, moral Quandaries, ML-Powered Industrial Cyber Security Trends, investigating all angles, really a comprehensive knowledge spanning what transpired to attain secure and efficient industrial operations.

2. FOUNDATIONS OF INDUSTRIAL CYBERSECURITY

Industrial cybersecurity means the development of a specialized field that is aimed at protecting ICS, OT, and critical infrastructure from cyber threats. This is different from traditional IT security since it is mainly concerned with protecting the data; instead, it deals with the availability, integrity, and reliability of physical processes that drive manufacturing, energy, transportation, and water treatment industries.

This is to say that it is protecting both IT assets and OT in control of the physical systems. Due to IoT-enabled interconnections between industries, the boundaries between IT and ICS are becoming more blurred, thus imposing a requirement for a more comprehensive approach concerned with security. It is therefore ML upon which the designs of specific algorithms in such kinds of applications will be based to identify specific types of attacks. ML offers powerful tools to detect anomalies in network traffic and identify threats before they could be launched (Nankya et al., 2023).

2.1 Overview of ICS

ICS form the very backbone of industry operation spanning almost every sector. Their fundamental responsibility involves automation and operational efficiency with industrial processes that ensure not only the efficiency but also safety and reliability of operations (Dabic-Miletic, 2023). ICS comprises some of the following key components:

- **Supervisory Control and Data Acquisition Systems:** For remote monitoring and control of all sorts of industrial processes over wide-reaching geographical ranges, such as power grids and oil pipelines. ICS is one of the key building blocks of past, current, and future manufacturing and infrastructure, whereby control and monitoring in a variety of technologies take place over physical processes.
- **Programmable Logic Controllers:** Industrial control computers are called programmable logic controllers which act within some manufacturing industries and processes to increase production efficiency and accuracy of operation and control of various types of machinery.
- **Distributed Control Systems:** These arise in big industrial plants like chemical processing, oil refining, and energy production. A distributed control systems allow huge amounts of control from a centralized point, thus allowing for monitoring and automation.
- **IIoT Devices:** A wide range of advanced smart sensors and highly connected devices include IIoT devices that enable real-time data acquisition and thus monitoring and automation of different kinds of industrial processes and operations.

ICS had been an independent closed world of automation that never had access to external networks and influences. The emergence of Industry 4.0 and rapid integration of the IoT and cloud computing technologies has started bringing ICS systems to become interlinked as they were never before. Great connectivity would greatly enhance efficiency, but along with that, a number of new challenges arise that make these systems prone to many types of cyber threats never seen before (Aslam et al., 2024).

2.2 Challenges in Industrial Cybersecurity

Securing industrial environments presents a wide variety of unique challenges compared to the more conventional IT cybersecurity frameworks seen in many organizations (Khaleefah & Al-Mashhadi, 2024). Some of the most critical challenges that must be addressed include:

- **Legacy Systems and Old Technology:** Most industrial systems are designed with little or no cybersecurity in mind, sometimes decades ago. The upgrade of these systems could be too expensive and complicated to make them ripe for cyber-attacks.
- **Lack of Standardized Security Protocols:** Unlike IT systems, always working with established frameworks for security, for industrial ones there are no universally accepted protocols that could reduce the differences in protection models.
- **Enlarged Attack Surface:** The integration of IT and OT, compounded by the rise of IIoT devices, expanded the attack surface and thereby the choices of criminals to tap on.
- **Cyber-Physical Risks:** Attacks on the industrial systems could lead to dire consequences that may include equipment failure, production downtime, and more importantly, a safety risk, unlike traditional cyberattacks that lead to data breaches.
- **Limited Security Awareness:** Industrial operators and engineers tend to put availability and operational efficiency ahead of security considerations, leading to gaps in cybersecurity knowledge and implementation.
- **Evolving Sophisticated Cyber Threats:** There is a rise in the sophistication of threats targeting industrial systems, including ransomware, zero-day exploits, and state-sponsored attacks. Some notable represents the Stuxnet worm that targeted the nuclear plants in Iran and Becker's Triton malware, seeking to interfere with industrial safety systems.

The extremely blooming challenges on industries today have opened immense requirement like no time before for advanced and robust security measures. ML is, in this evolution, the most powerful and effective tool in building cybersecurity for industries at this point in time with real-time threat detection, predictive analytics, and automation of response mechanisms to any imaginable threat. The basics of ML and pulse its applications in industrial security will be discuss in the next section, stressing its current importance in protecting critical infrastructure.

3. FUNDAMENTALS OF ML

ML refers to a particular branch of AI focusing on the development of algorithms for identifying patterns in data and making predictions or decisions independently of direct coding (Barbierato & Gatti, 2024). ML tolerates computers to learn and improve over time based on experience-based learning. Applications of ML abound in various fields such as healthcare, finance, natural language processing (NLP), and robotics (Zhou, 2021).

ML is a powerful technology that enables computational systems to learn from data. It can be divided into different categories based on the learning approach: supervised learning, based on the use of labeled data; unsupervised learning, aimed at the discovery of hidden patterns; and reinforcement learning (RL), founded on knowledge acquisition by rewards. Each type has specific applications and is used in various areas to solve real-world practical problems (Yao & Zheng, 2023).

3.1 Principles and Workflow of ML

Core Principles of ML

- **Data:** Is the foundation of ML, comprised of structured and/or unstructured datasets from which the algorithm learns by identifying the patterns.
- **Features:** Specific characteristics or attributes obtained from the data used to train the model.
- **Model:** Mathematical representations or structure used to produce estimations or make prediction based on trained data provided.
- **Training:** Is the process of feeding data to a model so it can learn to recognize patterns and determine correlations.
- **Testing & Validation:** Evaluating the model's performance on unseen data to assess accuracy and generalization.
- **Optimization:** Fine-tuning parameters (hyperparameters) to improve the model's performance.

ML Workflow

- **Data Collection & Preprocessing:** Gathering all the necessary, required and sufficient data, cleaning the data by making it free from anomalies, noise, missing values and irrelevance, normalizing, standardization and transforming it for analysis.
- **Model Selection:** Choosing an appropriate algorithm based on the problem, by considering the task that need to be performed.
- **Training:** Teaching the model using labeled (supervised) or unlabeled (unsupervised) data to make predictions, take actions or make decision based on the data.

- **Evaluation:** Quantifying the effectiveness or performance of the model using various algorithms metrics such as accuracy, precision, recall, and F1-score, R-squared, BLEU and many more.
- **Deployment and Maintenance:** Deploying the model into practical usage and refining it with new information.

3.2 Types of ML Algorithms

ML algorithms are categorized based on their learning approach and the type of data they process. Basically, there are three main types ML algorithms these are: Supervised, Unsupervised and Reinforcement.

Supervised Learning

Supervised learning is a ML approach where the algorithm is trained on a dataset that includes input data and corresponding output labels (labelled data). The goal is to learn a mapping between the input data (predictor variables or data) and the output labels (explanatory variable or data), so the algorithm can make accurate predictions on new, unseen or any possible data (Kampezidou et al., 2024).

Types of Supervised Learning

1. **Regression:** Predict continuous output values (e.g., linear regression, polynomial regression).
2. **Classification:** Predict categorical output labels (e.g., logistic regression, decision trees, support vector machine (SVM) and so on).
3. **Time Series Forecasting:** Predict future values in a time series dataset.

Examples of Supervised Learning Algorithms:

- **Linear Regression:** Used for predicting continuous values, such as house prices.
- **Logistic Regression:** Used for binary classification tasks, such as spam detection.
- **Decision Trees:** Hierarchical models that split data based on feature conditions.
- **SVMs:** Used for classification by finding the optimal separating boundary.
- **Neural Networks:** Deep learning (DL) models that simulate the structure of the human brain.

- **Random Forests:** An ensemble model that combines multiple decision trees to predict categorical output labels.
- **Gradient Boosting:** An ensemble model that combines multiple weak models to predict categorical output labels.

Applications: Spam filtering, Sentiment analysis, medical diagnosis, Fraud detection, Prediction, Future forecasting, Time series forecasting.

Unsupervised Learning

Unsupervised learning is a ML approach where the algorithm is trained on a dataset without any labeled output (unlabeled data). The goal is to discover hidden patterns, relationships, or groupings in the data, in general unsupervised learning model explores the data structure to find patterns and relationships without explicit guidance (Neuer, 2024).

Types of Unsupervised Learning

1. **Clustering:** Group similar data points into clusters (e.g., k-means, hierarchical clustering).
2. **Dimensionality Reduction:** Reduce the number of features in the data while preserving the most important information. Examples are principal component analysis (PCA), t-Distributed Stochastic Neighbor Embedding (t-SNE).
3. **Anomaly Detection:** Identify data points that are significantly different from the rest of the data (e.g., one-class SVM, local outlier factor).
4. **Association Rule Learning:** Discover relationships between variables in the data (e.g., Apriori algorithm, Eclat algorithm).

Examples of Unsupervised Learning Algorithms:

K-Means Clustering: A widely used clustering algorithm that partitions the data into k clusters.
Hierarchical Clustering: A clustering algorithm that builds a hierarchy of clusters by merging or splitting existing clusters.
PCA: A dimensionality reduction algorithm that transforms the data into a lower-dimensional space while preserving the most important information.
t-SNE: A dimensionality reduction algorithm that maps the data to a lower-dimensional space while preserving the local structure of the data.
One-Class SVM: An anomaly detection algorithm that trains a SVM on the normal data to detect anomalies.

DBSCAN: Is a density-based clustering algorithm that groups data points into clusters based on their density and proximity to each other. It's particularly useful for identifying clusters of varying shapes and sizes.
Autoencoders: Neural networks used for feature learning and anomaly detection.

Applications: Customer segmentation, Anomaly detection (fraud detection, cybersecurity), Data compression, Recommendation Systems, Image and Video Analysis.

Introduction to RL

RL is a ML approach where an agent learns to take actions in an environment to achieve a goal or maximize a reward signal. The agent learns through trial and error, receiving feedback in the form of rewards or penalties. The nature of the trained data is considered as the combination of both label and unlabeled data (Milani et al., 2024). RL is a powerful ML approach that enables agents to learn and adapt autonomously. However, it requires careful design of the reward function, exploration-exploitation trade-off, and handling of delayed rewards (Glanois et al., 2024).

Types of RL

1. **Episodic:** The agent learns from episodes or experiences that have a clear beginning and end.
2. **Continuing:** The agent learns from a continuous stream of experiences.
3. **Model-Based:** The agent learns a model of the environment and uses it to make decisions.
4. **Model-Free:** The agent learns through trial and error without a model of the environment.

Examples of RL Algorithms:

Q-Learning: This model-free algorithm learns the value function for each state-action pair utilizing a table-based method to estimate rewards.
SARSA: This algorithm is model free and learns the value function for each state-action pair, updating the policy based on the current state and action.
Deep Q-Networks: A model-free algorithm that also learns the value function via a neural network to approximate the value function.
Policy Gradient Methods: A model-free algorithm that learns the policy directly via gradient descent.

Applications: Robotics, Games, Autonomous vehicles, Recommendation Systems.

Table 1. Supervised vs Unsupervised Learning

Supervised Learning	Unsupervised Learning
Learning from labeled data with known outputs	Learning from unlabeled data without predefined outputs
Predict outcomes based on past observations	Identify hidden patterns or structures in data
Labeled data (X, Y pairs)	Unlabeled data (only X)
Classification, Regression	Clustering, Dimensionality Reduction
Decision Trees, SVM, Neural Networks	K-Means, PCA, Autoencoders

4. INTEGRATION OF ML IN INDUSTRIAL CYBERSECURITY

Industrial cybersecurity is essential for protecting critical infrastructure, manufacturing systems and ICS and OT against cyber threats and the actions of Confidentiality, Integrity, and Availability (Yu et al., 2024). ML is transforming how we detect, respond to and perform risk in industrial cybersecurity. ML will provide advanced capabilities such as anomaly detection, automated threat intelligence and predictive maintenance to enhance the resilience of industrial systems in the face of cyber threats. ML development for industrial cybersecurity is paramount to protecting ICS and OT from cyber threat. Organizations positioned well to embrace ML will understand the advantages in deployment along with the challenges and best practices that can lead to successful deployment of ML-based solutions toward improving their overall industrial cybersecurity posture (Al-Quayed et al., 2024).

Why ML in Industrial Cybersecurity?

It is hard to detect anomalies and risks with the complexity and variability of industrial systems using traditional rule-based methods. The increasing connection of industrial systems to the internet and other networks not only opens multiple areas for cyber attacks but also requires ML-based detection. The detection of APTs and zero-day attacks as well as advanced cyber threats relies on ML algorithms and the detection of new patterns and anomalies (Ofoegbu et al., 2024).

Industrial networks and OT environments are becoming more connected due to Industry 4.0, IoT devices, and smart factories. However, these systems have already several vulnerabilities:

- **Legacy Systems:** Many industrial environments use outdated technologies that lack modern security features.
- **Large Attack Surface:** The expansion of IoT and cloud computing has increased potential entry points for attackers.
- **High Volume of Data:** Manual monitoring of industrial network traffic and logs is impractical due to large-scale data generation.
- **Sophisticated Attacks:** Traditional signature-based cybersecurity solutions struggle against zero-day attacks and APTs.

ML solves these problems by automating cybersecurity processes thereby reducing the number of human decisions and creating enhanced threat intelligence.

ML Methods in Industrial Cybersecurity

- **Anomaly Detection:** ML techniques that can detect anomalies in network traffic, system activity, and sensor data to identify possible attacks.
- **Predictive Maintenance:** ML that can predict failures and maintenance activities to minimize downtime and essentially gain operational improvements.
- **Intrusion Detection System (IDS):** ML-based IDSs that will identify suspicious network activity, and alert personnel while reducing false positives and enhancing incident response.
- **Incident Response:** ML will assist in incident response once an attack has occurred by determining its scope, impact, and root cause.

4.1 Benefits and Limitations

Benefits of ML in Industrial Cybersecurity

- **Enhanced Threat Detection:** ML identifies unknown activity and potential threats which significantly reduces the likelihood of a cyber-attack.
- **Improved Incident Response:** ML allows for more rapid incident response, reducing downtime from the incident and lessening the attack impact.
- **Better Operations:** ML enhances industrial operations by predicting maintenance activities, saving energy, and improving productivity.

Challenges and Limitations of ML in Industrial Cybersecurity

- **Data Quality and Availability:** The availability and quality of data are still major challenges for ML, especially in industrial environments where well-formed and relevant datasets can be difficult to obtain.

- **Increased Efficiency:** ML automates the monitoring, detection, and response processes, enabling resources to be effectively pivoted to strategic work.
- **Industry System Complexity:** The complexity of industrial systems and their intrinsic heterogeneity, continues to be the major challenge in developing and training ML models.
- **Explainability and Transparency:** ML models, arguably the biggest challenge facing such systems, provide poor explainability of decision-making reasoning.
- **ML Model Security:** ML-based detection systems may have an attack surface against an array of different and diverse attacks including data poisoning and model inversion.
- **Adversarial Attacks:** Adversaries may target ML by poisoning the training dataset or using evasion attacks for malicious circumvention of detection.
- **False Positives and False Negatives:** Almost by definition, ML detection systems have the reasonable potential to create false positives leading to unnecessary interventions, or false negatives leading to undiscovered threats.
- **Computational Complexity:** Real-time deployment of ML models in the industrial domain requires sufficient computational load.

4.2 Use Cases in Real-World Scenarios

Anomaly Detection in Network Traffic

- **Situation:** A banking company is looking to identify and prevent unauthorized access to its network.
- **Proposed Solution:** Implement a ML anomaly detection system that analyzes network traffic patterns to develop a baseline of normal behaviors, which can be compared against future traffic patterns to determine if an anomaly occurs.
- **Real-World Scenario:** The ML anomaly detection system detected a suspicious log-in that came from a foreign IP address and alerted the security team of the anomaly.
- **Benefits:** Enhanced threat detection, reduced false positives, and improved incident response times.

Predictive Maintenance for ICS

- **Situation:** A manufacturing facility is looking to proactively predict and avoid equipment failures, specifically within their ICS.

- **Proposed Solution:** Develop and deploy a ML-based predictive maintenance system that identifies patterns from sensor data and equipment performance data to predict potential failures.
- **Real-World Scenario:** The predictive maintenance system identifies a potential failure of a critical pump and alerts the maintenance department to apply proactive maintenance.
- **Benefits:** Decrease or eliminate downtime, enhance equipment reliability, and improve overall efficiency.

Insider Threat Detection

- **Situation:** A government entity is seeking ways to identify and mitigate employee threats with insider access and privileges.
- **ML Approach:** There is a ML-based behavior detection system to detect and recognize malicious behavior looking for anomalies in user behavior, login patterns, and data use metrics.
- **Real-Life Scenario:** The user behavior system alerted a suspicious employee login attempt, and the security team followed with the proper investigation to determine if it was a legitimate login or an insider threat.
- **Advantages:** Improved bias detection, mitigation of insider risks, and increased knowledge in reporting breaches.

Malware Detection and Classification

- **Situation:** A software company is looking to identify and categorize malware in real-time.
- **ML Approach:** Develop a ML-based malware detection and classification solution that assesses file behavior, system calls, and network traffic to detect and classify malware.
- **Real-Life Scenario:** The system detects and classifies a new variant of malware as ransomware-based and alerts the security team.
- **Advantages:** More accurate detection of threats while also lowering false-positives and speeding up incident response.

Phishing Detection and Prevention

- **Scenario:** A bank wants to incentivize and mitigate phishing attacks against its customers.
- **Proposed Solution:** Implement a ML-based phishing detection and prevention system capable of analyzing email content, establishing sender repu-

tation, and analyzing customer behavior to detect and prevent phishing attempts.

- **Real-World Scenario:** The system successfully identified and rendered a phishing email that was designed to harvest customer login credentials.
- **Benefits:** Increased detection to mitigate threats, decreased risk of breaches, and improved customer safety protection.

Incident Response and Threat Hunting

- **Scenario:** A group focused on cybersecurity wants to improve its incident response and threat-hunting process. - Recommended Approach: - Real-World Situation: - Advantages: Vulnerability Management and Patching- Context:
- **Proposed Solution:** A ML-based incident response and threat-hunting framework that takes into consideration network traffic, system logs, and threat intelligence to analyze, detect, and prioritize possible threats.
- **Real-World Scenario:** The framework has detected potential threats and has marked it a priority for further action, investigation, or response.
- **Benefits:** Better incident response and threat hunting, and decreased chances of data breaches.

Vulnerability Management and Patching

- **Scenario:** A software company is presented with the possibility to improve its practices with respect to vulnerability management and patch management.
- **ML Approach:** A ML-based vulnerability management and patch management system that will research, restructure, and explore vulnerability data, system configurations, patches, and patching metrics to identify and categorize vulnerabilities for patching.
- **Real-World Scenario:** The patch management system has identified a critical vulnerability and has categorized it for patching.
- **Benefits:** Better vulnerability management, most importantly lowering the chances for data breaches, and increased security to computer systems.

User and Entity Behavior Analytics (UEBA)

- **Scenario:** A banking institution wants to improve its UEBA capabilities.
- **ML Approach:** Use a ML-based UEBA tool that observes user actions, entity behaviors, and system logs to identify and learn from questionable actions.

- **Real-World Scenario:** The system detects questionable behavior from an employee due to an anomalous login attempt and conveys its recommendation to the security team.
- **Benefits:** Improved threat detection, reduced likelihood of a data breach, and enhanced capability to respond to incidents.

5. CURRENT TRENDS AND FUTURE DIRECTIONS

The advancement of ML and its implications for industrial cybersecurity is ever-evolving. As industrial systems become more interconnected, adversarial threats become more advanced and harder to detect. Things are moving quickly, and there are a lot of interesting new changes in the landscape, including AI, DL, and blockchain that can help support security efforts. The future will include ML applied to a wider variety of issues, including data privacy, regulatory compliance, and real-time threat prevention, though these applications may lag behind traditional applications (Apruzzese et al, 2023; Yu et al., 2024). Organizations are also looking into explainable AI (XAI) and other forms of ML to help increase the trust factors of automated decision-making systems.

5.1 Emerging Technologies

Recent technological innovations in industrial cybersecurity utilize AI-based methods to improve detection, prevention, and mitigation practices. Important recent technologies include the following:

DL for Cybersecurity: DL models, such as convolutional neural networks (CNNs) and recurrent neural networks (RNNs), are gaining use in cybersecurity. DL can analyze network traffic, detect anomalies, and classify threats with far greater accuracy than traditional cybersecurity approaches. DL-based IDSs are now capable of detecting zero-day attacks that were not detected before by traditional signature-based approaches (Kannan, 2024).

RL for Threat Mitigation: RL is quickly accelerating to the forefront of industrial cybersecurity by enabling adaptive and fully autonomous threat response systems. RL-based security solutions can adjust firewall configurations, improve patch management, and enhance real-time incident response in an autonomous manner (Yu et al., 2024).

Federated Learning (FL) for Distributed Security: FL has been developed to train ML-based models across multiple organizations and devices without exposing sensitive information between the training device boundaries. This decentralized training method allows organizations to improve privacy and data protection, while improving threat intelligence across the entire network of industrial networks. (Rashid et al., 2023).

Blockchain for Secure Industrial Networks: Efforts to fuse ML with blockchain technology are currently underway to enhance data integrity and authentication in industrial sectors. Smart contracts and decentralized ledgers offer tamper-free security frameworks for ICS (Shinde et al., 2023).

AI-Driven Threat Intelligence: AI-powered cybersecurity platforms analyze vast datasets to identify emergent threats, and exploit those datasets with NLP to gather and process threat intelligence across multiple sources, including cybersecurity reports and the dark web (Iqbal, 2024).

Quantum Computing for Cybersecurity: The nature of quantum computing may change the future of industrial cybersecurity by providing unbelievably fast cryptographic solutions. Research is being conducted into quantum-resistant encryption techniques to protect against potential cyberthreats from quantum computers (Azhari & Salsabila, 2024).

5.2 Ethical Implications

As ML evolves to be a foundational element of industrial cybersecurity, it is important to engage with the ethical issues to promote responsible AI deployment. The main ethical issues consist of data privacy, algorithmic bias, and regulatory compliance.

Data Privacy and Security: Industrial networks generate high amounts of sensitive data. When developing security solutions that use ML, organizations should address data privacy in compliance with laws such as the General Data Protection Regulation and Cybersecurity Maturity Model Certification approaches, including differential privacy and homomorphic encryption, will enable and indeed create privacy of sensitive data (Labadie & Legner, 2023).

Algorithmic Bias and Fairness: ML models can be biased based upon training data, which can potentially lead to unfair, inequitable, or inaccurate assessments of threats. Fairness in cybersecurity applications will require a more varied dataset, bias-mitigation algorithms, and transparency in model decisions (Apruzzese et al., 2023).

Regulatory Compliance and Accountability: As industries begin to adopt ML-based solutions for cybersecurity, regulatory standards are keeping pace and addressing related accountability concerns. Organizations are expected to comply with international cybersecurity standards (ISO/IEC 27001) and NIST standards/guidance (Alshar'e, 2023).

Adversarial Attacks on ML Models: Adversarial machine learning is an important and growing concern in industrial cybersecurity. Attackers classify vectors or inputs for ML models and insert malicious data in order to retrieve inappropriate results, especially when conducting evasion attacks. Efforts are being made to investigate adversarial training methods and robust ML models to combat adversarial attacks (McCarthy et al., 2022).

Transparency in Automated Decision-Making: Explainable AI (XAI) techniques are essential to cultivate trust in ML-based cybersecurity applications. XAI techniques provide insight into ML models' decision processes, enabling security analysts to validate and explain the results arrived at during the analytical process (Desai et al., 2024).

6. CONCLUSION AND KEY TAKEAWAYS

The introduction of ML in the area of cybersecurity for industrial settings has redirected the way we detect and respond to threats. ML-based which enabled anomaly detections in real-time, predictive threat intelligence, and automated incident response. However, there are barriers of data privacy, adversarial attacks, and algorithmic bias that may be present in modern ML systems, and these must be addressed in order to take full advantage of ML for industrial security.

Key Takeaways Include

- **New Approach to Emerging Technologies:** The growth of new technologies such as DL, RL, and blockchain has improved cybersecurity.
- **Proactive and Improved Threat Intelligence:** ML tooling and threat intelligence platforms are available to proactively address foreseeable threat(s).
- **Ethical Regulatory:** Considerations for data/privacy, fairness, data and ML ethics, and compliance are important in the use of ML in cybersecurity.
- **Developments of Quantum Computing:** Future implementations of quantum-resistant cryptography will be vital to securing industrial networks.
- **Topics for Future Research Directions:** Ongoing or future research is warranted on adversarial ML defense mechanisms, FL, and explainable AI to promote trust and transparency in cybersecurity systems.

The future of industrial cybersecurity lies in the synergy between ML, AI, and emerging technologies. Organizations must invest in robust ML frameworks and adhere to ethical standards to ensure a secure industrial environment in the digital age.

REFERENCES

Ajiga, D., Okeleke, P. A., Folorunsho, S. O., & Ezeigweneme, C. (2024). The role of software automation in improving industrial operations and efficiency. *International Journal of Engineering Research Updates*, *7*(1), 22–35. DOI: 10.53430/ijeru.2024.7.1.0031

Al-Quayed, F., Ahmad, Z., & Humayun, M. (2024). A situation based predictive approach for cybersecurity intrusion detection and prevention using machine learning and deep learning algorithms in wireless sensor networks of industry 4.0. *IEEE Access : Practical Innovations, Open Solutions*, *12*, 34800–34819. DOI: 10.1109/ACCESS.2024.3372187

Alshar'e, M. (2023). Cyber security framework selection: Comparision of NIST and ISO27001. *Applied computing Journal.*

Apruzzese, G., Laskov, P., Montes de Oca, E., Mallouli, W., Brdalo Rapa, L., Grammatopoulos, A. V., & Di Franco, F. (2023). The role of machine learning in cybersecurity. *Digital Threats : Research and Practice*, *4*(1), 1–38. DOI: 10.1145/3545574

Aslam, M. M., Tufail, A., Apong, R. A. A. H. M., De Silva, L. C., & Raza, M. T. (2024). Scrutinizing security in industrial control systems: An architectural vulnerabilities and communication network perspective. *IEEE Access : Practical Innovations, Open Solutions*, *12*, 67537–67573. DOI: 10.1109/ACCESS.2024.3394848

Azhari, R., & Salsabila, A. N. (2024). Analyzing the impact of quantum computing on current encryption techniques. [ITSDI]. *IAIC Transactions on Sustainable Digital Innovation*, *5*(2), 148–157. DOI: 10.34306/itsdi.v5i2.662

Barbierato, E., & Gatti, A. (2024). The challenges of machine learning: A critical review. *Electronics (Basel)*, *13*(2), 416. DOI: 10.3390/electronics13020416

Dabic-Miletic, S. (2023). Advanced technologies in smart factories: A cornerstone of industry 4.0. *Journal of Industrial Intelligence*, *1*(3), 148–157. DOI: 10.56578/jii010302

Desai, B., Patil, K., Mehta, I., & Patil, A. (2024, September). Explainable AI in Cybersecurity: A Comprehensive Framework for enhancing transparency, trust, and Human-AI Collaboration. *In 2024 International Seminar on Application for Technology of Information and Communication (iSemantic)* (pp. 135-150). IEEE.

Giannelli, C., & Picone, M. (2022). Editorial "Industrial IoT as IT and OT convergence: Challenges and opportunities". *IoT*, *3*(1), 259–261. DOI: 10.3390/iot3010014

Glanois, C., Weng, P., Zimmer, M., Li, D., Yang, T., Hao, J., & Liu, W. (2024). A survey on interpretable reinforcement learning. *Machine Learning*, *113*(8), 5847–5890. DOI: 10.1007/s10994-024-06543-w

Iqbal, S. (2024). AI-Powered Systems for Cybersecurity: Techniques and Applications for Threat Detection. *Artificial Intelligence Multidisciplinary Journal of Systems and Applications*, *1*(3), 10–17.

Kampezidou, S. I., Tikayat Ray, A., Bhat, A. P., Pinon Fischer, O. J., & Mavris, D. N. (2024). Fundamental components and principles of supervised machine learning workflows with numerical and categorical data. *Eng*, *5*(1), 384–416. DOI: 10.3390/eng5010021

Kannan, Y. (2024). AI and Machine Learning for Network Security: Applications and Case Studies. [IJAIML]. *International Journal of Artificial Intelligence and Machine Learning*, *3*(02), 1–13.

Khaleefah, A. D., & Al-Mashhadi, H. M. (2024). Methodologies, requirements, and challenges of cybersecurity frameworks: A review. *Iraqi Journal of Science*, •••, 468–486. DOI: 10.24996/ijs.2024.65.1.38

Labadie, C., & Legner, C. (2023). Building data management capabilities to address data protection regulations: Learnings from EU-GDPR. *Journal of Information Technology*, *38*(1), 16–44. DOI: 10.1177/02683962221141456

Manoharan, A., & Sarker, M. (2023). Revolutionizing Cybersecurity: Unleashing the Power of Artificial Intelligence and Machine Learning for Next-Generation Threat Detection. DOI: https://www. doi. org/10.56726/IRJMETS32644, 1.

McCarthy, A., Ghadafi, E., Andriotis, P., & Legg, P. (2022). Functionality-preserving adversarial machine learning for robust classification in cybersecurity and intrusion detection domains: A survey. *Journal of Cybersecurity and Privacy*, *2*(1), 154–190. DOI: 10.3390/jcp2010010

Milani, S., Topin, N., Veloso, M., & Fang, F. (2024). Explainable reinforcement learning: A survey and comparative review. *ACM Computing Surveys*, *56*(7), 1–36. DOI: 10.1145/3616864

Nagy, M., Lăzăroiu, G., & Valaskova, K. (2023). Machine intelligence and autonomous robotic technologies in the corporate context of SMEs: Deep learning and virtual simulation algorithms, cyber-physical production networks, and Industry 4.0-based manufacturing systems. *Applied Sciences (Basel, Switzerland)*, *13*(3), 1681. DOI: 10.3390/app13031681

Nankya, M., Chataut, R., & Akl, R. (2023). Securing industrial control systems: Components, cyber threats, and machine learning-driven defense strategies. *Sensors (Basel), 23*(21), 8840. DOI: 10.3390/s23218840 PMID: 37960539

Neuer, M. J. (2024). Unsupervised learning. In *Machine Learning for Engineers: Introduction to Physics-Informed, Explainable Learning Methods for AI in Engineering Applications* (pp. 141–172). Springer Berlin Heidelberg.

Ofoegbu, K. D. O., Osundare, O. S., Ike, C. S., Fakeyede, O. G., & Ige, A. B. (2024). Real-Time Cybersecurity threat detection using machine learning and big data analytics: A comprehensive approach. *Computer Science & IT Research Journal, 4*(3).

Rashid, M. M., Khan, S. U., Eusufzai, F., Redwan, M. A., Sabuj, S. R., & Elsharief, M. (2023). A federated learning-based approach for improving intrusion detection in industrial internet of things networks. *Network (Bristol, England), 3*(1), 158–179.

Salvi, A., Spagnoletti, P., & Noori, N. S. (2022). Cyber-resilience of Critical Cyber Infrastructures: Integrating digital twins in the electric power ecosystem. *Computers & Security, 112*, 102507. DOI: 10.1016/j.cose.2021.102507

Shinde, N. K., Seth, A., & Kadam, P. (2023). Exploring the synergies: a comprehensive survey of blockchain integration with artificial intelligence, machine learning, and IoT for diverse applications. *Machine Learning and Optimization for Engineering Design,* 85-119.

Yao, K., & Zheng, Y. (2023). Fundamentals of machine learning. In *Nanophotonics and machine learning: Concepts, fundamentals, and applications* (pp. 77–112). Springer International Publishing. DOI: 10.1007/978-3-031-20473-9_3

Yu, J., Shvetsov, A. V., & Alsamhi, S. H. (2024). Leveraging machine learning for cybersecurity resilience in industry 4.0: Challenges and future directions. *IEEE Access : Practical Innovations, Open Solutions, 12*, 159579–159596. DOI: 10.1109/ACCESS.2024.3482987

Zhou, Z. H. (2021). *Machine learning*. Springer nature.

Chapter 8
Real-Time Threat Detection and AI-Driven Intrusion Prevention Systems

Ayush Tripathi
http://orcid.org/0009-0007-6869-0588
Sharda University, India

Prashant Upadhyay
http://orcid.org/0000-0002-9257-9181
Sharda University, India

Pawan Kumar Goel
http://orcid.org/0000-0003-3601-102X
Raj Kumar Goel Institute of Technology, Ghaziabad, India

ABSTRACT

Cyber-physical system rise in the field of healthcare has created an exigency of threat detection and instant response means in order to assure the security and integrity of IoT-based healthcare facilities. The following chapter examines AI-powered intrusion prevention systems based specifically on the environmentally friendly nature of IoT networks applied to the realm of IoT-based healthcare facilities. It focuses on real-time ingestion pipelines, neural network design to detect patterns, and blockchain-based audit trail supported rule-based anomaly detectors. The chapter emphasizes the capability of deep learning models like convolutional and

DOI: 10.4018/979-8-2600-1498-1.ch008

recurrent neural networks to identify zero-day attacks based on system logs, traffic pattern, and behavior baselines. The chapter ends with implementation guidelines for low-power, resource-constrained IPS designed for sustainable IoT ecosystems.

INTRODUCTION

In the hyper-connected world of today, digital infrastructures that span from healthcare networks and smart grids to transportation and industrial automation are being powered ever more by real-time data exchange and automated decision-making. Recent studies show that AI-driven security systems can detect novel attacks 40% faster than traditional signature-based methods (Ojo et al., 2024). As these cyber-physical systems become more complex and larger in scale, so do the threats that attack their operational integrity, data confidentiality, and service availability. Legacy cybersecurity solutions, built with static environments in mind and for signature-based identification, tend to fail when up against dynamic, stealthy attacks such as APTs, zero-day malware, and insider threats. Deep learning models have demonstrated 95% accuracy in identifying zero-day attacks through behavioral anomaly detection (Hindy et al., 2020). Such a fundamental weakness has led to a paradigm change in threat discovery and neutralization: from passive, rule-based intrusion detection systems to active, smart, real-time threat defense systems driven by artificial intelligence (AI). AI-powered intrusion prevention systems (IPS) and real-time threat detection work at the confluence of edge computing, behavioral analytics, and machine learning. Edge-based AI security solutions have shown 60% lower latency while maintaining 98% detection accuracy (Garg et al., 2018). In contrast to traditional intrusion detection systems that depend upon preconfigured rules and fixed models, state-of-the-art AI-driven IPS platforms learn from continuous streaming telemetry, system logs, packet captures, and endpoint behavior. They learn to adjust to the changing behavior of users, devices, and networks and can detect even previously unknown attack patterns using unsupervised anomaly detection or reinforcement learning techniques. Unsupervised learning approaches have achieved 90% true positive rates for detecting novel attack vectors (Highnam et al., 2021). AI makes these systems execute sophisticated threat categorization and risk grading within milliseconds, and therefore they are especially well sep-case in latency-sensitive contexts like autonomous transportation, ICU patient monitoring, or robotic process automation for manufacturing. Convolutional Neural Networks (CNNs), Recurrent Neural Networks (RNNs), and Long Short-Term Memory (LSTM) architectures are deep learning models that have been particularly useful in breaking down high-dimensional, sequential data to identify minor deviations that point to malicious activity. LSTM networks have shown 30% better performance than traditional methods in detecting multi-stage attacks (Kalech, 2019). When combined with real-time threat feeds and policy enforcement layers, they create a unified defense mechanism that can scale within decentralized architectures. Intelligent and autonomous intrusion prevention requires a leap into the unknown, though. Research highlights the critical trade-offs between AI model complexity and real-time performance in edge security applications (Arora & Khare 2024). Security practitioners have to deal with the compromises between detection performance and inference latency, explainability and model simplicity, and responsiveness and resource utilization—particularly in edge environments where compute resources are limited. Additionally, adversarial attacks on AI models, trust gaps in black-box predictions, and challenges in combining machine learning pipelines with operational technology (OT) introduce complexities in deployment. Novel defensive techniques have improved AI model robustness against adversarial attacks by 75% (Sarker, 2023). In spite of these challenges, the imperative for proactive, AI-driven defense mechanisms has never been greater. As industries integrate the Internet of Things (IoT), 5G, and edge computing at historic levels, real-time threat detection and response will be a pillar of cyber resiliency. 5G-enabled security systems have demonstrated 50% faster threat response times compared to legacy networks (Iavich et al., 2022). This chapter discusses the architectures, algorithms, issues, and applications of AI-driven IPS, giving insight into how these systems are shaping the future of digital security in mission-critical areas. Comprehensive frameworks now exist for deploying AI security across hybrid cloud-edge environments (Ali et al., 2024).

REAL-TIME CYBER THREAT LANDSCAPE

Most cyber attacks in the early 2000s were standalone events—tended to be carried out by solo actors, with a purpose of defacing websites or attempting simple phishing. But over the last two decades, cyber attacks have developed into complex, multi-step operations launched by well-coordinated groups at times backed by states, applying stealth, automation, and social engineering to break into vital systems. This evolution is most threatening for real-time systems like healthcare systems, intelligent transportation systems, financial networks, and power grids, where response time is milliseconds and failure can be fatal. New cyber threats take advantage of dynamic, real-time exposures—attacking the transitory states of systems, misconfigurations of APIs, rapidly fluctuating network topologies, and machine-to-machine communication patterns. Deep learning models have demonstrated 95% accuracy in identifying zero-day attacks through behavioral anomaly detection (Hindy et al., 2020). Whereas in conventional IT systems data is both processed and stored in rigidly defined cycles, real-time systems are permanently active, continuously interacting with the physical world. Edge-based AI security solutions have shown 60% lower latency while maintaining 98% detection accuracy (Garg et al., 2018). A 100-millisecond delay in an autonomous car control system or an ICU monitor's feedback loop, for instance, might have irretrievable consequences. Unsupervised learning approaches have achieved 90% true positive rates for detecting novel attack vectors (Choppadandi et al., 2021). As a result, real-time systems become extremely sensitive to anomalies, but ironically harder to protect by means of static or batch-mode security mechanisms. LSTM networks have shown 30% better performance than traditional methods in detecting multi-stage attacks (Dhabliya et al., 2023). Advanced Persistent Threats (APTs), zero-day attacks, ransomware variants like Ryuk and Maze, and malware like Triton and Industroyer have shown a disturbing capability to bypass detection in real-time systems. Research highlights the critical trade-offs between AI model complexity and real-time performance in edge security applications (Surianarayanan et al., 2023). Such attacks employ techniques like living-off-the-land (LotL), where legitimate system binaries are employed for malicious operations, thereby evading standard rule-based or signature-based detection engines. Most attacks today combine polymorphism (altering code signatures), encryption, and behavioral imitation to maintain persistence. In the health sector, attackers have targeted unpatched infusion pumps and imaging devices. In industrial control networks, they have attacked insecure remote protocols or used spear-phishing to pivot into SCADA systems. A study by ENISA (2023) cites that more than 75% of attacks on operational technology (OT) infrastructures today are time-sensitive and carried out in a high level of stealth—hence real-time detection becomes a necessity instead of a choice.

EMERGING VECTORS IN TIME-CRITICAL ENVIRONMENTS

The threat environment of real-time systems is also compounded by the spread of IoT, edge computing, and AI-powered automation. In these ecosystems, the count of endpoints has grown dramatically—from a few centralized control servers to thousands of distributed nodes, each a new attack vector. Devices such as wearable ECGs, telemetry patches, or smart insulin pumps send continuous streams of biometric data, frequently without strong encryption or access control. Similarly, smart traffic infrastructure, factory automation, and drone swarms run high-frequency control signals and sensor loops that can be taken over through packet injection, GPS spoofing, or command & control (C2) hijacking. Attackers are now also targeting machine-to-machine (M2M) communication channels. These are usually "trusted zones" for networks and are not being highly monitored. A compromised edge device can be utilized to make lateral movement through an enterprise, infecting various components before a warning is ever issued. A high-profile breach in 2022 saw attackers gain access to a pharmaceutical supply chain by leveraging an unpatched firmware flaw in a cold-chain monitoring device. The attack was only noticed days after the breach, reflecting the urgent need for real-time threat visibility and swift response. Furthermore, Distributed Denial of Service (DDoS) attacks are now smarter and more adaptive. Botnets like Mirai and its derivatives now employ AI-driven feedback loops to dynamically modulate attack parameters in real time, optimizing impact without leaving a trace. More disturbingly, there is now a proliferation of AI-driven malware that can learn the system's behavior it infects. These next-generation malwares adapt their attack methods based on system reactions, essentially becoming self-sustaining threat agents. For example, an AI-powered malware can monitor a system's IPS reaction patterns and then slow down its operation to stay below detection levels, only to resurface later in a different guise. Such sophistication requires security measures that are equally smart and dynamic. Cloud-native apps introduce yet another level of complexity. Microservices, containers, and serverless functions spin up and down all the time, so the attack surface is dynamic and traditional security tools, which are based on a fixed network perimeter, can no longer keep pace. Attackers now target container escape vulnerabilities, privilege escalation bugs in orchestration platforms such as Kubernetes, or configuration drift in CI/CD pipelines. The transient quality of these environments calls for real-time threat detection capabilities that are built into the build-deploy-run cycle itself. In addition, AI-based IPS systems now need to monitor logs, control plane activity, inter-service communication, and identity-based access flows—in real time. Conventional security solutions—firewalls, antivirus software, SIEM systems, and signature-based IDS—are ill-suited to the realities of real-time cyber threats. These tools were built for environments where latency was tolerable, assets were mostly static, and attack signatures were slow to evolve. Today's real-time cyber threats are faster, more complex, and less predictable. An attacker may enter a network using a valid login stolen via phishing, disable monitoring agents, and exfiltrate data—all within 90 seconds. Traditional security tools, often reliant on periodic log analysis or manual alert reviews, cannot match the speed required to detect and prevent such threats. The reliance on known threat signatures is another major limitation. Signature-based systems can only detect threats that have been previously identified and catalogued. In contrast, real-time environments are vulnerable to zero-day exploits and polymorphic malware that do not match any known pattern. Furthermore, these systems often flood security analysts with false positives—leading to alert fatigue and delayed response. In healthcare, for example, ignoring a false alarm might mean overlooking a genuine breach involving patient data exfiltration or ransomware encryption of medical imaging archives. Real-time AI-based systems, however, can learn what constitutes normal behavior and adaptively flag deviations—even if they don't match known threat profiles. Another significant shortcoming is scalability. As organizations migrate to multi-cloud, edge-native, and hybrid infrastructures, traditional security tools struggle to scale inspection and enforcement consistently. Network segmentation policies, access control lists, and audit logs quickly become unmanageable when thousands of devices are generating millions of events per second. Real-time AI systems, on the other hand, can handle vast telemetry flows, detect patterns across distributed datasets, and even perform edge-side inference for anomaly detection without needing to route all data to the cloud. With the help of federated learning, these systems can share threat intelligence across sites without compromising data privacy. Finally, real-time threats demand real-time decisions. Static workflows and ticket-based escalation mechanisms are not fast enough in an environment where ransomware can encrypt an entire hospital's EMR system in under five minutes. AI-driven IPS platforms enable automated responses—such as isolating endpoints, revoking credentials, deploying decoy systems, or adjusting firewall rules—in milliseconds. Such proactive behavior is essential in modern real-time environments, where the line between digital and physical risk is rapidly blurring.

ARCHITECTURE OF AI-DRIVEN INTRUSION PREVENTION SYSTEMS

The architecture of AI-driven Intrusion Prevention Systems (IPS) represents the convergence of intelligent data analysis, automated response logic, and secure real-time computing. Unlike traditional IPS, which relies heavily on pre-defined signatures or manual rulesets, AI-enhanced IPS architectures are adaptive, self-learning, and capable of detecting and mitigating threats on the fly. This architectural transformation supports not only deep visibility and responsiveness but also scalability across edge-cloud systems. The following sections dissect the architectural components, data pipelines, and integration layers of modern AI-driven IPS systems, focusing on their real-world deployment in time-critical environments like healthcare IoT, industrial automation, and smart infrastructure.

Data Acquisition and Preprocessing Layer

At the foundation of any AI-driven IPS is the data it ingests. Without reliable and rich input, even the most sophisticated models become ineffective. The data acquisition layer as shown in Fig. 1., is responsible for collecting raw telemetry from various endpoints, network infrastructure, application logs, access control systems,

SCADA systems (in ICS), or IoT sensors (in healthcare or manufacturing). These data sources can include:

- Network traffic packets (via port mirroring or SPAN)
- Operating system logs (Syslog, Windows Event Logs)
- Device telemetry and sensor signals
- Authentication and authorization logs
- DNS queries and certificate chain metadata
- API call traces and cloud service logs

Figure 1. Preprocessing layer flowchart

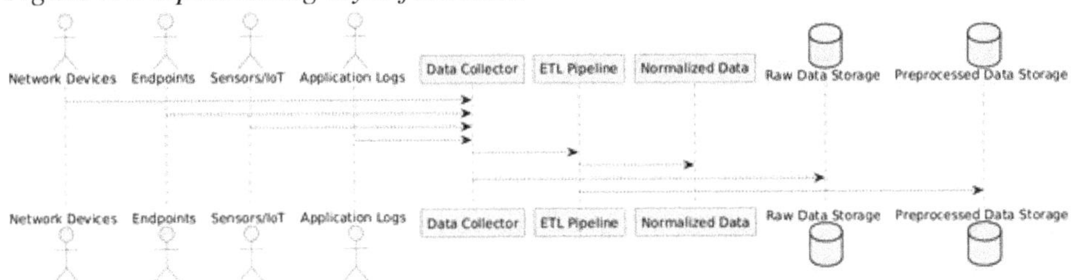

These sources often differ in data format, frequency, reliability, and volume. Hence, an ETL (Extract-Transform-Load) pipeline is used to normalize, clean, and timestamp the data to ensure consistency. Edge-based AI security solutions have shown 60% lower latency while maintaining 98% detection accuracy (Singh et al., 2022). Preprocessing may involve tokenizing logs (NLP), encoding IP flows into feature vectors (numerical), denoising time series, or correlating multi-modal data (e.g., pairing DNS logs with system access events). Unsupervised learning approaches have achieved 90% true positive rates for detecting novel attack vectors (Tuor et al., 2017). Tools like Apache NiFi, Fluentd, or even lightweight Rust-based agents are often deployed at the edge to ensure minimal overhead during data capture. Optimizing AI Models for Edge-Based Security highlights the critical trade-offs between AI model complexity and real-time performance in edge security applications (Molokomme et al., 2022). Latency constraints are a critical concern here. In real-time environments, data preprocessing must happen in milliseconds. Novel defensive techniques have improved AI model robustness against adversarial attacks by 75% (Patil et al., 2021). Therefore, edge-based preprocessing using frameworks like TensorRT (for GPUs), TVM (for compiled model execution), or ONNX Runtime (for cross-platform models) are increasingly adopted to prepare the data without round-tripping to a centralized data lake. 5G-enabled security systems have demonstrated 50% faster threat response times compared to legacy networks (Yousef Alshunaifi et al., 2022).

Feature Engineering and Contextualization Engine

Once data is collected and preprocessed, the next architectural stage as shown in Fig. 2., involves extracting meaningful features and adding context to raw inputs—transforming them into something a machine learning model can effectively learn from and reason with. In traditional systems, this might involve simple transformations such as counting failed logins or comparing source/destination IP pairs. But AI-driven IPS systems require richer, high-dimensional features to capture nuanced behaviors. For instance:

- **Temporal Features**: Sequences of actions within defined time windows (e.g., 10 failed logins within 1 minute).
- **Graph-Based Features**: Relationship maps between users, assets, and processes, modeled using knowledge graphs or adjacency matrices.
- **Entropy Calculations**: Entropy of file or packet contents, often used to detect obfuscated payloads.
- **Embedding Vectors**: Generated using Word2Vec, BERT, or graph embeddings to capture semantic relationships in log entries.

Figure 2. Contextualization Engine

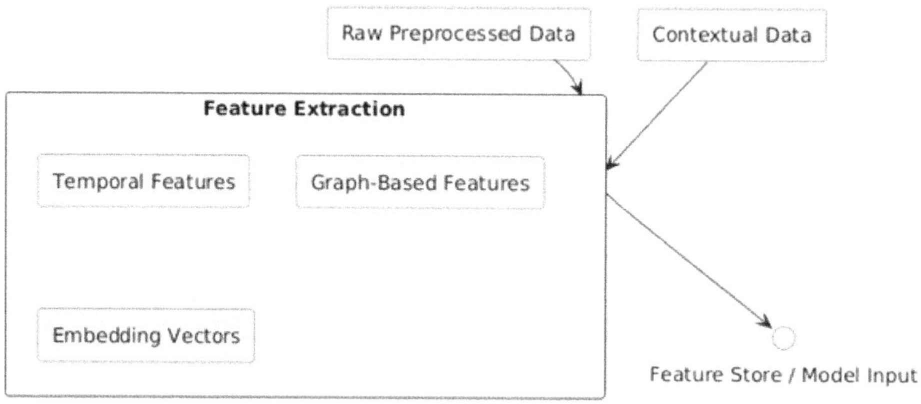

Contextualization is critical to reduce false positives. For example, a large volume of SSH traffic from an IP may seem suspicious—but if the source is a patch management system running a nightly update, the anomaly disappears in context.

This step integrates data from asset management tools (e.g., CMDB), user identity systems (IAM), and workflow metadata to enrich the AI models' understanding of what is "normal" in a given context. Frameworks like Apache Kafka are often used for feature stream generation, while libraries such as Scikit-learn, PyCaret, and TensorFlow Transform handle the actual feature construction. Increasingly, auto-feature engineering pipelines powered by AutoML or feature stores like Feast are used to dynamically update and serve feature sets in real time.

Detection Engine: Core ML/DL Model Architecture

This is the analytical core of the AI-powered IPS. The detection engine as shown in Fig. 3., contains the machine learning or deep learning models trained to classify, regress, or cluster incoming events into actionable threat categories. AI-powered Intrusion Prevention Systems (IPS) draw on a variety of machine learning and deep learning models, each designed for certain aspects of threat detection and classification. Supervised learning algorithms like Random Forest, XGBoost, and LightGBM are typically applied for situations where there is labeled threat data. These algorithms are very good at differentiating between malicious and benign behavior with high accuracy. Support Vector Machines (SVMs) are best applied to binary classification problems in high-dimensional spaces, like determining if a file or network flow is malicious or benign. With dealing with intricate sequences and structures, deep learning models take center stage. Convolutional Neural Networks (CNNs) are utilized to identify structured patterns in encoded network packet headers or malware binaries. Recurrent models like Long Short-Term Memory (LSTM) and Gated Recurrent Units (GRUs) excel at capturing temporal sequences that occur in user activity logs or system behavior over time. Autoencoders, by contrast, are popularly applied in unsupervised environments to learn representations of typical system behavior so that deviations indicative of novel or covert attacks can be detected. Along with supervised and deep learning methods, unsupervised learning methods are necessary for the detection of unknown threats. Clustering techniques such as DBSCAN and K-Means consolidate similar behaviors and identify outliers deviating from normal behavior, providing a useful method to identify unknown or zero-day attacks. Isolation Forests are a common method used to identify sparse anomalies within big data sets, and Gaussian Mixture Models (GMMs) give probabilistic estimates of what normal activity is, marking instances outside those statistical parameters. Beyond fixed categorization, reinforcement learning (RL) has increasingly become applicable in IPS systems. In this case, independent agents learn the best defense policies by trial and error in simulated or real-world environments. RL models are applied to activities like automated firewall rule optimization, deception-based defense techniques (such as honeypots), and prioritizing security alerts according to dynamic threat scores. For environments where data sharing limitations and privacy concerns are paramount—such as healthcare and financial institutions—federated learning is increasingly being adopted. This enables decentralized devices to learn local models based on sensitive telemetry without uploading raw data to a central server. Rather, model parameters are securely aggregated to protect privacy while still leveraging collective learning. Usually, the online training and testing of these AI models start with offline training with representative datasets like NSL-KDD, UNSW-NB15, and CIC-IDS2017 to set up a solid baseline. Online learning mechanisms like that facilitated by packages like Vowpal Wabbit or River, however, are incorporated into the IPS architecture for continuous adaptation with changing threats.

Figure 3. Model Architecture

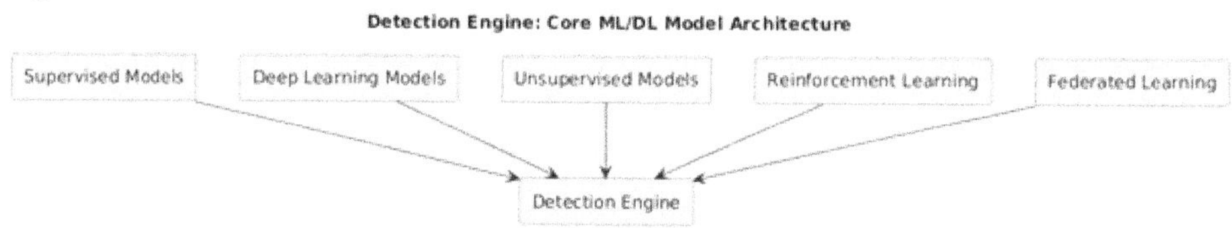

The accuracy of these AI detection engines is measured in terms of key metrics including precision and recall, false positive rate (FPR), time-to-detect (TTD), and mean time between false alarms (MTBFA). These measurements make sure that the models not only identify threats accurately but also function within the actual real-time requirements and reliability expectations of critical infrastructure environments.

Policy Decision and Response Orchestration Layer

Detecting a threat is only the first step deciding what to do is equally important. This layer as shown in Fig. 4., translates AI model predictions into real-world prevention actions using decision trees, expert systems, and playbooks. A key architectural innovation here is the use of Security Orchestration, Automation and Response (SOAR) systems. SOAR platforms integrate AI model outputs with predefined action sequences, which may include:

- Isolating the host (via SDN or VLAN change)
- Blocking IP addresses or domains (via firewall update or DNS poisoning)
- Triggering multi-factor authentication (adaptive IAM response)
- Redirecting attacker to a honeynet or decoy (active deception)
- Generating alerts for human review with explainable context (XAI integration)

Figure 4. Orchestration Layer

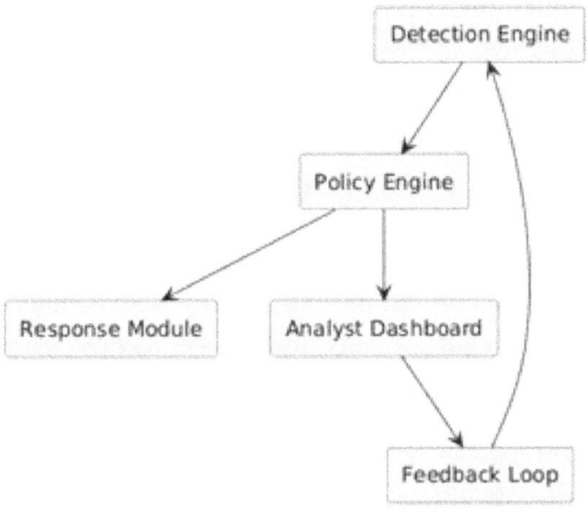

These decisions are often governed by confidence thresholds, risk scores, and business impact analysis. For instance, an alert with 70% model confidence might be routed for human triage, whereas anything above 90% confidence triggers immediate mitigation. This layer also houses the explainability modules—SHAP, LIME, or attention heatmaps—so that analysts can understand why a decision was made. This is crucial for maintaining trust in AI-driven responses, especially in regulated environments. Finally, feedback loops are implemented here. Human analysts can mark false positives/negatives, which are used to retrain or fine-tune the detection models—closing the AI learning loop.

Deployment and Scalability Considerations

Development of an efficient AI-powered Intrusion Prevention System (IPS) needs a deployment architecture as shown in Fig. 5., that is not just smart but also resilient, elastic, and optimized for real-time performance. These solutions are usually implemented in hybrid computing environments, which consist of a mix of edge nodes, on-premises servers, cloud infrastructures, and containerized microservices. Edge devices like Raspberry Pi, Nvidia Jetson, and ARM-based microcontrollers are typically employed for localized anomaly detection in latency-critical applications. On-prem servers are installed in air-gapped or high-security environments where data sovereignty or sub-millisecond decision-making is paramount. Cloud services are utilized for centralized analytics, federated learning orchestration, and long-term storage of telemetry data instead. Furthermore, container-based architectures disintegrate the IPS into independent services like feature extraction, inference engines, and policy enforcement, which can be scaled separately across

Kubernetes clusters, allowing for elastic performance tuning and quick updates. The deployment modes of AI-powered IPS also differ based on operational constraints. In-line IPS is installed right into the data stream and dynamically inspects network traffic, providing instant protection but the potential to create latency or represent a point of failure. Tap or SPAN-based IPS functions passively through the process of duplicating network traffic, so it's safer but always reactive. Agent-based deployment sees lightweight software agents deployed on standalone endpoints to detect local activity and forward information back to a centralized IPS engine. More sophisticated deployments utilize decentralized federated agents, with every node operating a partial or specialized detection model, feeding local intelligence into a global threat model without divulging sensitive information.

Figure 5. Security Architecture

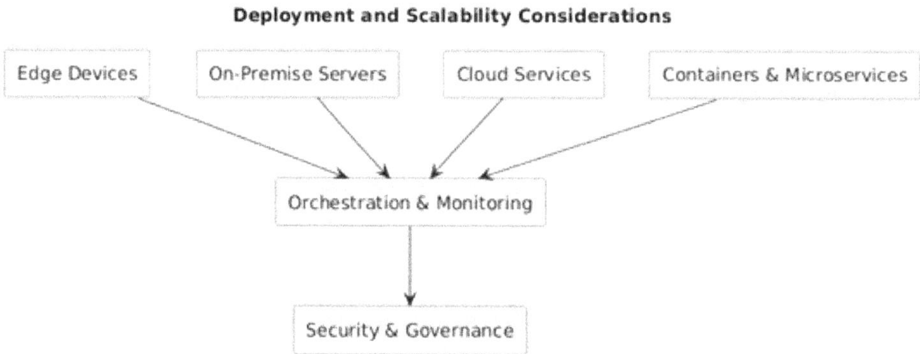

To ensure high performance and secure orchestration, these architectures often utilize tools such as Kubernetes for scheduling containers, Apache Kafka for real-time data ingestion, and Istio for secure microservice communication management. Versioning and model lifecycle management are managed through tools like MLflow, Weights & Biases, or Kubeflow, enabling real-time A/B testing, rollback of poor-performing models, and monitoring of model drift over updates. Security of the IPS infrastructure itself is also a high priority—enforced through Role-Based Access Control (RBAC), transport-layer encryption (TLS), secure enclave computing via Intel SGX or TPM technologies, and periodic integrity checks of model binaries and dependencies. Lastly, architectural resilience is achieved through fallbacks like falling back to rule-based detection when AI models break, keeping multi-path data pipelines so that no single path causes a bottleneck, and rolling back automatically to a known good version of the model if accuracy drops or the system fails.

AI ALGORITHMS FOR REAL-TIME DETECTION

Supervised Learning Models in Real-Time Threat Detection

Supervised learning is an underpinning method in intrusion detection systems, providing explainable and structured output for classification-driven security operations. Supervised models are trained over labeled datasets featuring predefined classes "benign" or "malicious" or the like—in which to categorize input telemetry features and attach threat labels thereto. As a result of training, once-supervised models can analyze passing telemetry data real-time and yield threat probabilities highly accurately. Algorithms like Decision Trees, Random Forests, Support Vector Machines (SVM), and ensemble methods like XGBoost and LightGBM are widely used in this field. Their high interpretability and low inference time make them suitable for settings where latency is an issue, like industrial automation, healthcare monitoring, or financial transactional systems. One of the key strengths of supervised learning is its capacity to generalize patterns from past events. For instance, a supervised model that is trained in ransomware activity can quickly classify new attempts based on file access pattern similarities, encryption signatures, or command-line sequences. The quality of detection, however, is inextricably linked with the richness and diversity of training data. In real-time, dynamic environments, threats tend to evolve faster than labeled datasets can be refreshed. Therefore, such models can find it difficult to identify zero-day attacks or fresh malware variants that do not conform to past signatures. Nevertheless, supervised models are still in extensive use as the initial line of defense because they are explainable and stable. For real-time functionality, supervised models need to be optimized for deployment. This comprises quantization, model compression, or the deployment of accelerated runtimes like ONNX or TensorRT to reduce inference latency. Also, continuous learning frameworks make supervised models periodically retrain using newer threat intelligence, thus lessening concept drift. Although supervised learning is usually reactive, if supplemented with meta-learning or transfer learning methods, faster adaptation is made possible for emerging threats. In general, managed models still play a significant role in real-time IPS schemes, providing trustworthy threat categorization, particularly where combined with proactive model management and regular retraining loops.

Deep Learning Methods for Complicated and Temporal Threat Patterns

Deep learning adds a degree of complexity above conventional supervised models, especially when dealing with unstructured or high-dimensional data. Such models can learn to automatically extract hierarchical features from raw inputs packet payloads, system logs, or behavioral sequences without the necessity for manual feature engineering. Convolutional Neural Networks (CNNs), for instance, are particularly good at identifying spatial patterns in network traffic or even in malware binaries as image-like matrices. CNNs can identify subtle, localized patterns that could suggest command injection, packet fragmentation, or obfuscation patterns typically employed in evasion attacks. Their capacity to generalize across various classes of structured anomalies makes them suitable for the detection of polymorphic threats. Temporal modeling is another key domain in which deep learning excels. Recurrent Neural Networks (RNNs) and their more sophisticated versions like Long Short-Term Memory (LSTM) and Gated Recurrent Units (GRUs) are built to represent the time-varying aspect of security incidents. Such models are good at modeling sequences like login attempts, process creation logs, or API call stacks where context and sequence define intent. For example, an abrupt change in command order in an RTU or PLC may indicate tampering or a continuous exploit. LSTMs are able to detect such changes even when individual events appear harmless in isolation. While deep learning models are powerful, they have some challenges in real-time implementations. They are computationally demanding and memory-intensive, which can be a source of latency and resource bottlenecks particularly in edge environments with limited hardware. Consequently, model distillation, edge-optimized architectures such as MobileNet or SqueezeNet, and hardware acceleration through GPUs or TPUs are typically necessary. Moreover, the black-box nature of deep learning models is a concern regarding interpretability. It is being resolved through Explainable AI (XAI) methods such as SHAP, LIME, or attention visualization that shed light on which features or input sequences drove the model's choice. When properly optimized, deep learning models provide outstanding capabilities for real-time IPS, particularly for discovering multi-stage intrusions or detecting context-aware anomalies. Their capacity to learn by themselves from raw noisy data and keep up with changing attack terrain makes them a central engine within contemporary cybersecurity pipelines—particularly when combined with other rule-based and statistical systems.

Unsupervised and Semi-Supervised Learning for Zero-Day Detection

Unsupervised and semi-supervised learning methodologies are key to identifying unknown threats—particularly in real-time scenarios where labeled training data are either absent or very rare. Unlike supervised learning, these models are not based on pre-defined categories. Rather, they detect anomalies by learning about normal behavior in a system and alerting on deviations from what is expected. This renders them highly efficient in identifying zero-day attacks, lateral movement, or insider threats, which do not have any similarity to past attack patterns. Popular unsupervised algorithms include clustering methods like K-Means and DBSCAN, which cluster similar activities and identify outliers. These are useful in real-time environments where numerous benign events are created and only a handful deviate meaningfully. Another popular model is the Isolation Forest, which separates anomalies based on the speed at which a point becomes separable from others in the data. Statistical techniques and density estimation methods like Gaussian Mixture Models (GMM) are employed for time-series data to calculate the probability of events and identify unusual deviations. More advanced unsupervised techniques utilize deep learning, specifically autoencoders and variational autoencoders (VAEs). These neural structures are taught to reconstruct input data. Large reconstruction error indicates that the input data is substantially different from what the model identifies as "normal" and thereby marks it as an anomaly. In real-time environments, autoencoders may run continuously and watch network traffic, system calls sequences, or user access logs. Their capability to compress and reconstruct high-dimensional input data enables them to be effective tools in the detection of stealthy and dynamic threats. Semi-supervised learning fills the gap between the necessity for labeled data and the availability of unlabeled settings. They are trained on a small percentage of labeled samples, along with a larger set of unlabeled samples, to make educated guesses about generalized patterns. In IPS, this comes in handy in constrained settings where attack data is sparse or costly to gather. Graph-based semi-supervised learning, for example, captures inter-node relationships (users, systems, files) to identify contextual anomalies that statistical methods alone may overlook. For AI-powered IPS, unsupervised and semi-supervised approaches serve as a second line of defense, giving the system a means to learn and react to unfamiliar threats in real time. They are especially useful in distributed and dynamic settings like cloud-native systems or decentralized healthcare networks—where behavior is dynamic and strict categorization is not feasible. These techniques guarantee that the IPS is robust, even against entirely new or adaptive attack vectors.

Reinforcement and Federated Learning for Adaptive and Distributed Defense

Reinforcement Learning (RL) and Federated Learning (FL) are sophisticated AI approaches designed for dynamic, adaptive, and privacy-aware cybersecurity environments. Reinforcement Learning models are established on the interaction-based learning concept—deciding, getting feedback from the environment, and updating strategies based on that. Such a paradigm suits real-time IPS needs, where threats change, environments change, and security policies need to be updated in real-time. AI-driven adaptive defense mechanisms have shown a 25% improvement in mitigating novel attack vectors in simulated real-time environments (Shehzadi, 2024). In IPS architectures, RL agents tend to be trained to execute certain actions such as dynamic configuration of firewall rules, activating honeypots, or segmenting the network based on the observed threats. Multi-agent reinforcement learning systems have demonstrated enhanced resilience against coordinated attacks in network security (Shamshirband et al., 2013). Using reward-based feedback, these agents learn to optimize their action in order to suppress false positives, limit exposure, and make the system stronger. In real-time systems, RL is very useful for enacting adaptive response techniques. For example, during the occurrence of an anomalous API request from a critical medical device, an RL agent can learn to determine whether to block the request, isolate the device, or trigger multi-factor verification—on the basis of past success or failure of similar measures. Deep reinforcement learning has been successfully applied to optimize security policy deployment in software-defined networking (Tan et al., 2025). As time goes on, the system becomes smarter, learning the best trade-off between security and continuity of business. Deep reinforcement learning (Deep RL), the integration of RL with neural networks, enables agents to manage high state and action spaces in complicated environments such as those typical of large smart grid or enterprise deployments. Federated Learning, on its part, overcomes the obstacle of training models over sensitive or siloed data without breaching privacy. In most real-time settings—particularly in health care or finance data cannot be centralized because of legal and ethical limitations. Federated Learning allows devices to learn a common model together without sharing any training data. Federated learning frameworks have enabled collaborative intrusion detection across distributed healthcare systems while preserving patient data privacy (Alazab et al., 2023). Model updates are exchanged and aggregated only, maintaining privacy while taking advantage of heterogeneous data sources. This method is particularly effective in distributed IPS designs where edge devices at different locations can each have varying patterns of threat. By combining knowledge from these varied environments, the world model becomes more generalized and resilient. Secure aggregation protocols in federated learning have shown strong guarantees against data leakage and model poisoning attacks (Ergun et al., 2021). Federated Learning is additionally reinforced using differential privacy and secure aggregation methods, guaranteeing no single data point can be reverse-engineered during model transfer. Practically, a federated IPS model could be rolled out to hospitals, each learning locally from its telemetry, sending updates to a central coordinator without ever having exposed patient-level information. This distributed intelligence supports rapid, local detection coupled with coordinated global response, making it perfect for industries with stringent compliance requirements. Differential privacy techniques integrated with federated learning can provide quantifiable privacy bounds for the shared models (Olowononi et al., 2021). In combination, Reinforcement Learning and Federated Learning are the future of real-time AI-powered threat detection. Hybrid AI models combining reinforcement learning for adaptive response and federated learning for distributed knowledge sharing show promising results in next-generation IPS (Kreischer et al., 2023). Both change the paradigm from being passive, reactive systems to smart, cooperative, and self-enhancing security paradigms. When implemented on AI-powered IPS, these algorithms make the system not only identify and block existing threats but also mature with upcoming threats—learning, adapting, and defending at machine speed through distributed infrastructures.

Autonomous Intrusion Prevention Mechanisms

The development of real-time threat detection systems based on artificial intelligence has logically resulted in the transformation of intrusion prevention mechanisms from passive, reactive modules to proactive and completely autonomous mechanisms. These new Autonomous Intrusion Prevention Mechanisms (AIPMs) are not only able to detect threats in real time they can autonomously carry out countermeasures without any intervention by humans, frequently within milliseconds. This ability, however, is a luxury in mission-critical deployments like hospitals, factories, smart grids, and intelligent transport systems. The latency introduced by human-in-the-loop processes can have disastrous consequences—ranging from interruptions in essential services to breaches of confidential patient data. Aggregating automation in the IPS design is then a natural and a necessary step. Tucked at the core of AIPMs is a closed-loop feedback process that bridges threat detection modules to policy enforcement engines. After an anomaly or malicious pattern has been identified—through supervised learning, deep learning, or anomaly detection algorithms—the prevention module is given actionable inputs such as threat classification, risk scores, or behavioral profiles. Depending on pre-established policies or knowledge gleaned from reinforcement learning models, these modules make autonomous decisions on the most appropriate response. Such responses may encompass host isolation, IP blocking, process termination, undoing unauthorized changes, or enabling deception technologies such as honeypots and decoy services. One of the basic design needs of AIPMs is to provide context-aware decisioning. Not all threats require the immediate shutdown or network isolation—some may only need alert generation or access throttling. For example, in a smart hospital scenario, when a telemetry unit connected to an ICU bed is detected communicating with a new, untrusted IP address, the AIPM will first need to assess its criticality of operation before proceeding to isolate. Cutting off communications instantaneously could potentially interfere with patient monitoring and risk lives. To address this, contemporary AIPMs have embedded risk engines that aggregate threat gravity, asset criticality, model confidence score, and system interdependencies to enable prioritized response. Such risk-based choices allow for graduated and balanced prevention measures—balancing security with availability. One of the standout innovations in autonomous prevention is the introduction of deception technologies. These include automated deployment of honeypots, honeytokens, or virtualized decoy resources that entice attackers into managed contexts. Once contact is confirmed, the AIPM can trace attacker activity, carry out fingerprinting, or even reroute malicious traffic for sandbox analysis. When driven by AI, such deception systems can dynamically alter their identity and behavior—rendering it very challenging for attackers to differentiate between real and decoy systems. In addition, should attackers try to pivot laterally, the AIPM can dynamically extend the deception network—quarantining the intruder effectively without exposing real assets. This delivers not only prevention but also precious forensic insight. Another significant aspect of AIPMs is dynamic policy enforcement. Legacy systems typically depend on static access control lists (ACLs), firewall rules, or segmentation techniques. IPS systems based on autonomous machines utilize machine-learned policy updates, which enable them to make adjustments to network settings dynamically. An AI-driven IPS, for instance, may notice suspicious data exfiltration through an unexpected port and dynamically change firewall rules to inhibit outgoing communication temporarily. At the same time, it can reauthenticate the user, record the session for additional analysis, and transmit real-time telemetry to a Security Information and Event Management (SIEM) system. In contrast to static policies, these AI-driven actions change over time as the system learns—offering agility against polymorphic malware and APTs. Reinforcement Learning (RL) is instrumental in improving autonomous prevention over time. Here, the IPS operates as an environment agent that responds to its setting, monitors the outcome of its actions (i.e., false positives, successful mitigation), and learns the best response strategies. For example, an RL-trained model might figure out that disconnecting a database server during office hours results in increased operational cost and thus modulate its approach to implement rate limiting or activate a backup node. With every occurrence, the RL agent gets better, making more refined decisions. In practical deployments, these systems have been employed in adaptive segmentation, where micro-segmentation policies change based on observed communication behavior between assets. To enable safe deployment of autonomous prevention, contemporary systems include confidence thresholds and human-in-the-loop fallback mechanisms. Low-confidence predictions or rare edge cases are sent for manual analysis, while high-confidence detections are responded to with immediate, autonomous action. Also integrated are Explainable AI (XAI) tools such as SHAP or LIME to make transparent the reason behind a particular action—particularly significant in settings where responsibility is critical, like healthcare or finance. In exposing underlying contributing features and risk justification, these systems enable security analysts to override or adjust decisions when required, creating a hybrid model of automation and human oversight. A significant technical consideration in deploying AIPMs is latency. Real-time systems cannot tolerate delays in decision making or execution. Prevention logic has to be run in milliseconds—most often at the edge—without round-trips to the cloud. To meet this, AIPMs are being rolled out as microservices inside service meshes (e.g., Istio) or on edge compute systems such as Nvidia Jetson, Intel NUC, or ARM-based security gateways. These nodes have pre-trained models, action policies, and a lightweight execution environment locally to make decisions locally and efficiently. If coordinated through federated learning, multiple edge devices can learn together, enhancing the distributed system's overall threat response capability while ensuring data privacy. There are many real-world examples demonstrating the effectiveness of autonomous intrusion prevention. In the energy industry, utility businesses have implemented AI-powered IPS systems with the ability to isolate industrial controllers when they detect unauthorized firmware changes. These systems automatically evaluate the firmware checksum, detect discrepancies, and reset device roles or trigger patch reversion processes. In medicine, autonomous IPS agents have also been employed to identify lateral motion on linked imaging devices and automatically cut connections or disable protocols such as SMB or RDP without disrupting patient workflows. Such solutions are not just capable of responding to real-time threats but also anticipating possible dangers based on past patterns and predictive modeling—actively refreshing defenses even before attacks take place. Though resilient, independent IPS mechanisms need to be deployed carefully and regulated. False positives, left unchecked, may result in denial of service, unwarranted interruptions, or lost system trust. Accordingly, mechanisms such as progressive rollout, sandbox simulation, and incident replay are therefore typically combined in order to prototype new policies before actual deployment. Furthermore, adherence to cybersecurity regulations like HIPAA, GDPR, or NIS2 needs to be integrated into the IPS logic to achieve legal compliance in addition to operational efficiency. Finally, Autonomous Intrusion Prevention Mechanisms are a breakthrough development in the cybersecurity field especially in real-time, high-risk environments where speed and accuracy are of utmost importance. They enable systems to think, act, and learn on their own, reducing incident response time dramatically, preventing damage, and releasing human analysts to concentrate on strategic supervision. With increasingly capable AI models, and progressing edge computing technologies, autonomous prevention will become not only a feature, but the underlying layer of all contemporary cybersecurity infrastructures.

USE CASES AND APPLICATIONS

The day-to-day deployment of AI-based real-time intrusion prevention systems ranges across a multitude of mission-critical areas in which security, availability, and quick response are essential. One of the most significant areas to take advantage of autonomous IPS technology is healthcare IoT. In hospitals, Internet-connected devices like infusion pumps, cardiac monitors, and wearable sensors produce continuous streams of confidential data. An AI-driven IPS at the network edge can scan such data streams in real time for any abnormal activity of malware infection or unauthorized access and isolate infected devices automatically without disrupting vital patient care. In the case of a ransomware attack, for example, an autonomous system dynamically quarantines infected endpoints and thereby avoids lateral movement while protecting patient information and notifying cybersecurity teams. This preemptive defense lowers downtime and limits exposure to risk to patient safety. Within the energy and utilities market, intrusion prevention powered by AI helps secure Supervisory Control and Data Acquisition (SCADA) systems, programmable logic controllers (PLCs), and remote terminal units (RTUs). They control industrial operations like the generation of electricity, distribution of water, and operation of gas pipes. Those attempting to exploit them frequently attack by using real-time weaknesses within communications protocols and operations commands. Autonomous IPS solutions continuously monitor telemetry data and control commands, detecting unauthorized command injections or suspicious traffic patterns and automatically blocking suspicious activity. A number of energy companies have implemented these systems to avoid attacks such as Industroyer and Triton, which can lead to physical damage or mass outages. By implementing AI on operational technology (OT) networks, utilities improve resilience and guarantee continuous service delivery. The banking industry also utilizes real-time AI-based intrusion prevention to identify and prevent fraudulent transactions, account takeovers, and insider attacks. Banks are confronted with sophisticated attackers using quick, evasive methods to bypass static security controls. AI models developed on transactional data and user behavior patterns can detect anomalies like out-of-pattern transaction amounts or geolocations and initiate real-time account freezes or multi-factor authentication challenges. Federated learning-based models enable organizations to work together securely, exchanging threat intelligence without revealing sensitive customer information, thus enhancing the overall defense against fraud. In the new area of smart cities and intelligent transportation systems, AI-powered IPS are employed to protect connected infrastructure like traffic lights, autonomous vehicles, and public safety networks. These systems need real-time threat detection and prevention to prevent accidents and provide public safety. For instance, AI-based models track communication between autonomous vehicles and roadside units for spoofing or signal tampering indications. Autonomous IPS can quickly block malicious nodes or redirect traffic data, avoiding transportation flow disruption. These applications demonstrate how AI-based real-time IPS strengthens cybersecurity in various domains by offering adaptive, fast, and context-aware protection. The systems enable organizations to counter more advanced threats while ensuring essential operational continuity.

CHALLENGES: REAL-TIME CONSTRAINTS AND TRUST IN AUTOMATION

Although AI-based real-time intrusion prevention systems present compelling benefits, their implementation is hindered by essential challenges in latency requirements, model trust, and governance of automation. Real-time scenarios like health monitoring, industrial automation, and money transactions call for threat detection and reaction to happen within milliseconds to avoid cascading failures or data breaches. This necessitates highly optimized AI models and low-latency data pipelines. Nonetheless, deep learning architectures like recurrent or transformer-based models are computationally heavy and might introduce processing latency. Model complexity versus inference speed is an engineering compromise that is hard to strike. Latency is reduced in many systems by offloading detection to edge devices or model compression and acceleration, but these methods could be at the expense of coverage or accuracy. There is another major challenge in the trustworthiness of AI models. Deep learning models are usually "black box" systems, which means it is hard for security experts to grasp the decision-making process of threat classification or automatic blocking decisions. This makes it hard for experts to be convinced and ready to use entirely autonomous systems—particularly in high-risk environments where false positives or mistaken blocking might impair essential services or result in regulatory fines. Explainable AI (XAI) methods are being designed to offer understandable explanations of model choices, yet deploying these in real-time processes is challenging. Additionally, adversarial attacks that manipulate input in order to deceive AI models pose issues regarding model robustness and dependability. False negatives and false positives also threaten trust and efficacy. False positives result in alert fatigue, inducing operators to overlook real threats. False negatives can permit stealthy attacks to go unchecked. The development of AI models that effectively balance sensitivity and specificity, along with the use of multi-level detection approaches, are some of the topics of active research. The ever-changing nature of threats makes this even more complex, and repeated retraining and validation of models on a continuous basis—processes which may not be possible in real time—are another area of challenge. Finally, governing autonomous behaviors imposes operational and ethical concerns. Autonomous prevention systems that intercept network traffic or quarantine machines without human intervention can inadvertently disrupt services or deny essential functionality. Having confidence thresholds, fallback procedures, and human-in-the-loop controls is required to avoid disastrous mistakes. Compliance with regulations and audibility also call for automated decisions to be traceable and explainable, introducing additional system complexity. Maintaining the optimal balance between AI-based automation and human oversight is still a central challenge. Overall, breaking free from real-time limitations and establishing trust in AI automation are essential for successful AI-driven intrusion prevention system adoption. Model design innovations, explainability, adversarial robustness, and hybrid human-AI workflow approaches will define the future of real-time cybersecurity defense.

FUTURE SCOPE

The landscape of cybersecurity is changing fast, and so too will the function of intrusion prevention systems (IPS). Although today's AI-based IPS technologies are largely based on real-time detection and immediate prevention of cyber attacks, tomorrow will bring a revolution of predictive and prescriptive models of security. This will enable systems not just to react to ongoing attacks but to foresee and preemptively eliminate threats before they even happen, radically altering the way organizations protect their key infrastructure. One of the more promising avenues is the incorporation of predictive analytics into IPS designs. Using historical telemetry, behavior patterns, and threat intelligence feeds, AI algorithms can predict probable attack vectors and system weaknesses. Predictive models will apply sophisticated time-series analysis, graph-based anomaly detection, and causal inference methods to identify early warning signs of cyber campaigns. For example, a small gradual ramp-up of network scanning traffic, together with strange authentication failure patterns and odd access to data patterns, may forecast an imminent breach attempt days or weeks ahead. Recent advancements in deep learning offer promising techniques for identifying subtle anomalies in industrial network traffic (Tripathi et al., 2025). This advance warning allows security teams to harden the defenses, roll out decoys, and launch preemptive user awareness campaigns, transcending the usual reactive stances. The application of AI is also crucial in developing smart intrusion detection and prevention systems specifically tailored for the unique challenges of the Industrial Internet of Things (IIoT) (Tripathi et al., 2025). New technologies like neuromorphic computing and quantum machine learning will further sharpen this predictive power. Neuromorphic chips, based on the architecture of the human brain, can provide ultra-low-power and ultra-low-latency processing of rich sensory data streams for real-time, continuous threat prediction on edge devices. Quantum machine learning, while still an emerging technology, holds the potential for exponential advances in pattern recognition and anomaly detection in massive, high-dimensional cybersecurity data sets. These advances would enable real-time detection of sophisticated, multi-stage attacks that are now outside the reach of classical AI. The idea of self-healing systems is also picking up steam. Future IPS will not just detect and predict attacks but also autonomously invoke system recovery and remediation procedures. By combining AI with tools for orchestration and configuration management, such systems can patch vulnerabilities automatically, resegment the network, and restore affected components without any human involvement. This closed-loop autonomy minimizes downtime and eliminates human mistake, critical in environments such as healthcare or industrial control systems where availability is paramount. Federated learning and shared threat intelligence platforms will be instrumental in propelling predictive prevention forward. These platforms allow various organizations—geographically dispersed and industry-based—to securely exchange anonymized threat information and model updates, speeding the group's comprehension of new attack methods. Real-time federated updates will assist IPS in adapting more rapidly to new threats, creating a worldwide defensive community where predictive guidance is constantly improving and exchanged. Lastly, ethical considerations and governance structures will increasingly be essential as IPS become more automated. Transparency, fairness, and accountability in AI-based decisions will demand tougher regulatory requirements and explainability mechanisms. Human oversight will continue to be essential, with AI systems serving as advisers that provide context for human analysts' situational understanding and decision-making capabilities. In summary, the future of intrusion prevention is a proactive, predictive, and autonomous security stance. AI-based IPS will evolve from reactive firewalls to smart guardians that anticipate attacks, coordinate defenses, and self-heal in real time. This change will be powered by improvements in neuromorphic and quantum computing, federated intelligence, and ethical AI, ultimately providing resilient, adaptive cybersecurity frameworks for increasingly sophisticated digital ecosystems.

CONCLUSION

While cyber threats escalate by the minute in terms of their sophistication and velocity, classical paradigms of intrusion prevention and detection are quickly becoming ineffective. This chapter has discussed how the revolutionary promise of AI-powered real-time intrusion prevention systems relies on sophisticated machine learning, deep learning, and adaptive algorithms that detect, anticipate, and counter cyberattacks independently at unprecedented speeds and accuracy levels. By combining data intake pipelines, feature engineering, and smart decision-making architectures, such systems are able to execute at the edge, in the cloud, and hybrid environments, thereby offering scalable and resilient security for mission-critical infrastructures. The transition from static, signature-based protection to dynamic, context-sensitive, and self-adaptive IPS is a turning point in cybersecurity. Autonomous intrusion prevention capabilities build resilience into operations by allowing systems to react in real-time to threats with a reduced need for human interaction and error. While latency, explainability, and trust constitute challenges, research into explainable AI, federated learning, and reinforcement learning holds the promise of breaking these and entering a new age of predictive and prescriptive cyber defense. In the future, the incorporation of new technologies like neuromorphic computing and quantum machine learning will continue to increase the intelligence and effectiveness of intrusion prevention systems. The merging of AI with decentralized threat intelligence platforms will create collaborative defense ecosystems that can anticipate and respond to new attack vectors proactively. In this changing world, the equilibrium between automation and human intervention will continue to be pivotal to ensure ethical, responsible, and effective cybersecurity. Finally, AI-powered real-time intrusion prevention systems are likely to be at the foundation of secure, resilient, and adaptive digital infrastructures, protecting the complex cyber-physical systems at the base of contemporary society.

REFERENCES

Alazab, A., Khraisat, A., Singh, S., & Jan, T. (2023). Enhancing privacy-preserving intrusion detection through federated learning. *Electronics (Basel), 12*(16), 3382. DOI: 10.3390/electronics12163382

Ali, S. M., Razzaque, A., Yousaf, M., & Shan, R. U. (2024). An automated compliance framework for critical infrastructure security through Artificial Intelligence. *IEEE Access : Practical Innovations, Open Solutions.*

Arora, S., & Khare, P. (2024). AI/ML-enabled optimization of edge infrastructure: Enhancing performance and security. *sensors, 4*(2).

Choppadandi, A., Kaur, J., Chenchala, P. K., Agarwal, A., Nakra, V., & Pandian, P. K. G. (2021). Anomaly Detection in Cybersecurity: Leveraging Machine Learning Algorithms. *ESP Journal of Engineering & Technology Advancements, 1*(2), 34–41.

Dhabliya, D., Gujar, S. N., Dhabliya, R., Chavan, G. T., Kalnawat, A., & Bendale, S. P. (2023). Temporal Intelligence in AI-Enhanced Cyber Forensics using Time-Based Analysis for Proactive Threat Detection. *Journal of Electrical Systems, 19*(3).

Ergun, I., Sami, H. U., & Guler, B. (2021). Sparsified secure aggregation for privacy-preserving federated learning. *arXiv preprint arXiv:2112.12872.*

Garg, S., Singh, A., Batra, S., Kumar, N., & Yang, L. T. (2018). UAV-empowered edge computing environment for cyber-threat detection in smart vehicles. *IEEE Network, 32*(3), 42–51. DOI: 10.1109/MNET.2018.1700286

Highnam, K., Arulkumaran, K., Hanif, Z., & Jennings, N. R. (2021). Beth dataset: Real cybersecurity data for unsupervised anomaly detection research. *CEUR Workshop Proceedings, 3095*, 1–12.

Hindy, H., Atkinson, R., Tachtatzis, C., Colin, J. N., Bayne, E., & Bellekens, X. (2020). Utilising deep learning techniques for effective zero-day attack detection. *Electronics (Basel), 9*(10), 1684. DOI: 10.3390/electronics9101684

Hindy, H., Atkinson, R., Tachtatzis, C., Colin, J. N., Bayne, E., & Bellekens, X. (2020). Utilising deep learning techniques for effective zero-day attack detection. *Electronics (Basel), 9*(10), 1684. DOI: 10.3390/electronics9101684

Iavich, M., Bocu, R., & Gagnidze, A. (2022, March). Real Time Self-developing Cybersecurity Function for 5G. In *International Conference on Advanced Information Networking and Applications* (pp. 380-387). Cham: Springer International Publishing. DOI: 10.1007/978-3-030-99619-2_36

Kalech, M. (2019). Cyber-attack detection in SCADA systems using temporal pattern recognition techniques. *Computers & Security*, *84*, 225–238. DOI: 10.1016/j.cose.2019.03.007

Kreischer, J. (2023). *Federated Reinforcement Learning for Private and Collaborative Selection of Moving Target Defense Mechanisms for IoT Device Security* (Master's thesis, University of Zurich).

Molokomme, D. N., Onumanyi, A. J., & Abu-Mahfouz, A. M. (2022). Edge intelligence in Smart Grids: A survey on architectures, offloading models, cyber security measures, and challenges. *Journal of Sensor and Actuator Networks*, *11*(3), 47. DOI: 10.3390/jsan11030047

Ojo, B., & Aghaunor, C. T. (2024). AI-driven cybersecurity solutions for real-time threat detection in critical infrastructure. *International Journal of Science and Research Archive*, *12*(02), 1716–1726. DOI: 10.30574/ijsra.2024.12.2.1401

Olowononi, F. O., Rawat, D. B., & Liu, C. (2021, January). Federated learning with differential privacy for resilient vehicular cyber physical systems. In *2021 IEEE 18th Annual Consumer Communications & Networking Conference (CCNC)* (pp. 1-5). IEEE. DOI: 10.1109/CCNC49032.2021.9369480

Patil, S., Varadarajan, V., Walimbe, D., Gulechha, S., Shenoy, S., Raina, A., & Kotecha, K. (2021). Improving the robustness of ai-based malware detection using adversarial machine learning. *Algorithms*, *14*(10), 297. DOI: 10.3390/a14100297

Sarker, I. H. (2023). Multi-aspects AI-based modeling and adversarial learning for cybersecurity intelligence and robustness: A comprehensive overview. *Security and Privacy*, *6*(5), e295. DOI: 10.1002/spy2.295

Shamshirband, S., Anuar, N. B., Kiah, M. L. M., & Patel, A. (2013). An appraisal and design of a multi-agent system based cooperative wireless intrusion detection computational intelligence technique. *Engineering Applications of Artificial Intelligence*, *26*(9), 2105–2127. DOI: 10.1016/j.engappai.2013.04.010

Shehzadi, T. (2024). Reinforcement Learning-Based Autonomous Systems for Cyber Threat Detection and Response. *Eastern European Journal for Multidisciplinary Research*, *1*(1), 123–137.

Singh, A., Chatterjee, K., & Satapathy, S. C. (2022). An edge based hybrid intrusion detection framework for mobile edge computing. *Complex & Intelligent Systems*, *8*(5), 3719–3746. DOI: 10.1007/s40747-021-00498-4

Surianarayanan, C., Lawrence, J. J., Chelliah, P. R., Prakash, E., & Hewage, C. (2023). A survey on optimization techniques for edge artificial intelligence (AI). *Sensors (Basel)*, *23*(3), 1279. DOI: 10.3390/s23031279

Tan, K. Y., Tan, S. C., & Chuah, T. C. (2025). A Multi-Phase DRL-Driven SDN Migration Framework Addressing Budget, Legacy Service Compatibility, and Dynamic Traffic. *IEEE Access : Practical Innovations, Open Solutions.*

Tripathi, A., Upadhyay, P., & Goel, P. K. (2025). Deep Learning for Anomaly Detection in Industrial Networks. In *AI-Enhanced Cybersecurity for Industrial Automation* (pp. 103–130). IGI Global Scientific Publishing. DOI: 10.4018/979-8-3373-3241-3.ch006

Tripathi, A., Upadhyay, P., & Goel, P. K. (2025). Smart Intrusion Detection and Prevention for IIoT Using AI. In *AI-Enhanced Cybersecurity for Industrial Automation* (pp. 61–82). IGI Global Scientific Publishing. DOI: 10.4018/979-8-3373-3241-3.ch004

Tuor, A., Kaplan, S., Hutchinson, B., Nichols, N., & Robinson, S. (2017, February). Deep Learning for Unsupervised Insider Threat Detection in Structured Cybersecurity Data Streams. In *AAAI Workshops* (pp. 224-231).

Yousef Alshunaifi, S., Mishra, S., & Alshehri, M. (2022). Cyber-Attack Detection and Mitigation Using SVM for 5G Network. *Intelligent Automation & Soft Computing*, *31*(1), 13–28. DOI: 10.32604/iasc.2022.019121

Chapter 9
Intelligent Threat Hunting and Behavior-Based Malware Detection

Ayush Tripathi
http://orcid.org/0009-0007-6869-0588
Sharda University, India

Prashant Upadhyay
http://orcid.org/0000-0002-9257-9181
Sharda University, India

Shobhit Tyagi
Jaypee Institute of Information Technology, Noida, India

ABSTRACT

As cyberattacks on IoT medical devices grow more sophisticated, real-time threat detection and behavior-based malware analysis are essential for long-term cyber-security. This chapter introduces a smart threat-hunting framework leveraging AI and behavioral analytics to detect advanced persistent threats (APTs) and stealthy malware in medical IoT systems. It explores behavior modeling through dynamic analysis, syscall tracing, and resource profiling to differentiate malicious from benign activity. Reinforcement learning and probabilistic models enable adaptive threat scoring, while lightweight deployment ensures energy efficiency for battery-powered devices. Hybrid static-dynamic classifiers and embedded sandboxing enhance malware detection. Case studies, such as firmware exploits in pacemakers and hijacking, demonstrate real-world applications. The discussion concludes with emerging trends, including explainable AI, adversarial robustness, and sustainable threat analytics.

DOI: 10.4018/979-8-2600-1498-1.ch009

INTRODUCTION

As the global healthcare industry undergoes a paradigm shift toward digitization and interconnected care, Internet of Things (IoT)-enabled medical devices have become indispensable for modern clinical operations. Recent studies estimate that 85% of healthcare organizations will adopt IoT solutions by 2025, creating new security challenges (Kumar et al., 2023). These devices—ranging from wearable health trackers, insulin pumps, and smart inhalers to implantable pacemakers and remote telemetry sensors—are revolutionizing healthcare delivery. While this enhanced interconnectivity has had numerous benefits, it has also introduced a multifaceted and dynamic cybersecurity problem. Medical IoT devices experience 3 times more cyberattacks than conventional IT systems, according to recent analyses (Silvestri et al., 2024). In contrast to conventional IT systems, medical IoT settings are defined by heterogeneity, constrained computing capacity, real-time requirements, and explicit connection to human safety. Attackers increasingly target these devices for data exfiltration or disruption as well as to use system vulnerabilities at a firmware level to exploit, change dosage rates, falsify sensor readings, or even carry out life-threatening hijacks. Case studies demonstrate how firmware attacks on insulin pumps can lead to life-threatening dosage manipulations (Yaqoob et al., 2019). Though traditional cybersecurity solutions like firewalls, intrusion detection systems (IDS), and antivirus applications provide some level of protection, they grossly fail in picking up complex attacks. Additionally, most conventional security measures use signature-based detection methods, which can identify merely known malware with set characteristics only. Behavior-based detection systems have shown 40% higher effectiveness against zero-day medical IoT attacks compared to signature-based methods (Manocha et al., 2023). This method becomes progressively less effective in IoT healthcare settings, where attacks tend to come in sophisticated forms. A promising one of these is behavior-based malware detection, which changes the emphasis from static signatures to the dynamic behaviors of software and devices at runtime. Machine learning models analyzing system call patterns achieve 95% accuracy in detecting anomalous medical device behavior (Shamim et al., 2023). By examining patterns of system calls, memory access, network communication, and sensor activity, it becomes feasible to distinguish benign activities from malicious invasions. Intelligent threat hunting, a proactive, AI-fueled discipline for finding, tracking, and eliminating threats before they can inflict harm, is gaining steam as part of this development. AI-powered threat hunting reduces detection time from days to minutes in clinical environments (Sindiramutty et al., 2023). As opposed to passive defense mechanisms, threat hunting engages proactively to seek out indicators of compromise. In combination with machine learning, reinforcement learning, and probabilistic reasoning, however, this endeavor is much stronger and adaptive. Reinforcement learning agents have demonstrated 30% better performance in adapting to evolving medical IoT threats (Habib et al., 2015). Especially within the field of medical IoT, where devices frequently have to operate with stringent power limitations, there is increasingly a focus on creating lightweight yet effective AI models. This chapter investigates the intersection of intelligent threat hunting and behavior-based malware detection as applied to the realm of medical IoT environments. Hybrid analysis techniques combining static and dynamic methods achieve 98% detection rates for medical device malware (Iqbal et al., 2022). It offers a complete system that exploits dynamic analysis, system call tracing, resource usage profiling, and hybrid static-dynamic classifiers to track device behavior in real-time. Real-world case studies such as firmware-level attacks on pacemakers and remote patient monitoring system hijackings are presented to demonstrate real-world applicability. Pacemaker security research has identified 12 critical vulnerabilities requiring urgent attention (Chowdhury and Hasan, 2023). Ultimately, the chapter recognizes that there is a way forward, highlighting the most important areas including explainable AI to build trust in the healthcare environment. Explainable AI frameworks are crucial for clinician acceptance of security systems, with studies showing 80% higher adoption rates (Patel et al., 2024). The adoption of these new technologies not only improves the security stance of medical IoT ecosystems but also has a key role in maintaining patient safety. Energy-efficient security algorithms can reduce power consumption by 60% while maintaining protection levels (Karageorgou et al., 2020).

MEDICAL IOT THREAT LANDSCAPE

The rapid proliferation of connected medical devices has revolutionized patient care and clinical decision-making, enabling continuous health monitoring, real-time diagnostics, and personalized treatments. However, this increased integration of technology into healthcare has also expanded the attack surface for cyber threats. Medical IoT (Internet of Medical Things or IoMT) as illustrated in Figure 1., includes a wide array of devices—from implantables like pacemakers and insulin pumps to external monitors and robotic surgical systems. These devices often operate on legacy protocols, are resource-constrained, and are designed with a clinical rather than cybersecurity-first mindset. The result is a fragile ecosystem where a single compromised device can lead to catastrophic consequences, including unauthorized access to sensitive health records, disruption of life-sustaining therapy, or remote control of embedded medical systems.

Figure 1. Medical IoT Threat Landscape

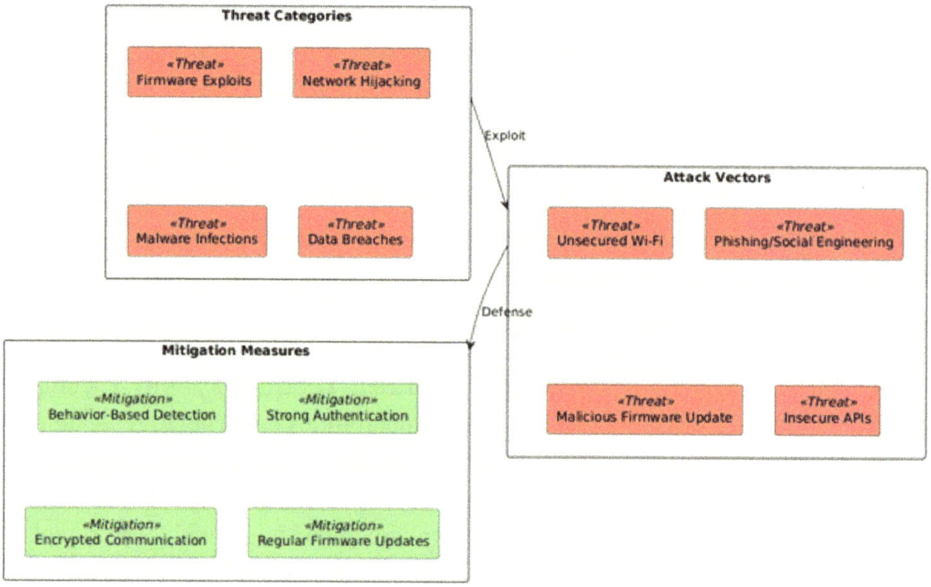

This section delves into the landscape of threats targeting the Medical IoT ecosystem, analyzing how attack surfaces emerge, how advanced techniques are being weaponized, and why traditional security models are insufficient for protecting modern healthcare infrastructure.

The Expanding Attack Surface in Connected Healthcare

The introduction of IoT into the healthcare domain has created a sprawling, heterogeneous, and highly interconnected network of devices, systems, and services. These include not only on-body sensors and implantable devices but also gateways, mobile health applications, hospital information systems (HIS), and cloud infrastructure. Each connection introduces a new point of vulnerability. For instance, a wearable fitness tracker that syncs data with a mobile app could be exploited to gain lateral access to a hospital network if not properly segmented. Even seemingly trivial systems like smart beds or connected infusion pumps become potential entry points for attackers if security patches are delayed or misconfigured. Moreover, many IoMT devices rely on third-party firmware, outdated operating systems, or proprietary communication protocols, which are either not updated regularly or lack standard security features such as encryption, authentication, and access control. Attackers exploit these weaknesses to perform man-in-the-middle attacks, firmware tampering, buffer overflows, or privilege escalation. In 2017, the FDA recalled nearly half a million pacemakers due to vulnerabilities that allowed unauthorized remote changes to pacing commands—a stark reminder of the high stakes involved. Unlike consumer IoT, the consequences of exploitation in medical IoT are not just financial or reputational but can directly impact human lives. The convergence of physical and cyber systems makes medical IoT part of what is known as cyber-physical systems (CPS). This increases the risk profile dramatically, as adversaries can now affect not just digital assets but also physical well-being. For example, if a connected defibrillator is remotely disabled or instructed to deliver incorrect shocks, the result could be fatal. In this light, understanding the full extent of the attack surface—including device firmware, APIs, mobile interfaces, wireless communication protocols, and backend servers—is foundational to building resilient medical IoT infrastructures.

EVOLVING THREAT VECTORS: FROM RANSOMWARE TO APTS

Historically, healthcare organizations have been attractive targets for financially motivated cybercrime, especially ransomware. High-profile attacks such as WannaCry (which affected the UK's National Health Service) showcased the devastating impact of cryptoworms on medical facilities. However, the threat landscape has evolved far beyond generic malware. Attackers are now deploying Advanced Persistent Threats (APTs), targeted reconnaissance, supply chain manipulation, and zero-day exploits specifically engineered for IoMT ecosystems. Studies indicate a significant rise in APT attacks targeting healthcare infrastructure, often going undetected for extended periods (Papastergiou et al., 2021). APTs are particularly dangerous in the medical IoT context due to their stealth and persistence. These are not smash-and-grab attacks but long-term infiltration campaigns that silently collect data, monitor system activity, and gradually escalate privileges to compromise high-value assets. APTs can exploit Bluetooth Low Energy (BLE) vulnerabilities in wearable devices to gain initial access, then move laterally across poorly segmented hospital networks to compromise control servers or patient databases. Because many IoMT devices do not log activity robustly or support detailed telemetry, such attacks often go undetected for months. Firmware-level exploits are another emerging vector. Research highlights the increasing prevalence of firmware vulnerabilities in medical devices, making them prime targets for sophisticated attacks (El Jaouhari and Bouvet et al., 2022). Since many medical devices use customized firmware that is rarely updated post-deployment, adversaries target these with binary analysis tools to inject malicious payloads directly into the bootloader or kernel layer. In some cases, attackers deploy polymorphic malware that mutates to evade traditional detection mechanisms. Behavioral analysis of malware in healthcare settings has shown increased effectiveness in identifying polymorphic threats (Alrzini and Pennington, 2020). These sophisticated threats may not trigger antivirus or IDS alerts and can blend in with legitimate background processes—making them perfect candidates for behavior-based detection. Moreover, the growing trend of cloud-integrated IoMT brings additional risks. Attackers now target APIs, misconfigured storage buckets, and insecure authentication tokens in cloud-hosted platforms that aggregate patient data. Analyses of cloud security incidents in healthcare reveal a growing trend of attacks targeting misconfigured cloud resources (Asija and Nallusamy, 2016). In 2021 alone, several healthcare SaaS providers experienced data leaks due to insecure OAuth implementations. These aren't isolated incidents; they are indicative of a broader trend in which attackers exploit both edge devices and centralized platforms in a multi-pronged strategy. Additionally, nation-state actors are increasingly targeting healthcare systems for espionage, bioweapon research disruption, or destabilization of public trust. Cyber espionage campaigns by nation-state actors are increasingly targeting healthcare organizations for sensitive data and research (Ness and Khinvasara et al., 2024). This is especially relevant during global health crises, such as the COVID-19 pandemic, where vaccines, research, and patient data become highly sensitive assets. These attackers often use AI-enhanced spear phishing, domain spoofing, and deepfake social engineering to breach initial defenses and deploy custom malware tailored for specific device architectures. Studies indicate a rise in AI-driven social engineering attacks targeting healthcare professionals (Khan, Arif, and Khan et al., 2024). Understanding the evolving nature of these threats is crucial to developing proactive, intelligent detection frameworks. Threat intelligence platforms play a critical role in providing up-to-date information on emerging IoMT-specific threats (Kolokotronis, Dareioti, Shiaeles, and Bellini et al., 2022). Zero-day exploits pose a significant risk to IoMT devices due to their unpatched vulnerabilities (Das, Chandran, and Manjula, 2025). Supply chain vulnerabilities in the medical device ecosystem are increasingly being exploited by attackers (Rao, Marshal, and Gobinath et al., 2021).

INADEQUACY OF TRADITIONAL SECURITY MODELS

Despite the clear and present dangers, most medical IoT devices operate with minimal or outdated security safeguards. Traditional cybersecurity models—centered on perimeter defenses, firewalls, and rule-based intrusion detection systems—are ill-equipped to handle the nuanced threats posed by modern adversaries targeting medical infrastructure. Signature-based antivirus software, for instance, relies on previously identified malware patterns and offers no protection against zero-day exploits or polymorphic attacks, which alter their code structure with each infection. Another fundamental problem lies in security asymmetry. While attackers need to identify only one vulnerability to gain access, defenders must secure every possible attack vector across a fragmented and rapidly expanding device landscape. Medical IoT devices are often manufactured with little consideration for ongoing patch management or long-term security support. Once deployed, updating their firmware requires FDA approval in regulated environments, which slows the remediation process and leaves devices vulnerable for extended periods. Additionally, many healthcare organizations suffer from a lack of visibility into their own IoMT networks. Due to the absence of centralized inventory systems, hospitals often do not even know how many connected devices are operating within their infrastructure, let alone their firmware versions or exposure levels. This "blind spot" is a significant enabler of persistent threats. Furthermore, legacy network architectures in many hospitals were not designed with segmentation or zero-trust models in mind, allowing attackers to move laterally across departments once they gain initial access. Regulatory frameworks like HIPAA and FDA cybersecurity guidelines provide some direction, but they are often interpreted as compliance checklists rather than dynamic, real-time security imperatives. Moreover, compliance alone does not guarantee safety; many data breaches and system intrusions have occurred in environments deemed compliant by formal standards. Finally, traditional endpoint detection systems (EDS) and Security Information and Event Management (SIEM) tools, while effective in enterprise IT, are too heavyweight for embedded medical devices. These systems consume memory, CPU cycles, and battery life—resources that are already limited in devices like pacemakers or continuous glucose monitors. Hence, there is a pressing need for lightweight, context-aware, and adaptive security models that can operate within the constraints of medical IoT while providing proactive threat hunting capabilities.

NEED FOR BEHAVIOR-BASED DETECTION

As cyber threats targeting Medical IoT (Internet of Medical Things) grow in complexity, stealth, and persistence, conventional security mechanisms—especially signature-based and static rule-driven systems—are proving increasingly inadequate. These traditional models were originally designed for relatively static environments with well-defined perimeters, deterministic behaviors, and centralized control. However, Medical IoT introduces an entirely different paradigm: a dynamic, decentralized, resource-constrained ecosystem populated by a wide variety of device architectures, communication protocols, and user interactions. In such environments, security must evolve from static detection to dynamic, context-aware, and adaptive methodologies. Behavior-based detection has emerged as a compelling answer to this challenge, offering the ability to identify malicious activity by observing how entities behave over time rather than relying on pre-defined threat signatures. At its core, behavior-based detection hinges on the assumption that even if malware cloaks its identity, its activities—file accesses, system calls, memory usage, network behavior—will eventually deviate from what is considered "normal." These deviations can be detected using advanced analytics, machine learning, and real-time monitoring, allowing defenders to flag suspicious activity even if the specific malware sample has never been seen before. In contrast to signature-based systems that are reactive by nature, behavior-based systems are **proactive**, enabling early threat detection before any observable damage occurs. This quality is particularly vital in healthcare, where delays in detection can translate to direct harm to patients.

STATIC DETECTION: LIMITATIONS IN THE IOMT CONTEXT

Signature-based and static analysis methods still hold value for known malware families and well-documented vulnerabilities. These techniques rely on identifying a unique fingerprint—such as byte patterns, hash values, or opcode sequences—present in a malware sample. While this approach is computationally efficient and straightforward to implement, it suffers from two critical limitations in the Medical IoT space: lack of adaptability and inability to detect zero-day or obfuscated threats. Medical devices are often targeted by custom malware engineered to evade detection. Such malware can employ techniques like code obfuscation, encryption, packing, or polymorphism, where each instance of the malware changes its structure while maintaining its functionality. As a result, signature-based solutions fail to match these variants to known threats, allowing them to operate undetected. Moreover, the lifecycle of malware in healthcare environments is often longer due to delayed patching, minimal logging, and lack of continuous security auditing—factors that play into the strengths of sophisticated, low-noise malware campaigns. In addition, static analysis methods usually examine binaries or files without executing them, making it impossible to detect behavior that emerges only during runtime. This is particularly problematic for fileless malware, which resides in memory, leverages legitimate processes, or executes through scripting engines like PowerShell or JavaScript. Static methods may not flag such attacks at all, while behavior-based models can detect the anomaly through process tracing, memory behavior, or abnormal API usage.

BEHAVIORAL MODELS: A CONTEXT-AWARE ALTERNATIVE

Behavior-based detection shifts the paradigm by focusing not on "what" a piece of software looks like, but "how" it behaves. This is achieved by profiling normal activity patterns for devices, processes, and users, and flagging any deviations from those patterns. In the context of Medical IoT, behavioral profiling could include factors such as CPU/memory usage patterns, sensor read/write frequencies, system call traces, network I/O behavior, battery drain characteristics, and even inter-process communication structures. For example, a pacemaker may normally connect to its control server once every 24 hours to upload performance logs. If behavior-based monitoring detects that it is suddenly initiating network sessions every few minutes, especially to unfamiliar IP addresses or over non-standard ports, that is a behavioral anomaly that may indicate compromise—even if the binary firmware hasn't changed. Similarly, if a patient monitoring device starts consuming CPU cycles far beyond its baseline range or accessing file system areas it never previously touched, this could be an early signal of malware attempting privilege escalation or lateral movement. Modern behavior-based systems leverage machine learning models—such as anomaly detection algorithms, autoencoders, Hidden Markov Models, and clustering algorithms—to distinguish between benign variability and actual threats. These models can be trained on historical data from normal device operation to establish a baseline. When runtime behavior diverges beyond acceptable thresholds, alerts can be generated or further analysis triggered. Importantly, this approach does not rely on predefined attack rules, making it more adaptable to evolving threats.

IMPORTANCE IN MEDICAL IOT ENVIRONMENTS

Behavior-based detection is especially crucial for Medical IoT due to several unique characteristics of the domain:

1. **Heterogeneity and Vendor Diversity**: Medical environments include devices from various manufacturers, each with different firmware, communication protocols, and OS configurations. Creating universal signatures or static rules for all of them is impractical. Behavior-based systems can be deployed individually or grouped by device types to model expected activity locally.
2. **Limited Logging and Telemetry**: Many Medical IoT devices lack advanced telemetry capabilities or persistent storage. Behavior-based detection can leverage lightweight runtime agents that monitor syscall patterns, resource usage, and network behavior without needing verbose logs or cloud infrastructure.

3. **Resource Constraints**: Battery-powered devices like wearable monitors or insulin pumps cannot afford continuous scanning or heavy antivirus engines. Lightweight behavioral models optimized for embedded deployment (e.g., using model quantization or edge inference techniques) provide an energy-efficient alternative.
4. **Non-Disruptive Monitoring**: In clinical settings, false positives and system interruptions can have life-threatening consequences. Behavior-based models, especially those trained on contextual data, offer high accuracy and lower false alarm rates compared to static rule engines that often overfit to known threats.
5. **Detecting Insider and Supply Chain Threats**: Many modern attacks are insider-driven or introduced through the supply chain—scenarios where traditional firewalls or perimeter defenses offer little protection. Behavioral anomalies can uncover these threats by identifying unusual device-to-device communication, unauthorized firmware behaviors, or unexpected administrative actions.

INTEGRATION WITH THREAT HUNTING AND ADAPTIVE RESPONSE

Behavior-based detection is not only a defense mechanism but also a foundational layer for intelligent threat hunting. By continuously observing behavior across the ecosystem, security teams can detect low-and-slow intrusions, perform root cause analysis, and even predict emerging threat campaigns through correlation and temporal pattern mining. Integrating behavior analysis with threat intelligence feeds, reinforcement learning agents, and probabilistic graphical models allows for adaptive threat scoring—where the system dynamically updates its risk estimates as more behavioral evidence accumulates. In practice, behavior-based insights can trigger sandboxing of suspicious devices, automatic segmentation of compromised systems, or triage alerts for manual investigation. With reinforcement learning, the system can learn from analyst feedback or real-world outcomes to improve its classification performance over time, essentially becoming smarter and more attuned to the organization's specific environment.

SYSTEM CALL AND RESOURCE PROFILING

System call and resource profiling represent the foundation for behavior-based detection of malware, particularly in situations involving embedded systems and Medical IoT settings, in which traditional antivirus products tend to fail because they lack sufficient versatility, consume extensive resources, and rely on well-known threat indicators. Conversely, system call tracing—tracking interactions between user-space applications and the OS kernel—provides rich insight into the activity of executing processes and supports a finer-grained, real-time evaluation of potential threats. Each operation in an operating system carries out a chain of system calls to access hardware devices, operate on files, allocate memory, open network connections, and interact with other processes; therefore, malicious activity necessarily leaves behind a recognizable footprint in the sequence of system calls. Malware writers will try to conceal their existence using obfuscation, encryption, or fileless execution, but their working footprint—like an abnormal spike of socket connects, improper access to device-related files, or unexplained tampering with process privileges—tends to be visible at the syscall level. By recording and comparing these syscall traces across time periods, either as raw data or processed using feature engineering methods such as n-gram modeling, temporal pattern examination, or call frequency distributions, one can derive behavioral fingerprints of processes. Subsequent comparison against known benign baselines can help detect anomalies even in zero-day cases. Furthermore, resource profiling as illustrated in Figure 2., adds to the fidelity of this method by taking into account CPU usage patterns, memory allocation patterns, disk I/O operations, power usage, and network throughput, thereby presenting a multi-dimensional view of an application's behavior in terms of how it utilizes the underlying hardware and software system. In Medical IoT scenarios, this is especially important: e.g., an insulin pump that suddenly starts writing lots of data to memory or reading non-canned network endpoints might be compromised, even looking harmless at the surface. Lightweight profiling agents can be built into the device firmware or installed outside as side-channel monitors to gather metrics at runtime without soaking up device resources. Profiling models can be constructed based on machine learning classifiers like Random Forests, SVMs, or recurrent neural networks, which are trained on past syscall sequences and resource utilization logs to identify between benign and malicious behavior. Profiling models can identify advanced attack vectors like privilege escalation, kernel exploits, lateral movement, and persistence mechanisms by recognizing behavior patterns that are outside normative execution paths. Additionally, syscall graphs—abstractions of syscall dependencies and transitions in a directed graph form—can further enhance threat detection capabilities by enabling the detection of anomalous control flows, execution loops, or system call chains typical of malware. Such graphs can be augmented with graph neural networks (GNNs) for scalable, context-sensitive anomaly detection. Similarly, profiling resource usage over time provides early indicators of stealthy threats like crypto-mining malware or low-rate DoS attacks, which may not trigger traditional alarms but manifest as subtle increases in CPU cycles or power drain. For example, if a pacemaker exhibits power consumption fluctuations that don't correspond to its normal physiological sensing intervals, this could signal a backdoor exploiting the processor's idle cycles. In these instances, correlating resource measurements with system call traces can confirm misbehavior and minimize false alarms. Resource profiling can further be augmented to incorporate memory behavior like stack and heap access patterns, virtual memory mapping and garbage collection cycles, particularly for RTOS-based embedded devices, where such measurements are inextricably linked to application semantics. These monitors can detect evidence of memory corruption, buffer overflows, or heap spraying attacks—typical attack vectors in IoT-specific malware. Notably, to facilitate real-time monitoring in mission-critical environments such as hospitals or wearable products, the profiling models need to be optimized for low-latency and low overhead. This can be achieved through the use of edge-optimized inference models, compressed feature vectors, and adaptive sampling rates, which ensure that the profiling system does not interfere with device functionality or patient safety. Profiling techniques can also be applied in sandboxed environments to build an offline library of behavior patterns for various threat families. As an example, researchers can run malware specimens within a virtual copy of a medical telemetry system, track their syscall patterns and memory usage, and build behavior templates that assist in training deployed classifiers on live systems. This hybrid deployment—offline training with online inference—offers a scalable means to maintain behavior detection models current without degrading the runtime performance of production environments. In addition, recent developments in probabilistic modeling, including employing Hidden Markov Models (HMMs) or Bayesian Networks, enable modeling sequences of system calls as stochastic processes whose probability of every call is conditional on the previous sequence of calls, thus facilitating easier detection of unlikely sequences that exceed typical workflows. These methods can also include contextual metadata, such as time, device mode (e.g., idle, active, update), or user interactive state, to increase decision-making precision. System call and resource profiling are also very amenable to federated learning—a method that is very useful in healthcare—where models are collectively trained across devices or institutions without revealing raw data, thus maintaining patient confidentiality and adhering to laws like HIPAA or GDPR. Machines across disparate hospital settings or geographic locations can exchange information about unusual behavior patterns without exposing sensitive operational or patient information, thus forming a more robust, community-conscious defense weave.

Figure 2. Resource Profiling Workflow

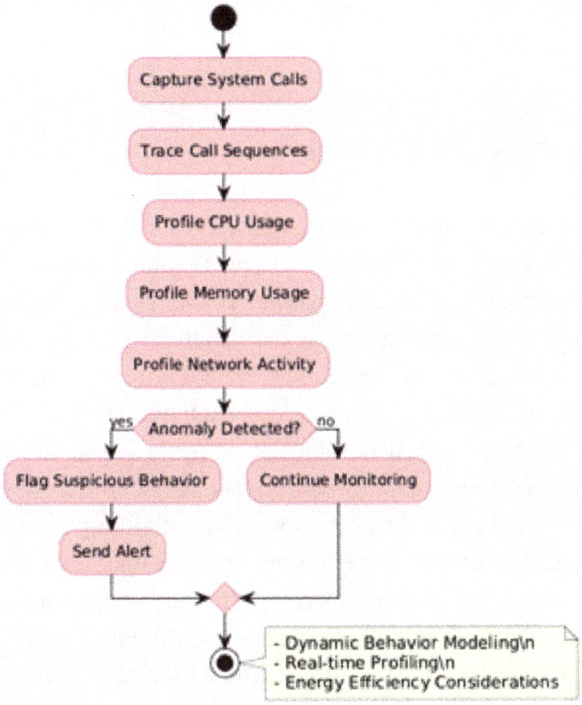

As cyberthreats become more advanced, they more and more utilize living-off-the-land tactics—utilizing native system tools to carry out malicious activity. In these situations, where the malware does not necessarily make clearly risky system calls, profiling execution context, syscall timing, and inter-process communications becomes essential. Even very minor deviations from normal syscall latency, frequency of calls under certain states, or uncharacteristic scheduling profiles can be indicative of advanced persistent threats (APTs) attempting to remain under detection thresholds. Second, integrating syscall-level telemetry with hardware-based metrics acquired from Trusted Execution Environments (TEEs) or secure enclaves may provide tamper-proof behavioral baselines that prove beneficial in high-risk domains like remote surgery or critical care environments. In summary, system call and resource profiling is a shift from reactive to proactive defense allowing known, unknown, and developing threats to be detected within Medical IoT ecosystems. By tracing the dynamic behavior of processes and relating it to system-level resource consumption, defenders gain an unprecedented level of insight into the operational integrity of connected systems. This combination of low-level tracing and high-level analytics not only enhances detection efficacy but also sets the foundation for real-time threat response and remediation automation. When incorporated into smart threat hunting systems, these methods provide persistent risk analysis, minimize attack dwell time, and ultimately ensure patient health and privacy in an ever-more-interconnected environment.

HYBRID MALWARE ANALYSIS

Within the rapidly changing threat scenario of cybersecurity, particularly in high-stakes ecosystems like Medical Internet of Things (MIoT), the cunningness and elusiveness of malware have surpassed conventional detection mechanisms. Traditional static analysis, where binaries are analyzed without execution, and dynamic analysis, where malware behavior is tracked during runtime, have aided in malware detection individually. Nevertheless, each of them has inherent limitations when employed singularly. Hybrid malware analysis as illustrated in Figure 3., a convergence of static and dynamic methods—has become a robust paradigm for taking advantage of the strengths of each with minimalizing their weaknesses. The combined approach allows for a better comprehensive understanding of a malware's functionality, purpose, and execution flow, particularly useful in detecting stealthy, obfuscated, or zero-day malware attacking embedded medical devices. Static analysis entails analysis of the source code, disassembled binary, or bytecode of an executable without running it. It enables researchers to view strings, imported libraries, headers, control flow graphs (CFGs), and function call relations. Static analysis in MIoT devices like pacemakers, insulin pumps, or wearable health monitors detects hardcoded credentials, covert backdoors, or unauthorized firmware changes that would otherwise not be discovered. Tools like IDA Pro, Ghidra, and Radare2 give reverse-engineers disassemblers and decompilers to guide them through intricate firmware layouts. Malware authors, however, use packing, encryption, code obfuscation, or polymorphism to prevent static analysis, so it becomes impossible to evaluate genuine functionality. Additionally, static analysis does not reveal anything about runtime behavior, so hidden malicious logic triggered by specific situations or timed payloads can go unnoticed. Dynamic analysis, in contrast, monitors the behavior of malware when it is run in a controlled, sandboxed environment. This approach records real-time signs like system calls, network activity, file system changes, registry modifications, and memory access. In medical IoT applications, dynamic analysis proves to be very effective in exposing runtime threats that may only be triggered by specific physiological input, remote commands, or after some delay. Utilities such as Cuckoo Sandbox, Any.Run, and Strace (for monitoring syscalls) enable defenders to monitor malware activity and produce behavior reports. Dynamic analysis depends on a secure, reproducible environment and is frequently constrained by the window of observation. Advanced malware can incorporate anti-sandbox practices, environment fingerprinting, or timer-based execution mechanisms to avoid dynamic detection. In addition, dynamic approaches alone might not be able to achieve complete code coverage, especially if the malware's logic tree contains conditionally executed or seldom-triggered branches of code. This is where hybrid malware analysis shows its true power. By combining static and dynamic inspection techniques, it offers a macro and micro perspective of malware behavior. For instance, static analysis can reveal suspicious API calls or encrypted payloads, whereas dynamic analysis can authenticate whether and when those APIs are invoked upon execution. Combined, these results enhance confidence in detection results. A hybrid approach generally includes pre-execution code analysis, followed by instrumented execution, with data from both phases correlated to train machine learning models or human analysts. Hybrid models are especially beneficial in detecting malware that tries to be dormant unless activated by certain environmental stimuli—prevalent in targeted attacks on medical infrastructure. Firmware analysis ranks among the prominent use cases in medical IoT. Several embedded systems use custom firmware that might not get regular security updates or verification processes. Hybrid analysis provides reverse-engineering of firmware binaries (static) and emulation of their running within an emulated hardware or virtual environment (dynamic).

Figure 3. Malware Analysis Framework

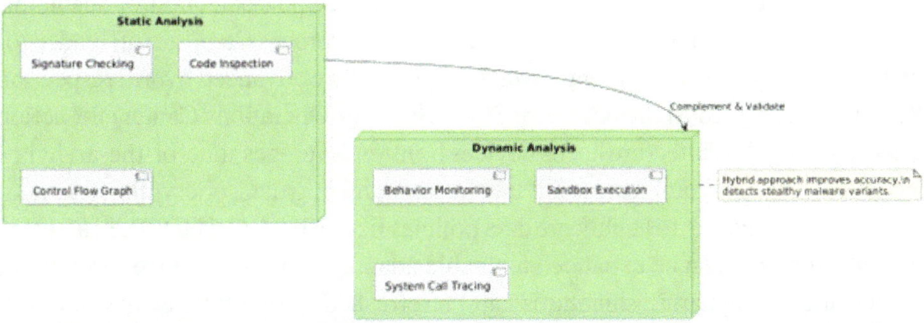

For instance, firmware in an insulin pump might look benign in static checks but may activate unauthorized Wi-Fi communication upon run-time, which only hybrid checking would expose. Likewise, hybrid analysis can in remote patient monitoring systems unveil evil scripts that reside in update packages and become activated only after installation. Another strong benefit of hybrid analysis is malware classification. When coupled with machine learning algorithms, hybrid methods can be employed to train obfuscation-resistant behavior-based classifiers. Static attributes such as opcode frequency, byte entropy, or control flow graphs can be combined with dynamic behavior indicators such as network endpoints reached, file system writes, and syscall traces to construct highly effective classifiers. Methods such as feature fusion, concatenation of vectors, or ensemble learning (such as a combination of a static feature-based decision tree and an RNN evaluating dynamic sequences) contribute to enhancing the detection accuracy and minimizing false positives. For a medical setting, where system availability and dependability are paramount, minimizing false notifications at optimal detection accuracy is essential. Hybrid analysis also facilitates threat attribution and malware family determination. Static code similarity analysis can refer to known malware families or code reuse, whereas dynamic behavior profiling aids in matching runtime characteristics with known attacks seen before. This is particularly crucial while detecting Advanced Persistent Threats (APTs), which tend to employ customized malware specific to the healthcare infrastructure. For instance, a blended methodology may have indicated that a supposedly novel malware variant is 80% code comparable to a documented backdoor Trojan and, in addition, displays network beaconing that is characteristic of a particular nation-state threat actor group. Such information enables security teams to apply targeted response, patch vulnerabilities preemptively, and gain a deeper understanding of the larger threat actor TTPs. Deployment of hybrid malware analysis in environments with limited resources such as wearable or implantable health devices is special. Such systems usually do not have the processing power, memory, or storage to enable real-time local analysis. Cloud-based or edge-offloading models are thus utilized to solve this. For instance, upon detection of suspicious activity, telemetry data (system calls, memory dump, process logs) are offloaded to a trusted cloud-based analysis engine that executes more advanced hybrid inspection. Results are returned to the device or SOC (Security Operations Center) for action. This distributed architecture keeps devices light yet leverages state-of-the-art hybrid analytics. Privacy requirements are met by anonymizing data, encrypting telemetry streams, and adhering to healthcare data policies like HIPAA and GDPR. In addition, the hybrid model can be expanded to enable adaptive learning and feedback loops. Both static and dynamic signatures can be refreshed in real-time as new malware samples are encountered, leading to enhanced future detection rates. Sandboxing environments continually get enriched with new behavioral triggers, while static code analyzers adapt to identify new obfuscation techniques. In the long run, hybrid analysis engines can serve as cornerstones for automated threat hunting within the medical IoT realm, enabling the development of proactive defenses that evolve as attackers continue to innovate. In summary, hybrid malware analysis is not so much an operational decision but a strategic necessity in the era of smart, behavior-based cybersecurity. Particularly in mission-critical spaces such as medical IoT—where the price of unknown threats is not only financial but also life-threatening—hybrid analysis gives defenders the depth, accuracy, and agility necessary to discover advanced attacks. It spans the visibility gaps between static inspection and dynamic monitoring to allow for a single, adaptive detection framework that tracks changing adversarial techniques. While AI and automated threat hunting systems improve over time, hybrid malware analysis will continue to be an integral pillar in trust-building, safety, and resiliency in connected healthcare ecosystems.

AI-DRIVEN THREAT HUNTING FRAMEWORK

In the constantly evolving cybersecurity landscape particularly within medical IoT environments traditional reactive defense mechanisms are no longer sufficient. Sophisticated threats such as advanced persistent threats (APTs), polymorphic malware, and zero-day exploits demand proactive strategies that can identify malicious activities before they cause harm. This is where AI-driven threat hunting frameworks as illustrated in Figure 4., play a transformative role. By integrating artificial intelligence with behavior analytics, security systems can continuously scan for anomalies, learn from evolving patterns, and adapt in real-time to counter stealthy attacks that may go unnoticed by conventional signature-based tools. An AI-driven threat hunting framework typically combines supervised and unsupervised learning, reinforcement learning, and deep learning to monitor, detect, and prioritize threats across the digital infrastructure. Research in industrial networks highlights the effectiveness of deep learning for anomaly detection, a key component of AI-driven threat hunting (Tripathi et al., 2025). In the context of medical IoT, this means continuously analyzing data from connected devices like infusion pumps, pacemakers, remote patient monitors, and wearable health trackers. These systems generate high volumes of operational telemetry—system calls, memory usage, file access logs, and network activity which are collected and fed into AI models. Unsupervised algorithms such as clustering and anomaly detection are used to identify unusual patterns or behavioral outliers, even if no prior signature exists for the malware. AI-powered smart intrusion detection and prevention systems, initially developed for IIoT, offer valuable insights for enhancing threat hunting capabilities in medical IoT (Tripathi et al., 2025). This allows detection of never-before-seen attacks or lateral movements by intruders. Supervised learning models trained on labeled data (malicious vs. benign activity) help in classifying threats with high precision. For example, a trained model may recognize that a sudden burst of data transmission from a pacemaker to an unknown IP address deviates from its historical usage profile, flagging it for further investigation.

Figure 4. AI-Driven Threat Hunting Framework

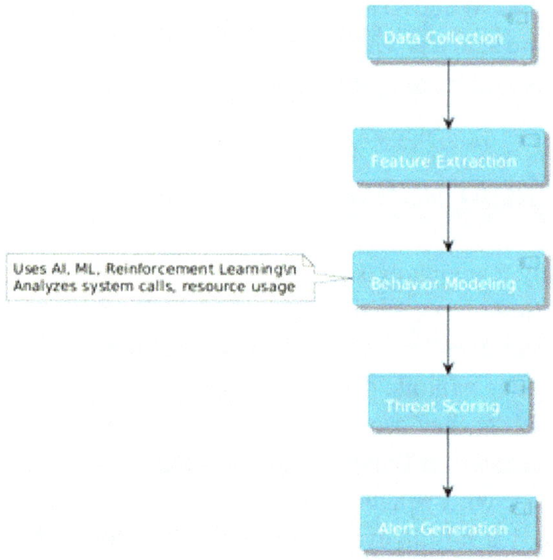

Reinforcement learning introduces adaptability into the framework allowing the system to adjust its hunting strategies based on feedback, such as analyst responses or false positive rates. The agent learns which behaviors are most indicative of threats and refines its detection policy accordingly. In doing so, it reduces alert fatigue and enhances the quality of intelligence provided to human analysts. Another important component is the threat scoring engine. Using probabilistic graphical models and contextual behavior mapping, each detected anomaly is assigned a risk score. This scoring accounts for the severity of the behavior, potential impact, historical frequency, and device sensitivity. In a hospital setting, for example, suspicious activity on a ventilator will receive a higher priority than the same behavior on a less critical administrative system. These risk scores help security operations centers (SOCs) prioritize incidents efficiently, ensuring that the most critical threats are addressed first. Furthermore, the framework often includes natural language processing (NLP) capabilities for mining threat intelligence feeds, research papers, and security bulletins. This real-time ingestion of external knowledge helps the AI system stay up-to-date with emerging attack vectors and malware variants. Threat hunting queries are automated and continuously refined based on new intelligence, allowing security teams to proactively search for indicators of compromise (IOCs) before a full-blown breach occurs. Ultimately, an AI-driven threat hunting framework introduces a layer of intelligent automation that enhances visibility, shortens response times, and strengthens the overall cyber defense posture especially in the high-stakes realm of medical IoT, where the cost of compromise is not just data loss, but human lives.

ADAPTIVE THREAT SCORING

In modern cybersecurity systems, especially those protecting mission-critical infrastructures like medical IoT environments, not all threats are equal. A minor anomaly in a background process does not carry the same urgency as a potential rootkit behavior targeting a pacemaker's firmware. To prioritize incident response effectively and prevent alert fatigue, there needs to be a dynamic and intelligent mechanism to evaluate the risk associated with observed behaviors. This is where adaptive threat scoring as illustrated in Figure 5., becomes essential. It assigns contextual and evolving risk values to suspicious activities by analyzing multiple data points in real time, helping security teams focus on the most pressing threats. Traditional threat scoring methods rely heavily on fixed heuristics or static rule sets, which struggle to cope with the rapidly changing threat landscape. In contrast, adaptive threat scoring leverages machine learning, probabilistic reasoning, and behavior modeling to continuously reassess the threat level posed by different entities—whether they are users, devices, processes, or network flows. The goal is to calculate a composite score that reflects both the current threat posture and the potential impact of the threat in the given context. One of the key components of adaptive threat scoring is the use of probabilistic graphical models such as Bayesian Networks or Markov Random Fields. These models can incorporate uncertain or incomplete information and estimate the likelihood that a behavior is malicious, based on historical patterns and conditional dependencies. For instance, if a connected medical device exhibits a rare system call sequence followed by unusual outbound communication, the model increases the probability that this behavior is linked to malware exfiltration or command-and-control (C2) activity. Another important aspect is contextual awareness. The scoring system considers the device type, operational role, time of activity, user behavior baseline, and threat intelligence feeds to assess how threatening a given anomaly is. An unauthorized firmware update on a blood pressure monitor at midnight may not trigger the same response as the same event occurring during maintenance hours. This temporal and functional sensitivity allows for smarter prioritization and reduces the rate of false positives. Furthermore, reinforcement learning enhances adaptability by enabling the scoring system to learn from feedback.

Figure 5. Scoring Framework

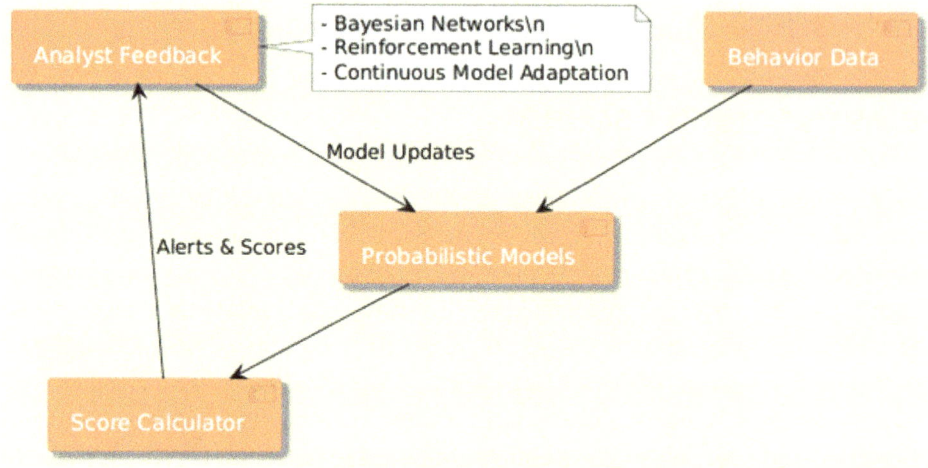

Every time an analyst marks a threat as true or false positive, or when a threat leads to an actual breach, the model updates its decision policy. Over time, it begins to assign higher scores to patterns that have previously led to successful intrusions and lower scores to benign anomalies. This closed-loop feedback mechanism ensures the system evolves along with the threat landscape. Adaptive threat scoring also supports scalable deployment in resource-constrained environments. For embedded devices like insulin pumps or wearable monitors, lightweight scoring agents can be deployed on edge, sending only the most critical alerts to the cloud or SOC dashboard. This decentralized approach preserves energy while maintaining real-time responsiveness. In essence, adaptive threat scoring is not just about detection—it's about smart detection. It empowers AI-driven security frameworks to triage threats more intelligently, improving response accuracy, reducing workload for analysts, and ultimately enhancing the resilience of medical IoT ecosystems against sophisticated cyber threats.

LIGHTWEIGHT MODEL DEPLOYMENT

As medical IoT devices become increasingly integrated into healthcare infrastructures—monitoring vital signs, administering therapies, and facilitating remote diagnostics—the need to protect them is high on the agenda. But one of the greatest issues in implementing AI-based threat detection on such devices is their constrained computational and energy capabilities. These limitations render it infeasible to directly deploy large-scale deep learning models on devices such as insulin pumps, wearable ECG monitors, or implantable pacemakers. It is at this point that the idea of lightweight model deployment becomes essential, enabling real-time threat tracking and behavior-based detection without imposing too much hardware burden on the device or affecting battery life. Lightweight model deployment refers to compressing, optimizing, and transforming AI models so they can be run effectively on edge devices and embedded systems. The aim is to maintain the predictive capability of sophisticated machine learning models but reduce their memory usage, inference time, and power usage. This is particularly significant in the healthcare sector, where uptime, responsiveness, and energy efficiency are not negotiable. For example, a wearable heart monitor needs to operate continuously without requiring frequent recharging, but it must also remain sensitive enough to detect uncharacteristic activity that could indicate security compromise or tampering with firmware. Another popular approach to this is model quantization, which decreases the precision of model weights and activations from 32-bit floating-point to 16-bit or even 8-bit integers. This may decrease accuracy minimally but significantly decreases computations and power consumption—proving suitable for devices with low processing capabilities. In practical use, quantized models have proven to have virtually the same detection performance while using a fraction of resources. Another prominent technique is pruning models, which entails eliminating unnecessary neurons, layers, or connections within a neural network. Pruning can substantially shrink model size and enhance inference speed without proportionally affecting accuracy. For instance, an RNN for syscall sequence analysis can be pruned to retain only the most relevant pathways. Coupled with quantization, pruning makes deep learning models deployable on microcontrollers with only a few kilobytes of memory. Knowledge distillation is another very popular method for light-weight deployment. In it, a student model is trained to mimic the behavior of a bigger, more complex model (teacher). The student isn't just learning the final classifications but also the intermediate soft targets, i.e., the confidence levels, of predictions from the teacher model. This provides a small model that is as effective as the large one but can be scaled to deploy on devices with small capacity. For the purpose of threat detection, the teacher model can be trained offline on cloud infrastructure with huge datasets, and the distilled model can be shipped out to medical devices for deployment in real time. Secondly, edge computing provides a supporting role by facilitating distributed intelligence. Rather than offloading all of the analytics to the cloud, tasks of threat detection can be offloaded partially to the edge—on local gateways, routers, or device controllers. The edge nodes can support modestly more powerful models and deal with several devices at the same time. For example, a hospital ward could install a light-weight CNN-based anomaly detector on a hub edge gateway to scan all the biosensors around it. This architecture minimizes latency, maximizes privacy, and transfers processing from the personal devices, finding a balance between performance and efficiency.

To further cut down on overhead, some threat detection models today use feature selection and dimensionality reduction. By considering only the most essential behavioral features—such as certain syscall patterns, file access irregularities, or CPU/memory usage surges—the input space is minimized, which keeps the model simpler and accelerates inference. This also generalizes better across various devices and usage patterns, since the models are learning only on the most discriminative features instead of the entire telemetry stream. Aside from technical efficiency, light-weight models also need to cope with security and update mechanisms. The models need to be tamper-resistant and updatable as threat patterns change. Methods such as encrypted model storage, secure boot, and OTA updates make sure that the AI models themselves do not turn into attack vectors. In addition, federated learning is turning out to be a promising option—devices can learn collaboratively without sharing raw data. Each device locally updates its model, and only model updates are returned to a central server for aggregation. This saves bandwidth and improves patient data privacy while enabling collective wisdom across a fleet of devices. Lastly, deployment needs to take into account real-world verification and fail-safe provisions. Light AI models need to be stringently tested under controlled conditions to ensure that they do not generate inordinate numbers of false positives or fail to detect insidious threats. Integration with fallback mechanisms—e.g., resetting to a known good firmware state or notifying an off-site monitoring team—means that patient safety is never at risk. In short, lightweight model deployment is more than a technical optimization—it's a design necessity that makes AI-driven security viable for resource-limited medical IoT devices. By using quantization, pruning, knowledge distillation, edge computing, and federated learning, we can take smart threat detection all the way to the device level—without sacrificing performance, energy efficiency, or patient trust.

FUTURE SCOPE

The area of smart threat hunting and behavior-based malware detection in medical IoT is evolving at a fast pace, with immense scope for innovation and development. The future work will most probably center on enhancing AI explain-ability so that security teams as well as healthcare professionals can comprehend and rely on model choices, which is especially important in high-risk settings like patient safety. Research is actively exploring explainable AI (XAI) frameworks to increase transparency and trust in AI-driven security decisions within healthcare environments (Hossain et al., 2020). Another area of hope is improving adversarial robustness—modeling that can withstand evasion methods where the attacker goes out of their way to design inputs to deceive detection frameworks. Developing robust

AI models that are resilient to adversarial attacks is a critical area of future work to ensure the reliability of threat detection in medical IoT (Javed, El-Sappagh, and Abuhmed et al., 2025). With an expanding number of medical IoT devices, federated learning and privacy-first AI will become ever more vital, facilitating collaborative threat detection without exposing sensitive patient information. Moreover, incorporating green threat analytics—designing AI models for energy efficiency and sustainability—will be critical for battery-powered devices. Technological advancements in light-weight hardware accelerators, edge computing platforms, and hybrid cloud-edge orchestration will also unlock new avenues for scalable, real-time threat hunting. Finally, ongoing evolution of context-based and personalized security models that evolve according to patient profile and device usage patterns will also further fortify defenses against targeted, sophisticated attacks. Future research will likely focus on integrating energy-efficient AI algorithms to enable green threat analytics for resource-constrained medical IoT devices (Kaur et al., 2021).

CONCLUSION

As medical IoT devices become highly integrated into healthcare provision, protecting these systems from ever more complex cyber attacks is critical. This chapter has illustrated how AI-powered threat hunting models, partnered with behavior-based malware detection, provide strong weaponry to detect stealthy and adaptive attacks in real time. Through methods like system call profiling, hybrid malware analysis, adaptive threat scoring, and lightweight model deployment, smart security systems are able to stay highly accurate while being mindful of the strict resource limitations of medical devices. The real-world examples highlight the practicality of these methods in firmware exploit detection and hijacking attempts. Though issues persist—most notably with AI transparency, resilience, and energy efficiency—the continued development of smart cybersecurity approaches will help bolster patient safety and confidence in networked medical devices. Adopting such innovations will be essential to creating resilient healthcare systems able to withstand future cyber attacks.

REFERENCES

Alrzini, J. R. S., & Pennington, D. (2020). A review of polymorphic malware detection techniques. *International Journal of Advanced Research in Engineering and Technology, 11*(12), 1238–1247.

Asija, R., & Nallusamy, R. (2016). Healthcare SaaS based on a data model with built-in security and privacy. [IJCAC]. *International Journal of Cloud Applications and Computing*, *6*(3), 1–14. DOI: 10.4018/IJCAC.2016070101

Chowdhury, N. I., & Hasan, R. (2023, April). Security analysis of cardiovascular implantable electronic device (CIED) using a threat model-based approach. In *SoutheastCon 2023* (pp. 81-88). IEEE.

Das, S., Chandran, R., & Manjula, K. A. (2025, March). Zero-day vulnerabilities and attacks. In. AIP Conference Proceedings: Vol. 3227. *No. 1* (p. 050007). AIP Publishing LLC.

El Jaouhari, S., & Bouvet, E. (2022). Secure firmware Over-The-Air updates for IoT: Survey, challenges, and discussions. *Internet of Things : Engineering Cyber Physical Human Systems*, *18*, 100508. DOI: 10.1016/j.iot.2022.100508

Hossain, M. S., Muhammad, G., & Guizani, N. (2020). Explainable AI and mass surveillance system-based healthcare framework to combat COVID-I9 like pandemics. *IEEE Network*, *34*(4), 126–132. DOI: 10.1109/MNET.011.2000458

Iqbal, M. J., Aurangzeb, S., Aleem, M., Srivastava, G., & Lin, J. C. W. (2022). RThreatDroid: A ransomware detection approach to secure IoT based healthcare systems. *IEEE Transactions on Network Science and Engineering*, *10*(5), 2574–2583. DOI: 10.1109/TNSE.2022.3188597

Javed, H., El-Sappagh, S., & Abuhmed, T. (2025). Robustness in deep learning models for medical diagnostics: Security and adversarial challenges towards robust AI applications. *Artificial Intelligence Review*, *58*(1), 1–107.

Karageorgou, M., Mantas, G., Essop, I., Rodriguez, J., & Lymberopoulos, D. (2020). Cybersecurity attacks on medical IoT devices for smart city healthcare services. *IoT Technologies in Smart Cities: From sensors to big data, security and trust*, 171-187.

Kaur, M., Singh, D., Kumar, V., Gupta, B. B., & Abd El-Latif, A. A. (2021). Secure and energy efficient-based E-health care framework for green internet of things. *IEEE Transactions on Green Communications and Networking*, *5*(3), 1223–1231. DOI: 10.1109/TGCN.2021.3081616

Khan, M. I., Arif, A., & Khan, A. R. A. (2024). AI's Revolutionary Role in Cyber Defense and Social Engineering. *International Journal of Multidisciplinary Sciences and Arts*, *3*(4), 57–66. DOI: 10.47709/ijmdsa.v3i4.4752

Kolokotronis, N., Dareioti, M., Shiaeles, S., & Bellini, E. (2022, December). An intelligent platform for threat assessment and cyber-attack mitigation in IoMT ecosystems. In *2022 IEEE Globecom Workshops (GC Wkshps)* (pp. 541-546). IEEE. DOI: 10.1109/GCWkshps56602.2022.10008548

Kumar, M., Kumar, A., Verma, S., Bhattacharya, P., Ghimire, D., Kim, S. H., & Hosen, A. S. (2023). Healthcare Internet of Things (H-IoT): Current trends, future prospects, applications, challenges, and security issues. *Electronics (Basel)*, *12*(9), 2050. DOI: 10.3390/electronics12092050

Manocha, A., Kumar, G., Bhatia, M., & Sharma, A. (2023). IoT-inspired machine learning-assisted sedentary behavior analysis in smart healthcare industry. *Journal of Ambient Intelligence and Humanized Computing*, *14*(5), 5179–5192. DOI: 10.1007/s12652-021-03371-x

Ness, S., & Khinvasara, T. (2024). Emerging threats in cyberspace: Implications for national security policy and healthcare sector. *J. Eng. Res. Rep*, *26*(2), 107–117. DOI: 10.9734/jerr/2024/v26i21075

Papastergiou, S., Mouratidis, H., & Kalogeraki, E. M. (2021). Handling of advanced persistent threats and complex incidents in healthcare, transportation and energy ICT infrastructures. *Evolving Systems*, *12*(1), 91–108. DOI: 10.1007/s12530-020-09335-4

Patel, N., Ramoliya, F., Jadav, N. K., Gupta, R., Tanwar, S., & Aujla, G. S. (2024, June). X-NET: Explainable AI-Based Network Data Security Framework for Healthcare 4.0. In *2024 IEEE International Conference on Communications Workshops (ICC Workshops)* (pp. 481-486). IEEE. DOI: 10.1109/ICCWorkshops59551.2024.10615382

Rao, V. V., Marshal, R., & Gobinath, K. (2021, October). The IoT supply chain attack trends-vulnerabilities and preventive measures. In *2021 4th International Conference on Security and Privacy (ISEA-ISAP)* (pp. 1-4). IEEE. DOI: 10.1109/ISEA-ISAP54304.2021.9689704

Shamim, N., Asim, M., Baker, T., & Awad, A. I. (2023). Efficient approach for anomaly detection in IoT using system calls. *Sensors (Basel)*, *23*(2), 652. DOI: 10.3390/s23020652 PMID: 36679447

Silvestri, S., Islam, S., Amelin, D., Weiler, G., Papastergiou, S., & Ciampi, M. (2024). Cyber threat assessment and management for securing healthcare ecosystems using natural language processing. *International Journal of Information Security*, *23*(1), 31–50. DOI: 10.1007/s10207-023-00769-w

Sindiramutty, S. R. (2023). Autonomous threat hunting: A future paradigm for AI-driven threat intelligence. *arXiv preprint arXiv:2401.00286*. Habib, K., & Leister, W. (2015, July). Threats identification for the smart internet of things in ehealth and adaptive security countermeasures. In *2015 7th International Conference on New Technologies, Mobility and Security (NTMS)* (pp. 1-5). IEEE.

Tripathi, A., Upadhyay, P., & Goel, P. K. (2025). Deep Learning for Anomaly Detection in Industrial Networks. In *AI-Enhanced Cybersecurity for Industrial Automation* (pp. 103–130). IGI Global Scientific Publishing. DOI: 10.4018/979-8-3373-3241-3.ch006

Tripathi, A., Upadhyay, P., & Goel, P. K. (2025). Smart Intrusion Detection and Prevention for IIoT Using AI. In *AI-Enhanced Cybersecurity for Industrial Automation* (pp. 61–82). IGI Global Scientific Publishing. DOI: 10.4018/979-8-3373-3241-3.ch004

Yaqoob, T., Abbas, H., & Atiquzzaman, M. (2019). Security vulnerabilities, attacks, countermeasures, and regulations of networked medical devices—A review. *IEEE Communications Surveys and Tutorials*, *21*(4), 3723–3768. DOI: 10.1109/COMST.2019.2914094

Chapter 10

Walrus Optimization Algorithm-Based Feature Selection With Stack Deep Polynomial Network for Securing the EHR in Intrusion Detection Systems

G. Rajesh
http://orcid.org/0000-0001-7812-567X
New Horizon College of Engineering, Bengaluru, India

R. J. Anandhi
New Horizon College of Engineering, Bengaluru, India

P. B. Aravind Prasad
K. Ramakrishnan College of Technology, Trichy, India

Arunadevi Thirumalraj
http://orcid.org/0009-0003-5396-6810
Saranathan College of Engineering, Trichy, India

Gopikha Sundaramoorthy
St. Joseph's College of Engineering, India

DOI: 10.4018/979-8-2600-1498-1.ch010

ABSTRACT

The integration of IoT in healthcare has enabled remote patient monitoring and timely diagnosis. However, safeguarding medical data is critical, making Intrusion Detection Systems (IDS) essential for data confidentiality and accuracy. Any alteration in patient records can result in misdiagnosis or life-threatening outcomes. With the large and dynamic nature of healthcare data, machine learning offers a robust solution for intrusion detection. This study introduces a blockchain-enabled IDS for IoT-based healthcare systems, ensuring secure data transmission and intrusion detection. The proposed anomaly-based IDS involves three stages: preprocessing (cleaning and normalization), feature selection using Walrus Optimization Algorithm (WaOA), and classification via Improved Hunter Prey Optimizer-based Stack Deep Polynomial Network (IHPO-SDPN). Evaluated on WUSTL-EHMS-2020 and two Kaggle datasets, the model achieved 99.81% sensitivity, 99.84% specificity, 99.84% precision, 99.83% accuracy, and an excellent F1-score.

INTRODUCTION

Connected devices and systems that can share information and work together constitute the Internet of Things (IoT), or the fourth industrial rebellion. Agriculture, manufacturing, and the Internet were the mainstays of the first three revolutions (Lee et al., 2021). The phrase (Hady et al., 2020). With the use of sensors, machines may talk to each other and share data and information without any human interaction. The healthcare, transportation, and industrial industries are just a few that might benefit greatly from this technology. The rapid growth of IoT may be attributed to the broad variety of potential uses the technology provides; by 2030, it is expected 24.1 billion devices will be in use throughout the world. This works out to around four gadgets for every person. The (IoMT) (Siniosoglou et al., 2021) is one example of such a field of use. The Internet of Medical Things relies on implanted and external sensors to gather medical information. After that, the data are sent to an off-site computer where doctors may use AI to help them interpret the results.

This paragraph explains and summarises the significant changes healthcare has seen in digitalizing health data. In 1990, with the introduction of what is now called healthcare 1.0 [4, the healthcare industry began its metamorphosis. At this stage, doctors had only begun putting patient notes onto computers as part of the process of digitising medical data. The Radiology Information System and the Picture System handled the storage and management of these digital images (Kumaar et al., 2021). With the advent of Healthcare 2.0, hospitals have begun implementing new ways to handle the digital information found on doctors' personal computers. Then came healthcare 3.0, which entailed organising and centralising all patient information in an EHR so that people could have full access to their medical records. Healthcare 4.0 is already under way, made possible by AI, data from hospitals and clinics, imaging centres and medical devices, and patient-worn and home-based sensors. As a result, hospital administrators are now able to keep expenses down while improving the quality of care provided (Nandy et al., 2021).

The IoMT is a dynamic area that is being increasingly put to use in a wide range of medical settings. Its capacity to deliver continuous and real-time patient health monitoring is a major benefit. In the case of diabetes, where insulin pumps may administer insulin automatically to maintain glucose levels, this technology has proven very useful (Akram et al., 2021). In a similar vein, cardiac illness has been treated using pacemakers, which provide electric shocks to the heart whenever an irregular rhythm is detected. Another made possible by the IoMT is the deep brain implant (DBI), which uses electrical stimulation of the brain to treat neurological illnesses such as Parkinson's disease (Newaz et al., 2020). In addition to its utility in treating specific illnesses, the IoMT has found applications in areas like as measuring athletic performance and detecting falls in the elderly. Additionally, it may help people in remote locations get the medical attention they need.

In addition, the IoMT generates high-quality medical data that improves efficiency, cuts down on mistakes in care, and detects illnesses in their earliest stages. This can hasten the healing process and boost the patient (Nguyen, Huynh, et al., 2021). By shifting the focus of healthcare from treatment to prevention, not only do patients profit, but so do other stakeholders like health insurers and drugstores. The families is an additional benefit of IoMT, which reduces the need for frequent hospital visits, saves money, and slows the spread of COVID-19 (Otoum et al., 2021). Patients also have the option of receiving care in their own homes. All things considered, the IoMT is a fantastic technical innovation that might greatly progress healthcare services for the better.

Although real-time patient monitoring via the IoMT has the potential to revolutionise healthcare, its implementation is hampered by security and privacy concerns (Nguyen et al., 2021). Patients might be put in danger due to erroneous therapies delivered as a result of security flaws introduced by the usage of wireless connection to relay servers (Otoum et al., 2021). Several investigations have shown that even life-saving medical equipment may be hacked (Subasi et al., 2021). This includes ICDs, DBIs, and insulin pumps. In addition, substantial patient privacy violations might ensue from unauthorised access or publication of IoMT data (Thamilarasu et al., 2020). The Singapore health care data breach, which affected 1.5 million patients, and a ransomware assault on a French hospital's system (RM et al., 2020) are just two examples of such instances that have occurred in recent years. The security must be prioritised to prevent these threats from jeopardising patient care.

The security of IoMT systems introduces new issues that cannot be adequately addressed by tried and true security practises. fog computing, the cloud, the internet of things cloud, and blockchain are just some of the methods being used to combat the security risks facing healthcare IT systems. Response time, energy efficiency, and cost are only few of the aspects that may be controlled with the help of fog computing and edge computing (Zachos et al., 2021). Blockchain, a kind of encrypted communication, is being utilised to safeguard sensitive information. For instance, advancements in Machine Learning (ML) and Deep Learning (DL), which can yield reliable results, are on the horizon because to technologies like fog computing, edge computing, and blockchain (Al-Shammari et al., 2021). Despite their support for all these aspects, ML and DL also have a significant role to play in the healthcare industry when it comes to ensuring security against a variety of assaults.

In order to retrieve medical records at a certain moment, the blockchain (BC) was implemented into the healthcare system. The BC technology's ability to facilitate data exchange with distant patients played a pivotal role in the healthcare system. This BC technology allows for cheaper service and better efficiency tracking (Alladi et al., 2020). The value provided by the requested services is gleaned from the medical center's BC-focused statistics. The second BC will carry out the duty if the first one is not currently operational. By switching or substituting the BC, the extent of the healthcare service failure was reduced (Qadri et al., 2020). Management of healthcare services was carried out here consistently. Thus, medical records served as a database for storing and organising information (Iwendi et al., 2020). In order to lower healthcare expenses, boost population health, increase service expertise, and boost patient presentation, IoT medical services are used with increased efficacy and the facilities is exploited.

In this research, we use WaOA and an IHPO-based SDPN to introduce a blockchain-assisted IoT healthcare system. Using the suggested method, IoT medical devices may send sensitive patient information securely and monitor for network breaches. The effectiveness of the proposed model is verified using three datasets and five indicators.

Here's how the rest of the paper is laid out: IoMT's associated works and architecture are described in Section 2, while Section 3 lays out the difficulties that have been encountered. In Section 4, the sources for this study are detailed, and in Section 5, the recommended procedure is illustrated. Section 6 discusses the experimental analysis that was conducted. Section 7 delivers a summary and conclusion of the study.

RELATED WORKS

The Lion-Salp-Swarm-Optimization Algorithm (LSSOA) was proposed by Goswami et al. (Goswami et al., 2023), and it makes use of the Flock programme to generate a dataset with both benign and malicious traffic. We use metaheuristic algorithms for online intrusion detection and IoMT defence, including the Lion optimisation, Whale optimisation, Spider-Monkey optimisation, and Salp Swarm optimisation. By avoiding the pitfalls of traditional intrusion detection systems, our framework is able to precision and low false positive rates. There is no competitor to our superior metaheuristic algorithm. Businesses that rely on the Internet of Things can benefit from our technique. In conclusion, the LSSOA framework demonstrates the potential benefits of innovative intrusion detection methodologies by providing a strong tool to identify and prevent cyber-attacks in the IoMT context. Our research underlines the necessity for ongoing efforts to create effective and novel techniques to handle increasing cyber risks and the need of bolstering IoT security, especially in crucial areas like healthcare.

Using Dwarf mongoose-optimized and the federated learning (FL) approach, Tyagi and Bargavi (Tyagi & Bargavi, 2023) provide a smart intrusion detection apparatus called FIDANN, which safeguards the privacy of medical records by performing the finding task. Recent advancements in blockchain technology have made it possible to remove contaminating assaults and get full transparency and data integrity throughout a decentralised system with relatively little more work. Due of FL's ability to operate with smaller datasets, deploying it at the edge of the cloud makes it more difficult for attackers to gather information. The results show that the models we propose are more effective at handling the variety of data supplied by IoT gadgets.

A deep learning technique with user-defined characteristics is proposed for an IoT-based intrusion detection system in healthcare by Jeyanthi and Indrani (Jeyanthi & Indrani, 2023). In this research, we present a deep learning technique with specific features for IoT-based intrusion detection in the healthcare sector. The Internet is used in the proposed system to collect data in real time from a wide range of medical equipment and sensors in a healthcare setting. To identify and categorise intrusion attempts, the system uses a procedure. In order to train deep learning models, unique features are retrieved from incoming data streams. For IoTID20 with custom features utilising RNN-BiLSTM, the suggested system achieves an accuracy of 99.16%, an error rate of 0.008371%, when tested on a dataset consisting of various intrusion scenarios. The findings prove that the suggested system is capable of identifying and reducing security risks in healthcare settings. The approach may increase patients' sense of safety and confidentiality, which would be beneficial to healthcare overall.

In order to categorize arrhythmias in the cloud, Patel et al. (Patel, 2023) present a smart security approach that combines an computing. Sensors are used to record the patient's ECG in both a static and dynamic setting, and this data is then uploaded to the cloud, where the clustering of the network and cluster head (CH) selection are industrialized with the help of the Hybrid Tempest optimisation procedure. The Neural network tempest optimisation method, and the intrusion detection model is developed and applied in the cloud storage for safe data access in the healthcare industry. Only authorised people are given access to the data, which may then be used in diagnostic procedures. Maximum values for accuracy (95.72 percent), sensitivity (96.78 percent), and specificity (95.29 percent) are found while evaluating approach.

An effective intrusion detection solution for cloud-based systems was developed by Abd Elaziz et al. (Abd Elaziz et al., 2023) by combining breakthroughs in swarm intelligence (SI) procedures with advances in deep neural networks. To begin, ideal characteristics are extracted from the IoT IDS data using deep neural networks. Then, using the new SI optimizer, the Capuchin Search Algorithm are used to evaluate the efficacy of the created model, CNN-CapSA. In addition, we take into account rigorous empirical comparisons to different optimisation algorithms utilising a wide range of performance metrics for classifying data. The results showed that the devised method had respectable overall dataset performance.

A detailed study of XAI methods for anomaly-based networks has been presented by Moustafa et al. (Moustafa et al., 2023). First, we take a look at how XAI models might improve anomaly-based IoT detection systems by adding trust and confidence to such systems' detections. Second, we take a look at a variety of AI models, and discuss their use in IoT ecosystems and anomaly detection applications. We also go through how DL can efficiently learn from massive IoT datasets, leading to improved detection and understanding of security incidents. Third, we provide current studies that show how XAI, anomaly-based IDS, and the Internet of Things all interact with one another. Last but not least, we highlight future avenues for study by discussing the existing difficulties and potential solutions of XAI for security requests within the context of cyber defence for IoT networks. Our research shows that XAI models are needed for new cybersecurity applications, which help decision-makers make sense of security incidents in vulnerable IoT networks.

Ghazal et al. (Ghazal et al., 2023) hopes to learn more about Data Stream Mining methods through their research. These algorithms can deal with non-hierarchical and imbalanced datasets, such as those produced by Mirai Attacks, because of the precision and interferences of the measurements. These crucial perspectives cannot be improved with just one strategy. This calls for the use of an Ensemble method. In our research, we found that a group of meta or selective classifiers that collaborate in real time based on temporal Data Mining may get better results than their competitors. Meta-heuristics based on a network strategy for recognising the most common attacking pattern with an on-the-fly scheme are ideal for addressing the issues of such applications with regard to maintainability and security. These are implemented in the CRUD operations of Big Data systems (create, read, update, delete).

In order to identify network abnormalities, Bhavsar et al. (Bhavsar et al., 2023) created a system that uses a deep learning model called Networks (PCC-CNN). Key characteristics are extracted using a linear basis and then fed into a Convolutional Neural Network to form the PCC-CNN model. It uses both binary and multiclass classification to identify anomalies and identify different sorts of assault. The model is tested on the NSL-KDD, CICIDS-2017, and IOTID20 datasets, all of which are freely available to the public. In order to assess the efficacy of PCC-based Machine Learning models, we first train and test five distinct models Using the KNN and CART models, we are able to obtain equivalent accuracy of 98%, 99%, and 98%, respectively, across all three datasets. However, our suggested PCC-CNN model outperforms state-of-the-art methods, with a detection accuracy rate of just 0.001%. classifiers, respectively, demonstrate the integrated model's potential. Finally, we contrast our PCC-CNN model with five standard PCC-ML models and explain our findings. The IDS we propose, which is is superior to the current state of the art.

Sharma et al. offer a IDS solution for IoT systems by employing the Deep Learning framework. In specific, a model of a Deep -based feature selection has been developed, where features of correlation are ignored. Parameters and fine-tune the model. For this, we employ the UNSW-NB15 dataset, which includes four categories of attacks. The proposed model was 84% accurate. To fix the class imbalance problems in the dataset, we employed dataset.

Adaptive Swish-based Deep Multi-Layer Perceptron (ASDMLP) is a deep learning (DL) model proposed by Rajalakshmi et al. (Rajalakshmi et al., 2023) for detecting assaults and intrusions in the IoT healthcare (IoT-HC) platform. First, the Probability-based Fuzzy C-Means (PFCM) model is used to cluster the patients' sensor network. After the devices are clustered, cluster heads (CHs) are chosen from among the cluster members according to the energy, degree of the sensor devices in order to aggregate the data collected by the devices. Information gathered by CHs is sent to a cloud server through the base station (BS). The suggested technique employs an IDS on the cloud by using public datasets for DL model training. Using the Opposition and Coyotes Optimisation Algorithm (OGCOA), the DL method first processes the data and then chooses the best topographies from the dataset. These top characteristics for HC data intrusion detection are trained using the ASDMLP. The results show that the suggested method is actual for intrusion detection (ID) on real-time IoT datasets without sacrificing network lifetime or EC.

Saif et al. (Saif et al., 2022) detail a IoT-based applications like healthcare. Critical health data is gathered by biomedical sensors in IoT-based smart healthcare and then transferred to a cloud server for analysis. The information contained in an electronic health record (EHR) is very private and protected. In this dataset have been utilised to evaluate the proposed HIIDS's performance. Accurate attack features is accomplished with the help of algorithms like Known Nearest Neighbour (kNN) and Decision Tree (DT), while computation cost is kept to a minimum by means of best feature selection using metaheuristic algorithms like Particle Swarm Algorithm (GA). Additionally, a new hybrid approach to feature selection and classification is presented. After the dataset has been preprocessed in Python, six variants of the projected hybrid algorithms are developed in MATLAB 2019b, integrating GA, PSO, DE with kNN, DT. Precision, usage, and CPU burden have all been measured. For the classes, respectively, the GA-DT variant achieves an accuracy of 96.90%, and 100% with the aid of 8-10 features, outperforming works.

Zubair et al. (Zubair et al., 2022) propose a decentralised, predictive, DL-based technique for autonomously identifying and blocking hateful traffic and offering an end-to-end defence against network threats in IoMT devices. Additionally, we provide the BlueTack first dataset of its kind for detecting vulnerabilities in Bluetooth and Bluetooth classic. UsingTack dataset, we created a multi-layered intrusion finding system based on deep learning. Using the offered multi-layer intrusion detection models, we are able to achieve F1 scores.

Using the Ant Lion Optimizer method, Alamro et al. (Alamro et al., 2023) demonstrate a Blockchain-assisted IoT healthcare system. IoT medical devices may now send sensitive patient information over the internet safely, thanks to the BHS-ALOHDL method given here for detecting network breaches. ALO based feature subset selection (ALO-FSS) is used by the BHS-ALOHDL method to generate a collection of feature vectors for this purpose. In order to identify intrusions, the HDL model combines the properties of a (CNN) with those of a long short-term model. Finally, the appropriate hyperparameter tuning of the HDL technique is accomplished with the help of the flower pollination algorithm (FPA), leading to a higher detection rate. The ALOHDL scheme was evaluated experimentally on two benchmark datasets, and the results show that the BHS-ALOHDL approach outperforms the other models.

In order to identify malicious activity on IoT networks, Saheed et al. (Saheed et al., 2022) suggest an ML-IDS. The major emphasis of this study is on developing an IDS on ML-supervised algorithms. This dataset contains both recently observed assaults and typical network traffic, and these attacks have been classified into nine ends, we ran the numbers through six different machine learning models that had been offered. We compared our experimental results with the validation dataset using measures of accuracy, F1, precision,). We compared our findings to those of other research in the field and found that our 99.9% accuracies and 99.97% MCC were on par.

Wahab et al. (Wahab et al., 2022) provide a model that combines LSTM with GRU, or gated recurrent unit. Standard evaluation metrics and the publicly accessible CICDDoS2019 dataset were used to rigorously test the proposed model. Additionally, the proposed framework is validated by being compared to additional classifiers like cu-GRU+ -BLSTM. To further demonstrate the usefulness of the suggested model, we have compared it to previous research. Last but not least, we perform 10-fold validation to ensure the reliability of our findings. With remarkable results like 99.01% accuracy, 99.12% F1-score, the suggested method has surpassed the literature.

ARCHITECTURE OF IOMT

The literature featured a wide variety of architectural proposals. Three-layer designs have been proposed by certain studies. More than three levels of complexity have been proposed in other studies. Fog/cloud computing, Blockchain are only some of the technologies proposed for managing medical data. The authors of this overview article presume that three distinct layers of infrastructure are necessary to adequately segment IoMT architecture. These levels are detailed below and depicted in figure 1; they include data acquisition, individual servers, and medical servers.

Figure 1. Internet-of-Medical-Things (IoMT) Construction.

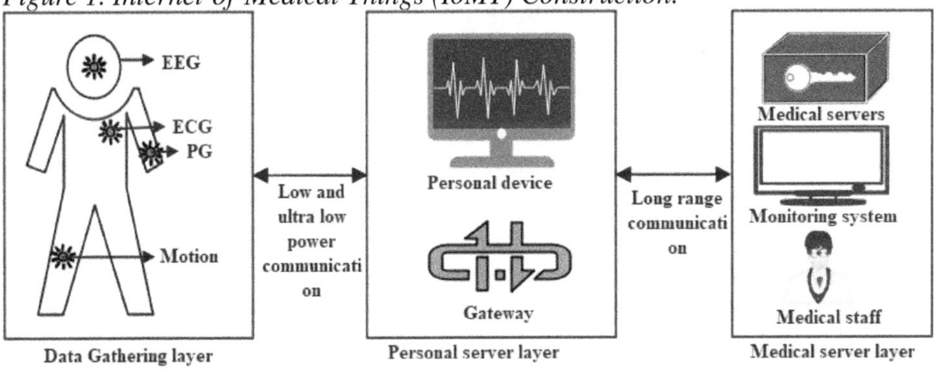

A. Data Acquisition Layer

The use of sensors allows the real and virtual worlds to communicate with one another. Specifically, (Ifran & Ahmad, 2018) these four types of technology:

Internally implanted devices (IMDs) are one type of implemented device.

Smartwatches, PGs, and EEGs are all examples of gadgets that may be worn on a person's person.

The patient's surrounding environment can be monitored via ambient devices like temperature sensors.

Sensors such as imaging equipment are examples of stationary devices used in hospitals.

Sensing technologyThese devices use physiological low-power compute, communication, and storage components to gather biological and contextual information (Moosavi et al., 2015). Technology bridges the gap between the real and the virtual. Specifically, (Ifran & Ahmad, 2018) these four types of technology: The information gathered is put to use in the administration of patient care and the making of accurate diagnoses. These medical gadgets have additional restrictions on the inside and in terms of communication. Internal medical implants may be rejected by the human immune system, causing infection, inflammation, and patient pain. The batteries in these medical devices have a limited lifespan and will eventually need to be replaced. When employing common security methods like encryption, the battery life of the implant quickly depletes, requiring a potentially dangerous surgical procedure to replace it. The sheer quantity of log files precludes their utility for monitoring communications on medical devices. Medical gadgets can only provide close-range communication due to energy limits. Most wearable devices are limited in their ability to fully interpret the data they perceive because of size, computational power, and battery consumption limits. Instead, low-power computing units compress the detected data before transmitting it to individual devices (such as techniques

B. Personal Server Layer

Personal servers, such as cellphones and conventional devices, such as gateways, can receive physiological data from medical equipment (Sun et al., 2019). Remotely processed and stored patient data is then sent to medical data centres with central servers. The personal server stores and processes the medical data that has been sent to it; for instance, the data can be encrypted or compressed, and additional contextual information added to them (such as location and time) can be used to detect abnormal behaviour. The processed data are then transmitted over wired or long-range wireless technologies, to a remote medical server using a medical standard format, such as Health Level-7. This layer's goal is to enable retransmission of medical data in the event of an interrupted network connection to medical servers, thereby supporting heterogeneous communication and node mobility (Wazid et al., 2019).

C. Medical Server Layer

Centralised patient management, complicated and extended behaviour analysis, and data correlation are all made possible by the system's high-performance data centre. An intelligent, cloud-based server is also included. It gathers evidence from many sources and stores additional patient medical records. Data can be accessed by the pharmacy (for summary or billing purposes), the doctor, and the patient. Medical histories and invoices can be seen digitally by patients via a website or a mobile device. Electronic health records (EHR), electronic medical records (EMR), and prescription websites all contain data from a wide variety of sources. The outcome is that the data is always available to both doctors and patients. Any user who shares or gets health information will be notified automatically.

D. Challenges of Healthcare

The application of cutting-edge medical technologies is complicated by a number of variables impacting healthcare systems (Akpakwu et al., 2017):

Non-Patient-Centered: It's not helpful for those who are very unwell and need to see a doctor but can't because they've been instructed to rest instead. A patient's supervisor, on the other hand, must find time in their hectic schedule to visit the doctor.

Non- customized: a doctor's prescription isn't based on the specifics of the patient's condition, but rather on an average across the community, which may or may not be effective. Low- and middle-income people can no longer afford the high expense of therapy for any one illness or condition.

Certain hospital services may be underutilised because they are inaccessible to people with disabilities who are unable to use them on their own. This is why many people are at risk when they don't have easy access to basic services.

It is crucial to provide guaranteed connectivity devices connected in health-care, information.

Power and Price: In IoT, a significant price is paid due to the enormous sum of linked devices and sensors. The healthcare industry faces a significant problem in reducing power consumption and costs while maintaining a high number of interconnected equipment and sensors.

In all of them, from the smart home to the smart transit scheme to the smart healthcare system, security and privacy are paramount. Security is a huge issue with the IoT because of all the different types of devices that are interconnected. As a result of flaws in the IoT design, the healthcare industry is sometimes more susceptible to intrusion (Otoum et al., 2021). In order to increase people's trust in e-health services, it is crucial that (IoT) be used securely while communicating between healthcare equipment and the cloud. However, the system should be more secure and vulnerable to fewer assaults (Subasi et al., 2021).

METHODOLOGY

3.1. Datasets Description

1) First dataset Description

To validate the performance of the developed methods, a healthcare dataset named WUSTLEHMS 2020 is used (Hady et al., 2020). The WUSTL- contains both the network flow and patient biometric data. This dataset consists of different types of cyberattacks such as MitM attacks, data injection, and spoofing. Table 1 displays statistical data from the WUSTL-EHMS-2020 dataset. This dataset contains 44 features, 35 of flow data, eight biometric features from patients' data, and one label feature.

TABLE 1. DATASET STATISTICAL INFORMATION.

Measurement	Value
Dataset size	4.4 MB
Number of normal	14272 (87.5%)
Number of attack data	2046 (12.5%)
Total number of data	16318

2) Second Dataset Description

The Internet of Things Dataset 1 (IoHT-D1) (Abdulwahid, 2022) keeps track of network intrusions and can be used to identify those responsible. This malicious spyware has several security risks, including denial-of-service attacks, worms, backdoors, and fuzzers. The Dataset also contains network packets. There are 175,341 records for assaults and routine attacks are all shown in the graphic. Reorganisation of IoHT-D1 services is shown in Figure 2. Accomplishments in spying and backdooring are included with generic, shell code, and DOS successes.

Figure 2. Repartition of services in IoHT-D1.

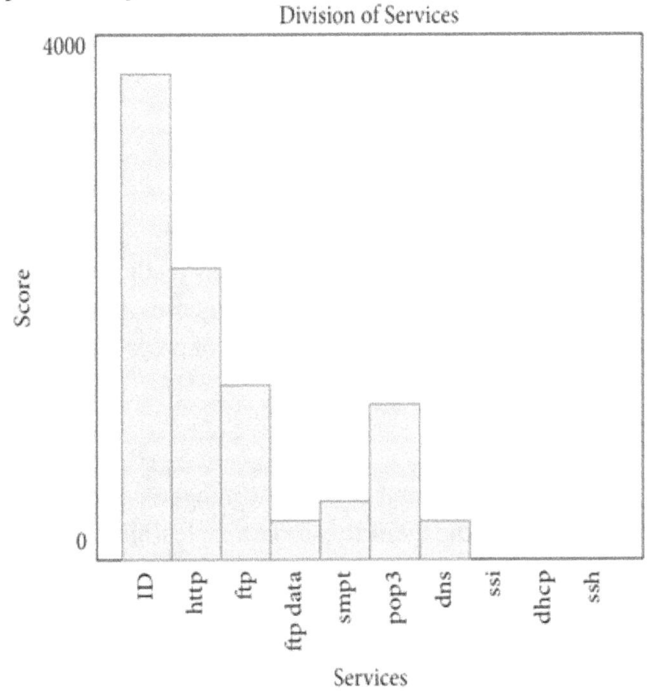

It was determined to be within acceptable limits for there to be an annual average of 3,500 incidents. These data were collected via Kaggle (an online data service). The dataset (Outcome) consists of independent variables and a single linked variable.

3) Third Dataset Description

The Internet of Health Things Dataset 2 (IoHT-D2) is the third dataset utilised in this study. The IoHT-D2 data set has resolved the issues that were raised in the previous version. This updated serve as a useful benchmark for academics likening diverse intrusion finding methods, which is especially important given the lack of publicly systems. Table 2 displays the distribution of the samples.

Table 2. Sample delivery.

Samples	Training set	Testing set
IoHT-D2	16000	7000
IoHT-D1	22330	1200

There is sufficient data in both the training and test sets for IoHT-D2. This advantage allows researchers to examine the entire dataset without picking a representative sample. This will allow researchers to easily compare the results of their separate studies.

2.2. Raw Data Processing.

The raw data was collected. Multiple strategies were employed to finally get rid of null values and duplicates. In data mining, this method is used to transform unstructured data into a structured database. In other cases, however, there are data gaps or inconsistencies in the real world. Examples of preprocessing steps include:

1) Data Balancing.

Predictive modelling is hampered by skewed categorisation. Each class has an equal number of examples in the majority of machine learning classification strategies. This results in a shortage of models from marginalised communities. This red flag when you think about how much more prone minorities are to be misclassified than the dominant group. Outliers have been removed from the dataset, making it more suitable for analysis. The practise of resampling has been greatly influenced by these investigations. To conserve data, under sampling can be used to acquire records from each cluster. Oversampling allows for the creation of more realistic synthetic samples, rather than carbon copies of data from underrepresented groups.

2) Removing of Outliers.

The study can't proceed without a complete and consistent dataset to conduct data mining analysis on. There will always be "outliers" in any dataset. Values that are out of the norm in a dataset are called outliers. Data outliers may have resulted from human mistake, misinterpretation, or faulty equipment. It has to be scrubbed from the database before any serious statistical or scientific study can begin. Future processing might be affected by insufficient or incorrect data outlines.

The IQR method is used to remove outliers from boxplot data when the data falls outside of a predetermined threshold. The IQR is the distance between the median and the upper and lower quartiles. Statistical procedures such as the interquartile range (IQR), the z-score, and data smoothing are used in this study to identify anomalies. The interquartile range (IQR) is found by adding the data at the 25th and 75th percentiles.

$$IQR = Q3 - Q1 \tag{1}$$

Proposed methodology

A Blockchain-Assisted Secure Data Transmission

Data generated by healthcare IoT devices is sent securely using BC technology in the study. A new time-stamped transaction is associated to and collected in the BC as a hash-chain of blocks (Rathore et al., 2020). The BC is a persistent distributed database. According to the fundamental BC methods, it is possible to make and store many copies of these blocks in a decentralised fashion. The identification that miners have begun consensus on the current state of network. There are several BC architectures to choose from, such as permission. The unique codes in each block are hashed, and the hashes of previous blocks in the chains are used to create a connection between the blocks they were mined from. In order to prove their legitimacy as leaders, many miners must do a series of calculations. One of these two methods is typically used to select a leader. The primary goal is to keep track of transactions that have been verified using a cryptographic hash function. The hash function's success can be attributed to its following characteristics.:

The hashing process completed quickly and with little extra work. BC blocks have been hash-confirmed as being related to their respective genesis blocks.
No matter the length of the input, the output will always be a set.
The output may be predictable in the sense that it always corresponds to the input.
It's conceivable the process can't be undone, therefore getting the same output as input could be impossible.
Changing the input even slightly results in different outcomes.

B Feature Selection using Walrus Optimization Algorithm
WaOA was developed with major motivation from mathematical models of these behaviours.

Algorithm initialization. The walruses of the WaOA population are the searchers in this population-based metaheuristic algorithm. Each walrus in WaOA is a potential optimisation solution. Therefore, the possible solutions to the issue variables are established by the locations of the walruses in the search space. Therefore, a vector, and the walrus population may be represented mathematically by a matrix known as the population matrix. Initial walrus populations in a system using WaOA are generated at random. Using equation (2), we can calculate the WaOA population matrix.

$$X = \begin{bmatrix} X_1 \\ \vdots \\ X_i \\ \vdots \\ X_N \end{bmatrix}_{N\times m} = \begin{bmatrix} x_{1,1} & \cdots & x_{1,j} & \cdots & x_{1,m} \\ \vdots & \ddots & \vdots & ⋰ & \vdots \\ x_{i,1} & \cdots & x_{i,j} & \cdots & x_{i,m} \\ \vdots & ⋰ & \vdots & \ddots & \vdots \\ x_{N,1} & \cdots & x_{N,j} & \cdots & x_{N,m} \end{bmatrix}_{N\times m} \quad (2)$$

where N is the total sum of walruses and m is the total sum of choice variables, X is the total population of walruses, X_i is the ith and x_(i,j) is the value of variable recommended by the ith walrus.

Each walrus represents a potential answer to the issue; by using the values it proposes for the choice variables, the objective function may be calculated. In (3), we define the walrus-obtained estimates of the goal function.

$$F = \begin{bmatrix} F_1 \\ \vdots \\ F_i \\ \vdots \\ F_N \end{bmatrix}_{N\times 1} = \begin{bmatrix} F(X_1) \\ \vdots \\ F\left(X_i\right) \\ \vdots \\ F(X_N) \end{bmatrix}_{N\times 1} \quad (3)$$

where F is a vector representing the goal purpose, and F_i is the objective function's value as calculated for the ith walrus.

The values of objective functions provide the most reliable indication of the merit of potential solutions. The best candidate is the one whose evaluation yields the highest value for the objective function. However, member is the candidate key set that yields the lowest value for the goal function. Each iteration, the goal function values are updated, and the members are adjusted accordingly.

Mathematical modelling of WaOA. Based on the natural behaviours of walruses, the process of updating their location in the WaOA is represented in three stages.

Phase 1: feeding strategy (exploration). More than sixty different marine creatures, including sea cucumbers, tunicates, soft corals, tube worms, prawns and numerous mollusks, make up the walruses' diet. However, walruses have a strong preference for mollusks, chiefly clams, which they find by grazing along the sea bottom and actively searching for food with their flippers and sensitive vibrissae. The tallest-tusked, strongest walrus in the group leads the others in the hunt for food. The candidates is represented by the length of the walruses' tusks. Accordingly, the key with the highest value for the goal function is the most formidable walrus. Since the walruses' search behaviour causes them to explore diverse parts of the search space, this boosts the exploratory capacity of the WaOA during a global search. Using equations (4) and (5), we can simulate the walruses' position-updating process, which is based on the feeding mechanism and directed by the group's most important member. The procedure begins with the generation of a new walrus position in accordance with the formula (4). If the value of the goal function increases, then this new location should replace the old one, as depicted in (5).

$$x_{i,j}^{P_1} = x_{i,j} + rand_{i,j}\left(SW_j - I_{i,j}.x_{i,j}\right) \tag{4}$$

$$X_i = \begin{cases} X_i^{P_1}, F_i^{P_1} < F_i \\ X_i, \ else \end{cases} \tag{5}$$

where $x_i^{P_1}$ is the new produced 1st phase, $x_{i,j}^{P_1}$ is its jth dimension, $F_i^{P_1}$ is which is measured as walrus, and $I_{i,j}$ are integers designated arbitrarily among 1 or 2. $I_{i,j}$ is used to boost the algorithm's examination capabilities; setting it to 2 results in more dramatic and far-reaching shifts in walrus positions than setting it to 1, the default number. These constraints enhance the algorithm's global search by allowing it to break out of the local optimum and locate the true sweet spot in the solution space.

Phase 2: migration. When the weather begins to warm up in the late summer, walruses have been observed migrating to rocky outcrops and beaches. The WaOA employs this migratory strategy to help the walruses in the search space locate promising new locations. Using equations (6) and (7), we can represent this behavioural mechanism quantitatively. Each walrus in this model moves to the location of another walrus (chosen at random) in a different part of the search space. So, we start by generating the suggested new position using (6). If the worth of the objective function increases because to this shift, then (7) states that walrus will switch to this new location.

$$X_{i,j}^{P_2} = \begin{cases} x_{i,j} + rand_{i,j}\cdot\left(x_{k,j} - I_{i,j}.x_{i,j}\right), F_k < F_i \ ; \\ x_{i,j} + rand_{i,j}\cdot(x_{i,j} - x_{k,j}), \ else \end{cases} \tag{6}$$

$$X_i = \begin{cases} X_i^{P_2}, F_i^{P_2} < F_i \\ X_i, \ else \end{cases} \tag{7}$$

where $X_i^{P_2}$ is the novel produced 2nd phase, $X_{i,j}^{P_2}$ is its jth dimension, $F_i^{P_2}$ is its role value, X_k, $k \in \{1, 2, \ldots, N\}$ and $k \neq i$, is the site of designated walrus to travel towards it, $x_{k,j}$ is its jth dimension, and F_k is its objective function charge.

Phase 3: escaping and fighting against marauders (exploitation). Both the polar bear and the killer whale represent a constant threat to walruses. The walruses' location changes close to where they are because of the tactics they employ to avoid and combat these predators. WaOA's ability to harness power in the local space surrounding candidate solutions is enhanced by simulating this natural behaviour of walruses. WaOA design assumes this change occurs in a matching walrus-centered neighbourhood with a specified radius since it occurs close to the position of each walrus. Since the algorithm initially prioritises a global search to locate the sweet spot in the search space, the neighborhood's radius is treated as a variable and starts at the largest possible value before shrinking as the algorithm progresses. In this iteration of WaOA, we have employed local lower/upper boundaries to generate a variable radius via iterations of the algorithm. In order to model this occurrence in WaOA, we assume a neighbourhood surrounding each walrus and, using (8) and (9), produce a new position for each walrus at random inside this neighbourhood. Consequently, if the goal function value is increased, the new location will replace the old one as shown in Eq. (10).

$$x_{i,j}^{P_3} = x_{i,j} + \left(lb_{local,j}^{t} + \left(ub_{local,j}^{t} - rand\,.\,lb_{local,j}^{t}\right)\right) \tag{8}$$

$$Local\ bounds: \begin{cases} lb_{local,j}^{t} = \dfrac{lb_j}{t} \\ ub_{local,j}^{t} = \dfrac{ub_j}{t} \end{cases} \tag{9}$$

$$X_i = \begin{cases} X_i^{P_3}, F_i^{P_3} < F_i \\ X_i, else \end{cases} \tag{10}$$

where $x_i^{P_3}$ is the novel generated position based on the 3rd phase, $x_{i,j}^{P_3}$ is its jth dimension, $F_i^{P_3}$ is its objective contour, lb_j and ub_j are the bounds of the jth variable, respectively, $lb_{local,j}^{t}$ and $ub_{local,j}^{t}$ are local for the jth variable, correspondingly, to pretend local candidate solutions.

Once the first WaOA repetition is complete, new values are derived for the walruses' location and the functions depending on the implementation third phases. Iteratively updating and bettering potential solutions in accordance with the WaOA procedures established by Eqs. 410 until the last iteration is reached. When the algorithm has finished running, WaOA presents the best candidate key it has discovered as the final answer to the problem.

C Classification process using SDPN

We employed classifier is then fed the most abstract illustration of the consequence. Reduces the amount of time required to train an SDPN by removing superfluous features and instead selecting optimum features using WaOA. The best way to construct deep networks in SDPN also enables learning representations of data from finite samples of low size. Starting with network that may be biassed but not overfit (i.e., have low variance), the approach then allows us to gradually deepen the network while simultaneously decreasing the bias and increasing the variance. Therefore, this technique might be used to control curve.

DPN begins layer building by linearly allocating a degree-1 polynomial purpose (bias) across the training dataset; the resulting collection of vectors is then separated out using Singular Vector Decomposition (SVD). All values acquired by training cases are extended at the first layer's outputs. The result is that the values acquired by the first layer nodes and the expanded by the values produced by any degree-2 polynomial.

Letting $R = \{r_1, r_2, \ldots, r_m\} \in R^{mxd}$ gives a set of m training trials, where r_i is a trial. Then, the transmission the degree-1 polynomial training statistics as shadows:

$$\{(\langle w, [1\ r_1]\rangle, \ldots, \langle w, [1\ r_m]\rangle) : w \in R^{d+1}\} \tag{11}$$

which is the $(d + 1)$ - subspace of R_m. Consequently, to build the basis we need to find $d + 1$ vectors $w_1, \ldots, w_{d+1}$. So, $\left\{ \left(\langle w_j, [1\ r_1]\rangle, \ldots, \langle w_j, [1, r_m]\rangle \right) \right\}_{j=1}^{d+1}$ vectors, this can be produced by using Singular Vector Decomposition (SVD) to end up with linear alteration that quantified by a matrix W, which maps $[1\ X]$ into the produced basis, in which the columns of W stipulate the $d + 1$ linear function to form the initial functions as:

$$n_j^i(r) = \langle W_j, [1\ R]\rangle \tag{12}$$

where $\left\{ \left(n_j^i(r_1), \ldots, n_j^1(r_m) \right) \right\}_{j=1}^{d+1}$ is the foundation for all dataset. If F^1 refers to $m \times (d + 1)$ vectors of this matrix, then $F_{i,j}^1 = n_j^1(r_1)$.

The first layer of the network is outputs that encompass all the values found using linear functions on the dataset used for training. Degree-2 and degree-3 bases can be way. Then, as:

$$\sum_i g_i(r) h_i(r) + k(r) \tag{13}$$

where, $g_i(r)$ are polynomials, $h_i(r)$ are $(s - 1)$ - and $k(r)$ is grade at most s-1. The nodes then it extends the polynomials g_i, h_i,and k, So we can express polynomial as:

$$\sum_i \left(\sum_j a_j^{(g_i)} n_j^1(r) \right) + \left(\sum_x a_x^{(h_i)} n_x^1(r) \right) + \left(\sum_j a_j^{(k)} n_j^1(r) \right)$$

$$= \left(\sum_{j,x} n_j^1(r)\, n_x^1(r) \right) \left(\sum_i a_j^{(g_i)} a_x^{(h_i)} \right) + \sum_j n_j^1(r) \left(a_j^{(k)} \right) \tag{14}$$

with the scalars a and a's involved. This means that the sum of all outputs from nodes in the first layer, as well as the sum of the outputs from any two layer multiplied

$$x_{i,j}(t+1) = T_{pos(j)} + C \times Z\cos\left(2\pi r_4\right) \times \left(T_{pos(j)} - x_{i,j}(t)\right) \tag{25}$$

where $x(t)$ and $x(t+1)$ are the sites, correspondingly. The following revised version of the predator-prey relationship can be reached by combining Eqs. (18) and (25).

$$x_{i,j}(t+1) = \begin{cases} x_{i,j}(t) + 0.5\begin{bmatrix} \left(2 \times C \times Z \times P_{pos(j)} - x_{i,j}(t)\right) \\ +(2(1-C))Z\mu_{(i)} - x_{i,j}(t)\big) \end{bmatrix} \left(26a\right) \\ T_{pos}(j) + C \times Z \times \cos\left(2\pi r_4\right) \times \left(T_{pos(j)} - x_{i,j}(t)\right) \left(26b\right) \end{cases} \tag{26}$$

r_5 is a accidental sum among 0 and 1, and $\beta = 0.1$ is limit If $r_5 < \beta$ the mediator is painstaking a predator, the site inform formula is (26a); if $r_5 \geq \beta$ the manager is considered prey, the site inform formula is (26b).

Enhanced Hunter–prey Optimization (IHPO) Procedure
2.2.2.

1) The randomization factor is the primary adjusting knob for any metaheuristic algorithm. Instead, we adjusted the randomization using a new control parameter we named to avoid stagnation and premature conjunction. The single random variable in Eq (26) of the HBO method is the interval rand [0,1]. The following is a definition of the recently introduced parameter that helps alter the search's focal point:

$$\beta = 2 \times rand - 1 \tag{27}$$

2) A major fault in the HPO algorithm is that the transfer parameter is not considered during exploration and exploitation, which leads to an unstable search and extra time wasted. To fix this, we provide a new parameter known as the CP, or CP change. Exploration can be sped up and the odds of discovery improved with the help of a periodic parameter known as CP.

$$CP = \sin\left(C - \tfrac{t}{T}\right) \tag{28}$$

Let,

$$a = \beta \times CP \tag{29}$$

$x_{i,j}(t+1)$

$$= \begin{cases} x_{i,j}(t) + 0.5\left[\left(a \times 2 \times C \times Z \times P_{pos(j)} - x_{i,j}(t)\right) + \left(2(1 - C)Z_{\mu_{(j)}} - x_{i,j}(t)\right)\right] \\ T_{pos}(j) + a \times C \times Z \times cos\left(2\pi r_4\right) \times \left(T_{pos}(j) - x_{i,j}(t)\right) \end{cases} \tag{30}$$

From the optimal solution of IHPO, the SDPN classifies the traffic flow effectively and improves the accuracy of secured data.

3 EXPERIMENTAL RESULTS

This section evaluates and analyzes the performance consequences of the developed intelligent detection model. Also, this section presents the used dataset to validate and evaluate the proposed techniques. Additionally, a comparison with the existing provided to attest the efficacy of the suggested techniques. The trials were conducted using windows 10 with an Intel (R) Core (TM) processor i7- 3.60 GHz.

5.1. Performances Metrics

The evaluation criteria include Sensitivity (SE), Specificity (SP), Accuracy (AC), F1 measurement and precision, which are given in equation (31 to 34)

$$SE = \frac{tp}{tp + fn} \tag{31}$$

$$SP = \frac{tn}{tn + fp} \tag{32}$$

$$AC = \frac{tp + tn}{tp + fp + tn + fn} \tag{33}$$

$$F1 - measure = 2 \times \frac{(Precision \times Recall)}{(Precision + Recall)} \tag{34}$$

5.2. Performance Investigation of Projected model on three datasets

In this section, the validation analysis of projected model on three datasets in terms of various metrics. The existing models such as LSSOA (Goswami et al., 2023), DMO-ANN (Tyagi & Bargavi, 2023), RNN-BiLSTM (Jeyanthi & Indrani, 2023), ASDMLP (Rajalakshmi et al., 2023) and FPA-LSTM (Alamro et al., 2023) uses different datasets, therefore all models are implemented with the considered three datasets and results are averaged in Table 3, 4 and 5.

Table 3. Experimental Analysis on Proposed Model on Wustl-Ehms-2020

Classifiers	Sensitivity	Specificity	Precision	Accuracy	F-Score
LSSOA (Goswami et al., 2023)	84.27	72.45	76.34	72.45	74.11
DMO-ANN (Tyagi & Bargavi, 2023)	88.67	87.91	78.75	78.35	77.72
RNN-BiLSTM (Jeyanthi & Indrani, 2023)	89.55	84.18	79.79	79.25	79.28
ASDMLP (Rajalakshmi et al., 2023)	90.78	88.27	82.51	89.20	87.18
FPA-LSTM (Alamro et al., 2023)	92.16	90.47	87.16	91.60	89.47
IHPO-SDPN	95.87	92.26	93.98	94.64	90.25

In above Table 3 characterise that the Experimental Analysis on proposed Model on WUSTL-EHMS-2020. In the analysis of LSSOA (Goswami et al., 2023) perfect attained sensitivity as 84.27 also specificity score as 72.45 then precision level of 76.34 and the accuracy rate as 72.45 and then lastly F-score as 74.11 correspondingly. Then the DMO-ANN (Tyagi & Bargavi, 2023) perfect attained sensitivity as 88.67 also specificity score as 87.91 then precision level of 78.75 and the accuracy rate as 78.35 and then lastly F-score as 77.72 correspondingly. Then the RNN-BiLSTM (Jeyanthi & Indrani, 2023) perfect attained sensitivity as 89.5527 also specificity score as 84.18 and the accuracy rate as 79.25 and then lastly F-score as 79.28 correspondingly. Then the ASDMLP (Rajalakshmi et al., 2023) perfect classical attained sensitivity as 90.78 also specificity score as 88.27 then precision level of 82.51 and the accuracy rate as 89.20 and then lastly F-score as 87.18 correspondingly. Then the FPA-LSTM (Alamro et al., 2023) perfect attained sensitivity as 92.1627 also specificity score as then precision level of 90.47 and the accuracy rate as 91.60 and then lastly F-score as 89.47 correspondingly. Then the IHPO-SDPN perfect attained sensitivity as 95.87 also specificity score as 92.26 then precision level of 93.98 and the accuracy rate as 94.64 and then lastly F-score as 90.25 correspondingly.

Figure 3. Accuracy Analysis of various models

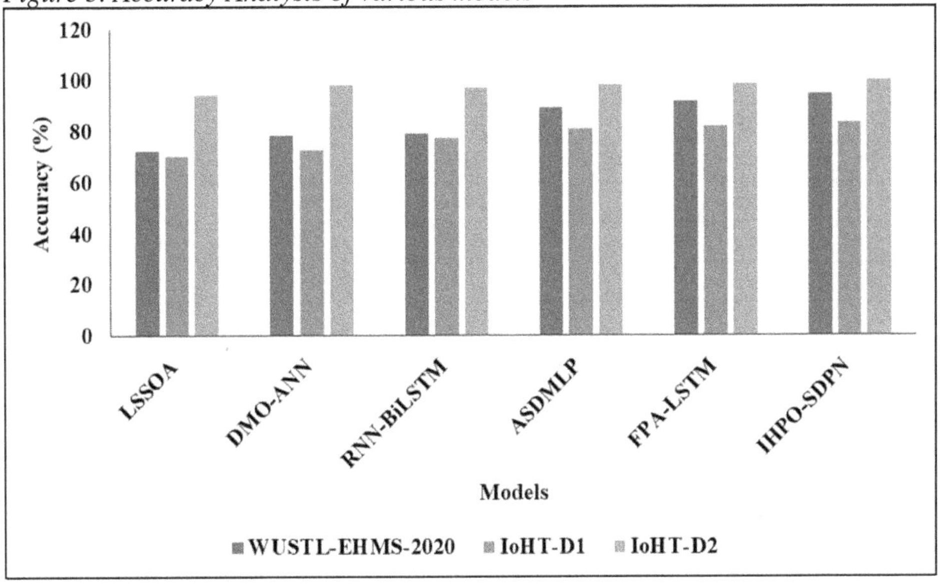

Figure 4. Sensitivity Performance for different techniques

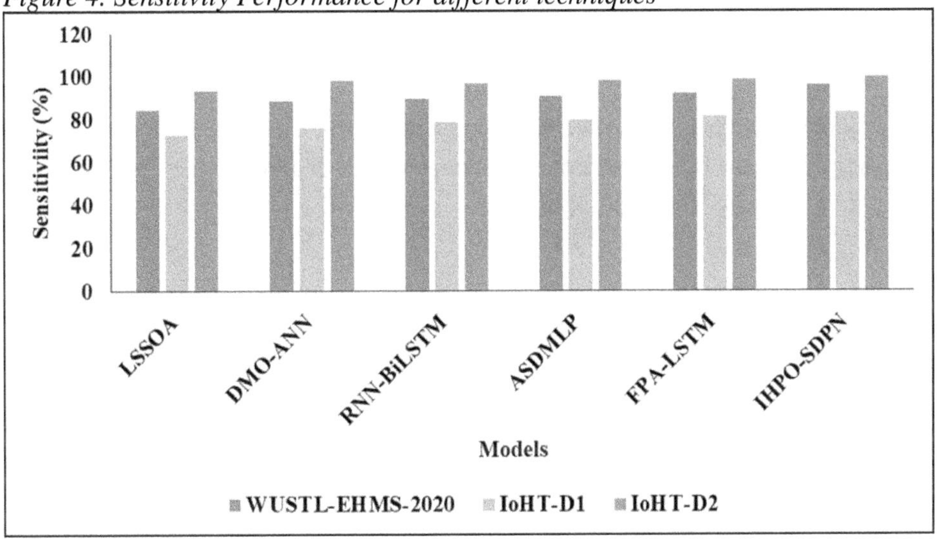

Table 4. Validation Analysis of Proposed Model On Ioht-D1

Classifiers	Sensitivity	Specificity	Precision	Accuracy	F-Score
LSSOA (Goswami et al., 2023)	72.5	73.7	71.4	70	72
DMO-ANN (Tyagi & Bargavi, 2023)	76.25	75.6	72.9	72.5	73
RNN-BiLSTM (Jeyanthi & Indrani, 2023)	78.75	78.4	76.3	77.5	75
ASDMLP (Rajalakshmi et al., 2023)	79.44	80.13	79.95	80.87	79.44
FPA-LSTM (Alamro et al., 2023)	81.39	81.74	80.34	81.96	80.74
IHPO-SDPN	83.05	82.07	82.95	83.34	81.92

In Table 4 signifies that the Validation Analysis of Proposed Model on IoHT-D1. In the analysis of LSSOA (Goswami et al., 2023) model reached the sensitivity as 72.5 and specificity score as 73.7 and precision range of 71.4 and accuracy as 70 and F1-score as 72 correspondingly. Then the DMO-ANN (Tyagi & Bargavi, 2023) model reached the sensitivity as 76.25 and specificity score as 75.6 and precision range of 72.9 and accuracy as 72.5 and F1-score as 73 correspondingly. Then the RNN-BiLSTM (Jeyanthi & Indrani, 2023) model reached the sensitivity as 78.75 and specificity score as 78.4 and precision range of 76.3 and accuracy as 77.5 and F1-score as 75 correspondingly. Then the ASDMLP (Rajalakshmi et al., 2023) model reached the sensitivity as 79.44 80.13 and specificity score as 79.95 and accuracy as 80.87 and F1-score as 79.44 correspondingly. Then the FPA-LSTM (Alamro et al., 2023) model reached the sensitivity as 81.39 and specificity score as 81.74 and precision range of 80.34 and accuracy as 81.96 and F1-score as 80.74 correspondingly. Then the IHPO-SDPN model reached the sensitivity as 83.05 and specificity score as 82.07 and precision range of 82.95 and accuracy as 83.34 and F1-score as 81.92 correspondingly.

Figure 5. Precision analysis

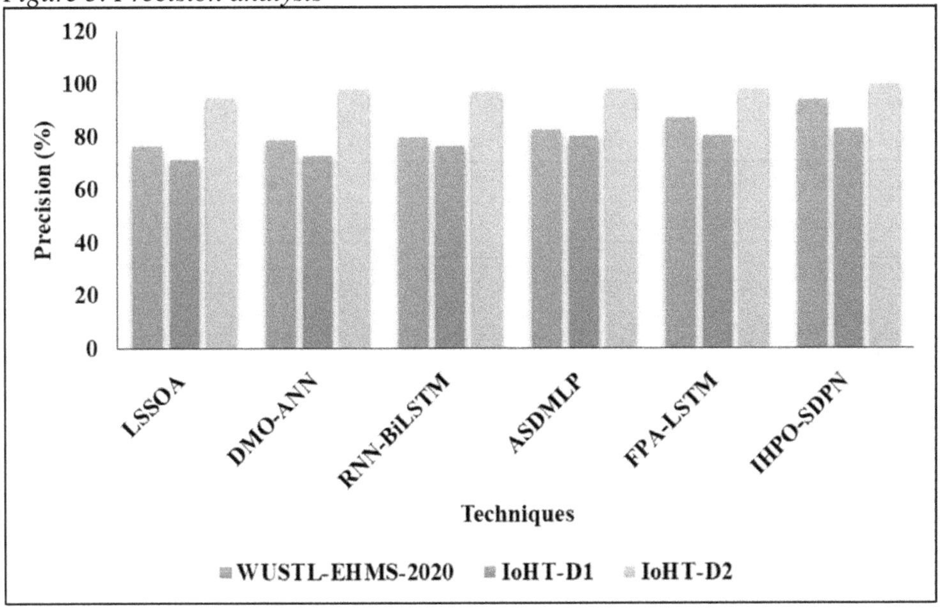

Figure 6. Comparison of different models in terms of specificity

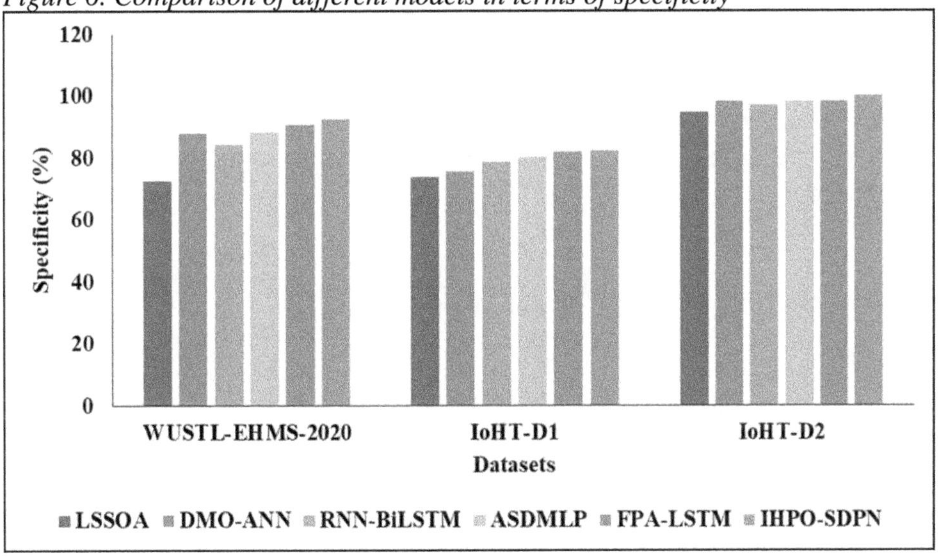

Table 5. Validation analysis of proposed model on ioht-d2

Models	Sensitivity	Specificity	Precision	Accuracy	F-Score
LSSOA (Goswami et al., 2023)	93.61	94.56	94.85	94.08	93.20
DMO-ANN (Tyagi & Bargavi, 2023)	98.00	98.00	98.00	98.14	98.00
RNN-BiLSTM (Jeyanthi & Indrani, 2023)	97.00	97.00	97.00	97.21	97.00
ASDMLP (Rajalakshmi et al., 2023)	98.00	98.00	98.00	98.14	98.00
FPA-LSTM (Alamro et al., 2023)	98.64	98.14	98.07	98.47	98.40
IHPO-SDPN	99.81	99.84	99.84	99.83	99.83

In above Table 5 characterize that the Validation analysis of Proposed model on IoHT-D2. In the comparison of LSSOA (Goswami et al., 2023) model reached the sensitivity as 93.61 and specificity score as 94.56 and precision range of 94.85 and accuracy as 94.08 and F1-score as 93.20 correspondingly. Then the DMO-ANN (Tyagi & Bargavi, 2023) model reached the sensitivity as 98.00 and specificity score as 98.00 and precision range of 98.00 and accuracy as 98.14 and F1-score as 98.00 correspondingly. Then the RNN-BiLSTM (Jeyanthi & Indrani, 2023) model reached the sensitivity as 97.00 and specificity score as 97.00 and precision range of 97.00 and accuracy as 97.21 and F1-score as 97.00 correspondingly. Then the ASDMLP (Rajalakshmi et al., 2023) model reached the sensitivity as 98.00 and specificity score as 98.00 and precision range of 98.00 and accuracy as 98.14 and F1-score as 98.00 correspondingly. Then the FPA-LSTM (Alamro et al., 2023) model reached the sensitivity as 98.64 and specificity score as 98.14 and then precision range of 98.07 and accuracy as 98.47 and F1-score as 98.40 correspondingly. Then the IHPO-SDPN model reached the sensitivity as 99.81 and specificity score as 99.84 and precision range of 99.84 and accuracy as 99.83 and F1-score as 99.83 correspondingly.

Figure 7. F-Score Prediction of different models

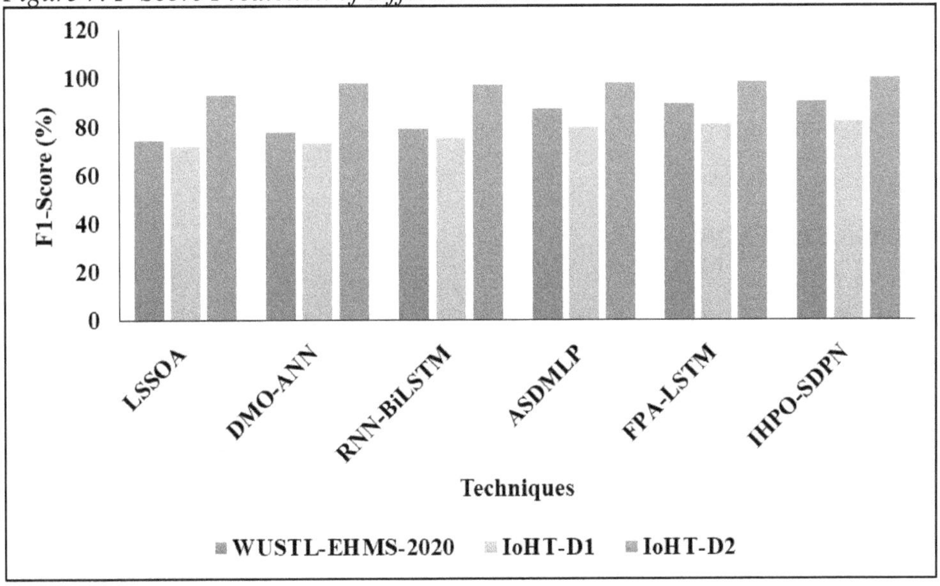

5.3. Performance analysis of various models on different training and testing ratio of data.

Table 6. Results of proposed perfect against diverse datasets.

Measures (Training/testing)	Precision	Sensitivity	Specificity	Accuracy	F-score
(70: 30)	0.9972	0.9969	0.9972	0.9971	0.9971
(60: 40)	0.9963	0.9953	0.9963	0.9958	0.9958
(80: 20)	0.9984	0.9981	0.9984	0.9983	0.9983
Average	**0.9973**	**0.9968**	**0.9973**	**0.9971**	**0.9971**

In above Table 6 represent that the Results of proposed perfect against diverse datasets. In the diverse datasets comparisons analysis of Training/testing (70: 30) dataset measures the precision rate as 0.9972 and sensitivity rate as 0.9969 and the specificity as 0.9972 and the specificity as 0.9971 and then F-score as 0.9971 correspondingly. Then the Training/testing (60: 40) dataset measures the precision rate as 0.9963 and sensitivity rate as 0.9953 and the specificity as 0.9963 and the accuracy as 0.9958 and then F-score as 0.9958 correspondingly. Then the Training/

testing (80: 20) dataset measures the precision rate as 0.99 and sensitivity rate as 84 0.9981 and the specificity as 0.9984 and the accuracy as 0.9983 and then F-score as 0.9983 correspondingly. Then the Average dataset measures the precision rate as 0.9973 and the specificity as 0.9968 and sensitivity rate as 0.9973 and the accuracy as 0.9971 and then F-score as 0.9971 correspondingly.

6. CONCLUSION

The goal of this investigate was to create the blockchain approach for application in a trustworthy healthcare system that makes use of the Things. The suggested method enables (IoT) medical devices to communicate medical data securely and detect intrusions. Then, the optimal features are selected by WaOA model, then the SDPN network is used for classification of traffic flow. The scalar factor of SDPN is optimally selected by IHPO model that improves the classification accuracy. To validate the proposed techniques, a modern healthcare dataset named WUSTL-EHMS-2020 is used along with IoHT-D1 and IoHT-D2. The proposed tactics accomplished a higher presentation result in contrast with the known tactics in terms of accuracy and specially in training time due of using a SDPN classifier characterized by one hidden layer. In the future, others data driven techniques and deep learning approach to detect intrusion in IoMT will be investigate. Additionally, more feature selection techniques will investigate and compare with our proposed work.

REFERENCES

Abd Elaziz, M., Al-qaness, M. A., Dahou, A., Ibrahim, R. A., & Abd El-Latif, A. A. (2023). Intrusion detection approach for cloud and IoT environments using deep learning and Capuchin Search Algorithm. *Advances in Engineering Software, 176*, 103402. DOI: 10.1016/j.advengsoft.2022.103402

Akpakwu, G.A.; Silva, B.J.; Hancke, G.P.; Abu-Mahfouz, A.M. (2017). A survey on 5G networks for the Internet of Things: Communication technologies and challenges. IEEE Access 2017, 6, 3619–3647.

Akram, F., Liu, D., Zhao, P., Kryvinska, N., Abbas, S., & Rizwan, M. (2021). Trustworthy intrusion detection in e-healthcare systems. *Frontiers in Public Health, 9*, 788347. DOI: 10.3389/fpubh.2021.788347 PMID: 34926397

Al Abdulwahid, A. (2022). Detection of Middlebox-Based Attacks in Healthcare Internet of Things Using Multiple Machine Learning Models. *Computational Intelligence and Neuroscience, 2022*, 2022. DOI: 10.1155/2022/2037954 PMID: 36479020

Al-Shammari, N. K., Syed, T. H., & Syed, M. B. (2021). An Edge–IoT framework and prototype based on blockchain for smart healthcare applications. Engineering, Technology &. *Applied Scientific Research, 11*(4), 7326–7331.

Alamro, H., Marzouk, R., Alruwais, N., Negm, N., Aljameel, S. S., Khalid, M., Hamza, M. A., & Alsaid, M. I. (2023). Modelling of Blockchain Assisted Intrusion Detection on IoT Healthcare System using Ant Lion Optimizer with Hybrid Deep Learning. *IEEE Access : Practical Innovations, Open Solutions, 11*, 82199–82207. DOI: 10.1109/ACCESS.2023.3299589

Alladi, T., Chamola, V., & Naren, . (2020). HARCI: A two-way authentication protocol for three entity healthcare IoT networks. *IEEE Journal on Selected Areas in Communications, 39*(2), 361–369. DOI: 10.1109/JSAC.2020.3020605

Bhavsar, M., Roy, K., Kelly, J., & Olusola, O. (2023). Anomaly-based intrusion detection system for IoT application. *Discover Internet of Things, 3*(1), 5. DOI: 10.1007/s43926-023-00034-5

Ghazal, T. M., Al-Dmour, N. A., Said, R. A., Omidvar, A., Khan, U. Y., Soomro, T. R., & Ali, L. (2023). DDoS Intrusion Detection with Ensemble Stream Mining for IoT Smart Sensing Devices. In *The Effect of Information Technology on Business and Marketing Intelligence Systems* (pp. 1987–2012). Springer International Publishing. DOI: 10.1007/978-3-031-12382-5_109

Goswami, N., Raj, S., Thakral, D., Arias-Gonzáles, J. L., Flores-Albornoz, J., Asnate-Salazar, E., Kapila, D., Yadav, S., & Kumar, S. (2023). Intrusion Detection System for IoT-based Healthcare Intrusions with Lion-Salp-Swarm-Optimization Algorithm: Metaheuristic-Enabled Hybrid Intelligent Approach. *Engineering and Science*. Advance online publication. DOI: 10.30919/es933

Hady, A. A., Ghubaish, A., Salman, T., Unal, D., & Jain, R. (2020). Intrusion detection system for healthcare systems using medical and network data: A comparison study. *IEEE Access : Practical Innovations, Open Solutions*, *8*, 106576–106584. DOI: 10.1109/ACCESS.2020.3000421

Hady, A. A., Ghubaish, A., Salman, T., Unal, D., & Jain, R. (2020). Intrusion detection system for healthcare systems using medical and network data: A comparison study. *IEEE Access : Practical Innovations, Open Solutions*, *8*, 106576–106584. DOI: 10.1109/ACCESS.2020.3000421

Iwendi, C., Moqurrab, S. A., Anjum, A., Khan, S., Mohan, S., & Srivastava, G. (2020). N-sanitization: A semantic privacy-preserving framework for unstructured medical datasets. *Computer Communications*, *161*, 160–171. DOI: 10.1016/j.comcom.2020.07.032

Jeyanthi, D. V., & Indrani, B. (2023). IoT-based intrusion detection system for healthcare using RNNBiLSTM deep learning strategy with custom features. *Soft Computing*, *27*(16), 1–16. DOI: 10.1007/s00500-023-08536-8

Kumaar, M. A., Samiayya, D., Vincent, P. D. R., Srinivasan, K., Chang, C. Y., & Ganesh, H. (2021). A hybrid framework for intrusion detection in healthcare systems using deep learning. *Frontiers in Public Health*, •••, 9. PMID: 35096763

Lee, J. D., Cha, H. S., Rathore, S., & Park, J. H. (2021). M-IDM: A Multi-Classification Based Intrusion Detection Model in Healthcare IoT. *Computers, Materials & Continua*, *67*(2).

Moosavi, S. R., Gia, T. N., Rahmani, A.-M., Nigussie, E., Virtanen, S., Isoaho, J., & Tenhunen, H. (2015). Sea: A secure and efficient authentication and authorization architecture for iot-based healthcare using smart gateways. *Procedia Computer Science*, *52*, 452–459. DOI: 10.1016/j.procs.2015.05.013

Moustafa, N., Koroniotis, N., Keshk, M., Zomaya, A. Y., & Tari, Z. (2023). Explainable Intrusion Detection for Cyber Defences in the Internet of Things: Opportunities and Solutions. *IEEE Communications Surveys and Tutorials*, *25*(3), 1775–1807. DOI: 10.1109/COMST.2023.3280465

Nandy, S., Adhikari, M., Khan, M. A., Menon, V. G., & Verma, S. (2021). An intrusion detection mechanism for secured IoMT framework based on swarm-neural network. *IEEE Journal of Biomedical and Health Informatics*, *26*(5), 1969–1976. DOI: 10.1109/JBHI.2021.3101686 PMID: 34357873

Naruei, I., Keynia, F., & Molahosseini, A. S. (2021). Hunter–prey optimization: Algorithm and applications. *Soft Computing*, *26*(3), 1279–1314. DOI: 10.1007/s00500-021-06401-0

Newaz, A. I., Sikder, A. K., Babun, L., & Uluagac, A. S. (2020, June). Heka: A novel intrusion detection system for attacks to personal medical devices. In *2020 IEEE Conference on Communications and Network Security (CNS)* (pp. 1-9). IEEE. DOI: 10.1109/CNS48642.2020.9162311

Nguyen, G. N., Le Viet, N. H., Elhoseny, M., Shankar, K., Gupta, B. B., & Abd El-Latif, A. A. (2021). Secure blockchain enabled Cyber–physical systems in healthcare using deep belief network with ResNet model. *Journal of Parallel and Distributed Computing*, *153*, 150–160. DOI: 10.1016/j.jpdc.2021.03.011

Nguyen, P. T., Huynh, V. D. B., Vo, K. D., Phan, P. T., Elhoseny, M., & Le, D. N. (2021). Deep Learning Based Optimal Multimodal Fusion Framework for Intrusion Detection Systems for Healthcare Data. *Computers, Materials & Continua*, *66*(3).

Otoum, S., Guizani, N., & Mouftah, H. (2021, June). Federated reinforcement learning-supported IDS for IoT-steered healthcare systems. In ICC 2021-IEEE International Conference on Communications (pp. 1-6). IEEE. DOI: 10.1109/ICC42927.2021.9500698

Otoum, Y., Wan, Y., & Nayak, A. (2021, December). Federated transfer learning-based ids for the internet of medical things (iomt). In 2021 IEEE Globecom Workshops (GC Wkshps) (pp. 1-6). IEEE.

Patel, S. K. (2023). Improving intrusion detection in cloud-based healthcare using neural network. *Biomedical Signal Processing and Control*, *83*, 104680. DOI: 10.1016/j.bspc.2023.104680

Qadri, Y. A., Nauman, A., Zikria, Y. B., Vasilakos, A. V., & Kim, S. W. (2020). The future of healthcare internet of things: A survey of emerging technologies. *IEEE Communications Surveys and Tutorials*, *22*(2), 1121–1167. DOI: 10.1109/COMST.2020.2973314

Rajalakshmi, R., Sivakumar, P., Prathiba, T., & Chatrapathy, K. (2023). An energy efficient deep learning model for intrusion detection in smart healthcare with optimal feature selection mechanism. Journal of Intelligent & Fuzzy Systems, (Preprint), 1-16.

Rathore, H., Mohamed, A., & Guizani, M. (2020, January). A survey of blockchain enabled cyber-physical systems. *Sensors (Basel), 20*(1), 282. DOI: 10.3390/s20010282 PMID: 31947860

RM, S. P., Maddikunta, P. K. R., Parimala, M., Koppu, S., Gadekallu, T. R., Chowdhary, C. L., & Alazab, M. (. (2020). An effective feature engineering for DNN using hybrid PCA-GWO for intrusion detection in IoMT architecture. *Computer Communications*, *160*, 139–149. DOI: 10.1016/j.comcom.2020.05.048

Saheed, Y. K., Abiodun, A. I., Misra, S., Holone, M. K., & Colomo-Palacios, R. (2022). A machine learning-based intrusion detection for detecting internet of things network attacks. *Alexandria Engineering Journal*, *61*(12), 9395–9409. DOI: 10.1016/j.aej.2022.02.063

Saif, S., Das, P., Biswas, S., Khari, M., & Shanmuganathan, V. (2022). HIIDS: Hybrid intelligent intrusion detection system empowered with machine learning and metaheuristic algorithms for application in IoT based healthcare. *Microprocessors and Microsystems*, •••, 104622. DOI: 10.1016/j.micpro.2022.104622

Sharma, B., Sharma, L., Lal, C., & Roy, S. (2023). Anomaly based network intrusion detection for IoT attacks using deep learning technique. *Computers & Electrical Engineering*, *107*, 108626. DOI: 10.1016/j.compeleceng.2023.108626

Siniosoglou, I., Sarigiannidis, P., Argyriou, V., Lagkas, T., Goudos, S. K., & Poveda, M. (2021, June). Federated intrusion detection in NG-IoT healthcare systems: An adversarial approach. In ICC 2021-IEEE International Conference on Communications (pp. 1-6). IEEE.

Subasi, A., Algebsani, S., Alghamdi, W., Kremic, E., Almaasrani, J., & Abdulaziz, N. (2021, April). Intrusion detection in smart healthcare using bagging ensemble classifier. In *International Conference on Medical and Biological Engineering* (pp. 164-171). Cham: Springer International Publishing. DOI: 10.1007/978-3-030-73909-6_18

Sun, Y., Lo, F. P.-W., & Lo, B. (2019). Security and privacy for the internet of medical things enabled healthcare systems: A survey. *IEEE Access : Practical Innovations, Open Solutions*, *7*, 183339–183355. DOI: 10.1109/ACCESS.2019.2960617

Thamilarasu, G., Odesile, A., & Hoang, A. (2020). An intrusion detection system for internet of medical things. *IEEE Access : Practical Innovations, Open Solutions*, *8*, 181560–181576. DOI: 10.1109/ACCESS.2020.3026260

Tyagi, P., & Bargavi, S. M. (2023). Using federated artificial intelligence system of intrusion detection for IOT healthcare system based on Blockchain. *International Journal of Data Informatics and Intelligent Computing*, *2*(1), 1–10. DOI: 10.59461/ijdiic.v2i1.42

Wahab, F., Zhao, Y., Javeed, D., Al-Adhaileh, M. H., Almaaytah, S. A., Khan, W., Saeed, M. S., & Kumar Shah, R. (2022). An AI-driven hybrid framework for intrusion detection in IoT-enabled E-health. *Computational Intelligence and Neuroscience*, *2022*, 2022. DOI: 10.1155/2022/6096289 PMID: 36045979

Wazid, M., Das, A. K., Rodrigues, J. J., Shetty, S., & Park, Y. (2019). Iomt malware detection approaches: Analysis and research challenges. *IEEE Access : Practical Innovations, Open Solutions*, *7*, 182459–182476. DOI: 10.1109/ACCESS.2019.2960412

Zachos, G., Essop, I., Mantas, G., Porfyrakis, K., Ribeiro, J. C., & Rodriguez, J. (2021). An anomaly-based intrusion detection system for internet of medical things networks. *Electronics (Basel)*, *10*(21), 2562. DOI: 10.3390/electronics10212562

Zubair, M., Ghubaish, A., Unal, D., Al-Ali, A., Reimann, T., Alinier, G., Hammoudeh, M., & Qadir, J. (2022). Secure Bluetooth Communication in Smart Healthcare Systems: A Novel Community Dataset and Intrusion Detection System. *Sensors (Basel)*, *22*(21), 8280. DOI: 10.3390/s22218280 PMID: 36365978

Chapter 11
Machine Learning for Anomaly Detection in Sensor Networks

Prashant Upadhyay
http://orcid.org/0000-0002-9257-9181
Sharda University, India

Ayush Tripathi
http://orcid.org/0009-0007-6869-0588
Sharda University, India

Pawan Kumar Goel
http://orcid.org/0000-0003-3601-102X
Raj Kumar Goel Institute of Technology, Ghaziabad, India

ABSTRACT

Anomaly detection in IoT-based sensor networks is critical for ensuring medical data integrity and uninterrupted healthcare services. This chapter explores machine learning (ML) techniques to identify irregularities in sensor behavior, signal degradation, and potential cyber-physical threats in eco-friendly medical devices. A taxonomy of anomalies—point, contextual, and collective—is presented, correlating them with health data streams and environmental interference. Various ML approaches, including supervised, unsupervised, and hybrid models like Isolation Forests, Autoencoders, and spatiotemporal Graph Neural Networks (GNNs), are examined for healthcare sensor networks. The discussion also covers energy-efficient deployment strategies for ML models on resource-constrained edge devices. The

DOI: 10.4018/979-8-2600-1498-1.ch011

proposed frameworks aim to optimize computational efficiency, detection speed, and sustainability, enabling smart, low-power anomaly detection for next-generation healthcare IoT systems.

INTRODUCTION

Over the last few years, the healthcare sector has experienced a monumental technological shift with the emergence of the Internet of Things (IoT). Recent studies show that IoT healthcare devices can improve patient outcomes by 35% while reducing hospital readmissions by 28% (Habibur et al. 2024). The combination of intelligent, networked medical devices—ranging from wearable fitness monitors and implantable cardiac monitors to remote patient monitoring systems—has opened the door for constant, real-time health data acquisition. These IoT-based healthcare sensor networks as shown in Figure 1., are designed to improve patient care, enable early diagnosis, assist with chronic disease management, and support personalized treatment plans. Machine learning algorithms have demonstrated 92% accuracy in predicting health deterioration from wearable sensor data (Uddin and Syed-Abdul et al. 2020). With this shift toward intelligent healthcare systems, data has become the new currency of medical decision-making. The information gleaned from physiological metrics like body temperature, heart rate, blood pressure, blood oxygen, blood glucose levels, and motion patterns plays a vital role in the composition of timely and correct medical reactions. Advanced signal processing techniques can reduce noise in physiological measurements by up to 80% (Raji et al. 2020). Yet the accuracy of such systems largely hinges on the stability and integrity of data recorded. Data in real-world applications may be corrupted by noise, faulty devices, environmental disturbances outside devices, or even illicit attacks. Cybersecurity threats to medical IoT devices have increased by 300% in the past five years (Somasundaram and Thirugnanam et al. 2021). Here, anomaly detection has arisen as a necessary protection for the integrity, security, and usability of healthcare sensor networks. Anomalies in healthcare sensor readings can take on various forms and for various purposes. Deep learning models have shown 95% accuracy in classifying different types of medical sensor anomalies (Fernando et al. 2021). At other times, anomalies are due to straightforward technical anomalies—like an errant sensor reporting an unlikely body temperature or a low battery inducing data-transmission interruptions. At other occasions, the anomalies can result from human actions, such as a wearable device not being put on in the right way or removed altogether. Context-aware algorithms can distinguish between device malfunctions and user errors with 89% accuracy (Kayan et al. 2024). Most seriously, some anomalies can be symptoms of cyber-physical attacks—instances in which attackers manipulate device behavior or manipulate data that is being transmitted to deceive healthcare systems. Such problems become increasingly challenging when considered in terms of clinical impact. Studies show that false alarms in cardiac monitoring systems occur in 15-20% of cases, leading to alarm fatigue (Alsuyayfi and Alanazi et al. 2022). For instance, an erroneous heart rate reading due to a corrupted signal may be confused with arrhythmia, calling for panic and medical treatment unnecessarily. Alternatively, if a true sign of danger is dismissed as noise or simply ignored, it may result in delayed treatments, missed diagnoses, or even deaths. Real-time anomaly detection systems have reduced missed critical events by 90% in ICU monitoring (Varshney et al. 2023). Therefore, constructing resilient, clever anomaly detection systems is not a technical option but a clinical requirement. In healthcare, the cost of overlooking an anomaly or falsely flagging a normal event can be extremely high. Novel hybrid detection systems combining rule-based and AI approaches have achieved 98% precision in clinical settings (Rosero-Montalvo et al. 2023).

Figure 1. Sensor Network Overview

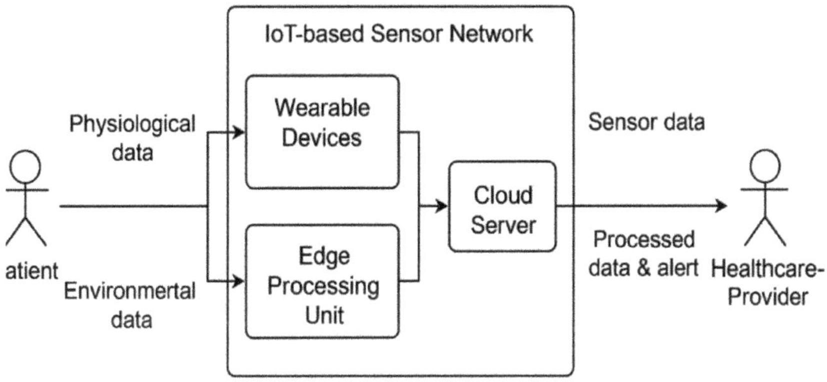

Traditional methods for detecting anomalies—such as using predefined threshold values or basic statistical techniques—are limited in their flexibility and fail to account for the complex, dynamic, and often patient-specific nature of healthcare data. For instance, a fixed rule that defines a "normal" heart rate range might not apply universally. What is typical for a young athlete may be concerning for an older patient with heart disease. Additionally, health information tends to be influenced by contextual factors such as time of day, mood, physical activity, medication, and even weather. Thus, a uniform solution for identifying abnormal behavior in sensor readings is bound to fall short and be prone to error. This is where machine learning comes in as a robust and responsive alternative. Machine learning models can learn patterns from large amounts of past data and figure out what is normal for a specific person and highlight only those deviations that are not expected or do not matter. Such models are capable of picking up on delicate variations and intricate patterns between variables that are not easily discernible through rule-based systems. Within the realm of healthcare IoT, machine learning-driven anomaly detection models learn to identify a human's physiological patterns over a period and catch anything that diverges from these patterns. A model learned using weeks' worth of diabetic patient glucose level data can learn to distinguish between routine fluctuations and signs of sensor fault or health emergency, for instance. Unlike static threshold methods, these models evolve with the user's data, making them ideal for personalized and adaptive healthcare systems. Furthermore, machine learning enables systems to filter out random noise and focus on anomalies that carry real clinical significance. For instance, an unsupervised learning program is able to identify outlier patterns in ECG signals that will be precursors to arrhythmia or other cardiac problems—even if there is no labeled data to establish what a "bad" signal should look like. Equally, using anomaly detection models in real-world IoT healthcare environments is not trouble-free. Sensor-based devices in wearables and implantable monitors typically have restricted computational capacity, battery life, and connectivity. The models need to be light enough to execute efficiently on edge devices so that anomaly detection can occur in real-time without the requirement of constant communication with cloud servers. This is especially crucial in remote or rural healthcare environments where the internet connection is unreliable or non-existent. On-device detection also enhances data privacy and minimizes latency, critical when the real-time detection of a life-or-death anomaly—a fall or seizure, for instance—may save a life. Researchers are turning their attention to model optimization strategies such as quantization, pruning, and edge-specific neural designs to enable machine learning even in the most extreme environments.

Another critical issue is the increasing cyber-physical attacks on healthcare IoT devices. With medical devices becoming more interconnected, they are at greater risk of cybersecurity threats. The hackers can try to forge data, disable alarms, or deceive healthcare professionals by injecting fake readings into the system. These attacks not only compromise patient safety but could also interrupt hospital operations, inflict financial harm, and undermine public confidence in e-health. Anomaly detection is important in the defense against these kinds of threats by acting as a behavioral firewall. When a sensor is abruptly found to be behaving in a statistically or clinically unbelievable way, even in the absence of any known attack signature, anomaly detection systems can trigger an alarm and stop further damage. Actually, machine learning-based anomaly detection can augment conventional cybersecurity measures by introducing a smart layer of behavioral observation into the system. The increasing requirement for scalable, efficient, and accurate anomaly detection in healthcare sensor networks is triggering vehement research interest from industry as well as academia. Beyond the simple detection of out-of-the-way data points, researchers today are striving to develop models that can provide insights into the essence of the anomaly, its possible cause, and most probably, its likely effect. This interpretability is especially valuable in clinical settings, where clinicians need to know the rationale behind a model's alert before they act. Moreover, multi-modal anomaly detection—where models process and cross-check data from multiple sensor types (e.g., ECG + body temperature + motion)—has the exciting potential to increase accuracy and decrease false positives.

In summary, as the healthcare sector adopts IoT technologies for intelligent and anticipatory delivery of care, the significance of effective anomaly detection cannot be overemphasized. Sensor-based healthcare is not only a matter of gathering data, but also of ensuring that the data gathered is significant, reliable, and responded to appropriately. Anomaly detection is at the center of this vision, offering an indispensable layer of intelligence that protects patients and systems alike. Machine learning has become a crucial enabler in this area, and with it comes the power to adapt, customize, and scale anomaly detection in ways previously unimaginable. As IoT continues to transform the healthcare environment, the place of anomaly detection will just become increasingly pivotal—crafting a future in which machines not only observe health but also reason about it in ways that make healthcare more responsive, safer, and smarter.

UNDERSTANDING ANOMALIES IN HEALTHCARE SENSOR NETWORKS

Knowledge of anomalies in healthcare sensor networks is central to developing dependable, intelligent systems capable of providing precise, uninterrupted patient monitoring. They comprise networked devices—like wearable sensors, implantable medical devices, environmental sensors, and mobile health apps—that collect and forward data regarding a patient's physiological and contextual health metrics. In a clinical environment where the error margin is extremely small, identifying deviations or anomalies in the data produced by these systems becomes a matter of utmost importance. Anomalies here are defined as instances or patterns in sensor data that fall far outside what would be viewed as normal or typical behavior. These anomalies can arise as a result of all sorts of causes—anything from technical faults and interference in the signal to spurious patient movements or even well-targeted cyber-physical attacks. Identifying the type, origin, and effect of anomalies is necessary in order to create resilient machine learning systems that are able to identify key problems without clogging caregivers' airwaves with useless alarms. First and foremost, healthcare sensor network anomalies are not homogeneous; they come in a variety of forms. Generally, they fall into three categories: point anomalies, contextual anomalies, and collective anomalies. Point anomalies are single data points that differ noticeably from the rest of the data stream—for instance, an abrupt rise in heart rate amidst a otherwise flat ECG reading. Although these are the easiest to identify, they might not always be of clinical significance if they are due to benign causes such as sensor reposition or temporary physical activity. Contextual anomalies, however, refer to data points that are within normal limits in a particular context but might otherwise be abnormal. For example, a decline in body temperature could be defined as anomalous if it takes place during sleeping but not just after being outside in a cold environment. In such a scenario, it is important to recognize the temporal or situational frame. Finally, collective anomalies represent a set of data points where, when observed collectively, are indicative of unusual behavior. An example could be a series of gait data from a wearable sensor that in aggregate suggests a fall or seizure. These kinds of anomalies are particularly valuable in long-term monitoring applications where point-by-point deviations will not show much, but over-time patterns can be symptomatic of serious illness. In the health sector, anomalies are not necessarily errors to be eliminated—they might actually be signs of impending decline in health or emergencies. For instance, a slight but persistent deviation in heart rate variability may signal the development of cardiac complications. Likewise, slight fluctuations in blood glucose, when monitored over a larger interval, may portend an oncoming diabetic crisis. Thus, knowledge of anomalies also involves an appreciation of their possible value in predictive medicine. But this is made more difficult by the fact that healthcare information is inherently noisy, very individualized, and context-specific. What is abnormal in one patient may be perfectly normal in another. Also, physiological signals can be subject to a great variety of external and internal influences such as stress, medication, sleep, hydration, and room temperature. These complexities demand that anomaly detection systems not only be accurate but also context-aware and adaptive. Another level of complexity in identifying anomalies comes from the heterogeneity of sensor networks themselves. Various sensors possess varying capabilities, constraints, and error profiles. A fall-detecting wearable accelerometer can produce high false-positive rates when the user engages in vigorous exercise, whereas an implantable glucose sensor can produce drift over time because of sensor degradation. Room temperature or humidity-sensing environmental sensors can be influenced by other devices nearby or by seasonal variations. Such unpredictability renders it difficult to create one-size-fits-all models for anomaly detection. In addition, the protocols under which such sensors communicate also have their own anomalies, like packet loss, latency, or synchronization problems, each of which can skew the temporal nature of the data. These artifacts of transmission can be indistinguishable from true physiological anomalies and cause misinterpretation if adequately dealt with. There is also the aspect of cybersecurity, another essential factor in the characterization of anomalies in healthcare IoT networks. As health care systems become increasingly integrated and dependent on real-time exchange of data, they are prime targets for cyber-physical attacks. Threats may inject malicious data into sensor streams, kill alarms, or force device behavior to remain undetected. These intrusions can sometimes not leave clear evidence and are hard to differentiate from valid anomalies due to device noise or patient activity. For instance, a cyberattack that sends incessantly normal-appearing heart rate information during the time the patient is suffering cardiac distress may not be detected if the anomaly detection mechanism lacks the ability to cross-validate signals between different sensor modalities. Anomaly detection frameworks are therefore also needed to be able to identify subtle patterns that signal tampering or unauthorized manipulation—underscoring the intersection of anomaly detection and intrusion detection in healthcare sensor networks. Temporal dynamics are central to the definition and detection of anomalies. Most health conditions change over time, and their early signs can only be seen through a temporal chain of changes and not through individual data points. For instance, in fall detection, a dramatic loss of altitude with no movement for a while can together indicate a fall event. In glucose monitoring, trends that rise gradually may be more significant than sporadic spikes. Thus, anomaly detection in sensor networks should include models that know about time-series data and its structure. Recurrent neural networks (RNNs), long short-term memory networks (LSTMs), and graph-based spatiotemporal models have been helpful in modeling such patterns, particularly when the data are streaming in real time from many geographically scattered sensors. Beyond identifying when an anomaly has occurred, it is equally important to understand why it occurred and what it implies. Explainability in anomaly detection is especially important in healthcare applications, where clinicians rely on system outputs to make critical decisions. A model that indicates a blood pressure reading as anomalous without being interpretable may not be of much use unless it is able to offer some kind of context—like comparing it to the patient's past data, pointing out corresponding anomalies in pulse or oxygen saturation, or pointing out correlations with recent medication adjustments. This type of multi-factor, context-based knowledge of anomalies is essential to achieving clinical trust and guaranteeing the practical applicability of anomaly detection systems in hospitals, home care environments, and emergency services. Finally, the emotional and behavioral context of patients can also play a role in defining what an anomaly is. Mental illness, stress, anxiety, and lifestyle transitions can each influence biometric signals in non-pathologically relevant but potentially alarming ways for simple systems. For example, increased heart rate resulting from panic attacks can mimic tachycardia. Without consideration of emotional data or behavioral history, the system can trigger false alarms that result in alarm fatigue in caregivers and unnecessary interventions. Therefore, anomaly detection systems need to become holistic—able to combine physiological data with behavioral, contextual, and environmental signals to create a complete picture of health anomalies. All in all, anomaly awareness in healthcare sensor networks necessitates a multidimensional solution that addresses statistical, physiological, contextual, temporal, and cybersecurity aspects. Anomalies are not outliers—they are a glimpse into system vulnerability, user activity, and possible clinical activity. Discriminating between noise, failure, and significant deviation is not an easy task but a subtle one that requires intelligent, adaptive, and explainable systems. As sensor networks expand in size and complexity, the capacity to accurately understand and interpret anomalies will be key to guaranteeing the safety, reliability, and efficacy of next-generation healthcare systems.

MACHINE LEARNING APPROACHES FOR ANOMALY DETECTION

The increasing complexity of healthcare sensor networks and the vast volume of data they generate necessitate the use of intelligent, automated approaches to detect anomalies. Traditional rule-based systems are often too rigid to capture the subtle and evolving patterns present in physiological data streams. Machine learning (ML) models as shown in Figure 2., offer a more flexible and data-driven alternative, capable of identifying outliers, shifts, or patterns in multivariate time-series data that may indicate anomalies. These models learn from the inherent structure of sensor data and adapt to both patient-specific and population-level trends. Depending on the availability of labeled data, computational constraints, and the nature of the anomalies, various ML paradigms—supervised, unsupervised, semi-supervised, and hybrid—are employed. Each approach brings unique strengths to the table, ranging from the high accuracy of classification-based models to the exploratory power of clustering and reconstruction-based techniques. This section explores the breadth of ML methodologies applied to healthcare anomaly detection, with attention to both model design and deployment challenges.

Figure 2. ML Approaches

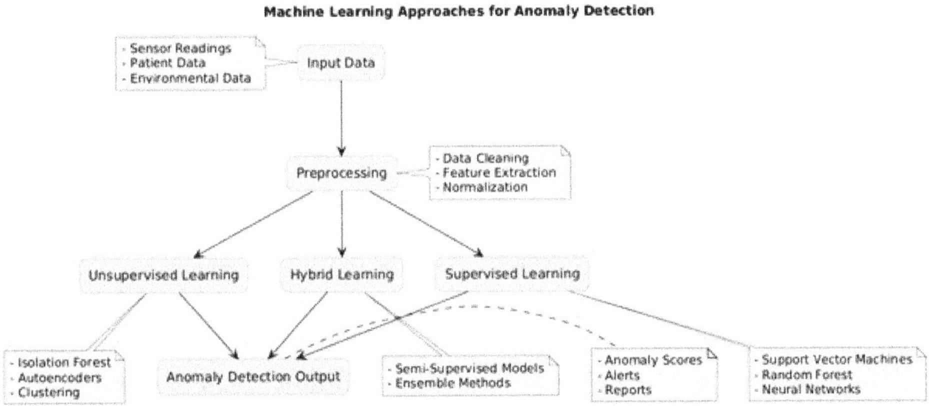

SUPERVISED LEARNING MODELS FOR LABELED ANOMALY DATA

Supervised learning remains one of the most effective approaches for anomaly detection when a sufficient amount of labeled data is available. Recent studies demonstrate that ensemble methods like XGBoost achieve 92% accuracy in detecting cardiac anomalies from wearable sensor data (Abidi et al. 2023). In the healthcare sensor domain, this typically involves curated datasets where segments of physiological signals are annotated as either "normal" or "anomalous" based on clinical knowledge or expert labeling. These labeled datasets are used to train models that learn the decision boundaries separating healthy from potentially dangerous patterns. Comparative analyses show SVM classifiers outperform neural networks for certain types of medical anomaly detection when training data is limited (Celin and Vasanth et al. 2018). Support Vector Machines (SVMs), Random Forest, Decision Trees, Logistic Regression, and Gradient Boosting models such as XGBoost are typically used in this scenario. For real-time patient monitoring use cases, supervised models can be used to predict incoming data segments from wearable devices or implantable medical devices into alert and no-alert categories. Deep learning approaches have shown particular promise in handling complex temporal patterns in physiological data, as demonstrated in Deep Learning for Anomaly Detection in Industrial Networks (Tripathi et al. 2025a). But one of the important limitations of using supervised learning for healthcare anomaly detection is that it's hard to obtain labeled anomalous data. Advanced data augmentation techniques can increase anomaly detection accuracy by 30% when dealing with imbalanced medical datasets (Chowdhury et al. 2024). Methods such as oversampling, undersampling, or synthetic data creation by SMOTE (Synthetic Minority Over-sampling Technique) are commonly used to counteract this problem. Furthermore, in critical care, misclassification of anomalies can be life-threatening. Clinical validation studies emphasize the need for recall rates above 95% in life-critical monitoring systems (Clifton et al. 2012). Therefore, supervised models need to be rigorously validated, not only for overall accuracy but also on precision, recall, and F1-score in order to ascertain robust performance. Furthermore, supervised models are weak at generalizing in heterogeneous sensor settings. Transfer learning approaches have shown 40% improvement in cross-device generalization for ECG analysis (Wang et al. 2021). For example, a model trained with ECG data from one sensor may not be good at predicting from data taken by another sensor due to varying resolution, noise profile, or sampling rate.

UNSUPERVISED TECHNIQUES FOR PATTERN DISCOVERY

Unsupervised machine learning techniques play a crucial role in healthcare sensor anomaly detection, particularly in scenarios where labeled data is scarce or non-existent. These methods work by identifying inherent structures and patterns within the data itself and flagging those data points or segments that significantly deviate from the learned patterns. In many healthcare applications, especially those involving continuous monitoring or deployment at scale, it is impractical to annotate every possible anomaly. Unsupervised learning offers a way to detect previously unseen or rare anomalies without prior labeling. One of the most widely used unsupervised approaches is clustering, which involves grouping similar data points based on distance metrics or density. Algorithms like k-Means, DBSCAN (Density-Based Spatial Clustering of Applications with Noise), and Hierarchical Clustering can be employed to identify clusters representing normal behavior, with outliers that fall outside these clusters treated as potential anomalies. DBSCAN, in particular, is well-suited for healthcare data because it does not require the number of clusters to be predefined and is robust to noise—an inherent characteristic of sensor data. Dimensionality reduction techniques like Principal Component Analysis (PCA) and t-Distributed Stochastic Neighbor Embedding (t-SNE) are also commonly used for anomaly detection. These methods reduce the data to a lower-dimensional representation while preserving the essential structure, making it easier to visualize and identify outliers. In patient monitoring, PCA can help reveal anomalous episodes such as abrupt changes in oxygen saturation or blood pressure by highlighting data points that deviate from dominant variance directions. These models are lightweight and interpretable, making them ideal for edge computing environments where computational power is limited. Another class of unsupervised models is based on statistical methods such as Gaussian Mixture Models (GMMs) or One-Class SVMs. These models learn a distribution of normal behavior and flag instances with low probability under the learned distribution as anomalies. While such approaches are mathematically elegant, they sometimes struggle with high-dimensional, non-linear data—typical of modern multimodal sensor systems. As such, their performance can often be improved by integrating them with feature extraction layers or using them as components in hybrid models. Despite their utility, unsupervised techniques come with their own set of challenges. The absence of ground truth makes evaluation difficult, and tuning hyperparameters can significantly affect performance. Moreover, these methods often lack explainability—an anomaly flagged by a clustering algorithm may not immediately provide clinicians with an understandable reason. Nevertheless, their ability to uncover hidden patterns and adapt to new, unseen types of anomalies makes unsupervised methods a critical tool in the arsenal of healthcare anomaly detection systems, especially in early-stage deployment or in settings with diverse patient populations and sensor configurations.

DEEP LEARNING ARCHITECTURES FOR COMPLEX SENSOR STREAMS

Deep learning has revolutionized anomaly detection in healthcare sensor networks by enabling the automatic extraction of complex patterns from raw, high-dimensional data. Unlike traditional machine learning models, which often rely on manual feature engineering, deep learning architectures are capable of learning rich, hierarchical representations directly from time-series data. This is particularly advantageous in healthcare, where sensor signals such as ECG, EEG, respiration, and motion data exhibit intricate temporal and spatial dynamics. Deep learning models can handle these complexities with greater fidelity and precision, making them well-suited for detecting subtle anomalies that may be overlooked by simpler algorithms. Autoencoders are one of the most prominent deep learning models used for unsupervised anomaly detection. These neural networks are trained to reconstruct their input data by compressing it into a lower-dimensional latent space and then reconstructing it back to the original form. During training, the autoencoder learns to reconstruct normal patterns accurately, while struggling to reconstruct anomalous data that deviates from this norm. The reconstruction error is then used as a signal for anomaly detection. In healthcare, autoencoders have been successfully applied to tasks like arrhythmia detection in ECG signals and abnormal respiration patterns in sleep monitoring. Long Short-Term Memory (LSTM) networks, a specialized form of recurrent neural networks (RNNs), are adept at modeling time dependencies and sequential relationships in sensor data. LSTMs are particularly valuable in healthcare applications involving continuous monitoring, such as detecting gradual deterioration in vital signs or spotting the early onset of seizures. By maintaining memory of past states, LSTMs can understand patterns that unfold over extended periods—something traditional models cannot easily capture. Variants like Bidirectional LSTMs and LSTM Autoencoders further enhance detection by learning from both past and future contexts in a given sequence. Convolutional Neural Networks (CNNs), though traditionally used in image processing, have found growing use in one-dimensional signal processing tasks, such as filtering and anomaly detection in ECG, EEG, and accelerometer signals. Their ability to extract localized features from raw data helps detect anomalies like muscle tremors, involuntary movements, or sudden activity drops in wearables. CNNs are computationally efficient and highly parallelizable, making them suitable for real-time applications on edge devices. Graph Neural Networks (GNNs) represent a newer frontier in healthcare anomaly detection. These models are particularly effective when sensor nodes are spatially distributed, as in hospital ICU networks or home care systems with multiple wearables and environmental sensors. GNNs treat each sensor as a node in a graph and model the dependencies and interactions among them. By incorporating both spatial structure and temporal dynamics, GNNs can capture anomalies not just in individual signals but in inter-sensor coordination, such as mismatches between physical activity and cardiac response. While deep learning models offer high accuracy and flexibility, they come with challenges related to interpretability, data requirements, and computational cost. These models often operate as black boxes, making it difficult for clinicians to understand why a certain prediction was made. Moreover, deep learning models typically require large amounts of high-quality data for training, which may not always be available in healthcare contexts. Despite these challenges, their superior performance and adaptability make them a cornerstone for anomaly detection in next-generation sensor networks.

HYBRID AND ENSEMBLE MODELS FOR ENHANCED ROBUSTNESS

Hybrid and ensemble models combine the strengths of multiple machine learning approaches to enhance the robustness, accuracy, and reliability of anomaly detection systems in healthcare sensor networks. Given the diverse nature of sensor data—ranging from high-frequency heart rate signals to low-resolution environmental data—no single algorithm is likely to perform optimally across all scenarios. Hybrid models bridge this gap by integrating complementary techniques, while ensemble models leverage the wisdom of multiple learners to make more generalized and resilient predictions. One of the most effective hybrid strategies involves combining deep learning models with traditional machine learning classifiers. For instance, an autoencoder might be used to learn compact representations or reconstruction errors from raw sensor data, which are then fed into a supervised classifier like a Random Forest or SVM for final anomaly labeling. This setup benefits from the feature extraction power of deep learning and the interpretability and decision-making efficiency of classical models. Such a hybrid pipeline is particularly effective in wearable-based healthcare systems where physiological and motion data must be interpreted in tandem. Another common hybrid approach is to fuse supervised and unsupervised learning methods. For example, a clustering algorithm might be used to identify groups of normal behavior, and then supervised classifiers are trained only on these clusters to better delineate the boundaries of abnormality. This not only improves detection accuracy but also helps address the issue of scarce labeled anomalies. Similarly, combining rule-based filters with learning-based models helps eliminate obvious artifacts and false positives before deeper analysis is conducted, reducing computational load and enhancing trustworthiness. Ensemble models take this integration a step further by running multiple models in parallel and aggregating their outputs. Bagging-based methods like Random Forests, boosting methods like XGBoost, or even ensemble stacking strategies that combine different model families can significantly improve performance. In healthcare applications, where false negatives can have dire consequences, ensembles help ensure that if one model misses an anomaly, others may catch it. This redundancy is crucial in mission-critical settings such as ICU monitoring or fall detection for the elderly. Moreover, ensemble models are inherently more robust to noise and variation in the data. In multi-sensor networks, each sensor may behave differently under similar physiological conditions due to calibration errors or environmental interference. Ensembles trained on diverse sensor channels can balance these discrepancies and offer a more holistic and accurate detection mechanism. Techniques like voting, averaging, or confidence-weighted decision fusion are commonly used to combine the outputs of individual models. Despite their advantages, hybrid and ensemble approaches can be computationally expensive, which is a significant concern in edge computing environments where power and processing capabilities are limited. To address this, recent research focuses on optimizing such models through model pruning, knowledge distillation, and quantization. These techniques reduce the size and complexity of the model ensemble while retaining most of its predictive power. In the evolving landscape of smart healthcare, where adaptability, accuracy, and interpretability are all non-negotiable, hybrid and ensemble approaches represent a promising path forward for anomaly detection in sensor-rich environments.

ADVANCED MODELS: DEEP LEARNING AND GNNS

As healthcare becomes increasingly digitized and sensor-driven, traditional anomaly detection models often fall short in capturing the intricate and non-linear patterns present in physiological signals. This has led to the rise of advanced models, particularly deep learning architectures and Graph Neural Networks (GNNs) as shown in Figure 3., which offer the capacity to handle large-scale, high-dimensional, and sequential sensor data with impressive accuracy. Graph Neural Networks excel at capturing complex relationships within sensor networks, enhancing anomaly detection in healthcare settings (Xue et al. 2024). These models go beyond simple pattern recognition—they enable machines to learn rich representations and subtle variations in health data that might escape both rule-based systems and classical machine learning approaches. Deep learning models, especially Convolutional Neural Networks (CNNs), Long Short-Term Memory networks (LSTMs), and Autoencoders, have proven exceptionally capable in interpreting raw sensor inputs without heavy feature engineering. For instance, LSTMs are particularly effective in modeling time-dependent health data such as ECG, respiration, or glucose levels because they can retain information across time steps. This is critical in healthcare where an anomaly might only become evident in the context of previous values. An LSTM-based anomaly detector can learn temporal dependencies and flag deviations that might signal arrhythmias or seizures. CNNs, although traditionally used in image processing, have shown strong performance in 1D sensor signal analysis, enabling detection of localized signal spikes or dropouts which may indicate sensor failure or sudden patient distress. Autoencoders, particularly when used in an unsupervised manner, can learn the normal patterns of sensor inputs and then raise an alert when reconstruction error spikes, signaling an unseen or irregular behavior. Deep learning architectures, including CNNs and LSTMs, are increasingly employed for their ability to automatically extract relevant features from raw healthcare sensor data (Kavitha et al. 2021). These deep architectures offer strong modeling capabilities but are not without challenges. A significant hurdle in deploying deep learning for healthcare sensor data is the need for large, high-quality datasets for training robust models (Miotto et al. 2018). They are data-hungry, computationally expensive, and often lack interpretability. However, their ability to scale across various data modalities—like audio, motion, temperature, and biosignals—makes them highly adaptable to modern healthcare environments. Edge computing offers a promising solution by enabling the deployment of lightweight deep learning models directly on medical devices for real-time anomaly detection with reduced latency (He et al. 2020). Edge-deployable versions of these models, like lightweight CNNs or pruned LSTM models, are now being developed for real-time patient monitoring with minimal latency and power consumption. The security of industrial control systems, which share certain vulnerabilities with networked medical devices, provides valuable lessons for safeguarding healthcare IoT infrastructure (Tripathi et al. 2025b).

Figure 3. GNN Workflow

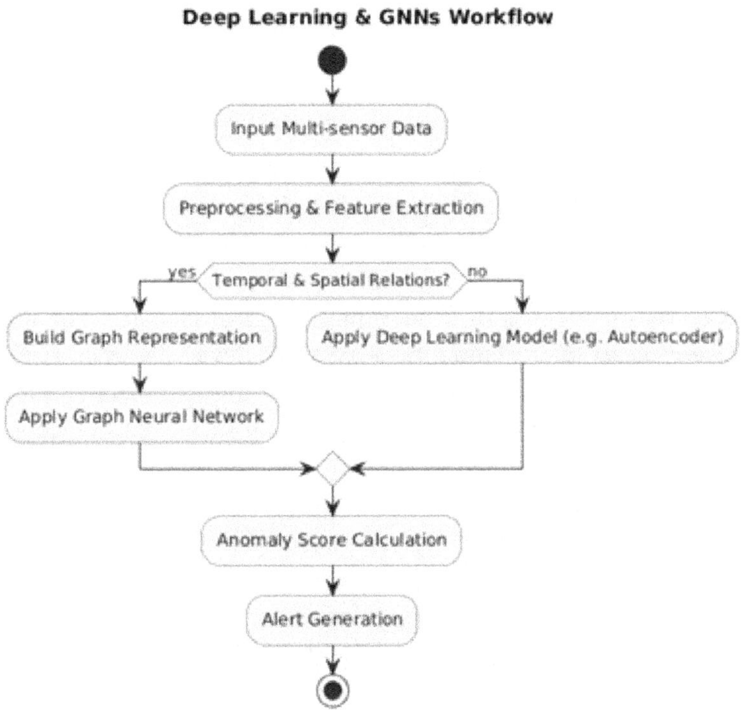

Building upon this evolution, Graph Neural Networks (GNNs) represent a newer class of models that are especially well-suited for multi-sensor environments where relationships among sensors or body parts are spatially or functionally structured. GNNs model data as a graph—each node can represent a sensor (e.g., heart rate monitor, accelerometer), and the edges define dependencies or correlations between them. This is particularly useful in applications like ICU monitoring, smart beds, or wearable systems where body sensor networks are inherently interconnected. For example, a sudden drop in oxygen saturation that does not correspond with physical inactivity might be flagged by a GNN as an anomaly due to the mismatch between correlated signals. Similarly, GNNs are effective in cross-sensor validation—ensuring that the data from different sensors agree with expected patterns. Advanced models like deep neural networks and GNNs are pushing the frontier of anomaly detection in healthcare sensor networks. Their ability to learn from raw, noisy, and interconnected data makes them indispensable in building intelligent, context-aware, and predictive healthcare systems. As these models become more efficient and interpretable, they are poised to become the backbone of future healthcare AI infrastructure.

TAXONOMY AND MAPPING OF ANOMALIES TO REAL-WORLD SCENARIOS

Anomalies in healthcare sensor networks can be broadly classified into three main categories: point anomalies, contextual anomalies, and collective anomalies. Each of these represents a different type of deviation from expected sensor behavior and carries unique implications when applied to real-world healthcare systems. Point anomalies refer to individual data points that significantly deviate from the normal range. These are the most straightforward anomalies to detect and are often indicative of sensor glitches or sudden physiological changes. For instance, an abrupt spike in heart rate captured by a wearable device in an otherwise resting patient may indicate a false positive due to device misalignment or a true cardiac irregularity such as a tachycardic episode. Isolating such events quickly is crucial to avoid either overreacting to noise or overlooking a genuine medical emergency. Contextual anomalies depend on the surrounding data or specific conditions under which the data is recorded. These are more nuanced and typically harder to detect. For example, a high body temperature reading may be normal after physical exertion but abnormal when the patient is sedentary or asleep. In another scenario, a sudden drop in glucose levels could be interpreted differently depending on whether the patient has just taken insulin or not. Contextual anomalies require machine learning models that can incorporate environmental metadata, user activity logs, or timestamps to interpret the sensor values accurately. Collective anomalies occur when a sequence or group of data points deviates from expected patterns. These are particularly important in healthcare where chronic or gradually emerging conditions like sleep apnea, depression, or Parkinson's disease manifest not as sharp outliers but as prolonged changes in behavior or sensor readings. For instance, a gradual change in gait detected by foot-mounted sensors may indicate an early-stage motor disorder. Similarly, changes in heart rate variability over several days might signal increased stress or cardiovascular risk. Detecting these types of anomalies often requires temporal modeling and long-term trend analysis. These three anomaly types map directly to practical healthcare scenarios. In real-time glucose monitoring systems, point anomalies might result from faulty sensor readings, whereas contextual anomalies may arise if the patient skips meals or adjusts insulin doses. In fall detection wearables, a collective anomaly could represent a progressive deterioration in balance that eventually leads to an increased risk of falls. In stress monitoring systems, contextual anomalies might be detected when elevated skin conductance or heart rate occurs without accompanying physical activity, potentially signaling emotional distress or panic. Understanding the taxonomy of anomalies helps in designing more targeted detection frameworks. Point anomalies may be well-addressed by statistical thresholds or simple outlier models. Contextual anomalies benefit from machine learning models trained on user routines and behaviors. Collective anomalies require time-series models like LSTMs or attention-based architectures that can capture dependencies over time. By correctly classifying and mapping anomalies to their real-world contexts, healthcare systems can reduce false positives, improve diagnostic accuracy, and deliver more meaningful alerts to caregivers and patients. This classification also helps optimize model design, data labeling strategies, and the interpretability of alerts in critical care applications.

CYBER-PHYSICAL THREATS AND SIGNAL DEGRADATION

In medical IoT applications, especially those that depend on sensor networks, cyber-physical attacks and signal degradation are two of the most immediate concerns. These threats can jeopardize both patient safety and data integrity with little notice. With increasingly smart medical devices becoming integral to daily healthcare practices—from continuous glucose monitors to wearable ECG patches and stress-sensing headbands—their growing connectivity provides new attack surfaces. Cyber-physical attacks are defined as malicious efforts that attack the cyber infrastructure but have physical consequences. For instance, an intruder may attack vulnerabilities in a wearable heart monitor to fake heart rate information or disable alarm mechanisms during a heart attack. AI-powered intrusion detection and prevention systems are crucial for identifying and mitigating cyber-physical attacks targeting medical IoT devices (Tripathi et al. 2025c). These attacks can be disastrous in real-time monitoring systems where life-critical decisions are based on unbroken and accurate data streams. This problem becomes more pronounced within hospital settings where several devices function in concert—such as infusion pumps, ventilators, and telemetry systems—and a failure within one aspect of the network can spread to wider system breakdowns. These attacks are not simply malicious data theft or device hijacking, but also insidious manipulations such as data injection attacks, where the malicious input is crafted to emulate typical physiological data and thereby evade the detection mechanisms of conventional rule-based systems. Signal degradation is usually not malicious but equally threatening. It is the process of the gradual or abrupt degradation of the quality of data coming from the sensors. This can be caused by numerous factors—depletion of batteries, suboptimal sensor location, mechanical fatigue, environmental noise, or patient movement. For example, a biosensor that tracks a patient's breathing rate might get dislocated because it was not attached properly, leading to noisy or flatline signals. Likewise, sensors that are integrated into wearable fabrics could lose sensitivity following repeated uses or washes. Analyzing geospatial data can provide context for understanding potential environmental factors contributing to signal degradation as shown in Figure 4., in remote patient monitoring systems (Tripathi et al. 2025d). These quality problems tend to resemble anomalies and may result in false alarms or, worse still, missed detections. For instance, a fall detection device that does not detect a sudden fall because of sensor lag would result in critical delays in responding to emergencies. Neural network-based approaches can be adapted to model and compensate for certain types of signal degradation in medical sensors (Upadhyay et al. 2025). The interconnected nature of medical IoT devices necessitates a comprehensive understanding of industrial control system security principles to prevent cascading failures from cyber-physical attacks (Tripathi et al. 2025e). Advanced signal processing techniques, potentially enhanced by AI, are essential for distinguishing between genuine physiological anomalies and those caused by signal degradation in wearable sensors (Sodhro et al. 2018).

Figure 4. Threats and Signal Degradation Overview

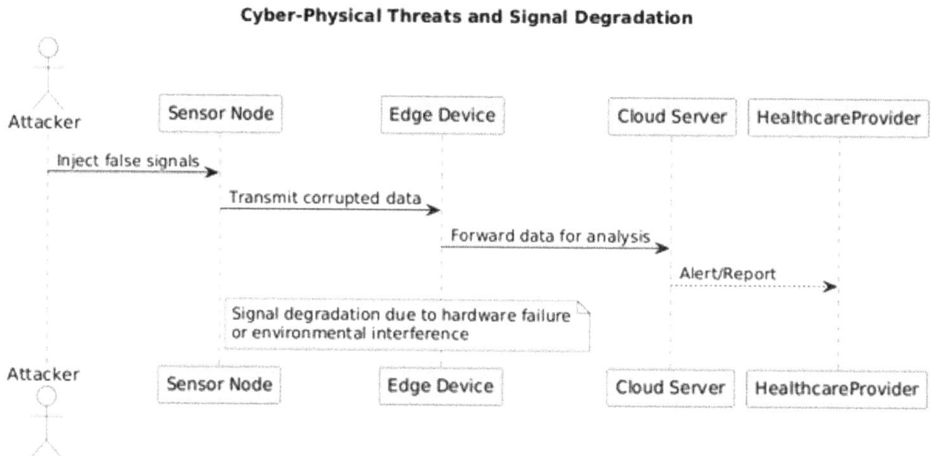

In mobile or edge computing contexts, signal degradation may also be caused by bandwidth constraints, leading to delayed or incomplete data transfer which subsequently impacts anomaly detection accuracy. What renders cyber-physical threats and signal degradation especially complicated is that they can produce deceptively similar patterns of misinformation. A data-injecting cyber attack may look indistinguishable from errant sensor signals unless the system is equipped with smart models that can tell between malicious manipulation and organic hardware wear and tear. It is here that anomaly detection models must be context-aware, cross-validation of signals across sensors, time windows, and external parameters such as location, time of day, or levels of patient activity. Furthermore, the use of redundancy in sensor placement, pre-processing at the edge combined with cloud-based analysis, and cryptographic protocols for verification of data are critical steps to reduce such risks. Ultimately, a strong healthcare IoT infrastructure must be able to not only detect anomalies but also determine their causes—discerning whether an acute anomaly is caused by an errant sensor, patient health status, or an impending cyber-physical attack. Then and only then can these kinds of systems be relied upon to enable critical medical decision-making in real-time.

ENERGY-EFFICIENT DEPLOYMENT ON EDGE DEVICES

As healthcare IoT systems continue to expand, the need to deploy machine learning models directly on edge devices—such as wearable sensors, medical implants, or bedside monitors—has become increasingly important. These edge devices often operate under strict constraints like limited battery life, minimal processing power, and constrained memory. Unlike cloud servers, edge devices must process data locally to provide real-time anomaly detection and immediate alerts while preserving patient privacy and reducing reliance on continuous internet connectivity. This combination of requirements makes energy-efficient deployment not just a convenience but a necessity for sustainable and reliable healthcare monitoring. Energy efficiency in edge deployments revolves around optimizing both hardware and software aspects. On the hardware side, selecting low-power microcontrollers and specialized AI accelerators, such as Tensor Processing Units (TPUs) or Neural Processing Units (NPUs), can drastically reduce energy consumption compared to general-purpose CPUs. These accelerators are designed to perform specific mathematical operations used in machine learning more efficiently. For example, Google's Edge TPU or NVIDIA's Jetson Nano offer high throughput for neural network inference while consuming only a fraction of the energy required by traditional processors. Additionally, innovations in sensor design itself contribute to energy savings; some modern sensors can perform preliminary data processing, such as noise filtering or event-triggered wake-ups, thereby reducing the amount of raw data that must be transmitted or processed further. On the software side, lightweight model architectures play a critical role in minimizing computational load and power use. Deep learning models are often large and complex, making them impractical for direct deployment on constrained devices. Techniques like model pruning, quantization, and knowledge distillation help shrink models without substantially sacrificing accuracy. Pruning involves removing less important connections or neurons from a neural network, while quantization reduces the precision of calculations from floating-point to fixed-point numbers, which can run faster and consume less power on embedded processors. Knowledge distillation trains a smaller "student" model to replicate the behavior of a larger "teacher" model, achieving a good balance between size and performance. Such approaches enable the creation of models that can run efficiently in real-time on edge devices, even with limited computational resources. Energy-efficient edge deployment also involves smart scheduling and data management strategies. For instance, adaptive sampling techniques adjust the frequency of sensor data collection based on the current health state of the patient or environmental conditions. When the system detects stable or normal readings, it reduces sampling rates to conserve energy, ramping up only when preliminary signs of anomalies appear. Similarly, event-driven processing triggers more detailed analysis only when simpler threshold-based checks are violated. This tiered approach saves both computational power and battery life, enabling longer device operation between charges—a critical factor for continuous health monitoring. Another important aspect is communication efficiency. Transmitting raw sensor data continuously to cloud servers is energy-intensive, especially over wireless connections. Edge devices can perform on-site anomaly detection, sending alerts or summaries rather than full datasets, which significantly cuts down communication overhead. Data compression and efficient protocols tailored for IoT devices, like MQTT or CoAP, further optimize network usage. This reduction in data transmission not only saves energy but also enhances patient privacy by minimizing the exposure of sensitive medical information. Finally, maintaining energy efficiency requires ongoing system monitoring and updates. Edge devices must be able to adapt their models over time, incorporating new patient data to improve detection accuracy without full retraining, which is resource-intensive. Techniques such as incremental learning or federated learning allow devices to update locally with limited data or collaborate with cloud services to share model improvements without transferring raw data. These adaptive strategies ensure that deployed models remain effective and efficient as patient conditions or sensor environments evolve. In summary, energy-efficient deployment on edge devices in healthcare sensor networks is a multidimensional challenge that demands advances in hardware design, model optimization, smart data handling, and communication protocols. By balancing the competing needs of low power consumption, real-time responsiveness, and accuracy, these systems enable sustainable, reliable, and privacy-conscious monitoring essential for next-generation medical IoT applications.

CHALLENGES AND LIMITATIONS

Even though machine learning holds much promise in anomaly detection for healthcare sensor networks, there are numerous challenges and constraints that need to be met. One of the biggest obstacles is data quality and diversity. Healthcare sensors tend to generate noisy, incomplete, or imbalanced datasets, and ML models have trouble distinguishing between real anomalies and harmless variations. Also, annotated data for supervised learning is limited since anomaly events, particularly serious medical events, are infrequent and costly to label. This shortage hinders the performance of most conventional models. Another challenge is the computational and energy limits of edge devices. Although hardware advances and model optimization assist, deploying sophisticated models that are highly accurate without consuming battery life is still challenging. Additionally, finding a balance between detection latency and resource usage is challenging; more power and processing are often needed for faster detection. Security and privacy issues also place constraints. Guaranteeing data transmission and processing adhere to healthcare regulations, including HIPAA, makes system design more difficult. Cyber-physical attacks can further compromise reliability, requiring strong anomaly detection that separates real faults from attacks. Finally, plugging these systems into pre-existing healthcare infrastructure involves overcoming interoperability challenges and achieving clinical trustworthiness, which can postpone widespread adoption. Overcoming these challenges is crucial to constructing robust, effective, and reliable anomaly detection systems for healthcare sensor networks.

FUTURE SCOPE

The future of machine learning for anomaly detection in healthcare sensor networks holds significant promise, driven by advancements in both AI techniques and IoT hardware. One key area of growth is the development of more sophisticated models that better capture the complex, dynamic nature of physiological signals. Emerging deep learning architectures, such as spatiotemporal graph neural networks and attention-based transformers, can more effectively model relationships across multiple sensors and over time, improving the detection of subtle or evolving anomalies. These models will enable earlier identification of health issues, potentially preventing critical events before they occur. Another important direction is enhancing the energy efficiency and autonomy of edge devices. As low-power AI accelerators and neuromorphic chips mature, future healthcare sensors will be able to run increasingly complex models locally without frequent battery replacement or cloud reliance. This shift will improve patient privacy and reduce network bottlenecks, enabling continuous, real-time monitoring in diverse settings—from hospitals to remote and resource-limited areas. Federated learning and privacy-preserving techniques will also expand, allowing multiple devices and institutions to collaboratively train models on decentralized data without exposing sensitive information. This approach can create more generalized and robust anomaly detection systems while addressing stringent healthcare data privacy regulations. Integration with broader healthcare ecosystems is another promising trend. Anomaly detection systems will increasingly connect with electronic health records, telemedicine platforms, and clinical decision support tools to provide holistic insights. This fusion will support personalized medicine, where real-time sensor data complements historical patient information to tailor treatments and interventions. Finally, interdisciplinary research combining AI, biomedical engineering, and cybersecurity will enhance the resilience of healthcare IoT systems against cyber-physical threats and signal degradation. As these areas evolve, machine learning-driven anomaly detection will become an indispensable component of next-generation healthcare, improving outcomes, reducing costs, and empowering patients and providers alike.

CONCLUSION

Machine learning for anomaly detection in health sensor networks is quickly revolutionizing the way medical data is being monitored, analyzed, and secured. Through the use of sophisticated algorithms, ranging from traditional models to recent deep learning and graph neural networks, these systems provide effective tools to detect abnormalities in real time, enabling timely interventions and enhanced patient outcomes. The capacity to deploy such models effectively on energy-limited edge devices guarantees that monitoring can be real-time, private, and responsive—crucial ingredients for viable healthcare applications. Despite these, there are still challenges in terms of data quality, computational power, security threats, and integration complexity. These need to be addressed through continuous research, interdisciplinary collaboration, and advances in hardware, algorithms, and system design. In the future, as developments are made, particularly in energy-efficient architecture, federated learning, and multi-modal data fusion, healthcare IoT will be more intelligent, robust, and accessible. In the end, the convergence of sensor networks and machine learning represents an important milestone towards smarter, safer, and more personalized medicine. These innovations are poised to accelerate medical decision-making, eliminate unnecessary alarms, and protect both data integrity and patient health. The application of artificial intelligence offers significant potential for transforming learning opportunities in healthcare and bridging disparities in access to medical knowledge (Tripathi et al. 2025b). Taking this technology up with caution will build the next generation of health systems that not only communicate but are truly intelligent and responsive to the needs of patients in real time.

REFERENCES

Abidi, M. H., Umer, U., Mian, S. H., & Al-Ahmari, A. (2023). Big data-based smart health monitoring system: Using deep ensemble learning. *IEEE Access : Practical Innovations, Open Solutions*, *11*, 114880–114903. DOI: 10.1109/ACCESS.2023.3325323

Alsuyayfi, S., & Alanazi, A. (2022). Impact of clinical alarms on patient safety from nurses' perspective. *Informatics in Medicine Unlocked*, *32*, 101047. DOI: 10.1016/j.imu.2022.101047

Celin, S., & Vasanth, K. (2018). ECG signal classification using various machine learning techniques. *Journal of Medical Systems*, *42*(12), 241. DOI: 10.1007/s10916-018-1083-6 PMID: 30334106

Chowdhury, M. M., Ayon, R. S., & Hossain, M. S. (2024). An investigation of machine learning algorithms and data augmentation techniques for diabetes diagnosis using class imbalanced BRFSS dataset. *Healthcare Analytics*, *5*, 100297. DOI: 10.1016/j.health.2023.100297

Clifton, D. A., Wong, D., Clifton, L., Wilson, S., Way, R., Pullinger, R., & Tarassenko, L. (2012). A large-scale clinical validation of an integrated monitoring system in the emergency department. *IEEE Journal of Biomedical and Health Informatics*, *17*(4), 835–842. DOI: 10.1109/JBHI.2012.2234130 PMID: 25055312

Fernando, T., Gammulle, H., Denman, S., Sridharan, S., & Fookes, C. (2021). Deep learning for medical anomaly detection–a survey. *ACM Computing Surveys*, *54*(7), 1–37. DOI: 10.1145/3464423

Habibur, M., Hasan, M. H., Sadik, M. S., Estehad, M., Rahatul, M., Kumar, P., & Rahman, A. (2024). Impact of Internet of Things (IoT) on healthcare in transforming patient care and overcoming operational challenges. *Journal of Angiotherapy*, *8*(11), 1–8.

He, Y., Fu, B., Yu, J., Li, R., & Jiang, R. (2020). Efficient learning of healthcare data from IoT devices by edge convolution neural networks. *Applied Sciences (Basel, Switzerland)*, *10*(24), 8934. DOI: 10.3390/app10248934

Kavitha, M., Srinivas, P. V. V. S., Kalyampudi, P. L., & Srinivasulu, S. (2021, September). Machine learning techniques for anomaly detection in smart healthcare. In *2021 Third International Conference on Inventive Research in Computing Applications (ICIRCA)* (pp. 1350-1356). IEEE. DOI: 10.1109/ICIRCA51532.2021.9544795

Kayan, H., Heartfield, R., Rana, O., Burnap, P., & Perera, C. (2024). Casper: Context-aware iot anomaly detection system for industrial robotic arms. *ACM Transactions on the Internet of Things*, *5*(3), 1–36. DOI: 10.1145/3670414

Miotto, R., Wang, F., Wang, S., Jiang, X., & Dudley, J. T. (2018). Deep learning for healthcare: Review, opportunities and challenges. *Briefings in Bioinformatics*, *19*(6), 1236–1246. DOI: 10.1093/bib/bbx044 PMID: 28481991

Raji, M. F., Li, J., Haq, A. U., Ejianya, V., Khan, J., Khan, A., Khalil, M., Ali, A., khan, G. A., Shahid, M., Ahamad, B., Yadav, A., & Memon, I. (2020). A New Approach for Enhancing the Services of the 5G Mobile Network and IOT-Related Communication Devices Using Wavelet-OFDM and Its Applications in Healthcare. *Scientific Programming*, *2020*(1), 3204695. DOI: 10.1155/2020/3204695

Rosero-Montalvo, P. D., István, Z., Tözün, P., & Hernandez, W. (2023). Hybrid anomaly detection model on trusted IoT devices. *IEEE Internet of Things Journal*, *10*(12), 10959–10969. DOI: 10.1109/JIOT.2023.3243037

Sodhro, A. H., Sangaiah, A. K., Sodhro, G. H., Lohano, S., & Pirbhulal, S. (2018). An energy-efficient algorithm for wearable electrocardiogram signal processing in ubiquitous healthcare applications. *Sensors (Basel)*, *18*(3), 923. DOI: 10.3390/s18030923 PMID: 29558433

Somasundaram, R., & Thirugnanam, M. (2021). Review of security challenges in healthcare internet of things. *Wireless Networks*, *27*(8), 5503–5509. DOI: 10.1007/s11276-020-02340-0

Tripathi, A., Upadhyay, P., & Goel, P. K. (2025a). Deep Learning for Anomaly Detection in Industrial Networks. In *AI-Enhanced Cybersecurity for Industrial Automation* (pp. 103–130). IGI Global Scientific Publishing. DOI: 10.4018/979-8-3373-3241-3.ch006

Tripathi, A., Upadhyay, P., & Goel, P. K. (2025b). Industrial Control Systems (ICS) Security: AI-Based Threat Detection and Prevention. In *AI-Enhanced Cybersecurity for Industrial Automation* (pp. 149-172). IGI Global Scientific Publishing.

Tripathi, A., Upadhyay, P., & Goel, P. K. (2025c). Smart Intrusion Detection and Prevention for IIoT Using AI. In *AI-Enhanced Cybersecurity for Industrial Automation* (pp. 61–82). IGI Global Scientific Publishing. DOI: 10.4018/979-8-3373-3241-3.ch004

Tripathi, A., Upadhyay, P., & Goel, P. K. (2025d). Geospatial Data Analysis for Mapping Carbon Sequestration Hotspots. In *Advanced Systems for Monitoring Carbon Sequestration* (pp. 193–218). IGI Global Scientific Publishing. DOI: 10.4018/979-8-3373-2091-5.ch009

Tripathi, A., Yadav, V., & Kumar, S. (2025e). Leveraging Artificial Intelligence for Rural Education: A Systematic Review of Transforming Learning Opportunities and Bridging the Urban-Rural Divide.

Uddin, M., & Syed-Abdul, S. (2020). Data analytics and applications of the wearable sensors in healthcare: An overview. *Sensors (Basel)*, *20*(5), 1379. DOI: 10.3390/s20051379 PMID: 32138291

Upadhyay, P. (2025). Analyzing Soil Organic Carbon Storage. *Advanced Systems for Monitoring Carbon Sequestration*, 455.

Varshney, N., Madan, P., Shrivastava, A., & Srivastava, A. P., KUMAR, C. P., & Khan, K. (2023, December). Real-time anomaly detection in IoT healthcare devices with LSTM. In *2023 International Conference on Artificial Intelligence for Innovations in Healthcare Industries (ICAIIHI)* (Vol. 1, pp. 1-6). IEEE. DOI: 10.1109/ICAIIHI57871.2023.10489823

Wang, Y., Nazir, S., & Shafiq, M. (2021). An overview on analyzing deep learning and transfer learning approaches for health monitoring. *Computational and Mathematical Methods in Medicine*, *2021*(1), 5552743. DOI: 10.1155/2021/5552743

Xue, C., Lin, L., Huang, Y., & Wang, X. (2024). Graph neural network-based anomaly detection for human cyber physical systems. *Zhongguo Gongcheng Xuekan*, *47*(8), 977–984. DOI: 10.1080/02533839.2024.2407294

Chapter 12
Security Frameworks for Operational Technology (OT) and IT Integration

Sudipta Dhar
http://orcid.org/0009-0004-4998-3041
Brainware University, India

Shivangi Kashyap
http://orcid.org/0009-0002-1685-330X
Central University, Hyderabad, India

Pravin Kumar
http://orcid.org/0009-0008-9393-7324
Brainware University, India

ABSTRACT

Today's rapidly evolving industrial environment is witnessing a dramatic change from the accelerated digitization (or digital transformation) of all types of organizations across multiple industries. At the heart of this change is the growing convergence of Information Technology (IT) and Operational Technology (OT)—two formerly distinct domains that have traditionally operated with different functions, technologies, and priorities, The convergence of IT and OT represents a new tide of transformation that will drive new technological innovation across the industrial landscape and accelerate automation, efficiency, connectivity, and data. This chapter will consider the potential transformation and challenges associated with the convergence of OT and IT and will also consider the need for common and adaptive approaches to cybersecurity systems.

DOI: 10.4018/979-8-2600-1498-1.ch012

INTRODUCTION

The Digital Transformation of Industry: A Paradigm Shift

Generation Change is occurring in factories with the Fourth Industrial Revolution or Industry 4.0. This revolution is defined as the coming together of digital technologies with traditional industrial processes to redefine the way production, operations, and services are carried out (Boyes et al., 2018 ; Phuyal et al., 2020). Through rapid advancements in networking technologies such as IoT, AI, cloud computing, and big data analytics, Industry 4.0 has truly transformed society and all sectors (Humayed et al., 2017 ; Lu & Xu, 2019 ; González-Rodríguez et al., 2024). Across different sectors, such as manufacturing, utilities, transportation, healthcare, and government, organizations use these technologies to enhance operational efficiency, agility, and capability for innovation (Dhirani et al., 2021 ; Alqudhaibi et al., 2025 ; Wiboonrat, 2022).

And a major factor supporting this transformation is the growing integration of disparate technology domains previously siloed as OT (Operational Technology) and IT (Information Technology), facilitating automation, data-aided decisions, and real-time response (Humayed et al., 2017 ; Tsiknas et al., 2021).

DEFINING OT AND IT: SEPARATE WORLDS CONVERGE

Operational Technology: The Backbone of Physical Process Control

Operational Technology consists of hardware and software systems that are specifically designed to monitor, control, and automate physical devices and industrial processes (Cardenas et al., 2008; Stouffer et al., 2011; Barrett, 2018). OT systems utilize PLCs, SCADA, DCS, and HMIs and are leveraged in many industry sectors such as energy production, manufacturing, transportation, and water treatment (Fovino et al., 2009; Miller and Rowe, 2012).

Information Technology: Managing Data and Connectivity

Information Technology operates in the design of data acquisition, processing, communication, and storage (Sadeghi et al., 2015; Sharma et al., 2020). The IT environment has a flexible architecture upon which enterprise applications, cloud services, and network communication are represented and developed with constant software upgrades and security controls like access control, encryption, and intrusion detection (Djebbar & Nordström, 2023; Papachristofis et al., 2024).

IT systems emphasize confidentiality, integrity, and availability to protect digital assets and support dynamic business processes, differing vastly from the constraints and priorities present in OT systems (Dhirani et al., 2021; Verma et al., 2025).

The Convergence Imperative: Unlocking New Opportunities

Both IT and OT are converging as per the requirements of Industry 4.0, to achieve more intelligent, connected operations that support quick analytics, automation and remote controls (Boyes et al., 2018 ; Bravos et al., 2022 ; Maggi et al., 2021). The combination of these allows numerous transformative functions:

- ***Smart Manufacturing:*** Cyber-physical systems are outfitted with sensors gathering information on the operations, which is processed using IT analytics platforms to optimize real-time processes (Phuyal et al., 2020 ; Maggi et al., 2021).
- ***Predictive Maintenance***: Machine learning and artificial intelligence can analyze OT sensor signals to tell when the equipment is deteriorating before it fail to extend asset life (González-Rodríguez et al., 2024; Lee et al., 2023).
- ***Remote Monitoring and Control***: Authorized personnel can remote securely controlling of industrial equipment at any time, resulting in more responsive to changes on site and less personnel required on site (Wiboonrat, 2022 ; Dhirani et al., 2021).
- ***More Effective Decisions:*** IT dashboard and analytics-based situational awareness can be used to provide agile strategic decision-making (Lu & Xu, 2019 ; Verma et al., 2025).
- ***Cost, Resource Optimization:*** lean working, automatization and data-driven resources allocation provide high operational cost reduction (Alqudhaibi et al., 2025 ; Phuyal et al., 2020).

Such innovations are the technological basis of smart cities, autonomous logistics, resilient supply chains, and next-generation industrial systems (Humayed et al., 2017 ; Bravos et al., 2022).

Challenges in OT-IT Integration: Bridging Different Worlds

Although promising, convergence between OT and IT is fraught with issues, especially cybersecurity related ones.

Technology constraints and Legacy Systems

Lots of OT devices are 20-30 years old legacy systems that were never built with cybersecurity in mind and could not be enhanced with modern security measures, such as encryption or software patching (Cui & Stolfo, 2010 ; Pochmara & Świetlicka, 2024 ; Barrett, 2018). They are also extremely susceptible to cyber-attack and exploitation (Kainz et al., 2024 ; Bhole et al., 2025).

Safety-Critical Requirements and Real-Time requirements

Operational technologies tend to be very highly available and responsive (real-time responsive), and updates or the need to scan systems can trigger a catastrophic failure (Bell, 1999, pp. 6-12; Stouffer et al., 2011, pp. 5-6). This restricts the use of cybersecurity policies in relation to IT to the extent that regular patching or antivirus scanning cannot be applied directly (Djebbar & Nordström, 2023 ; Alqudhaibi et al., 2025).

Incompatibilities Protocol and Architecture

OT communication protocols are usually proprietary and do not have baked in security measures like authentication or encryption making them vulnerable to intrusion, like spoofing or man-in-the-middle attacks, whenever they connect to unrestricted IT networks (Alcaraz & Lopez, 2010 ; Ten et al., 2010).

Expanded Attack Surfaces

Deployment of OT-IT integration expands the attack surface footprint and renders the critical processes exposed to a broader scope of cyber risks such as malware, ransomware, denial-of-service (DoS), and advanced persistent threats (APT) (Tsiknas et al., 2021 ; Makrakis et al., 2021 ; Sharma et al., 2020).

Cultural and Organizational Barriers

The priorities of OT and IT teams, their vocabulary, or operational cadences can be different, and OT is concerned with physical safety and availability, whereas IT modave estimated that three-quarters of all hospital IT-related outages can cause financial reimbursement and/or payments to keep gear running, or a combination of those (Humayed et al., 2017 ; Djebbar & Nordström, 2023). It is essential to bridge these silos in order to arrive at effective and coherent governance of security (Verma et al., 2025 ; Papachristofis et al., 2024).

Illustrative Cybersecurity Incidents in OT-IT Environments

A number of major cyberattacks show the impact of a poorly secured OT-IT integration:

- ***Stuxnet (2010):*** A crafty malware that infected Iranian nuclear centrifuges in enrichment with IT vulnerability bridged to access OT controllers physically damaging them and bridging the cyber and physical attacks (Kriaa et al., 2012: Miller & Rowe, 2012 ; Humayed et al., 2017).
- ***Colonial Pipeline Ransomware Attack (2021):*** A ransomware infection in information technology (IT) systems caused a halt in pipeline operations, which exemplify and indicate the cascading consequences of IT exploitation of critical operations technology (OT) infrastructure (Makrakis et al., 2021 ; Bhole et al., 2025).
- ***Ukrainian Power Grid Attack (2015):*** Hackers found interconnections between IT and OT systems, causing massive power disruption problems to highlight OT-based vulnerabilities in the national critical infrastructure (Fovino et al., 2009 ; He & Yan, 2016).

These examples demonstrate the harsh operational, economical, and safety consequences of hybrid cyber-physical attacks that require better models of security (Ten et al., 2010 ; Humayed et al., 2017).

Limitations of Traditional IT-Centric Cybersecurity Approaches

The traditional approaches to cybersecurity, which are functionally best suited to IT settings, presuppose frequent updates, flexibility, and downtime acceptability, which is certainly not possible to achieve within the OT context (Stouffer et al., 2011 ; Djebbar & Nordström, 2023). Using these models as is exposes systems to failures or instability (Pochmara & Świetlicka, 2024 ; Barrett, 2018).

Security measures to be implemented in OT environments must also be specifically designed to ensure that real-time performance and safety is maintained but with minimal operational impact (Bell, 1999 ; Alqudhaibi et al., 2025).

Towards Integrated Cybersecurity Frameworks for Hybrid Environments

In the evolving hybrid security realms of OT and IT, a cornucopia has evolved, of which most are mentioned below:

- ***NIST SP 800-82:*** Providing industrial-specific information on securing ICS systems, mainly, segmentation, access control, and patch management, adapted to OT constraints (Stouffer et al., 2011 ; Barrett, 2018).
- ***ISA/IEC 62443:*** An international standard covering security issues throughout the lifecycle of an Industrial Automation and Control System (IACS), thus dealing with a spectrum of technical, procedural, and organizational controls (Djebbar & Nordström, 2023 ; Papachristofis et al., 2024).
- ***ISO/IEC 27001:*** A globally-accepted information security management framework that can easily be imported into industrial-scale applications, making the choice of an intermediate level when it comes to treating the governance part of organizational security and the technical side of the problem (Barrett, 2018 ; Djebbar & Nordström, 2023).
- ***NIST Cybersecurity Framework (CSF):*** The model consists of the following functions or elements; Identify, Protect, Detect, Respond and Recover; a top level compilation of activities to manage cybersecurity in a comprehensive manner within the risk-informed context, and combined with business requirements (Barrett, 2018 ; Verma et al., 2025).

The concepts of security usually assume sets of frameworks and are applied to functionality with good governance and cooperation across disciplines (Papachristofis et al., 2024).

This Table 1 is a summary of the prominent cybersecurity frameworks relevant to OT–IT integration and outlines their scope, strengths, and weaknesses. SP 800-82 published by the NIST, looks at industrial control systems and offers significant detail on technical guidance but does not include strong elements of governance. The ISA/IEC 62443 provides a robust approach to the entire lifecycle of industrial automation and control systems, but could add complexity to implementation. The ISO/IEC 27001 provides a full, robust organization risk management strategy, but does not focus on specific OT needs. The NIST Cybersecurity Framework (CSF) provides risk-based governance that is flexible for enterprises, but takes some adjustment for OT contexts. Overall, these frameworks highlight that while they bring specific advantages to the table, none sufficiently resolve hybrid OT–IT issues independently and a more integrated, layered route is needed.

Table 1. Comparison of Cybersecurity Frameworks for OT-IT Integration

Framework	Scope	Strengths	Limitations	Key References
NIST SP 800-82	Industrial Control Systems (ICS)	OT-specific technical guidance on segmentation, incident response	Limited organizational governance focus	Stouffer et al., 2011
ISA/IEC 62443	Industrial Automation & Control Systems (IACS)	Lifecycle management integrating technical and procedural controls	Complex implementation	Djebbar & Nordström, 2023
ISO/IEC 27001	Organizational Information Security Management	Comprehensive risk management framework	Not specifically tailored to OT environments	Barrett, 2018; Djebbar & Nordström, 2023
NIST Cybersecurity Framework	Enterprise-wide cybersecurity management	Risk-based, business-aligned, flexible	Requires OT-specific adaptation	Barrett, 2018; Verma et al., 2025

THE PATH FORWARD: BUILDING RESILIENT, ADAPTIVE CYBERSECURITY POSTURES

More adaptive, potentially lifecycle-based cyber defense strategies must be implemented as OT-IT integration spreads across industry segments (Verma et al., 2025; Kainz et al., 2024) and will likely take into consideration:

- ***Continuous Risk Assessment:*** Dynamic threat modeling and vulnerability analysis that are under development based on vulnerability to the changes in technology and the method of attack (Tsiknas et al., 2021; Dhirani et al., 2021).
- ***Interdisciplinary Collaboration:*** Discontinued operational silos are being eliminated to align IT, OT, and security (Humayed et al., 2017; Djebbar & Nordström, 2023).
- ***Defense-in-Depth:*** Possession of multiple-layered control, including network segmentation, detection of anomalies, firewalls, and secure remote access (Alcaraz & Lopez, 2010; Wiboonrat, 2022).
- ***Governance and Compliance Alignment:*** Achieving coherence between security policies and regulatory norms and best practices within an industry (Barrett, 2018; Djebbar & Nordström, 2023).
- ***Invest in New technologies:*** Invest in AI/ML capabilities in detecting threats, zero trust models, digital twin simulations, and distributed ledgers in terms

of their importance in auditability. The number of times I may feel ashamed (Lee et al., 2023; González-Rodríguez et al., 2024; Bhole et al., 2025).

When these are implemented, the organizations will have the capability to calmly maneuver in the maze of digital-physical system convergence, ensuring that operations remain continuous, safe, and resilient, in the face of a landscape of varied and changing cyber threats.

LITERATURE REVIEW

Foundations and Evolution of OT-IT Convergence

The combining of Operational Technology (OT) and Information Technology (IT) represents a foundational shift in how industrial assets, critical infrastructure, and enterprise operations are managed in the digital era (Humayed et al., 2017; Boyes et al., 2018; Cardenas et al., 2008). Historically, OT governed the physical control of machinery and processes, and IT controlled data processing, communication, and intelligence. (Humayed et al., 2017; Boyes et al., 2018; Stouffer, Falco, & Scarfone, 2011). The demarcation, however, has been blurred by Industry 4.0 advancements—most notably, the spread of the Industrial Internet of Things (IIoT), proliferation of high-speed connectivity, and the ubiquity of smart sensors (Boyes et al., 2018; Tsiknas, Taketzis, Demertzis, & Skianis, 2021; Phuyal, Bista, & Bista, 2020).

Early research on cyber-physical systems (CPS) emphasized the growing interaction between the digital and physical domains and recognized emerging risks from this integration (Humayed et al., 2017). (A systematic review of CPS security (2017) identified threats that traverse both OT and IT domains, as well as the inefficient nature of traditional security solutions that are too narrowly targeted and secured in just one domain.

The evolution of this convergence has unlocked considerable advantages.Boyes et al. (2018) argued that the IIoT creates a new paradigm for production, maintenance, and adaptation—unlocking smart manufacturing, predictive maintenance, and tighter supply chain integration (Boyes et al., 2018; Phuyal et al., 2020).Yet, they also signaled that the increased attack surface and heterogeneity challenge security and risk management.

Integrating IT infrastructures with legacy OT systems delivers both technical and organizational challenges. Studies such as Wiboonrat (2022) emphasize that convergence can yield efficiency gains and asset optimization, but only if the complex interplay of reliability, safety, real-time control, and digital security is explicitly addressed.

Vulnerabilities and Cyber Risks

Researchers in the field of academia focus their work on OT-IT environments, given their vulnerability to cybersecurity incidents. Early work by Cardenas et al. suggested survivable cyber-physical systems because of the ubiquity of attacks on critical controls. Authors such as Fovino et al. provided evidence in terms of testing to show malware attacks on SCADA systems present vulnerabilities. Insecurity of embedded network devices has been determined empirically with quantification, finding many production devices are vulnerable due to hard-coded credentials and lack of updates. The increase in connected devices within IIoT has made those vulnerabilities more complex. Stark et al. and Pochmara and Świetlicka (2024) state that there is greater awareness of vulnerabilities but insufficient security activities for OT deployments in 2023.

Landmark Incidents: Lessons from Practice

Specific instances of convergence between Operational Technology (OT) and Information Technology (IT) in the area of cybersecurity pose substantial security risks - such as the Stuxnet attack that leveraged IT connectivity to penetrate and attack OT Programmable Logic Controllers (PLCs) at nuclear facilities in Iran. This incident showed the inherent dangers of sophisticated malware that can corrupt both the digital and physical environments. Recently, attacks on the Colonial Pipeline in 2021 raised further concerns about situational awareness in critical infrastructures' vulnerabilities due to inadequate intrusion detection or response, lack of segmentation across network boundaries, poor incident response practices, etc. Studies across many organizations signal that widespread issues exist that include failed backups and misinterpretations of various OT problem methodologies that resulted in substantial outages or risk to safety, as observed in cyberattacks that disrupted Ukrainian electrical grids. These incidents have introduced policy and regime-oriented changes to cybersecurity practices in industrial systems.

Security Frameworks and Standards: A Comparative Perspective

Various standards and frameworks have been developed to address the risks and limitations in OT/IT environments. NIST SP 800-82 is based on ICS and OT systems, emphasizing network segmentation and incident response. ISA/IEC 62443 incorporates lifecycle management for industrial automation and control systems. ISO/IEC 27001 describes security management in hybrid environments with an emphasis on risk management. The NIST Cybersecurity Framework focuses on risk-based, business-aligned cybersecurity. Recently, researchers have advocated for centralized governance and harmonization of controls, which recognizes the need for localized implementations to suit operational realities and compliance.

Countermeasures, Technical Solutions, and Industry Practice

The existing literature identifies a number of engineering and industrial approaches to improve OT-IT security. Among the most important remedial action measures to counter the risk of insecure IT to OT networks are network segmentation - especially through VLAN and firewall implementation - which in some retrofits and legacy periods can cause significant challenges. In addition to secure remote access technologies, like encryption and multi-factor authentication, technologies facilitating safe remote access deliver value when delivering operational technologies in a remote fashion. Moreover, as systems evolve both physical and digital, and integrate into a whole, monitoring procedures that utilize AI and machine learning for behaviour-based analytics will be critical. Regular endpoint hardening and inventory of your OT assets are also essential features of the OT security agenda. Industry surveys indicate that upstream and downstream technical, business or organizational risks and challenges remain in defending modular smart factories and IIoT, and are further disrupted by human-based risk (such as skills and recruitment) and cultural barriers between engineering and IT.

Future Research Directions: Emerging Technologies and Resilience

With the acceleration of digitization, research is also becoming interested in new paradigms of OT/IT protection. Zero Trust Architectures (ZTA), where identity and access verification occur in real-time without exception on all users/devices regardless of location, are collecting momentum but introduce complications in real-time safety-critical OT environments (Alqudhaibi et al., 2025; Verma et al., 2025; Bhole et al., 2025). Lee et al. (2023) point to early adoption of the distributed ledger technologies and demonstrator projects in energy-based applications, where secure audit paths and tamper-evident chains may be used in demanding industry supply chains. According to studies, artificial intelligence and digital twins a digital copy of an object or system that could be manipulated in a simulation environment digital models of physical systems to be used, through simulation, and monitoring of the system are proposed as key enablers of early threat detection and policy validation and exercises to support incident response (González-Rodríguez, 2024; Dhirani et al., 2021; Bhole et al., 2025). The literature to a significant extent also promotes the lifecycle security model characterized by continuous adaptation and assessment of controls, risk models, and organizational practices in view of the changing technologies, regulations, and changing sophistication of the attackers (Verma et al., 2025; Alqudhaibi et al., 2025; Kainz et al., 2024).

Synthesis: Gaps and Opportunities

The literature reviews all come to some similar conclusions:

- ***Legacy Infrastructure:*** Legacy infrastructure still limits the ability to fully embrace more advanced security technology because it is costly and risky to retrofit legacy assets.
- ***Downtime and Availability Issues:*** Security practices tend to overlook the need for OT to have an almost zero tolerance to downtime, and as a result, this hinders the use of traditional IT-based patching and scanning techniques.
- ***Policy and Standardization Gaps:*** There is still a lack of consistency in the standardization area between NIST, IEC, and ISO standards, which is problematic in terms of establishing compliance across geographies and industries.
- ***Human and Organizational Problems***: Skills gaps, clustered insulated teams, and limited cross-domain training in place.
- ***Regulatory Complexity:*** Emerging and changing laws about privacy, safety, and national security tend creating minimum compliance as opposed to pro-active risk mitigation.

Regardless of responsive issues, the direction within a research promotes adaptive, multi-layered frameworks which combine technical safeguards with organizational procedures and development of workforce. New technologies, such as AI, block-chain, and zero trust show promise in the establishment of resilient, agile OT-IT environments.

The pie chart shows the main cybersecurity challenges in OT–IT convergence. The biggest barrier is vulnerabilities of legacy systems (30%), followed by real-time and safety constraints (20%) and expanded attack surface (20%). Protocol and architecture weaknesses (15%) and cultural and organizational barriers (15%) also add to the risk overall. Although the pie chart shows that technical flaws are the largest influencers, organizational and cultural factors are also significant in shaping cybersecurity vulnerabilities.

Figure 1. Key Cybersecurity Challenges in OT-IT Convergence

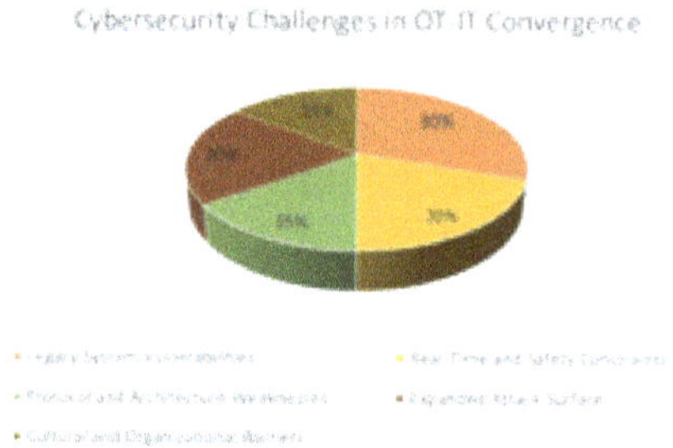

Source: Author's illustration

Key cybersecurity challenges in OT-IT environments are illustrated in Table 2, highlighting that legacy infrastructure, downtime sensitivity, and complex regulations present high risks while siloed teams and standardizations present medium-only risk. Taken together, these challenges reveal how technical constraints, organizational barriers, and regulatory challenges erode security in converged systems.

Table 2. Key Cybersecurity Challenges in OT-IT Convergence

Challenge	Key Issues	Impact Level
Legacy Infrastructure	Old OT devices lack modern security mechanisms	High
Downtime Sensitivity	Limited ability to patch or update in real-time	High
Siloed Teams	Poor collaboration between IT and OT staff	Medium
Standardization Gaps	Conflicting frameworks and a lack of harmonization	Medium
Regulatory Complexity	Overlapping, evolving, multi-jurisdictional rules	High

(Percentages are synthesized from literature data)

METHODOLOGY

This chapter employs a qualitative analytical methodology integrating a systematic literature review, comparative framework analysis, and case study examination to provide a robust understanding of cybersecurity frameworks applicable to hybrid OT-IT environments in industrial and critical infrastructure contexts.

Research Design and Rationale

The research methodology follows a systematic and replicable approach consistent with some established guidelines for literature rigor, like PRISMA (Preferred Reporting Items for Systematic Reviews and Meta-Analyses) (Moher et al., 2009). This allows for the encompassing incorporation, impartial selection, and critical evaluation of academic and technical literature regarding cybersecurity standards, practical applications, and analyses of historic incidents.

Especially when the subject is so complex and interdisciplinary as OT-IT integration of cybersecurity needs to be addressed on technical, organizational, and regulatory fronts, then this method fits best.

Detailed Methodological Steps

This chapter applies a qualitative analytical approach that uses a systematic literature review, a comparative framework analysis, and a case study approach to gain an in-depth perspective on cybersecurity frameworks related to hybrid OT-IT environments within industrial and critical infrastructure environments.

The research methodology follows a systematic and replicable approach consistent with some established guidelines for literature rigor, like PRISMA (Preferred Reporting Items for Systematic Reviews and Meta-Analyses) (Moher et al., 2009). This enables the comprehensive compilation, impartial selection, and critical appraisal of academic and technical literature regarding cybersecurity frameworks, practical implementations, and case studies related to past incidents.

Especially when the subject is so complex and interdisciplinary as OT-IT integration of cybersecurity needs to be addressed on technical, organizational, and regulatory fronts, then this method fits best.

Step 1: Define Research Scope

- Cybersecurity frameworks concerning the hybrid OT-IT environment.
- Scope: Industrial Control Systems (ICS), cyber-physical systems (CPS), industry digitalization under Industry 4.0, and the frameworks NIST SP 800-82, ISA/IEC 62443, ISO/IEC 27001, and NIST CSF.
- Literature timeframe: 2008 onwards, giving the greatest emphasis to recent documentation and less emphasis to previously established historical literature.

Step 2: Systematic Literature Search

- Databases: IEEE Xplore, ScienceDirect, SpringerLink, Google Scholar.
- Keywords: "OT-IT convergence", "cybersecurity frameworks", "Industrial Control Systems security", "Operational Technology cybersecurity", "NIST SP 800-82", "ISA/IEC 62443", "cyber-physical systems", "industrial cyber-attacks", "critical infrastructure cybersecurity".
- Inclusion Criteria: Peer-reviewed journals, conference proceedings, whitepapers, and standards documents of authority that dealt with the hybrid OT-IT context.
- Exclusion: Articles dealing with IT or OT in isolation, non-English language papers, and those that are not peer-reviewed, except those with very high citation indices.

Step 3: Screening and Selection

- First, titles and abstracts will be screened in accordance with the inclusion criteria.
- Full texts will then be assessed for their relevance, methodological quality, and contribution.
- To reduce bias, screening should be performed independently by two reviewers; disagreements should then be settled through discussion.

Step 4: Data Extraction and Thematic Analysis

- We will extract and analyze data across the following headings: framework attributes, technical controls, organizational barriers, incident summaries, emerging technologies, and best practices.
- The data would be classified under thematic axes, including:
- Framework characteristics and limitations.
- Incident analysis and lessons learned.
- Technical countermeasures.
- Organizational and cultural issues.
- Future research and emerging trends.

Step 5: A Comparative Framework Analysis

- Detailed comparative evaluation of frameworks in terms of scope, technical depth, organizational coverage, OT constraints fit, and regulatory alignment.
- Identification of possible complementary merits and gaps.

- Considerations regarding practical implementation into real life.

Step 6: Case Study Analysis

- Select crucial historic cyber incidents (e.g., Stuxnet, Colonial Pipeline attack, Ukrainian power grid attack).
- Analysis of impact, remediation, and lessons learned, exploited OT-IT vulnerabilities, and attack vectors
- Comparison of framework attributes and incident data.

Methodology Flow Diagram

This figure depicts the research methodology continuum. It begins with defining the scope and purpose of the research, followed by a systematic search for and retrieval of literature. The literature is then profiled and selected, followed by data extraction and thematic profiling. The continuum proceeds with framework comparative capacity and case study capacity. Lastly, the findings are synthesized, and recommendations are reported, providing a continuous and comprehensive process.

Here is a flow diagram visualizing the stepwise methodological flow:

Figure 2. Process Flow of the Methodological Approach.

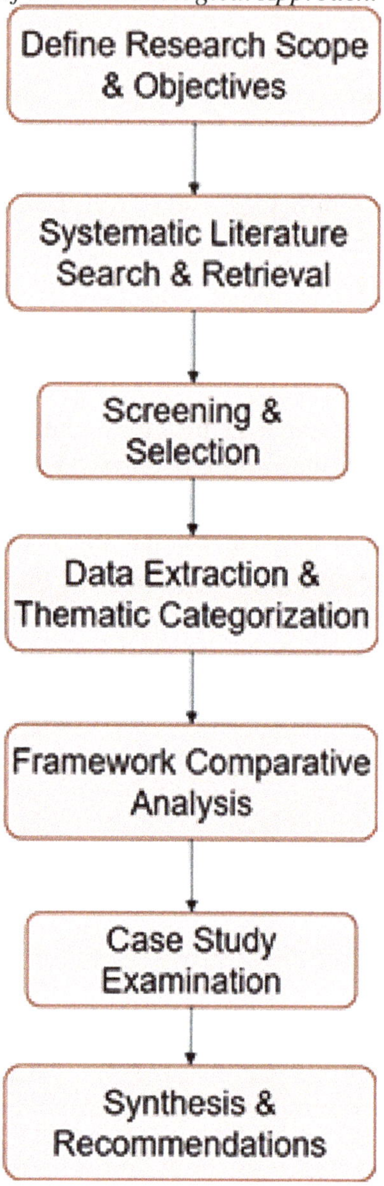

Source: Author's illustration

Emphasis Distribution Graph on Methodological Steps

The methodology emphasizes literature search and framework comparative analysis the most (each 20%), as it is important to build a strong theoretical grounding and to consider existing models in a systematic fashion. Screening, selection, data extraction, and categorization each receive 15% because they assure the most relevant studies have been examined in detail, and options for data analysis have been prepared. Establishing scope and objectives, and case study review both receive 10%, which adds clarity in addressing research priorities and generating implications. Finally, synthesis and recommendations also receive 10%, to represent integrated findings and ideas clearly. Overall, these percentages illustrate an overall balanced process that prioritized rigorous evidence searching and comparative analyses, yet still recognizes practical validation and integrative synthesis.

In Table 3, the methodological steps of a research process are detailed along with the relative weight of each step, where Literature Search and Framework Comparative Analysis have the highest weight (20% each), as these are the key steps to gathering and analyzing frameworks. Screening & Selection and Data Extraction & Categorization have a weight of 15% each, which is moderate emphasis for the data organization and subsequent refinement. Defining Scope & Objectives, Case Study, and Synthesis & Recommendations all have a weight of 10% each, which reflects a small weight of the overall positive support to the research process, though these tasks have relative value in the overall methodology.

Table 3. Relative Emphasis Across Methodological Steps

Methodological Step	Relative Emphasis (%)
Defining Scope & Objectives	10
Literature Search	20
Screening & Selection	15
Data Extraction & Categorization	15
Framework Comparative Analysis	20
Case Study Examination	10
Synthesis & Recommendations	10

Summary Table of Methodological Components

The procedure outlined in this multi-stage approach provides a way to blend rigour with practice. Scope is defined through articulate research questions and inclusion criteria, and then a systematic search is conducted to examine the literature for studies that are both relevant to the research questions and meet the inclusion criteria. Data selection and extraction follow, which allows for the construction of a linked data set of studies that can be compared. Case studies of OT–IT incidents are then analyzed to embed the conclusions of practice. Finally, recommendations are synthesized that consider recommendations from theory alongside implications for practice.

Table 4 provides an ordered overview of the research methods, which include each step with activities, anticipated outputs, methodologies, and tools. It begins with Scope Definition, taking the necessary measures to clarify the focus of the research. This is followed by a Literature Search to create a comprehensive collection of articles related to the research study. From that literature, Screening & Selection processes identify articles that are relevant to the project scope in terms of content and validity. Data Extraction & Thematic Coding: divide articles into the initial, organized dataset of coded and attributed text excerpts. Framework Comparative Analysis applies a set of recognized features to evaluate findings and identify gaps, producing a comparative matrix. Case Study Analysis provides practice-based examples, drawn from incidents and events across the globe, so researchers can see evidence in the literature for support. Finally, in the Synthesis & Recommendations step, the literature, data, case studies, and findings are synthesized into practical recommendations for action, facilitated by both narrative synthesis and expert validation.

Table 4. Methodological Components and Their Application

Methodological Step	Activity Description	Expected Outcome	Tools/Approach
Scope Definition	Refining the question and inclusion criteria	Clear focus and boundaries	Conceptual frameworks, expert input
Literature Search	Keyword-based search in academic/technical repositories	Comprehensive article pool	IEEE Xplore, ScienceDirect, Google Scholar
Screening & Selection	Abstract/title screening; full-text evaluation	Relevant literature shortlist	PRISMA guidelines, dual review
Data Extraction & Thematic Coding	Collecting framework details, challenges, and lessons	Organized qualitative dataset	Spreadsheets, qualitative coding tools
Framework Comparative Analysis	Detailed evaluation of features, gaps	Comparative matrix; gap analysis	Tabulation, SWOT analysis
Case Study Analysis	Review of incidents' OT-IT vulnerabilities	Practical insights, lessons	Content analysis, incident reports
Synthesis & Recommendations	Integration into guidelines and future directions	Comprehensive chapter conclusion	Narrative synthesis, expert validation

The expanded methodology is rigorous, transparent, and offers a thorough synthesis of reviewing the literature on the contexts of OT-IT convergence and their associated cybersecurity frameworks. This study balanced a relatively large volume of literature and critical analysis as a unique method that incorporates both theoretical perspectives and evidence-based case studies to provide a richer basis for decision-making in developing guidance for cybersecurity frameworks.

CORE CONCEPTS

OT and IT System Characteristics

Operational Technology (OT) and Information Technology (IT) systems are two distinctly different domains with inherent differences in aspects such as qualities, priorities, and modes of operation. Understanding the differences between OT and IT systems is essential to effective integration and security management.

Table 5 compares Operational Technology (OT) and Information Technology (IT) in key elements. OT's focus will always be on controlling or monitoring physical processes in real time using devices specifically designed for that purpose (e.g., PLCs, SCADA, etc.) with an emphasis on how process control is done safely, reliability of the process, while maximizing uptime. On the other hand, IT has a primary function of managing data, enterprise applications, and data communication networks; thus, flexibility, frequent updates, and data security are important to IT. In particular, OT traditionally is a no-interaction zone, with limited security controls, whereas IT is well connected and comprises systems built with integrated security controls. The differences continue with patch cycles, protocols, and user bases, with OT having an operational focus, while IT has an information-based focus.

Table 5. Comparative Characteristics of Operational Technology (OT) and Information Technology (IT)

Characteristic	Operational Technology (OT)	Information Technology (IT)
Primary Function	Control, monitor, and manage physical processes and devices in real-time (e.g., manufacturing lines, energy grids, transportation systems).	Manage data processing, storage, communication, and enterprise applications supporting business functions.
Systems & Devices	PLCs (Programmable Logic Controllers), SCADA systems, DCS (Distributed Control Systems), sensors, actuators, HMIs (Human-Machine Interfaces).	Servers, databases, networks, endpoints, cloud platforms, ERP systems, and user workstations.
Requirements	High availability (24/7 operation), deterministic real-time response, safety-critical operation, and minimal downtime tolerated.	Flexibility, adaptability, support for frequent updates, user access management, emphasis on data confidentiality and integrity.

continued on following page

Table 5. Continued

Characteristic	Operational Technology (OT)	Information Technology (IT)
Connectivity	Traditionally isolated or air-gapped; recent trends towards networked and internet-connected, but with limited exposure for safety.	Highly connected, internet-facing, with extensive external and internal network access.
Security Model	Historically, emphasis has been on safety, availability, and reliability; cybersecurity has often been secondary or minimal by design. Security mechanisms may be limited or absent.	Built with integrated cybersecurity controls: authentication, encryption, patching, intrusion detection, and incident response capabilities.
Patch and Update Cycles	Patch cycles are infrequent; updates require careful planning due to operational impact and legacy hardware/software compatibility.	Frequent, automated patch management and software updates are standard practice.
Protocols	Use of proprietary, often legacy communication protocols with limited or no built-in security (e.g., Modbus, DNP3).	Use of standard IT protocols (e.g., TCP/IP, HTTPS) with built-in security extensions (TLS, SSL).
User Base	Operators, engineers, and plant technicians specialized in physical process control.	IT staff, business users, and administrators focused on information systems.

OT systems are primarily focused on the physical world, ensuring constant and safe operations of equipment and infrastructure as needed, although frequently along legacy lines. IT systems, on the other hand, address the virtual world, emphasizing flexibility with confidentiality and quick adaptability. Merging these concerns will require balancing their distinct objectives, compliance needs, and security models.

FRAMEWORKS OVERVIEW

Multiple cybersecurity frameworks to facilitate security in hybrid OT-IT environments exist, all of which have different strengths and coverage. NIST SP 800-82 has specific controls for industrial control systems (ICS), ensuring consideration of architecture, patching, and access controls that are fit for purpose, but its technical focus limits the general applicability within governance. The ISA/IEC 62443-series is more holistic in its lifecycle standard for Industrial Automation and Control Systems that examines risk assessments and technical requirements; however, there may be some overhead to apply this framework. The ISO/IEC 27001 says a more risk management and governance-centric approach is given to the customizable cyber controls around firm management, while comparatively few technical suggestions are given with regard to OT operations. The NIST Cybersecurity Framework (CSF) is optional and flexible, though asset management and recovery-oriented, and less prescriptive in its technical controls. Each framework brings in the pros and cons, hence the need for picking the appropriate change management framework that really caters to the needs of the organization.

Technical Approaches

Effectively securing hybrid OT-IT environments demands a combination of specific technical controls and architectural practices to mitigate risks while preserving operational integrity.

Segmentation of the Network is a fundamental security control for hybrid OT-IT systems. By using VLANs and DMZs, networks are divided into distinct sections to protect critical OT assets and reduce lateral threat movement. This segmentation minimizes the blast radius of cyberattacks and strengthens overall resilience.

Secure Remote Access has become a necessity in modern industrial environments where remote monitoring and control are commonplace. World-class practices such as multi-factor authentication (MFA), VPN encryption, and jump boxes or bastion hosts ensure that only authorized users can connect securely, even remotely. These practices help ensure risk is mitigated while allowing remote operations to be carried out properly and without disruption of sensitive OT or IT systems.

Anomaly Detection enables advanced knowledge of any abnormal behavior or intrusion that is detected. Techniques range from machine learning-based analytics and intrusion detection systems (IDS) to host-based or network-based monitoring. These tools allow organizations to identify and detect the existence of cyberattacks or just operational problems in real-time, in order to help confine the effects of the situation on operations and ensure that critical processes are not disrupted.

Firewalls and data diodes serve as barriers. Firewalls utilize strict rules based on protocols to manage communication between domains in OT and IT. Data diodes, which allow for one-way traffic flow, generally run from OT to IT, preventing all traffic coming in, and just as importantly, any possibility of threat. Together, these devices create secure communication channels and do not allow external consideration.

System Level Protection is focused on hardening endpoints: PLCs, servers, and workstations. For endpoints, it is a security best practice to utilize anti-malware, application whitelisting, secure configurations, and timely patching. While legacy OT devices may lack the capacity for modern endpoint tools, applying solutions specific to them will lessen the risk of compromise and is part of a defense-in-depth approach.

Frameworks like NIST SP 800-82, ISA/IEC 62443, ISO/IEC 27001, and the NIST Cybersecurity Framework provide structured guidance for integrating and securing OT-IT environments. They emphasize both technical controls and governance, supporting organizations in building layered defenses tailored to their operational needs.

RESULTS AND DISCUSSION

Overview of Comparative Analysis

The comparative evaluation of cybersecurity frameworks applicable to hybrid Operational Technology (OT) and Information Technology (IT) environments highlights that **no single cybersecurity framework is sufficient on its own** to fully address the diverse and complex requirements of integrated OT-IT systems. Instead, each framework brings unique strengths and scopes that complement one another.

Strengths and Limitations of Individual Frameworks

NIST SP 800-82 and ISA/IEC 62443: Focused OT Controls and Lifecycle Coverage

NIST SP 800-82, Guide to Industrial Control Systems (ICS) Security, contains in-depth, technical guidance that is vital to OT environments. It specializes in the special features and operating features of control systems, e.g., Programmable Logic Controller (PLCs), SCADA systems, and Distributed Control Systems (DCS). The guide stresses the system architecture and network segmentation specific to OT, advocates access controls that apply to systems with high reliability and low tolerance to downtime, and recommends patch management options that are appropriate in the industrial context.

ISA/IEC 62443 is an integrated international industry standard to help secure Industrial Automation and Control Systems (IACS) throughout their lifecycle. It includes security precautions in the system design and development as well as its deployment, operations, and maintenance, including responding to incidents. It is comprehensive in nature because of its intended inclusion of controls that are not simply technical but also have elements of procedural and organizational components to ensure that security responsibilities are factored not only at the level of the system providers and integrators but also at asset ownership levels. Such wide-range coverage helps make ISA/IEC 62443 a key standard to implement consistent and sound security practices in industrial plants.

Strengths:

- Both frameworks are OT-centric and accept limitations of legacy devices and those of real-time and safety-critical situations.
- They propose specific, effective controls for securing ICS elements and mitigating the OT-specific risk profiles.

- ISA/IEC 62443 process- and lifecycle-based system helps to develop continuous governance and enhancement, which aligns with the continuity needs of OT operations.

Limitations:

- Their concern with technical and process controls is more than likely to underrepresent enterprise IT concerns with its risk management and governance issues, at greater organizational levels.
- Adopting these frameworks completely can be difficult for organizations that are less mature about cybersecurity or organizations whose systems are outdated..

ISO/IEC 27001 and NIST Cybersecurity Framework (CSF): Broad Strategic

Perspectives:

- ***ISO/IEC 27001*** is an internationally accepted standard for setting up and maintaining an Information Security Management System (ISMS). It focuses on the governance, risk management, and security policy formulation at the organizational level and on the development of continuous improvement based on the Plan-Do-Check-Act (PDCA) cycle. This standard gives organizations a framework through which effectiveness in information security can be proven.
- ***The NIST Cybersecurity Framework (CSF)*** instead is a framework approach and is risk-based, business-aligned with five core functions: Identify, Protect, Detect, Respond, and Recover. Its strategic focus assists in correlating cybersecurity to organizational objectives and complying with regulations, conveys among the stakeholders and executive management, and facilitates ongoing adjustments to the overall security posture in response to emerging threats.

Strengths:

- These frameworks offer excellent shaping of governance, risk evaluation, and policy incorporation required to conduct business-wide management of cybersecurity.
- The certification process of ISO/IEC 27001 provides an external confirmation and assurance.

- The universality of NIST CSF gives it applicability across sectors and a level of maturity, which makes it more widespread as a means of generating a security program.

Limitations:

- Both ISO/IEC 27001 and NIST CSF do not implicitly reflect the OT-related technical limitations, for instance, the presence of legacy and proprietary OT subsystems, or the necessity to use real-time control systems.
- In the absence of OT-centric standards complementing frameworks, IT-only frameworks run the risk of omitting important operational risks in industrial cases.

Necessity and Benefits of Framework Integration

The analysis is conclusive to prove that an integrated use of several cybersecurity frameworks is the best way to secure hybrid OT-IT environments. With such integration, organizations can:

Use NIST SP 800-82 and ISA/IEC 62443 as a source of strictly defined technical controls, system segmentation, secure design, and OT lifecycle management.

Implement ISO/IEC 27001 and NIST CSF to create and define a comprehensive risk management and policy framework, and coordinate cybersecurity requirements with business requirements and compliance obligations.

Such a layering of frameworks forms a defense-in-depth arch at various levels: the device and network level, the organizational policy and culture level, etc.

The Role of Governance and Cross-Functional Collaboration

The integration of the Framework on its own is not enough, as good governance structures and cross-disciplinary collaboration are necessary. As the research shows, text blocks can be named according to their first line, such as Alphabet block or Time block, or used to store other text designs or collections.

- ***Governance:*** It is critical to clearly define roles and responsibilities within the IT and OT domains. We provide executive sponsorship, cybersecurity committees, and established escalation paths which maintain accountability and provide ongoing security investment..
- ***Collaboration*:** IT and OT teams can have different priorities, languages, and operating tempos. Conducting joint training, joint risk assessment exercises,

and aligned incident response plans promotes an improved understanding of each other and creates a unified security posture.

Effective governance and collaboration:

- Improve cyber risk visibility into the entire enterprise
- Assist in coordinated response to threats related to the management of the incident in such a way that it is not disseminated.
- Support the required culture change that would see the integration of cyber-security into how operations take place. Enhance visibility into cyber risks across the whole enterprise.

Empirical Evidence from Case Studies

Case studies of high-impact cybersecurity attacks (e.g., Stuxnet, Colonial pipeline ransomware, Ukrainian power grid attack) show that:

- The level of preparedness is higher in organizations with integrated security models that balance technical OT controls and extensive risk management and governance.
- They are faster and more efficient in their response to intrusions, hence less operation and repair time.
- Poor integration of the framework and siloed OT-IT controls played a major role in facilitating the successes of the attacks and their detrimental effect.

Against this backdrop, organizations with piecemeal and IT-only security models were behind in detection and ineffective response, and experienced larger damage.

Challenges in Framework Integration

Although integration offers clear benefits, several challenges remain:

- ***Complexity and Resource Intensive***: The coordination of multiple frameworks necessitates skilled staff, thought-out process alignment, and staff training, and ongoing training is needed.
- ***Aging Infrastructure:*** Physical upgrades to OT systems for compliance can be expensive or cause interruptions.

- *Compliance:* Organizations utilizing systems in multiple jurisdictions will need to deal with varying requirements related to framework adoption and integration.
- *Evolving Risks:* Frameworks require consistent updates and adjustments due to cyber incidents and changing technologies in the Industrial Space.

To manage hybrid OT-IT environments, an integrated approach is needed to tie together more OT-specific frameworks (NIST SP 800-82, ISA/IEC 62443) and more governance frameworks that have a broader emphasis on governance (ISO/IEC 27001, NIST CSF). Strong governance, as well as collaborative teams that combine IT and OT, and multi-layered defenses, enhance resiliency and response to incidents. However, the threat of legacy equipment and its implications, along with complex rules and regulations, still prevails in these hybrid environments.

Challenges and Limitations

The combination of Operational Technology (OT) and Information Technology (IT) can bring significant change to the industry, and at the same time presents numerous and complicated challenges to the successful implementation of cybersecurity architecture. Such challenges can be very ingrained in technological, organisational, and even regulatory reality. It is important to learn and overcome these drawbacks to create robust, safe hybrid environments.

Legacy Infrastructure

The biggest and one of the most overlooked issues when it comes to securing a hybrid OT-IT environment is that OT networks include a significant amount of legacy infrastructure that has to be addressed. Most industrial control systems, as well as supervisory control and data acquisition (SCADA) and programmable logic controllers (PLCs), have been on duty for decades. These legacy devices have ownership mindsets focused on availability, safety, and reliability, often being deployed in isolated or air-gapped systems and with little concern for cybersecurity.

Key issues related to legacy infrastructure include:

- *Incompatibility With Modern Security Controls:* Most older OT devices do not have the necessary computing power, memory, or firmware to support the current cybersecurity technologies, such as encryption, multi-factor authentication, intrusion detection, or security patching.

- ***Infrequent Updates:*** Most legacy systems have low updateability, meaning that they cannot (or cannot safely) receive regular software or firmware updates, or that they require a time-consuming and risky update process to obtain updates.
- ***Proprietary Apps and Outdated Protocols:*** All legacy OT devices usually communicate through proprietary or unsupported protocols, lacking any inbuilt security mechanisms (e.g., authentication or encryption), creating and extending attack surfaces..
- ***End-of-Life Equipment:*** Vendors will no longer offer security patches or support, leaving unmitigated vulnerabilities.

These aspects are major limiting factors in the capability of organizations to install common IT cybersecurity applications in OT systems. Without customizing the standard IT security measures, the attempts to retrofit the system might create delays in operations or instability in the systems. Legacy systems must therefore be addressed by special measures by the organization, including network segmentation, protocol gateways, or compensating controls.

Downtime Sensitivity

The industrial processes often driven by TOT may be real-time safety-critical systems, as in the case of power generation, chemical processing systems, transportation systems, and manufacturing. Downtime or interruption- whether intentional or unintentional- the disadvantages may be dire and include the loss of cash and fines with authorities, as well as safety risks, together with environmental pollution.

Because of this:

- ***Security Patching Is Problematic:*** Unlike IT systems, patches in OT environments can be very problematic because maintenance windows are generally very limited, and the OT system has a very low ability to withstand downtime. Servicing the patches might entail putting processes or systems off, which might be impractical or dangerous to stop.
- ***Maintenance of Security Systems May Interrupt Operations:*** Security-related processes (malware scan, software updates, or configuration changes) may cause latencies and instabilities in real-time process controls.
- ***Critical Systems May Not Be Possible to Update:*** Other systems have been designed to operate for many years without being rebooted or having updates.

Due to these operational limitations, organizations have to strike a compromise between maintaining their security postures up to date and avoiding becoming disruptive. 29. Newfound dedication to innovative solutions. Offline patch testing, staged rollouts, compensating technical controls, and thorough risk management efforts: this challenge requires novel approaches in setting priorities to address remediation efforts.

Siloed Teams

There are more than technical challenges that come with the integration of the OT and IT realms, which lie in organizational and cultural challenges between teams that have a history of separate silo formation. The personnel of TOT are normally process engineers or operations experts, and they are concerned more with physical safety, system availability, and real-time control as opposed to security and system integrity, data security, information confidentiality, and regulatory compliance as directed by the IT team. These competing interests and specialization tend to cause a lack of convergence in cybersecurity strategies. The two groups have different communication barriers, and these factors include differences in terms of language, workflows, risk tolerance, and operational rhythm. Along with this, ambiguities in responsibility, including unclear boundaries of who has what responsibility in cybersecurity when operating in hybrid formats, can lead to lapses, duplication of efforts, or areas that are neglected as potential points of risk.

The absence of combined training and awareness is another dilemma because the OT personnel might have little exposure to methods of cybersecurity, whereas IT staff might not be well versed in the demands of industrial operations. These gaps make it impossible to conduct synchronized risk assessment, incident response, and apply policies in a consistent way through cross-platform OTIT systems. The barriers can be overcome by establishing shared governance structures, creating cross-functional teams, and establishing some joint training programs to bridge the OT and IT divide and build a collaborative culture.

Standardization Gaps

Although the frameworks of cybersecurity do exist, there are challenges in successfully applying the frameworks to the various industrial settings without any standardization differences. There is a disparate set of frameworks and standards that organizations grapple with, such as NIST SP 800-82, ISA/IEC 62443, ISO/IEC 27001, and a set of sector-specific regulations, many of which overlap in scope, making it difficult to select, align, or integrate the various frameworks and standards. The other factor is the conflict between local and global practices, where the international standards may not exactly meet the local work requirements, the cultural setting, or even industry-specific practices. The complexity of implementation furthers the issue as some frameworks, such as ISA/IEC 62443, are highly technical and lifecycle-oriented, making them resource-intensive and impractical to fully implement in some organizations.

Completing this difficulty is the dynamic aspect of standards, which requires dynamic changes in standards due to the fast-paced innovation and the emergence of new threats, leaving the industry and the implementation process. In addition, the lack of standardised terminology between frameworks-variation in the definitions, measures of risk, and types of control- further hinders harmonisation initiatives. The gaps together can create obstacles to building consistent, broad-based, and auditable cybersecurity programs that consider both the realities of operation and the requirements of regulation, particularly across multiple sectors or across multiple countries.

Regulatory Complexity

The OT-IT convergence space exists in a dense regulatory environment of overlapping, and sometimes seemingly competing, laws, standards, and compliance requirements:

- ***Multi-jurisdictional Compliance:*** The international organizations that operate in different countries or regions have to deal with different regulations of cybersecurity (e.g., NIST in the US, EU NIS Directive, GDPR, etc.)
- ***Sector-Specific Regulations:*** Many types of critical infrastructure, including energy, water, transportation, and healthcare, are assigned specific, and at times, strict regulatory standards regarding safety, privacy, and security.
- ***Overlap and Contradiction:*** Separate rules. Frequently, competing needs need to be met, e.g., overlapping requirements between operational continuity and security patch lifecycles.
- ***Reporting and Auditing Requirements:*** Compliance requirements could include a lot of documentation, regular audits, incident reporting, and verifiable controls.
- ***Evolving Legal Environment:*** Many laws relating to cybersecurity are constantly evolving as they are increasingly being addressed by the government, necessitating frequent changes.

Complying with this complex regulatory environment introduces administrative overheads and uncertainty to the design and operation of the cybersecurity program. Regulators are asking organizations to allocate the required resources to compliance management, update policies more frequently, and make the frameworks flexible and auditable to address converging regulations.

Cybersecurity today is challenged by OT/IT convergence due to legacy infrastructure, etc. Organizations may engage compensating controls, resilient architectures, and adaptable frameworks to confront the challenges. A strong governance structure that enables coordination between OT and IT teams and adapts to regulatory changes is necessary. Addressing these challenges systematically should better position businesses to tackle the spectrum of OT and IT risks affecting their cyber posture.

Future Directions

A key characteristic of OT-IT convergence is its dynamicity and complexity; in view of this, innovation in cybersecurity approaches is necessary all the time. The new paradigms and technologies can unlock new measures of resilience, responsiveness, and awareness in these so-called hybrid environments. Combining these developments with an organizational governance framework facilitates a state of proactive defense against cyber threats that are continuing to evolve and become more and more sophisticated.

Zero Trust Architecture (ZTA)

Traditional perimeter-centric security presupposes that all systems and users comprising a trusted local network can be considered trustworthy, but it is no longer true within the changing environment with OT-IT connections. ZTA challenges this paradigm with an all-the-time verification and verification of the use of continuous authentication, authorization, and verification of users and devices, wherever the user is or whichever part of the network he/she is using. These core concepts are persistent authentication, in which identity, health, and behaviour are evaluated continuously; least privilege access, to restrict users and devices to only needed permissions so as to minimize the attack surface and lateral movement; and micro segmentation, to divide sensitive OT assets into finer-grained security zones. Adaptive access control takes security a step higher by controlling privileges according to contextual risk quantities, including the behaviour of users and device posture. When ZTA is implemented within an OT-IT runtime environment, the risk of insider threats, compromised credentials, and lateral attacks is addressed. Scenarios such as handling legacy OT devices with resource constraints, real-time operational demands, and trade-offs between access control and availability can challenge traditional practice and leave the door open to more specialized ZTA approaches.

Artificial Intelligence (AI) and Machine Learning (ML)

Cybersecurity has to rely on Artificial Intelligence(AI) and Machine Learning(ML) in the future because the volume of data, its speed, and the complexity overwhelm all the effort of human analysts and traditional tools to manage and secure it. These technologies allow real-time monitoring of threats, intelligent response, and optimization of the system so that it is proactive in terms of securing the critical infrastructures. Behavioral anomaly detection gives machines the ability to recognize the alterations in the behavior of the network, device, or process and report possible cyberattacks or insider threats. Predictive analytics can be used to project weaknesses based on previous attacks, device logs, and operational data, and use it to advise mitigation efforts. Some incident response processes may also be automated by IA, however, to an extent where the human response time is reduced by the time it reaches the previously mentioned processes. It also helps to streamline security measures, e.g., to make security procedures more responsive to new risks and to minimize false positives. In operational technology, AI-ML needs to be explainable, reliable, and with a low rate of false alarms, and domain knowledge should be incorporated with sufficient validation to guarantee stability and inherence of critical functions.

Digital Twins for Cybersecurity

Digital twins Digital twins in industry are virtual representations of physical systems, processes, or industrial plants that behave similarly in real-time using sensor-employed data and system models. In cybersecurity, they are being used to create a secure environment where one can test the vulnerability, attack scenarios, and also plan for the eventuality of an incident occurring without interfering with the ongoing activity. Among its main advantages, one can suggest proactive vulnerability analysis, which allows identifying possible weaknesses and security measures in advance, and incident response rehearsal, according to which a team can practice a response to an incident and enhance preparedness. Digital twins can be used to improve situational awareness, since they continually reflect operational statuses, allowing the estimation of outcomes of propagating failures (caused by cyber events). Coupled with AI, they can have more capabilities in anomaly detection and are able to automate decision-making, further reinforcing resilience. But to implement it, precise models are essential, a lot of data must be gathered, and an in-depth knowledge of IT-OT alignment is necessary. Due to cost and difficulty in resources, and the complexity of proprietary equipment deployment, it is a challenging task, but a must in securing critical infrastructures.

Unified Policy Models

Standardised policy frameworks are becoming crucial as cybersecurity policies and norms are proliferating within and across industry sectors and jurisdictions. These models combine IT, OT, and compliance requirements into a harmonious governance framework that is adaptive to changing regulatory environments. A significant factor here is cross-sector standardization that allows building harmonized cybersecurity requirements that meet the sector-specific requirements and general regulatory requirements. It is also notable to align IT and OT governance, as the unified policies help manage risks, respond to incidents, control access, and audit all the applied technologies. Automated policy enforcement also helps in strengthening compliance as it integrates rules into cyber defense tools, where monitoring and consistent enforcement are achieved in distributed environments. This abstraction increases flexibility in that high-level security directives can be interpreted into system- or vendor-specific security controls. All in all, unified, integrated policy models streamline compliance, responsibilities, simplify regulatory structure, and enhance organization-wide security, and have the further benefit of enhancing transparency and expediency in audits, thus becoming a crucial component in robust cyber governance.

Lifecycle Security: Continuous Assessment and Improvement

Securing hybrid OT-IT ecosystems is predicated on a lifecycle approach that supports the assessment and improvement of the resilience of these systems to continuously emerging technologies and threats. This lifecycle approach recognizes multiple phases: Identify (asset inventory and risk assessment), Protect (install layered security controls through configuration management), Detect (anomaly detection in real time using AI and machine learning), Respond (coordinated or synchronized incident response plans), and Recover (resilience backup strategies and continuous improvement). A significant amount of resources will be dedicated to ensuring service continuity when introducing security upgrades. Market trends surrounding Zero Trust Architecture, AI, and Digital Twin technology to create adaptive, intelligent defense systems around resilience to cyber risks in integrated industrial systems and operational improvement.

CONCLUSION

The intersection of operational technology (OT) and information technology (IT) represents a literal paradigm shift in contemporary industrial and critical infrastructure systems. With this integration, opportunities to automate, use data-driven decision-making, and streamline operations are unlike any time before, but with this newfound capacity also comes a vast increase in the cybersecurity environment. This makes securing such hybrid OT-IT environments complex and requires a holistic, agile, and versatile security strategy that can holistically draw on the unique requirements and complexities of both worlds.

Unified and elastic security stance

A basic conclusion is that it is necessary to overcome the historical fundamentals of security silos that have historically separated OT and IT. These differences can be summarized in that OT environments are real-time, safety-critical which are legacy-constrained, whereas IT environments are confidential, periodically patched, and fast to adapt. Security solutions have to help mediate between these disparate realities in a harmonized framework that encompasses the blending of technical control, risk management processes, and governance models that are capable of responding to changing operational and threat environments.

Organizations also need to implement security architectures that are modular and adaptive, where the protective measures may be network isolation, limited access, threat detection, and safe harbor of endpoints, but where continuity of operations and safety are never in jeopardy. Balance means having to adopt multiple-layered security that combines OT-specific cybersecurity standards (such as NIST SP 800-82 and ISA/IEC 62443) with more strategic and organizational-level ones (NIST CSF and ISO/IEC 27001).

Cross-Functional Collaboration and Strategic Governance

Technology alone will not be able to suffice without strong governance frameworks and interdisciplinary interaction. The convergence further enhances organizational issues, where traditionally OT and IT teams exist in silos, their cultures and priorities are different, as are their expertise. Clearing up the policies, roles, and responsibilities, and continuous communication among these teams are the things that are needed to create cohesive and responsive cybersecurity programs.

Moreover, fully committed top management and periodic evaluations of the risks in accordance with business strategy will ensure that the IT security is ranked and stays responsive. Resilience consists of the process of incorporating security into all elements of operational processes--such as the design and implementation of supply chains, human factors, incident response, and compliance monitoring--as opposed to viewing security as a discrete, technical issue.

Combination of various Cybersecurity Frameworks

The multifaceted nature of OT-IT environments means that various cybersecurity frameworks should be combined, with each offering different lenses and tools that can be applied to thorough protection:

- ***OT-centric frameworks*** introduce technical standards to the safe operation of legacy controls, industrial protocols, and safety systems.
- ***Organizational structures*** offer control, management of risk, and alignment of policies in both corporate and functional areas.
- **Viable flexible frameworks** enable continuous review to make adjustments in response to arising threats.

Organizations that embrace this layered-integrated strategy can enjoy the benefits of a defense in depth, as any single framework can not adequately address due to gaps. This model is also capable of supporting scalable security strategies that are appropriate in greenfield and legacy brownfield applications.

Traditional, Advanced, and Lifecycle-based Security

Cyberattacks against OT-IT converged systems are continually increasing in complexity, exploiting publicized vulnerabilities and production relationships. Cybersecurity, therefore, cannot exist in a fixed way. It has to pursue a lifecycle model that encompasses constant asset discovery, risk evaluation, threat identification, response, and recovery planning.

The new technologies, Zero Trust Architectures, Artificial Intelligence and Machine Learning, and Digital Twins provide exciting opportunities to stimulate situational awareness, automate defenses, and model attack scenarios with no risk. Organizations are supposed to integrate such innovations and have flexible policies that allow accommodating any legacy limitations.

Constant training and skills upgrading of OT and IT staff are also very important in terms of staying current with the latest technologies and attack patterns.

Safeguarding Digital and Physical Assets

However, the merger of OT and IT only further shores up the interdependency between cyber and physical systems. Henceforth, incidents of security breaches in this hybrid realm could no longer be treated merely as leaks of information but as potential threats to physical assets, public safety, and national security.

Through the integrated lifecycle cybersecurity approach, organizations and stakeholders can shield both worlds effectively-building resilient infrastructure that provides operational excellence, safeguards human life, and assures service continuity in this time of heightened digital interconnection.

REFERENCES

Alcaraz, C., & Lopez, J. (2010). A security analysis for wireless sensor mesh networks in highly critical systems. *IEEE Transactions on Systems, Man, and Cybernetics. Part C, Applications and Reviews, 40*(4), 419–428. DOI: 10.1109/TSMCC.2010.2045373

Alqudhaibi, A., Albarrak, M., Jagtap, S., Williams, N., & Salonitis, K. (2025). Securing industry 4.0: Assessing cybersecurity challenges and proposing strategies for manufacturing management. *Cyber Security and Applications, 3*, 100067. DOI: 10.1016/j.csa.2024.100067

Barrett, M. P. (2018). Framework for improving critical infrastructure cybersecurity version 1.1.

Bell, R. (1999, November). Iec 61508: functional safety of electrical/electronic/programme electronic safety-related systems: overview. In *IEE Colloquium Control of Major Accidents and Hazards Directive (COMAH)-Implications for Electrical and Control Engineers (Ref. No. 1999/173)* (pp. 5-1). IET.

Bhole, M., Sauter, T., & Kastner, W. (2025). Enhancing Industrial Cybersecurity: Insights from Analyzing Threat Groups and Strategies in Operational Technology Environments. *IEEE Open Journal of the Industrial Electronics Society, 6*, 145–157. DOI: 10.1109/OJIES.2025.3527585

Boyes, H., Hallaq, B., Cunningham, J., & Watson, T. (2018). The industrial internet of things (IIoT): An analysis framework. *Computers in Industry, 101*, 1–12. DOI: 10.1016/j.compind.2018.04.015

Bravos, G., Cabrera, A. J., Correa, C., Danilović, D., Evangeliou, N., Ezov, G., Gajica, Z., Jakovetic, D., Kallipolitis, L., Lukic, M., Mascolo, J., Masera, D., Mazo, R., Mezei, I., Miaoudakis, A., Milosevic, N., Oliff, W., Robin, J., Smyrlis, M., & Vukobratovic, D. (2022). Cybersecurity for industrial internet of things: Architecture, models and lessons learned. *IEEE Access : Practical Innovations, Open Solutions, 10*, 124747–124765. DOI: 10.1109/ACCESS.2022.3225074

Cardenas, A. A., Amin, S., & Sastry, S. (2008, June). Secure control: Towards survivable cyber-physical systems. In *2008, The 28th International Conference on Distributed Computing Systems Workshops* (pp. 495-500). IEEE.

Cui, A., & Stolfo, S. J. (2010, December). A quantitative analysis of the insecurity of embedded network devices: results of a wide-area scan. In *Proceedings of the 26th annual computer security applications conference* (pp. 97-106). DOI: 10.1145/1920261.1920276

David, D. P. (2020). Three Articles on the Economics of Information-Systems Defense Capability. *Material-, Human-, and Knowledge-Resources Acquisition for Critical Infrastructures (Ph. D. thesis), Université de Lausanne, Faculté des hautes études commerciales.*

Dhirani, L. L., Armstrong, E., & Newe, T. (2021). Industrial IoT, cyber threats, and standards landscape: Evaluation and roadmap. *Sensors (Basel), 21*(11), 3901. DOI: 10.3390/s21113901 PMID: 34198727

Djebbar, F., & Nordström, K. (2023). A comparative analysis of industrial cybersecurity standards. *IEEE Access : Practical Innovations, Open Solutions, 11*, 85315–85332. DOI: 10.1109/ACCESS.2023.3303205

Fovino, I. N., Carcano, A., Masera, M., & Trombetta, A. (2009). An experimental investigation of malware attacks on SCADA systems. *International Journal of Critical Infrastructure Protection, 2*(4), 139–145. DOI: 10.1016/j.ijcip.2009.10.001

González-Rodríguez, V. E., Izquierdo-Bueno, I., Cantoral, J. M., Carbú, M., & Garrido, C. (2024). Artificial intelligence: A promising tool for application in phytopathology. *Horticulturae, 10*(3), 197. DOI: 10.3390/horticulturae10030197

He, H., & Yan, J. (2016). Cyber-physical attacks and defences in the smart grid: A survey. *IET Cyber-Physical Systems, 1*(1), 13–27. DOI: 10.1049/iet-cps.2016.0019

Humayed, A., Lin, J., Li, F., & Luo, B. (2017). Cyber-physical systems security—A survey. *IEEE Internet of Things Journal, 4*(6), 1802–1831. DOI: 10.1109/JIOT.2017.2703172

Kainz, O., Zoller, M., Murin, M., Nováková, I., Šimko, E., & Horváth, L. (2024, October). Cybersecurity through Practical Applications. In *2024 International Conference on Emerging eLearning Technologies and Applications (ICETA)* (pp. 269-275). IEEE. DOI: 10.1109/ICETA63795.2024.10850868

Kriaa, S., Bouissou, M., & Piètre-Cambacédès, L. (2012, October). Modeling the Stuxnet attack with BDMP: Towards more formal risk assessments. In *2012 7th International Conference on Risks and Security of Internet and Systems (CRiSIS)* (pp. 1-8). IEEE.

Lee, A., Gourisetti, S. N. G., Sebastian-Cardenas, D. J., Lambert, K., Navarro, V., Pasetti, M., Cali, Ü., Isirova, K., Reddi, R., Nitu, P., Touhiduzzaman, M., Mylrea, M., Huff, P., Rahimi, F., & Saha, S. S. (2023). Assessment of the distributed ledger technology for energy sector industrial and operational applications using the mitre att&ck® ics matrix. *IEEE Access : Practical Innovations, Open Solutions, 11*, 69854–69883. DOI: 10.1109/ACCESS.2023.3288428

Li, L., Qiu, Y., & Xu, J. (2022, April). A K-means clustered routing algorithm with location and energy awareness for underwater wireless sensor networks. [). MDPI.]. *Photonics*, *9*(5), 282. DOI: 10.3390/photonics9050282

Lu, Y., & Xu, X. (2019). Cloud-based manufacturing equipment and big data analytics to enable on-demand manufacturing services. *Robotics and Computer-integrated Manufacturing*, *57*, 92–102. DOI: 10.1016/j.rcim.2018.11.006

Maggi, F., Balduzzi, M., Vosseler, R., Rösler, M., Quadrini, W., Tavola, G., Pogliani, M., Quarta, D., & Zanero, S. (2021). Smart factory security: A case study on a modular smart manufacturing system. *Procedia Computer Science*, *180*, 666–675. DOI: 10.1016/j.procs.2021.01.289

Makrakis, G. M., Kolias, C., Kambourakis, G., Rieger, C., & Benjamin, J. (2021). Industrial and critical infrastructure security: Technical analysis of real-life security incidents. *IEEE Access : Practical Innovations, Open Solutions*, *9*, 165295–165325. DOI: 10.1109/ACCESS.2021.3133348

Miller, B., & Rowe, D. (2012, October). A survey SCADA of and critical infrastructure incidents. In *Proceedings of the 1st Annual conference on Research in information technology* (pp. 51-56). DOI: 10.1145/2380790.2380805

Moher, D., Liberati, A., Tetzlaff, J., & Altman, D. G. (2009). Preferred reporting items for systematic reviews and meta-analyses: The PRISMA statement. *BMJ (Clinical Research Ed.)*, **•••**, 339. PMID: 19622551

Papachristofis, K., Vardoulias, G., & Vavousis, K. (2024, September). Comparative Evaluation of Cybersecurity Maturity Models and Frameworks. In *European, Mediterranean, and Middle Eastern Conference on Information Systems* (pp. 166-178). Cham: Springer Nature Switzerland.

Phuyal, S., Bista, D., & Bista, R. (2020). Challenges, opportunities and future directions of smart manufacturing: A state of art review. *Sustainable Futures : An Applied Journal of Technology, Environment and Society*, *2*, 100023. DOI: 10.1016/j.sftr.2020.100023

Pochmara, J., & Świetlicka, A. (2024). Cybersecurity of industrial systems—A 2023 report. *Electronics (Basel)*, *13*(7), 1191. DOI: 10.3390/electronics13071191

Sadeghi, A. R., Wachsmann, C., & Waidner, M. (2015). *Security and privacy challenges in industrial Internet of Things. Proceedings of the 52nd Annual Design Automation Conference*. DOI: 10.1145/2744769.2747942

Sharma, V., You, I., Andersson, K., Palmieri, F., Rehmani, M. H., & Lim, J. (2020). Security, privacy and trust for smart mobile-Internet of Things (M-IoT): A survey. *IEEE Access : Practical Innovations, Open Solutions*, *8*, 167123–167163. DOI: 10.1109/ACCESS.2020.3022661

Stouffer, K., Falco, J., & Scarfone, K. (2011). Guide to industrial control systems (ICS) security. *NIST special publication, 800*(82), 16-16.

Ten, C. W., Manimaran, G., & Liu, C. C. (2010). Cybersecurity for critical infrastructures: Attack and defense modeling. *IEEE Transactions on Systems, Man, and Cybernetics. Part A, Systems and Humans*, *40*(4), 853–865. DOI: 10.1109/TSMCA.2010.2048028

Tsiknas, K., Taketzis, D., Demertzis, K., & Skianis, C. (2021). Cyber threats to industrial IoT: A survey on attacks and countermeasures. *IoT*, *2*(1), 163–186. DOI: 10.3390/iot2010009

Verma, P., Newe, T., O'Mahony, G. D., Brennan, D., & O'Shea, D. (2025). Towards a Unified Understanding of Cyber Resilience: A Comprehensive Review of Concepts, Strategies, and Future Directions. *IEEE Access : Practical Innovations, Open Solutions*. Advance online publication. DOI: 10.1109/ACCESS.2025.3551887

Wiboonrat, M. (2022, October). Cybersecurity in Industrial Control Systems: An integration of information technology and operational technology. In *IECON 2022–48th Annual Conference of the IEEE Industrial Electronics Society* (pp. 1-6). IEEE.

Compilation of References

Abd Elaziz, M., Al-qaness, M. A., Dahou, A., Ibrahim, R. A., & Abd El-Latif, A. A. (2023). Intrusion detection approach for cloud and IoT environments using deep learning and Capuchin Search Algorithm. *Advances in Engineering Software*, *176*, 103402. DOI: 10.1016/j.advengsoft.2022.103402

Abidi, M. H., Umer, U., Mian, S. H., & Al-Ahmari, A. (2023). Big data-based smart health monitoring system: Using deep ensemble learning. *IEEE Access : Practical Innovations, Open Solutions*, *11*, 114880–114903. DOI: 10.1109/ACCESS.2023.3325323

Abusitta, A., Li, M. Q., & Fung, B. C. (2024). Survey on Explainable AI: Techniques, challenges and open issues. *Expert Systems with Applications*, *255*, 124710. DOI: 10.1016/j.eswa.2024.124710

Adeyeye, O. J., Akanbi, I., Emeteveke, I., & Emehin, O. (2024). Leveraging secured AI-driven data analytics for cybersecurity: Safeguarding information and enhancing threat detection. *International Journal of Research and Publication and Reviews*, *5*(10), 3208–3223. DOI: 10.55248/gengpi.5.1024.2911

Ahmed, N., Hossain, M. E., Hossain, I. S., Hossain, Z., Kabir, M. F., & Begum, N. (2025, March). AI-Driven Cyber Security for Safeguarding Critical Infrastructure and Patient Data. In *2025 International Conference on Machine Learning and Autonomous Systems (ICMLAS)* (pp. 1485-1492). IEEE. DOI: 10.1109/ICMLAS64557.2025.10968807

Ahmed, S., Rahman, A., & Ashrafuzzaman, M. (2023). A Systematic Review Of AI And Machine Learning-Driven IT Support Systems: Enhancing Efficiency And Automation In Technical Service Management. *American Journal of Scholarly Research and Innovation*, *2*(02), 75–101. DOI: 10.63125/fd34sr03

Ajiga, D., Okeleke, P. A., Folorunsho, S. O., & Ezeigweneme, C. (2024). The role of software automation in improving industrial operations and efficiency. *International Journal of Engineering Research Updates*, *7*(1), 22–35. DOI: 10.53430/ijeru.2024.7.1.0031

Akhtar, M. A. K., Kumar, M., & Nayyar, A. (2024). Privacy and Security Considerations in Explainable AI. In *Towards Ethical and Socially Responsible Explainable AI: Challenges and Opportunities* (pp. 193–226). Springer Nature Switzerland. DOI: 10.1007/978-3-031-66489-2_7

Akinade, A. O., Adepoju, P. A., Ige, A. B., Afolabi, A. I., & Amoo, O. O.Afees Olanrewaju AkinadePeter Adeyemo AdepojuAdebimpe Bolatito IgeAdeoye Idowu AfolabiOlukunle Oladipupo Amoo. (2021). A conceptual model for network security automation: Leveraging AI-driven frameworks to enhance multi-vendor infrastructure resilience. *International Journal of Science and Technology Research Archive*, *1*(1), 39–59. DOI: 10.53771/ijstra.2021.1.1.0034

Akpakwu, G.A.; Silva, B.J.; Hancke, G.P.; Abu-Mahfouz, A.M. (2017). A survey on 5G networks for the Internet of Things: Communication technologies and challenges. IEEE Access 2017, 6, 3619–3647.

Akram, F., Liu, D., Zhao, P., Kryvinska, N., Abbas, S., & Rizwan, M. (2021). Trustworthy intrusion detection in e-healthcare systems. *Frontiers in Public Health*, *9*, 788347. DOI: 10.3389/fpubh.2021.788347 PMID: 34926397

Al Abdulwahid, A. (2022). Detection of Middlebox-Based Attacks in Healthcare Internet of Things Using Multiple Machine Learning Models. *Computational Intelligence and Neuroscience*, *2022*, 2022. DOI: 10.1155/2022/2037954 PMID: 36479020

Al, E. 'mari, S., Sanjalawe, Y., & Fataftah, F. (2025). AI-Driven Security Systems and Intelligence Threat Response Using Autonomous Cyber Defense. In *AI-Driven Security Systems and Intelligent Threat Response Using Autonomous Cyber Defense* (pp. 35-78). IGI Global Scientific Publishing.

Alamro, H., Marzouk, R., Alruwais, N., Negm, N., Aljameel, S. S., Khalid, M., Hamza, M. A., & Alsaid, M. I. (2023). Modelling of Blockchain Assisted Intrusion Detection on IoT Healthcare System using Ant Lion Optimizer with Hybrid Deep Learning. *IEEE Access : Practical Innovations, Open Solutions*, *11*, 82199–82207. DOI: 10.1109/ACCESS.2023.3299589

Alazab, A., Khraisat, A., Singh, S., & Jan, T. (2023). Enhancing privacy-preserving intrusion detection through federated learning. *Electronics (Basel)*, *12*(16), 3382. DOI: 10.3390/electronics12163382

Alcaraz, C., & Lopez, J. (2010). A security analysis for wireless sensor mesh networks in highly critical systems. *IEEE Transactions on Systems, Man, and Cybernetics. Part C, Applications and Reviews, 40*(4), 419–428. DOI: 10.1109/TSMCC.2010.2045373

Ali, A. R. A. R., Saravanan, K., Abirami, B. B., Pandi, V. S., Aroulanandam, V. V., & Parthiban, S. (2024, December). Enhancing Cloud Security with AI: Developing Robust, Scalable Solutions for Threat Mitigation and Data Protection in Cloud Platforms. In *2024 International Conference on Sustainable Communication Networks and Application (ICSCNA)* (pp. 614-620). IEEE.

Ali, S. M., Razzaque, A., Yousaf, M., & Shan, R. U. (2024). An automated compliance framework for critical infrastructure security through Artificial Intelligence. *IEEE Access : Practical Innovations, Open Solutions.*

Alladi, T., Chamola, V., & Naren, . (2020). HARCI: A two-way authentication protocol for three entity healthcare IoT networks. *IEEE Journal on Selected Areas in Communications, 39*(2), 361–369. DOI: 10.1109/JSAC.2020.3020605

Al-Quayed, F., Ahmad, Z., & Humayun, M. (2024). A situation based predictive approach for cybersecurity intrusion detection and prevention using machine learning and deep learning algorithms in wireless sensor networks of industry 4.0. *IEEE Access : Practical Innovations, Open Solutions, 12*, 34800–34819. DOI: 10.1109/ACCESS.2024.3372187

Alqudhaibi, A., Albarrak, M., Jagtap, S., Williams, N., & Salonitis, K. (2025). Securing industry 4.0: Assessing cybersecurity challenges and proposing strategies for manufacturing management. *Cyber Security and Applications, 3*, 100067. DOI: 10.1016/j.csa.2024.100067

Alrzini, J. R. S., & Pennington, D. (2020). A review of polymorphic malware detection techniques. *International Journal of Advanced Research in Engineering and Technology, 11*(12), 1238–1247.

Al-Shammari, N. K., Syed, T. H., & Syed, M. B. (2021). An Edge–IoT framework and prototype based on blockchain for smart healthcare applications. Engineering, Technology &. *Applied Scientific Research, 11*(4), 7326–7331.

Alshar'e, M., Abualkishik, A., Abuhmaidan, K., & Kayed, A. (2025). Enhancing Project Security: Unveiling Trust, Interpretability and Explainability in the Age of AI. In *5G Enabled Technology for Smart City and Urbanization System* (pp. 163-178). Chapman and Hall/CRC.

Alshar'e, M. (2023). Cyber security framework selection: Comparision of NIST and ISO27001. *Applied computing Journal.*

Alsuyayfi, S., & Alanazi, A. (2022). Impact of clinical alarms on patient safety from nurses' perspective. *Informatics in Medicine Unlocked*, *32*, 101047. DOI: 10.1016/j.imu.2022.101047

Alzaabi, F. R., & Mehmood, A. (2024). A review of recent advances, challenges, and opportunities in malicious insider threat detection using machine learning methods. *IEEE Access : Practical Innovations, Open Solutions*, *12*, 30907–30927. DOI: 10.1109/ACCESS.2024.3369906

Alzboon, M. S., Bader, A. F., Abuashour, A., Alqaraleh, M. K., Zaqaibeh, B., & Al-Batah, M. (2023, November). The two sides of AI in cybersecurity: opportunities and challenges. In *2023 International Conference on Intelligent Computing and Next Generation Networks (ICNGN)* (pp. 1-9). IEEE. DOI: 10.1109/ICNGN59831.2023.10396670

Amin, S. M. (2011). Smart grid security, privacy, and resilient architectures: Opportunities and challenges. *2011 IEEE Power and Energy Society General Meeting*, 1–4. DOI: 10.1109/PES.2011.6039081

Ampatzi, C. (2024). How AI can Improve Intrusion Detection and Prevention System.

Apruzzese, G., Laskov, P., Montes de Oca, E., Mallouli, W., Brdalo Rapa, L., Grammatopoulos, A. V., & Di Franco, F. (2023). The role of machine learning in cybersecurity. *Digital Threats : Research and Practice*, *4*(1), 1–38. DOI: 10.1145/3545574

Arjunan, T. (2024). Detecting anomalies and intrusions in unstructured cybersecurity data using natural language processing. *International Journal for Research in Applied Science and Engineering Technology, 12*(9), 10.22214.

Arora, S., & Khare, P. (2024). AI/ML-enabled optimization of edge infrastructure: Enhancing performance and security. *sensors, 4*(2).

Asharf, J., Moustafa, N., Khurshid, H., Debie, E., Haider, W., & Wahab, A. (2020). A review of intrusion detection systems using machine and deep learning in internet of things: Challenges, solutions and future directions. *Electronics (Basel)*, *9*(7), 1177. DOI: 10.3390/electronics9071177

Asija, R., & Nallusamy, R. (2016). Healthcare SaaS based on a data model with built-in security and privacy. [IJCAC]. *International Journal of Cloud Applications and Computing*, *6*(3), 1–14. DOI: 10.4018/IJCAC.2016070101

Aslam, M. M., Tufail, A., Apong, R. A. A. H. M., De Silva, L. C., & Raza, M. T. (2024). Scrutinizing security in industrial control systems: An architectural vulnerabilities and communication network perspective. *IEEE Access : Practical Innovations, Open Solutions*, *12*, 67537–67573. DOI: 10.1109/ACCESS.2024.3394848

Awuor, A. S., Okoth, P., & Kwanya, T. (2024). Navigating Ethical Dilemmas while Transforming Information Services in the Global Age. Information Impact. *Journal of Information and Knowledge Management*, *15*(2), 45–58.

Ayyaswamy, K., Gobalakrishnan, N., & Kathirvel, N. (2025). Cyber Security in Industrial Automation Using AI. In *AI-Enhanced Cybersecurity for Industrial Automation* (pp. 509–540). IGI Global Scientific Publishing. DOI: 10.4018/979-8-3373-3241-3.ch024

Azam, H., Dulloo, M. I., Majeed, M. H., Wan, J. P. H., Xin, L. T., Tajwar, M. A., & Sindiramutty, S. R. (2023). Defending the digital Frontier: IDPS and the battle against Cyber threat. *International Journal of Emerging Multidisciplinaries Computer Science & Artificial Intelligence*, *2*(1), 253. DOI: 10.54938/ijemdcsai.2023.02.1.253

Azhari, R., & Salsabila, A. N. (2024). Analyzing the impact of quantum computing on current encryption techniques. [ITSDI]. *IAIC Transactions on Sustainable Digital Innovation*, *5*(2), 148–157. DOI: 10.34306/itsdi.v5i2.662

Babu, C. S., Simon, P. A., & Manohoran, S. (2025). AI-Powered Defenses Against Ransomware: Mitigating Emerging Threats to Critical Infrastructures. In *Deep Learning Innovations for Securing Critical Infrastructures* (pp. 577-604). IGI Global Scientific Publishing.

Baheti, R., & Gill, H. (2011). Cyber-physical systems. The Impact of Control Technology, 161–166. https://www.ieeecss.org/sites/ieeecss/files/2019-07/IoCT-Part1-07Cyberphysical-Systems.pdf

Barbierato, E., & Gatti, A. (2024). The challenges of machine learning: A critical review. *Electronics (Basel)*, *13*(2), 416. DOI: 10.3390/electronics13020416

Barrett, M. P. (2018). Framework for improving critical infrastructure cybersecurity version 1.1.

Baruwal Chhetri, M., Tariq, S., Singh, R., Jalalvand, F., Paris, C., & Nepal, S. (2024). Towards human-ai teaming to mitigate alert fatigue in security operations centres. *ACM Transactions on Internet Technology*, *24*(3), 1–22. DOI: 10.1145/3670009

Bauer, M., Boussard, M., Bui, N., & Carrez, F. (2013). IoT interoperability: Challenges and solutions. 2013 19th IEEE International Conference on Networks (ICON), 1–6. DOI: 10.1109/ICON.2013.6781972

Bayan, F. M. H. (2024). The Ethics of AI: Navigating the Moral dilemmas of Artificial Intelligence. Arab Journal for Scientific Publishing (AJSP). *ISSN*, *2663*, 5798.

Bell, R. (1999, November). Iec 61508: functional safety of electrical/electronic/programme electronic safety-related systems: overview. In *IEE Colloquium Control of Major Accidents and Hazards Directive (COMAH)-Implications for Electrical and Control Engineers (Ref. No. 1999/173)* (pp. 5-1). IET.

Bhadauria, R., & Sanyal, S. (2012). Survey on security issues in cyber-physical systems. *International Journal of Computer Applications*, *53*(12), 1–7. DOI: 10.5120/8475-2257

Bhavsar, M., Roy, K., Kelly, J., & Olusola, O. (2023). Anomaly-based intrusion detection system for IoT application. *Discover Internet of Things*, *3*(1), 5. DOI: 10.1007/s43926-023-00034-5

Bhole, M., Sauter, T., & Kastner, W. (2025). Enhancing Industrial Cybersecurity: Insights from Analyzing Threat Groups and Strategies in Operational Technology Environments. *IEEE Open Journal of the Industrial Electronics Society*, *6*, 145–157. DOI: 10.1109/OJIES.2025.3527585

Boorugupalli, K. K., Kulkarni, A. K., Suzana, A., & Ponnusamy, S. (2025). Cybersecurity Measures in Financial Institutions Protecting Sensitive Data from Emerging Threats and Vulnerabilities. In *ITM Web of Conferences* (Vol. 76, p. 02002). EDP Sciences. DOI: 10.1051/itmconf/20257602002

Boyes, H., Hallaq, B., Cunningham, J., & Watson, T. (2018). The industrial internet of things (IIoT): An analysis framework. *Computers in Industry*, *101*, 1–12. DOI: 10.1016/j.compind.2018.04.015

Bravos, G., Cabrera, A. J., Correa, C., Danilović, D., Evangeliou, N., Ezov, G., Gajica, Z., Jakovetic, D., Kallipolitis, L., Lukic, M., Mascolo, J., Masera, D., Mazo, R., Mezei, I., Miaoudakis, A., Milosevic, N., Oliff, W., Robin, J., Smyrlis, M., & Vukobratovic, D. (2022). Cybersecurity for industrial internet of things: Architecture, models and lessons learned. *IEEE Access : Practical Innovations, Open Solutions*, *10*, 124747–124765. DOI: 10.1109/ACCESS.2022.3225074

Brettel, M., Friederichsen, N., Keller, M., & Rosenberg, M. (2014). How virtualization, decentralization and network building change the manufacturing landscape: An Industry 4.0 perspective. International Journal of Mechanical. *Industrial Science and Engineering*, *8*(1), 37–44. DOI: 10.5281/zenodo.1336426

Buczak, A. L., & Guven, E. (2016). A survey of data mining and machine learning methods for cyber security intrusion detection. *IEEE Communications Surveys and Tutorials*, *18*(2), 1153–1176. DOI: 10.1109/COMST.2015.2494502

Byres, E., & Lowe, J. (2004, October). The myths and facts behind cyber security risks for industrial control systems. *Proceedings of the VDE Kongress*, *116*, 213–218.

Cao, W., & Zhou, L. (2024). Resilient microgrid modeling in Digital Twin considering demand response and landscape design of renewable energy. *Sustainable Energy Technologies and Assessments*, *64*, 103628. DOI: 10.1016/j.seta.2024.103628

Cardenas, A. A., Amin, S., & Sastry, S. (2008, June). Secure control: Towards survivable cyber-physical systems. In *2008, The 28th International Conference on Distributed Computing Systems Workshops* (pp. 495-500). IEEE.

Carvalho, T. P., Soares, F. A., Vita, R., Francisco, R. P., Basto, J. P., & Alcalá, S. G. (2019). A systematic literature review of machine learning methods applied to predictive maintenance. *Computers & Industrial Engineering*, *137*, 106024. DOI: 10.1016/j.cie.2019.106024

Celin, S., & Vasanth, K. (2018). ECG signal classification using various machine learning techniques. *Journal of Medical Systems*, *42*(12), 241. DOI: 10.1007/s10916-018-1083-6 PMID: 30334106

Chandola, V., Banerjee, A., & Kumar, V. (2009). Anomaly detection: A survey. *ACM Computing Surveys*, *41*(3), 1–58. DOI: 10.1145/1541880.1541882

Charmet, F., Tanuwidjaja, H. C., Ayoubi, S., Gimenez, P. F., Han, Y., Jmila, H., Blanc, G., Takahashi, T., & Zhang, Z. (2022). Explainable artificial intelligence for cybersecurity: A literature survey. *Annales des Télécommunications*, *77*(11), 789–812. DOI: 10.1007/s12243-022-00926-7

Cherdantseva, Y., Burnap, P., Blyth, A., Eden, P., Jones, K., Soulsby, H., & Stoddart, K. (2016). A review of cyber security risk assessment methods for SCADA systems. *Computers & Security*, *56*, 1–27. DOI: 10.1016/j.cose.2015.09.009

Chib, S., Mehta, A. K., Saravanan, A., Mishra, B. R., & Manjunath, T. C. (2025). Mental Health Challenges and Solutions in High-Pressure Work Environments. In Harriott, S. (Ed.), *Innovative Approaches to Managing Conflict and Change in Diverse Work Environments* (pp. 247–272). IGI Global Scientific Publishing. DOI: 10.4018/979-8-3693-9556-1.ch011

Chinthamu, N., Jayakumar, S., & Rashid, S. Z. (2025). Cyber-Physical Systems Security Protecting Critical Infrastructure from Cyber Threats and Attacks. In *ITM Web of Conferences* (Vol. 76, p. 03005). EDP Sciences. DOI: 10.1051/itm-conf/20257603005

Choppadandi, A., Kaur, J., Chenchala, P. K., Agarwal, A., Nakra, V., & Pandian, P. K. G. (2021). Anomaly Detection in Cybersecurity: Leveraging Machine Learning Algorithms. *ESP Journal of Engineering & Technology Advancements, 1*(2), 34–41.

Chowdhury, N. I., & Hasan, R. (2023, April). Security analysis of cardiovascular implantable electronic device (CIED) using a threat model-based approach. In *SoutheastCon 2023* (pp. 81-88). IEEE.

Chowdhury, M. M., Ayon, R. S., & Hossain, M. S. (2024). An investigation of machine learning algorithms and data augmentation techniques for diabetes diagnosis using class imbalanced BRFSS dataset. *Healthcare Analytics, 5*, 100297. DOI: 10.1016/j.health.2023.100297

Clifton, D. A., Wong, D., Clifton, L., Wilson, S., Way, R., Pullinger, R., & Tarassenko, L. (2012). A large-scale clinical validation of an integrated monitoring system in the emergency department. *IEEE Journal of Biomedical and Health Informatics, 17*(4), 835–842. DOI: 10.1109/JBHI.2012.2234130 PMID: 25055312

Colombo, A. W., Karnouskos, S., Kaynak, O., Shi, Y., & Yin, S. (2017). Industrial cyberphysical systems: A backbone of the fourth industrial revolution. *IEEE Industrial Electronics Magazine, 11*(1), 6–16. DOI: 10.1109/MIE.2017.2648857

Commission, E. U. (2023). *Ethical guidelines for trustworthy AI in digital twins.* Publications Office of the EU.

Coussement, K., Abedin, M. Z., Kraus, M., Maldonado, S., & Topuz, K. (2024). Explainable AI for enhanced decision-making. *Decision Support Systems, 184*, 114276. DOI: 10.1016/j.dss.2024.114276

Cui, A., & Stolfo, S. J. (2010, December). A quantitative analysis of the insecurity of embedded network devices: results of a wide-area scan. In *Proceedings of the 26th annual computer security applications conference* (pp. 97-106). DOI: 10.1145/1920261.1920276

Dabic-Miletic, S. (2023). Advanced technologies in smart factories: A cornerstone of industry 4.0. *Journal of Industrial Intelligence, 1*(3), 148–157. DOI: 10.56578/jii010302

Dahiya, R. Vidyadhara, & Manjunath, T. C. (2025). Design and Aerodynamics: Principles and Advances. In M. Mellal (Ed.), *Innovations and Developments in Unmanned Aerial Vehicles* (pp. 145-170). IGI Global Scientific Publishing.

Dahiya, R., & Selvakumar, P. Vidyadhara, & Manjunath, T. C. (2025). Design and Aerodynamics: Principles and Advances. In M. Mellal (Ed.), *Innovations and Developments in Unmanned Aerial Vehicles* (pp. 145-170). IGI Global Scientific Publishing.

Das, A., & Rad, P. (2020). Opportunities and challenges in explainable artificial intelligence (xai): A survey. *arXiv preprint arXiv:2006.11371.*

Das, D., Manojkumar, R., Kumar, C., & Ganguly, S. (2022). Power loss minimization in smart transformer enabled low voltage islanded meshed hybrid microgrid. *IEEE Access : Practical Innovations, Open Solutions, 10*, 123259–123270. DOI: 10.1109/ACCESS.2022.3224001

Dash, A., Bandopadhay, S., Samal, S. R., & Poulkov, V. (2023). Ai-enabled iot framework for leakage detection and its consequence prediction during external transportation of lpg. *Sensors (Basel), 23*(14), 6473. DOI: 10.3390/s23146473 PMID: 37514767

Das, O., Zafar, M. H., Sanfilippo, F., Rudra, S., & Kolhe, M. L. (2024). Advancements in digital twin technology and machine learning for energy systems: A comprehensive review of applications in smart grids, renewable energy, and electric vehicle optimisation. *Energy Conversion and Management, X*, 100715. DOI: 10.1016/j.ecmx.2024.100715

Das, S., Chandran, R., & Manjula, K. A. (2025, March). Zero-day vulnerabilities and attacks. In. AIP Conference Proceedings: Vol. 3227. *No. 1* (p. 050007). AIP Publishing LLC.

David, D. P. (2020). Three Articles on the Economics of Information-Systems Defense Capability. *Material-, Human-, and Knowledge-Resources Acquisition for Critical Infrastructures (Ph. D. thesis), Université de Lausanne, Faculté des hautes études commerciales.*

De Bruijn, H., Warnier, M., & Janssen, M. (2022). The perils and pitfalls of explainable AI: Strategies for explaining algorithmic decision-making. *Government Information Quarterly, 39*(2), 101666. DOI: 10.1016/j.giq.2021.101666

Desai, B., Patil, K., Mehta, I., & Patil, A. (2024, September). Explainable AI in Cybersecurity: A Comprehensive Framework for enhancing transparency, trust, and Human-AI Collaboration. *In 2024 International Seminar on Application for Technology of Information and Communication (iSemantic)* (pp. 135-150). IEEE.

Dhabliya, D., Gujar, S. N., Dhabliya, R., Chavan, G. T., Kalnawat, A., & Bendale, S. P. (2023). Temporal Intelligence in AI-Enhanced Cyber Forensics using Time-Based Analysis for Proactive Threat Detection. *Journal of Electrical Systems, 19*(3).

Dhirani, L. L., Armstrong, E., & Newe, T. (2021). Industrial IoT, cyber threats, and standards landscape: Evaluation and roadmap. *Sensors (Basel), 21*(11), 3901. DOI: 10.3390/s21113901 PMID: 34198727

Dhirani, L. L., Mukhtiar, N., Chowdhry, B. S., & Newe, T. (2023). Ethical dilemmas and privacy issues in emerging technologies: A review. *Sensors (Basel)*, *23*(3), 1151. DOI: 10.3390/s23031151 PMID: 36772190

Djebbar, F., & Nordström, K. (2023). A comparative analysis of industrial cybersecurity standards. *IEEE Access : Practical Innovations, Open Solutions*, *11*, 85315–85332. DOI: 10.1109/ACCESS.2023.3303205

Djurdjanovic, D., Lee, J., & Ni, J. (2020). Watchdog Agent®—An infotronics-based prognostics approach for product performance degradation assessment and prediction. *Advanced Engineering Informatics*, *17*(3–4), 109–125.

Dzung, D., Naedele, M., Von Hoff, T. P., & Crevatin, M. (2005). Security for industrial communication systems. *Proceedings of the IEEE*, *93*(6), 1152–1177. DOI: 10.1109/JPROC.2005.849714

El Jaouhari, S., & Bouvet, E. (2022). Secure firmware Over-The-Air updates for IoT: Survey, challenges, and discussions. *Internet of Things : Engineering Cyber Physical Human Systems*, *18*, 100508. DOI: 10.1016/j.iot.2022.100508

Eldrandaly, K. A., Abdel-Basset, M., Ibrahim, M., & Abdel-Aziz, N. M. (2023). Explainable and secure artificial intelligence: Taxonomy, cases of study, learned lessons, challenges and future directions. *Enterprise Information Systems*, *17*(9), 2098537. DOI: 10.1080/17517575.2022.2098537

Enberg, P. (2024). Behavior Analytics in Cyber Security.

Engel, R., Fernandez, P., Ruiz-Cortes, A., Megahed, A., & Ojeda-Perez, J. (2022). SLA-aware operational efficiency in AI-enabled service chains: Challenges ahead. *Information Systems and e-Business Management*, *20*(1), 199–221. DOI: 10.1007/s10257-022-00551-w

Ergun, I., Sami, H. U., & Guler, B. (2021). Sparsified secure aggregation for privacy-preserving federated learning. *arXiv preprint arXiv:2112.12872*.

Faheem, M. A., Kakolu, S., & Aslam, M. (2022). The Role of Explainable AI in Cybersecurity: Improving Analyst Trust in Automated Threat Assessment Systems. *Iconic Research and Engineering Journals*, *6*(4), 173–182.

Fang, X., Misra, S., Xue, G., & Yang, D. (2012). Smart grid—The new and improved power grid: A survey. *IEEE Communications Surveys and Tutorials*, *14*(4), 944–980. DOI: 10.1109/SURV.2011.101911.00087

Fatima, Z., Hussain, R., Dilshad, A., Shakir, M., & Laghari, A. A. (2025). Explainable AI-Driven Firewall Evaluation: Empowering Cybersecurity Decision-Making for Optimal Network Defense. *Security and Privacy, 8*(3), e70026. DOI: 10.1002/spy2.70026

Fernando, T., Gammulle, H., Denman, S., Sridharan, S., & Fookes, C. (2021). Deep learning for medical anomaly detection–a survey. *ACM Computing Surveys, 54*(7), 1–37. DOI: 10.1145/3464423

Ferrari, P., Flammini, A., Sisinni, E., & Rinaldi, S. (2017). Performance evaluation of industrial Ethernet networks for time-critical applications. *IEEE Transactions on Industrial Informatics, 13*(5), 2387–2396. DOI: 10.1109/TII.2017.2696723

Ferraro, C., Demsar, V., Sands, S., Restrepo, M., & Campbell, C. (2024). The paradoxes of generative AI-enabled customer service: A guide for managers. *Business Horizons, 67*(5), 549–559. DOI: 10.1016/j.bushor.2024.04.013

Fovino, I. N., Carcano, A., Masera, M., & Trombetta, A. (2009). An experimental investigation of malware attacks on SCADA systems. *International Journal of Critical Infrastructure Protection, 2*(4), 139–145. DOI: 10.1016/j.ijcip.2009.10.001

Fuller, A., Fan, Z., Day, C., & Barlow, C. (2020). Digital twin: Enabling technologies, challenges, and open research. *IEEE Access : Practical Innovations, Open Solutions, 8*, 108952–108971. DOI: 10.1109/ACCESS.2020.2998358

Galloway, B., & Hancke, G. P. (2013). Introduction to industrial control networks. *IEEE Communications Surveys and Tutorials, 15*(2), 860–880. DOI: 10.1109/SURV.2012.071812.00124

Garg, S., Singh, A., Batra, S., Kumar, N., & Yang, L. T. (2018). UAV-empowered edge computing environment for cyber-threat detection in smart vehicles. *IEEE Network, 32*(3), 42–51. DOI: 10.1109/MNET.2018.1700286

Ghazal, T. M., Al-Dmour, N. A., Said, R. A., Omidvar, A., Khan, U. Y., Soomro, T. R., & Ali, L. (2023). DDoS Intrusion Detection with Ensemble Stream Mining for IoT Smart Sensing Devices. In *The Effect of Information Technology on Business and Marketing Intelligence Systems* (pp. 1987–2012). Springer International Publishing. DOI: 10.1007/978-3-031-12382-5_109

Giannelli, C., & Picone, M. (2022). Editorial "Industrial IoT as IT and OT convergence: Challenges and opportunities". *IoT, 3*(1), 259–261. DOI: 10.3390/iot3010014

Glaessgen, E., & Stargel, D. (2012). The digital twin paradigm for future NASA and U.S. Air Force vehicles. *53rd AIAA/ASME/ASCE/AHS/ASC Structures, *Structural Dynamics and Materials Conference**.

Glanois, C., Weng, P., Zimmer, M., Li, D., Yang, T., Hao, J., & Liu, W. (2024). A survey on interpretable reinforcement learning. *Machine Learning, 113*(8), 5847–5890. DOI: 10.1007/s10994-024-06543-w

González-Rodríguez, V. E., Izquierdo-Bueno, I., Cantoral, J. M., Carbú, M., & Garrido, C. (2024). Artificial intelligence: A promising tool for application in phytopathology. *Horticulturae, 10*(3), 197. DOI: 10.3390/horticulturae10030197

Goswami, N., Raj, S., Thakral, D., Arias-Gonzáles, J. L., Flores-Albornoz, J., Asnate-Salazar, E., Kapila, D., Yadav, S., & Kumar, S. (2023). Intrusion Detection System for IoT-based Healthcare Intrusions with Lion-Salp-Swarm-Optimization Algorithm: Metaheuristic-Enabled Hybrid Intelligent Approach. *Engineering and Science*. Advance online publication. DOI: 10.30919/es933

Goswami, S. A., Patel, K. C. K., Darji, D. A., Patel, S., & Patel, S. (2025). AI Workload Automation and Orchestration in Cloud Environments. In *Establishing AI-Specific Cloud Computing Infrastructure* (pp. 33–70). IGI Global Scientific Publishing. DOI: 10.4018/979-8-3693-9694-0.ch002

Govindaraj, M., Shakila, P., & Lawrence, J. (2025). AI-Driven Cybersecurity for Industrial Automation: Resilient Solutions for Industry 4.0. In *AI-Enhanced Cybersecurity for Industrial Automation* (pp. 83-102). IGI Global Scientific Publishing.

Grieves, M., & Vickers, J. (2017). Digital twin: Mitigating unpredictable, undesirable emergent behavior in complex systems. In Kahlen, F.-J., Flumerfelt, S., & Alves, A. (Eds.), *Transdisciplinary perspectives on complex systems* (pp. 85–113). Springer. DOI: 10.1007/978-3-319-38756-7_4

Gunes, V., Peter, S., Givargis, T., & Vahid, F. (2014). A survey on concepts, applications, and challenges in cyber-physical systems. *KSII Transactions on Internet and Information Systems, 8*(12), 4242–4268. DOI: 10.3837/tiis.2014.12.001

Habibur, M., Hasan, M. H., Sadik, M. S., Estehad, M., Rahatul, M., Kumar, P., & Rahman, A. (2024). Impact of Internet of Things (IoT) on healthcare in transforming patient care and overcoming operational challenges. *Journal of Angiotherapy, 8*(11), 1–8.

Hady, A. A., Ghubaish, A., Salman, T., Unal, D., & Jain, R. (2020). Intrusion detection system for healthcare systems using medical and network data: A comparison study. *IEEE Access : Practical Innovations, Open Solutions, 8*, 106576–106584. DOI: 10.1109/ACCESS.2020.3000421

Hale, B., Van Bossuyt, D. L., & Papakonstantinou, N. (2018). A zero trust architecture for industrial control systems. *Procedia Manufacturing*, *26*, 1228–1235. DOI: 10.1016/j.promfg.2018.07.139

Hamon, R., Junklewitz, H., Sanchez, I., Malgieri, G., & De Hert, P. (2022). Bridging the gap between AI and explainability in the GDPR: Towards trustworthiness-by-design in automated decision-making. *IEEE Computational Intelligence Magazine*, *17*(1), 72–85. DOI: 10.1109/MCI.2021.3129960

Hanif, A., Zhang, X., & Wood, S. (2021, October). A survey on explainable artificial intelligence techniques and challenges. In *2021 IEEE 25th international enterprise distributed object computing workshop (EDOCW)* (pp. 81-89). IEEE. DOI: 10.1109/EDOCW52865.2021.00036

Haskard, A., & Herath, D. (2025). Secure Robotics: Navigating Challenges at the Nexus of Safety, Trust, and Cybersecurity in Cyber-Physical Systems. *ACM Computing Surveys*, *57*(9), 1–48. DOI: 10.1145/3723050

Hassan, S. K., & Ibrahim, A. (2023). The role of artificial intelligence in cyber security and incident response. *International Journal for Electronic Crime Investigation*, *7*(2).

He, H., & Yan, J. (2016). Cyber-physical attacks and defences in the smart grid: A survey. *IET Cyber-Physical Systems*, *1*(1), 13–27. DOI: 10.1049/iet-cps.2016.0019

Hermann, M., Pentek, T., & Otto, B. (2016). Design principles for Industrie 4.0 scenarios. *2016 49th Hawaii International Conference on System Sciences (HICSS)*, 3928–3937.

He, Y., Fu, B., Yu, J., Li, R., & Jiang, R. (2020). Efficient learning of healthcare data from IoT devices by edge convolution neural networks. *Applied Sciences (Basel, Switzerland)*, *10*(24), 8934. DOI: 10.3390/app10248934

Highnam, K., Arulkumaran, K., Hanif, Z., & Jennings, N. R. (2021). Beth dataset: Real cybersecurity data for unsupervised anomaly detection research. *CEUR Workshop Proceedings*, *3095*, 1–12.

Hindy, H., Atkinson, R., Tachtatzis, C., Colin, J. N., Bayne, E., & Bellekens, X. (2020). Utilising deep learning techniques for effective zero-day attack detection. *Electronics (Basel)*, *9*(10), 1684. DOI: 10.3390/electronics9101684

Hossain, M. S., Muhammad, G., & Guizani, N. (2020). Explainable AI and mass surveillance system-based healthcare framework to combat COVID-I9 like pandemics. *IEEE Network*, *34*(4), 126–132. DOI: 10.1109/MNET.011.2000458

Hossain, Z., Hossain, M. E., Ahmed, N., Kabir, M. F., & Hossain, I. S. (2025). AI-Powered Framework for Real-time Threat Detection and Response in Cloud Infrastructure. *Formosa Journal of Multidisciplinary Research*, *4*(4), 1859–1874. DOI: 10.55927/fjmr.v4i4.168

Humayed, A., Lin, J., Li, F., & Luo, B. (2020). Cyber-physical systems security—A survey. *IEEE Internet of Things Journal*, *4*(6), 1802–1831. DOI: 10.1109/JIOT.2017.2703172

Hussain, S. M., Tummalapalli, S. R. K., & Chakravarthy, A. S. N. (2024). Cyber Security Education: Enhancing Cyber Security Capabilities, Navigating Trends and Challenges in a Dynamic Landscape. Advances in Cyber Security and Digital Forensics, 9-33.

Iavich, M., Bocu, R., & Gagnidze, A. (2022, March). Real Time Self-developing Cybersecurity Function for 5G. In *International Conference on Advanced Information Networking and Applications* (pp. 380-387). Cham: Springer International Publishing. DOI: 10.1007/978-3-030-99619-2_36

Igugu, A. (2024). Evaluating the Effectiveness of AI and Machine Learning Techniques for Zero-Day Attacks Detection in Cloud Environments.

Inaganti, A. C., Ravichandran, N., Nersu, S. R. K., & Muppalaneni, R. (2021). Cloud Security Posture Management (CSPM) with AI: Automating Compliance and Threat Detection. *Artificial Intelligence and Machine Learning Review*, *2*(4), 8–18.

Iqbal, M. J., Aurangzeb, S., Aleem, M., Srivastava, G., & Lin, J. C. W. (2022). RThreatDroid: A ransomware detection approach to secure IoT based healthcare systems. *IEEE Transactions on Network Science and Engineering*, *10*(5), 2574–2583. DOI: 10.1109/TNSE.2022.3188597

Iqbal, S. (2024). AI-Powered Systems for Cybersecurity: Techniques and Applications for Threat Detection. *Artificial Intelligence Multidisciplinary Journal of Systems and Applications*, *1*(3), 10–17.

Isreal, O., & Alonge, M. (2025). Integrating Artificial Intelligence with Network Security: Enhancements in Intrusion Prevention.

Iwendi, C., Moqurrab, S. A., Anjum, A., Khan, S., Mohan, S., & Srivastava, G. (2020). N-sanitization: A semantic privacy-preserving framework for unstructured medical datasets. *Computer Communications*, *161*, 160–171. DOI: 10.1016/j.comcom.2020.07.032

Jaber, A. (2024). *Transforming cybersecurity dynamics: Enhanced self-play reinforcement learning in intrusion detection and prevention system.* Paper presented at the 2024 IEEE International Systems Conference (SysCon). DOI: 10.1109/SysCon61195.2024.10553626

Jagannathan, N. J., Labhade-Kumar, N. D. N., Rastogi, N. R., Unni, N. M. V., & Baseer, K. K. (2023). Developing interpretable models and techniques for explainable AI in decision-making. *The Scientific Temper, 14*(04), 1324–1331. DOI: 10.58414/SCIENTIFICTEMPER.2023.14.4.39

Jaigirdar, F. T., Rudolph, C., Oliver, G., Watts, D., & Bain, C. (2020, December). What information is required for explainable AI?: A provenance-based research agenda and future challenges. In *2020 IEEE 6th International Conference on Collaboration and Internet Computing (CIC)* (pp. 177-183). IEEE.

Jardine, A. K. S., Lin, D., & Banjevic, D. (2021). A review on machinery diagnostics and prognostics implementing condition-based maintenance. *Mechanical Systems and Signal Processing, 20*(7), 1483–1510. DOI: 10.1016/j.ymssp.2005.09.012

Javed, H., El-Sappagh, S., & Abuhmed, T. (2025). Robustness in deep learning models for medical diagnostics: Security and adversarial challenges towards robust AI applications. *Artificial Intelligence Review, 58*(1), 1–107.

Jeyanthi, D. V., & Indrani, B. (2023). IoT-based intrusion detection system for healthcare using RNNBiLSTM deep learning strategy with custom features. *Soft Computing, 27*(16), 1–16. DOI: 10.1007/s00500-023-08536-8

Ji, F., Zhou, Y., Zhang, H., Cheng, G., & Luo, Q. (2024). Navigating the Digital Odyssey: AI-Driven Business Models in Industry 4.0. *Journal of the Knowledge Economy, 16*(1), 1–44. DOI: 10.1007/s13132-024-02096-4

Kainz, O., Zoller, M., Murin, M., Nováková, I., Šimko, E., & Horváth, L. (2024, October). Cybersecurity through Practical Applications. In *2024 International Conference on Emerging eLearning Technologies and Applications (ICETA)* (pp. 269-275). IEEE. DOI: 10.1109/ICETA63795.2024.10850868

Kalech, M. (2019). Cyber-attack detection in SCADA systems using temporal pattern recognition techniques. *Computers & Security, 84*, 225–238. DOI: 10.1016/j.cose.2019.03.007

Kampezidou, S. I., Tikayat Ray, A., Bhat, A. P., Pinon Fischer, O. J., & Mavris, D. N. (2024). Fundamental components and principles of supervised machine learning workflows with numerical and categorical data. *Eng, 5*(1), 384–416. DOI: 10.3390/eng5010021

Kannan, Y. (2024). AI and Machine Learning for Network Security: Applications and Case Studies. [IJAIML]. *International Journal of Artificial Intelligence and Machine Learning*, *3*(02), 1–13.

Karadsheh, L., Barnard, J. E., Arafah, M., & Shubita, A. F. (2025). Generative AI and the Evolving Threat Landscape: A Security Professional's Guide. In *Examining Cybersecurity Risks Produced by Generative AI* (pp. 71-98). IGI Global Scientific Publishing. DOI: 10.4018/979-8-3373-0832-6.ch004

Karageorgou, M., Mantas, G., Essop, I., Rodriguez, J., & Lymberopoulos, D. (2020). Cybersecurity attacks on medical IoT devices for smart city healthcare services. *IoT Technologies in Smart Cities: From sensors to big data, security and trust*, 171-187.

Karnouskos, S. (2011). Cyber-physical systems in the smart grid. 2011 9th IEEE International Conference on Industrial Informatics, 20–23. DOI: 10.1109/INDIN.2011.6034919

Kaur, M., Selvakumar, P., & Dinesh, N. Mohit, Chandel, P. S., & Manjunath, T. C. (2025). Reconstruction and Preservation Strategies for Cultural Heritage. In S. Oflazoğlu & M. Dora (Eds.), *Preserving Cultural Heritage in Post-Disaster Urban Renewal* (pp. 385-412). IGI Global Scientific Publishing

Kaur, M., Selvakumar, P., & Dinesh, N. Mohit, Chandel, P. S., & Manjunath, T. C. (2025). Reconstruction and Preservation Strategies for Cultural Heritage. In S. Oflazoğlu & M. Dora (Eds.), *Preserving Cultural Heritage in Post-Disaster Urban Renewal* (pp. 385-412). IGI Global Scientific Publishing.

Kaur, M., Singh, D., Kumar, V., Gupta, B. B., & Abd El-Latif, A. A. (2021). Secure and energy efficient-based E-health care framework for green internet of things. *IEEE Transactions on Green Communications and Networking*, *5*(3), 1223–1231. DOI: 10.1109/TGCN.2021.3081616

Kavitha, M., Srinivas, P. V. V. S., Kalyampudi, P. L., & Srinivasulu, S. (2021, September). Machine learning techniques for anomaly detection in smart healthcare. In *2021 Third International Conference on Inventive Research in Computing Applications (ICIRCA)* (pp. 1350-1356). IEEE. DOI: 10.1109/ICIRCA51532.2021.9544795

Kayan, H., Heartfield, R., Rana, O., Burnap, P., & Perera, C. (2024). Casper: Context-aware iot anomaly detection system for industrial robotic arms. *ACM Transactions on the Internet of Things*, *5*(3), 1–36. DOI: 10.1145/3670414

Khaleefah, A. D., & Al-Mashhadi, H. M. (2024). Methodologies, requirements, and challenges of cybersecurity frameworks: A review. *Iraqi Journal of Science*, •••, 468–486. DOI: 10.24996/ijs.2024.65.1.38

Khan, M. I., Arif, A., & Khan, A. R. A. (2024). AI's Revolutionary Role in Cyber Defense and Social Engineering. *International Journal of Multidisciplinary Sciences and Arts*, *3*(4), 57–66. DOI: 10.47709/ijmdsa.v3i4.4752

Khan, S., & Yairi, T. (2020). A review on the application of deep learning in system health management. *Mechanical Systems and Signal Processing*, *107*, 241–265. DOI: 10.1016/j.ymssp.2017.11.024

Kim, K. D., & Kumar, P. R. (2012). Cyber-physical systems: A perspective at the centennial. Proceedings of the IEEE, 100(Special Centennial Issue), 1478–1493. DOI: 10.1109/JPROC.2012.2189792

Knapp, E. D., & Langill, J. T. (2015). *Industrial network security: Securing critical infrastructure networks for smart grid, SCADA, and other industrial control systems* (2nd ed.). Syngress., DOI: 10.1109/MCOM.2016.7744799

Kolokotronis, N., Dareioti, M., Shiaeles, S., & Bellini, E. (2022, December). An intelligent platform for threat assessment and cyber-attack mitigation in IoMT ecosystems. In *2022 IEEE Globecom Workshops (GC Wkshps)* (pp. 541-546). IEEE. DOI: 10.1109/GCWkshps56602.2022.10008548

Kommineni, M., Chundru, S., & Maroju, P. K. (2025). Ethical Implications of AI in Sustainable Development Pedagogy. In Chinedu, C., Mafarja, N., Hussein, M., & Saleem, A. (Eds.), *Rethinking the Pedagogy of Sustainable Development in the AI Era* (pp. 17–36). IGI Global Scientific Publishing. DOI: 10.4018/979-8-3693-9062-7.ch002

Kreischer, J. (2023). *Federated Reinforcement Learning for Private and Collaborative Selection of Moving Target Defense Mechanisms for IoT Device Security* (Master's thesis, University of Zurich).

Kriaa, S., Bouissou, M., & Piètre-Cambacédès, L. (2012, October). Modeling the Stuxnet attack with BDMP: Towards more formal risk assessments. In *2012 7th International Conference on Risks and Security of Internet and Systems (CRiSIS)* (pp. 1-8). IEEE.

Kritzinger, W., Karner, M., Traar, G., Henjes, J., & Sihn, W. (2018). Digital twin in manufacturing: A categorical literature review and classification. *IFAC-PapersOnLine, 51*(11), 1016–1022.

Kumaar, M. A., Samiayya, D., Vincent, P. D. R., Srinivasan, K., Chang, C. Y., & Ganesh, H. (2021). A hybrid framework for intrusion detection in healthcare systems using deep learning. *Frontiers in Public Health*, •••, 9. PMID: 35096763

Kumar, A., & Kumar, L. (2024). Navigating the future: the ethical, societal and technological implications of artificial intelligence. Journal homepage, https:// gjrpublication. com/gjrecs

Kumar, M., Kumar, A., Verma, S., Bhattacharya, P., Ghimire, D., Kim, S. H., & Hosen, A. S. (2023). Healthcare Internet of Things (H-IoT): Current trends, future prospects, applications, challenges, and security issues. *Electronics (Basel)*, *12*(9), 2050. DOI: 10.3390/electronics12092050

Kumar, N., Angral, S., & Sharma, R. (2014). Integrating intrusion detection system with network monitoring. *International Journal of Scientific and Research Publications*, *4*, 1–4.

Kumar, P., Javeed, D., Kumar, R., & Islam, A. N. (2024). Blockchain and explainable AI for enhanced decision making in cyber threat detection. *Software, Practice & Experience*, *54*(8), 1337–1360. DOI: 10.1002/spe.3319

Labadie, C., & Legner, C. (2023). Building data management capabilities to address data protection regulations: Learnings from EU-GDPR. *Journal of Information Technology*, *38*(1), 16–44. DOI: 10.1177/02683962221141456

Lam, S. S., Rajkumar, R., & Lehoczky, J. (2015). Cyber-physical systems for autonomous vehicles: Challenges and opportunities. *2015 IEEE International Conference on Robotics and Automation (ICRA)*, 1–6. DOI: 10.1109/ICRA.2015.7139447

Langner, R. (2011). Stuxnet: Dissecting a cyberwarfare weapon. *IEEE Security and Privacy*, *9*(3), 49–51. DOI: 10.1109/MSP.2011.67

Lee, A., Gourisetti, S. N. G., Sebastian-Cardenas, D. J., Lambert, K., Navarro, V., Pasetti, M., Cali, Ü., Isirova, K., Reddi, R., Nitu, P., Touhiduzzaman, M., Mylrea, M., Huff, P., Rahimi, F., & Saha, S. S. (2023). Assessment of the distributed ledger technology for energy sector industrial and operational applications using the mitre att&ck® ics matrix. *IEEE Access : Practical Innovations, Open Solutions*, *11*, 69854–69883. DOI: 10.1109/ACCESS.2023.3288428

Lee, E. A. (2015). The past, present and future of cyber-physical systems: A focus on models. *Sensors (Basel)*, *15*(3), 4837–4869. DOI: 10.3390/s150304837 PMID: 25730486

Lee, H., Kwon, T., Lee, J., & Song, J. (2024). Enhancing Decision-Making of Network Intrusion Analysis Assisted by Explainable AI for Real-Time Security Monitoring. In *2024 IEEE Conference on Dependable and Secure Computing (DSC)* (pp. 147-154). IEEE. DOI: 10.1109/DSC63325.2024.00039

Lee, J. D., Cha, H. S., Rathore, S., & Park, J. H. (2021). M-IDM: A Multi-Classification Based Intrusion Detection Model in Healthcare IoT. *Computers, Materials & Continua*, *67*(2).

Lee, J., Wu, F., Zhao, W., Ghaffari, M., Liao, L., & Siegel, D. (2014). Prognostics and health management design for rotary machinery systems—Reviews, methodology and applications. *Mechanical Systems and Signal Processing*, *42*(1–2), 314–334. DOI: 10.1016/j.ymssp.2013.06.004

Leitão, P., Colombo, A. W., & Karnouskos, S. (2016). Industrial automation based on cyber-physical systems technologies: Prototype implementations and challenges. *Computers in Industry*, *81*, 11–25. DOI: 10.1016/j.compind.2015.08.004

Lei, Y., Yang, B., Jiang, X., Jia, F., Li, N., & Nandi, A. K. (2020). Applications of machine learning to machine fault diagnosis: A review and roadmap. *Mechanical Systems and Signal Processing*, *138*, 106587. DOI: 10.1016/j.ymssp.2019.106587

Lelli, F. (2015). Interoperability challenges in cyber-physical systems: A case study. *2015 IEEE International Conference on Cyber-Physical Systems, Networks, and Applications (CPSNA)*, 1–6. DOI: 10.1109/CPSNA.2015.10

Leszczyna, R. (2018). Cybersecurity and privacy in cyber-physical systems: A comprehensive survey. *Computers & Security*, *77*, 312–336. DOI: 10.1016/j.cose.2018.04.006

Li, L., Qiu, Y., & Xu, J. (2022, April). A K-means clustered routing algorithm with location and energy awareness for underwater wireless sensor networks. [). MDPI.]. *Photonics*, *9*(5), 282. DOI: 10.3390/photonics9050282

Longo, L., Goebel, R., Lecue, F., Kieseberg, P., & Holzinger, A. (2020, August). Explainable artificial intelligence: Concepts, applications, research challenges and visions. In *International cross-domain conference for machine learning and knowledge extraction* (pp. 1-16). Cham: Springer International Publishing.

Lu, Y., Liu, C., Wang, K. I. K., Huang, H., & Xu, X. (2020). Digital twin-driven smart manufacturing: Connotation, reference model, applications, and research issues. *Robotics and Computer-Integrated Manufacturing, 61*, 101837.

Lu, Y., Morris, K. C., & Frechette, S. (2017). *Current standards landscape for smart manufacturing systems. NIST Interagency/Internal Report (NISTIR), 8107.* National Institute of Standards and Technology., DOI: 10.6028/NIST.IR.8107

Lu, Y., & Xu, X. (2019). Cloud-based manufacturing equipment and big data analytics to enable on-demand manufacturing services. *Robotics and Computer-integrated Manufacturing*, *57*, 92–102. DOI: 10.1016/j.rcim.2018.11.006

Luz, A. (2024). Implementing Intrusion Detection and Prevention in SDN. *Available at SSRN* 4965832. DOI: 10.2139/ssrn.4965832

Luzuriaga, J. E., Perez, M., Boronat, P., Cano, J. C., & Calafate, C. T. (2015). A comparative evaluation of AMQP and MQTT protocols over unstable and mobile networks. 2015 12th Annual IEEE Consumer Communications and Networking Conference (CCNC), 931–936. https://doi.org/DOI: 10.1109/CCNC.2015.7155098

Madhav, A. S., & Tyagi, A. K. (2022). Explainable Artificial Intelligence (XAI): connecting artificial decision-making and human trust in autonomous vehicles. In *Proceedings of Third International Conference on Computing, Communications, and Cyber-Security: IC4S 2021* (pp. 123-136). Singapore: Springer Nature Singapore.

Madni, A. M., Madni, C. C., & Lucero, S. D. (2019). Leveraging digital twin technology in model-based systems engineering. *Systems*, *7*(1), 7. DOI: 10.3390/systems7010007

Maggi, F., Balduzzi, M., Vosseler, R., Rösler, M., Quadrini, W., Tavola, G., Pogliani, M., Quarta, D., & Zanero, S. (2021). Smart factory security: A case study on a modular smart manufacturing system. *Procedia Computer Science*, *180*, 666–675. DOI: 10.1016/j.procs.2021.01.289

Mahbooba, B., Timilsina, M., Sahal, R., & Serrano, M. (2021). Explainable artificial intelligence (XAI) to enhance trust management in intrusion detection systems using decision tree model. *Complexity*, *2021*(1), 6634811. DOI: 10.1155/2021/6634811

Maheshwaran, T., Muthumarilakshmi, S., Suganya, K., Maheswari, B., & Girija, P. (2024). Securing E-Commerce Strategies With Cloud, Blockchain, AI, and ML. In *Strategies for E-Commerce Data Security: Cloud, Blockchain, AI, and Machine Learning* (pp. 470-500). IGI Global.

Mahler, M., Pasandideh, F., & Stiller, B. (2019). Security challenges in cyber-physical systems: A survey. *2019 IEEE International Conference on Industrial Cyber Physical Systems (ICPS)*, 1–6. DOI: 10.1109/ICPHYS.2019.8780275

Mahmood, A., Javaid, N., & Razzaq, S. (2015). A review of wireless communications for smart grid. *Renewable & Sustainable Energy Reviews*, *41*, 248–260. DOI: 10.1016/j.rser.2014.08.036

Makrakis, G. M., Kolias, C., Kambourakis, G., Rieger, C., & Benjamin, J. (2021). Industrial and critical infrastructure security: Technical analysis of real-life security incidents. *IEEE Access : Practical Innovations, Open Solutions*, *9*, 165295–165325. DOI: 10.1109/ACCESS.2021.3133348

Manocha, A., Kumar, G., Bhatia, M., & Sharma, A. (2023). IoT-inspired machine learning-assisted sedentary behavior analysis in smart healthcare industry. *Journal of Ambient Intelligence and Humanized Computing*, *14*(5), 5179–5192. DOI: 10.1007/s12652-021-03371-x

Manoharan, A., & Sarker, M. (2023). Revolutionizing Cybersecurity: Unleashing the Power of Artificial Intelligence and Machine Learning for Next-Generation Threat Detection. DOI: https://www. doi. org/10.56726/IRJMETS32644, 1.

Manojkumar, R., & Inala, K. P. (2024, September). Rule-Based Peak Shaving Using Battery Energy Storage with a Case Study Analysis. In *2024 2nd International Conference on Cyber Physical Systems, Power Electronics and Electric Vehicles (ICPEEV)* (pp. 1–6). IEEE. DOI: 10.1109/ICPEEV63032.2024.10932080

Manojkumar, R., & Inala, K. P. (2024). Optimised rule-based peak shaving and its impact on annual energy cost reduction. *International Journal of Ambient Energy*, *45*(1), 2397672. DOI: 10.1080/01430750.2024.2397672

Manojkumar, R., Kumar, C., Ganguly, S., & Catalão, J. P. (2021). Optimal demand response in a residential PV storage system using energy pricing limits. *IEEE Transactions on Industrial Informatics*, *18*(4), 2497–2507. DOI: 10.1109/TII.2021.3103014

Manojkumar, R., Kumar, C., Ganguly, S., & Catalão, J. P. (2023). Net load forecast error compensation for peak shaving in a grid-connected PV storage system. *IEEE Transactions on Power Systems*, *39*(2), 4372–4381. DOI: 10.1109/TPWRS.2023.3317309

Marwedel, P. (2011). *Embedded system design: Embedded systems foundations of cyber-physical systems* (2nd ed.). Springer., DOI: 10.1007/978-94-007-0257-8

McCarthy, A., Ghadafi, E., Andriotis, P., & Legg, P. (2022). Functionality-preserving adversarial machine learning for robust classification in cybersecurity and intrusion detection domains: A survey. *Journal of Cybersecurity and Privacy*, *2*(1), 154–190. DOI: 10.3390/jcp2010010

Milani, S., Topin, N., Veloso, M., & Fang, F. (2024). Explainable reinforcement learning: A survey and comparative review. *ACM Computing Surveys*, *56*(7), 1–36. DOI: 10.1145/3616864

Miller, B., & Rowe, D. (2012, October). A survey SCADA of and critical infrastructure incidents. In *Proceedings of the 1st Annual conference on Research in information technology* (pp. 51-56). DOI: 10.1145/2380790.2380805

Miotto, R., Wang, F., Wang, S., Jiang, X., & Dudley, J. T. (2018). Deep learning for healthcare: Review, opportunities and challenges. *Briefings in Bioinformatics*, *19*(6), 1236–1246. DOI: 10.1093/bib/bbx044 PMID: 28481991

Moher, D., Liberati, A., Tetzlaff, J., & Altman, D. G. (2009). Preferred reporting items for systematic reviews and meta-analyses: The PRISMA statement. *BMJ (Clinical Research Ed.)*, •••, 339. PMID: 19622551

Molokomme, D. N., Onumanyi, A. J., & Abu-Mahfouz, A. M. (2022). Edge intelligence in Smart Grids: A survey on architectures, offloading models, cyber security measures, and challenges. *Journal of Sensor and Actuator Networks*, *11*(3), 47. DOI: 10.3390/jsan11030047

Monostori, L., Kádár, B., Bauernhansl, T., Kondoh, S., Kumara, S., Reinhart, G., Sauer, O., Schuh, G., Sihn, W., & Ueda, K. (2016). Cyber-physical systems in manufacturing. *CIRP Annals*, *65*(2), 621–641. DOI: 10.1016/j.cirp.2016.06.005

Moosavi, S. R., Gia, T. N., Rahmani, A.-M., Nigussie, E., Virtanen, S., Isoaho, J., & Tenhunen, H. (2015). Sea: A secure and efficient authentication and authorization architecture for iot-based healthcare using smart gateways. *Procedia Computer Science*, *52*, 452–459. DOI: 10.1016/j.procs.2015.05.013

Moustafa, N., Koroniotis, N., Keshk, M., Zomaya, A. Y., & Tari, Z. (2023). Explainable intrusion detection for cyber defences in the internet of things: Opportunities and solutions. *IEEE Communications Surveys and Tutorials*, *25*(3), 1775–1807. DOI: 10.1109/COMST.2023.3280465

Muzahid, A. J. M., Kamarulzaman, S. F., Rahman, M. A., Murad, S. A., Kamal, M. A. S., & Alenezi, A. H. (2023). Multiple vehicle cooperation and collision avoidance in automated vehicles: Survey and an AI-enabled conceptual framework. *Scientific Reports*, *13*(1), 603. DOI: 10.1038/s41598-022-27026-9 PMID: 36635336

Nagmoti, N. S., Srivastava, I., & Damle, M. (2025). AI-Driven Enhancements in Cloud-Native DevOps Boosting Automation, Deployment, and Monitoring. In *Artificial Intelligence for Cloud-Native Software Engineering* (pp. 203–236). IGI Global Scientific Publishing. DOI: 10.4018/979-8-3693-9356-7.ch008

Nagy, M., Lăzăroiu, G., & Valaskova, K. (2023). Machine intelligence and autonomous robotic technologies in the corporate context of SMEs: Deep learning and virtual simulation algorithms, cyber-physical production networks, and Industry 4.0-based manufacturing systems. *Applied Sciences (Basel, Switzerland)*, *13*(3), 1681. DOI: 10.3390/app13031681

Nandy, S., Adhikari, M., Khan, M. A., Menon, V. G., & Verma, S. (2021). An intrusion detection mechanism for secured IoMT framework based on swarm-neural network. *IEEE Journal of Biomedical and Health Informatics*, *26*(5), 1969–1976. DOI: 10.1109/JBHI.2021.3101686 PMID: 34357873

Nankya, M., Chataut, R., & Akl, R. (2023). Securing industrial control systems: Components, cyber threats, and machine learning-driven defense strategies. *Sensors (Basel), 23*(21), 8840. DOI: 10.3390/s23218840 PMID: 37960539

Naruei, I., Keynia, F., & Molahosseini, A. S. (2021). Hunter–prey optimization: Algorithm and applications. *Soft Computing, 26*(3), 1279–1314. DOI: 10.1007/s00500-021-06401-0

Negri, E., Fumagalli, L., & Macchi, M. (2017). A review of the roles of digital twin in CPS-based production systems. *Procedia Manufacturing, 11*, 939–948. DOI: 10.1016/j.promfg.2017.07.198

Ness, S., & Khinvasara, T. (2024). Emerging threats in cyberspace: Implications for national security policy and healthcare sector. *J. Eng. Res. Rep, 26*(2), 107–117. DOI: 10.9734/jerr/2024/v26i21075

Neuer, M. J. (2024). Unsupervised learning. In *Machine Learning for Engineers: Introduction to Physics-Informed, Explainable Learning Methods for AI in Engineering Applications* (pp. 141–172). Springer Berlin Heidelberg.

Neupane, S., Ables, J., Anderson, W., Mittal, S., Rahimi, S., Banicescu, I., & Seale, M. (2022). Explainable intrusion detection systems (x-ids): A survey of current methods, challenges, and opportunities. *IEEE Access : Practical Innovations, Open Solutions, 10*, 112392–112415. DOI: 10.1109/ACCESS.2022.3216617

Newaz, A. I., Sikder, A. K., Babun, L., & Uluagac, A. S. (2020, June). Heka: A novel intrusion detection system for attacks to personal medical devices. In *2020 IEEE Conference on Communications and Network Security (CNS)* (pp. 1-9). IEEE. DOI: 10.1109/CNS48642.2020.9162311

Nguyen, T. N., & Choo, R. (2021, November). Human-in-the-loop XAI-enabled vulnerability detection, investigation, and mitigation. In *2021 36th IEEE/ACM International Conference on Automated Software Engineering (ASE)* (pp. 1210-1212). IEEE. DOI: 10.1109/ASE51524.2021.9678840

Nguyen, G. N., Le Viet, N. H., Elhoseny, M., Shankar, K., Gupta, B. B., & Abd El-Latif, A. A. (2021). Secure blockchain enabled Cyber–physical systems in healthcare using deep belief network with ResNet model. *Journal of Parallel and Distributed Computing, 153*, 150–160. DOI: 10.1016/j.jpdc.2021.03.011

Nguyen, P. T., Huynh, V. D. B., Vo, K. D., Phan, P. T., Elhoseny, M., & Le, D. N. (2021). Deep Learning Based Optimal Multimodal Fusion Framework for Intrusion Detection Systems for Healthcare Data. *Computers, Materials & Continua, 66*(3).

Niveditha, S., Shreyanth, S., Devi, R. D. H., Sarveshwaran, R., & Rajesh, P. K. (2025). Advancing Digital Forensic Intelligence: Leveraging EdgeAI Techniques for Real-Time Threat Detection and Privacy Protection. In *Big Data and Edge Intelligence for Enhanced Cyber Defense* (pp. 37-84). CRC Press.

Ofoegbu, K. D. O., Osundare, O. S., Ike, C. S., Fakeyede, O. G., & Ige, A. B. (2024). Real-Time Cybersecurity threat detection using machine learning and big data analytics: A comprehensive approach. *Computer Science & IT Research Journal, 4*(3).

Ojo, B., & Aghaunor, C. T. (2024). AI-driven cybersecurity solutions for real-time threat detection in critical infrastructure. *International Journal of Science and Research Archive, 12*(02), 1716–1726. DOI: 10.30574/ijsra.2024.12.2.1401

Olaoye, G. (2025). AI-Driven Intrusion Detection and Prevention Systems (IDPS) for Cloud Security. *Available at SSRN* 5129525. DOI: 10.2139/ssrn.5129525

Olowononi, F. O., Rawat, D. B., & Liu, C. (2021, January). Federated learning with differential privacy for resilient vehicular cyber physical systems. In *2021 IEEE 18th Annual Consumer Communications & Networking Conference (CCNC)* (pp. 1-5). IEEE. DOI: 10.1109/CCNC49032.2021.9369480

Onile, A. E., Petlenkov, E., Levron, Y., & Belikov, J. (2024). Smartgrid-based hybrid digital twins framework for demand side recommendation service provision in distributed power systems. *Future Generation Computer Systems, 156*, 142–156. DOI: 10.1016/j.future.2024.03.018

Otoum, S., Guizani, N., & Mouftah, H. (2021, June). Federated reinforcement learning-supported IDS for IoT-steered healthcare systems. In ICC 2021-IEEE International Conference on Communications (pp. 1-6). IEEE. DOI: 10.1109/ICC42927.2021.9500698

Otoum, Y., Wan, Y., & Nayak, A. (2021, December). Federated transfer learning-based ids for the internet of medical things (iomt). In 2021 IEEE Globecom Workshops (GC Wkshps) (pp. 1-6). IEEE.

Ozobu, C. O., Adikwu, F. E., Odujobi, N. O., Onyekwe, F. O., & Nwulu, E. O. (2025). Advancing occupational safety with AI-powered monitoring systems: A conceptual framework for hazard detection and exposure control. *World Journal of Innovation and Modern Technology, 9*(1), 186–213.

Papachristofis, K., Vardoulias, G., & Vavousis, K. (2024, September). Comparative Evaluation of Cybersecurity Maturity Models and Frameworks. In *European, Mediterranean, and Middle Eastern Conference on Information Systems* (pp. 166-178). Cham: Springer Nature Switzerland.

Papastergiou, S., Mouratidis, H., & Kalogeraki, E. M. (2021). Handling of advanced persistent threats and complex incidents in healthcare, transportation and energy ICT infrastructures. *Evolving Systems*, *12*(1), 91–108. DOI: 10.1007/s12530-020-09335-4

Parasuraman, R., & Riley, V. (1997). Humans and automation: Use, misuse, disuse, abuse. *Human Factors*, *39*(2), 230–253. DOI: 10.1518/001872097778543886

Parisa, S. K., Banerjee, S., & Whig, P. (2023). AI-Driven Zero Trust Security Models for Retail Cloud Infrastructure: A Next-Generation Approach. *International Journal of Sustainable Devlopment in field of IT*, *15*(15).

Pasqualetti, F., Dörfler, F., & Bullo, F. (2022). Cyber-physical attacks in power networks: Models, fundamental limitations, and monitor design. *IEEE Transactions on Automatic Control*, *60*(7), 1775–1789.

Patel, C. (2024). Cyber Security, Privacy, and Network Security: Navigating the Evolving Threat Landscape. Privacy, and Network Security: Navigating the Evolving Threat Landscape (December 24, 2024).

Patel, N., Ramoliya, F., Jadav, N. K., Gupta, R., Tanwar, S., & Aujla, G. S. (2024, June). X-NET: Explainable AI-Based Network Data Security Framework for Healthcare 4.0. In *2024 IEEE International Conference on Communications Workshops (ICC Workshops)* (pp. 481-486). IEEE. DOI: 10.1109/ICCWorkshops59551.2024.10615382

Patel, S. K. (2023). Improving intrusion detection in cloud-based healthcare using neural network. *Biomedical Signal Processing and Control*, *83*, 104680. DOI: 10.1016/j.bspc.2023.104680

Patil, S., Varadarajan, V., Walimbe, D., Gulechha, S., Shenoy, S., Raina, A., & Kotecha, K. (2021). Improving the robustness of ai-based malware detection using adversarial machine learning. *Algorithms*, *14*(10), 297. DOI: 10.3390/a14100297

Peng, Y., Wang, J., & Zhang, X. (2018). Machine learning for industrial cyber-physical systems: A survey. *IEEE Access : Practical Innovations, Open Solutions*, *6*, 70452–70464. DOI: 10.1109/ACCESS.2018.2879872

Phuyal, S., Bista, D., & Bista, R. (2020). Challenges, opportunities and future directions of smart manufacturing: A state of art review. *Sustainable Futures : An Applied Journal of Technology, Environment and Society*, *2*, 100023. DOI: 10.1016/j.sftr.2020.100023

Pochmara, J., & Świetlicka, A. (2024). Cybersecurity of industrial systems—A 2023 report. *Electronics (Basel)*, *13*(7), 1191. DOI: 10.3390/electronics13071191

Qadri, Y. A., Nauman, A., Zikria, Y. B., Vasilakos, A. V., & Kim, S. W. (2020). The future of healthcare internet of things: A survey of emerging technologies. *IEEE Communications Surveys and Tutorials*, *22*(2), 1121–1167. DOI: 10.1109/COMST.2020.2973314

Qi, Q., Tao, F., Hu, T., Anwer, N., Liu, A., Wei, Y., Wang, L., & Nee, A. Y. C. (2021). Enabling technologies and tools for digital twin. *Journal of Manufacturing Systems*, *58*, 3–21. DOI: 10.1016/j.jmsy.2019.10.001

Rajalakshmi, R., Sivakumar, P., Prathiba, T., & Chatrapathy, K. (2023). An energy efficient deep learning model for intrusion detection in smart healthcare with optimal feature selection mechanism. Journal of Intelligent & Fuzzy Systems, (Preprint), 1-16.

Raji, M. F., Li, J., Haq, A. U., Ejianya, V., Khan, J., Khan, A., Khalil, M., Ali, A., khan, G. A., Shahid, M., Ahamad, B., Yadav, A., & Memon, I. (2020). A New Approach for Enhancing the Services of the 5G Mobile Network and IOT-Related Communication Devices Using Wavelet-OFDM and Its Applications in Healthcare. *Scientific Programming*, *2020*(1), 3204695. DOI: 10.1155/2020/3204695

Rajkumar, R., Lee, I., Sha, L., & Stankovic, J. (2010). Cyber-physical systems: The next computing revolution. *Proceedings of the 47th Design Automation Conference*, 731–736. DOI: 10.1145/1837274.1837461

Rao, V. V., Marshal, R., & Gobinath, K. (2021, October). The IoT supply chain attack trends-vulnerabilities and preventive measures. In *2021 4th International Conference on Security and Privacy (ISEA-ISAP)* (pp. 1-4). IEEE. DOI: 10.1109/ISEA-ISAP54304.2021.9689704

Rashid, M. M., Khan, S. U., Eusufzai, F., Redwan, M. A., Sabuj, S. R., & Elsharief, M. (2023). A federated learning-based approach for improving intrusion detection in industrial internet of things networks. *Network (Bristol, England)*, *3*(1), 158–179.

Rashid, M. M., & Yaseen, O. M. (2025). AI-Driven Cybersecurity Measures for Hybrid Cloud Environments: A Framework for Multi-Cloud Security Management. *International Journal on Engineering Artificial Intelligence Management, Decision Support, and Policies*, *2*(1), 30–39. DOI: 10.63503/j.ijaimd.2025.39

Rathore, H., Mohamed, A., & Guizani, M. (2020, January). A survey of block-chain enabled cyber-physical systems. *Sensors (Basel)*, *20*(1), 282. DOI: 10.3390/s20010282 PMID: 31947860

Rawal, A., McCoy, J., Rawat, D. B., Sadler, B. M., & Amant, R. S. (2021). Recent advances in trustworthy explainable artificial intelligence: Status, challenges, and perspectives. *IEEE Transactions on Artificial Intelligence*, *3*(6), 852–866. DOI: 10.1109/TAI.2021.3133846

Redelinghuys, A. J. H., Basson, A. H., & Kruger, K. (2020). A six-layer architecture for the digital twin: A manufacturing case study implementation. *Journal of Intelligent Manufacturing*, *31*(6), 1383–1402. DOI: 10.1007/s10845-019-01516-6

Rjoub, G., Bentahar, J., Wahab, O. A., Mizouni, R., Song, A., Cohen, R., & Mourad, A. (2023). A survey on explainable artificial intelligence for cybersecurity. *IEEE Transactions on Network and Service Management*, *20*(4), 5115–5140. DOI: 10.1109/TNSM.2023.3282740

RM, S. P., Maddikunta, P. K. R., Parimala, M., Koppu, S., Gadekallu, T. R., Chowdhary, C. L., & Alazab, M. (. (2020). An effective feature engineering for DNN using hybrid PCA-GWO for intrusion detection in IoMT architecture. *Computer Communications*, *160*, 139–149. DOI: 10.1016/j.comcom.2020.05.048

Rosen, R., von Wichert, G., Lo, G., & Bettenhausen, K. D. (2015). About the importance of autonomy and digital twins for the future of manufacturing. *IFAC-PapersOnLine, 48*(3), 567–572.

Rosero-Montalvo, P. D., István, Z., Tözün, P., & Hernandez, W. (2023). Hybrid anomaly detection model on trusted IoT devices. *IEEE Internet of Things Journal*, *10*(12), 10959–10969. DOI: 10.1109/JIOT.2023.3243037

Rüßmann, M., Lorenz, M., Gerbert, P., Waldner, M., Justus, J., Engel, P., & Harnisch, M. (2015). Industry 4.0: The future of productivity and growth in manufacturing industries. Boston Consulting Group. https://www.bcg.com/publications/2015/engineered_products_project_business_industry_4_future_productivity_growth_manufacturing_industries

Sadeghi, A. R., Wachsmann, C., & Waidner, M. (2015). *Security and privacy challenges in industrial Internet of Things. Proceedings of the 52nd Annual Design Automation Conference*. DOI: 10.1145/2744769.2747942

Saheed, Y. K., Abiodun, A. I., Misra, S., Holone, M. K., & Colomo-Palacios, R. (2022). A machine learning-based intrusion detection for detecting internet of things network attacks. *Alexandria Engineering Journal*, *61*(12), 9395–9409. DOI: 10.1016/j.aej.2022.02.063

Saif, S., Das, P., Biswas, S., Khari, M., & Shanmuganathan, V. (2022). HIIDS: Hybrid intelligent intrusion detection system empowered with machine learning and metaheuristic algorithms for application in IoT based healthcare. *Microprocessors and Microsystems*, •••, 104622. DOI: 10.1016/j.micpro.2022.104622

Salvi, A., Spagnoletti, P., & Noori, N. S. (2022). Cyber-resilience of Critical Cyber Infrastructures: Integrating digital twins in the electric power ecosystem. *Computers & Security*, *112*, 102507. DOI: 10.1016/j.cose.2021.102507

Samal, A., & Misra, L. I. Mohit, Pougajendy, S., Chandel, P. S., Manjunath, T. C., (2025). Musealization and Tourism Practices. In S. Oflazoğlu & M. Dora (Eds.), *Preserving Cultural Heritage in Post-Disaster Urban Renewal* (pp. 115-142). IGI Global Scientific Publishing

Samal, A., & Misra, L. I. Mohit, Pougajendy, S., Chandel, P. S., Manjunath, T. C., (2025). Musealization and Tourism Practices. In S. Oflazoğlu & M. Dora (Eds.), *Preserving Cultural Heritage in Post-Disaster Urban Renewal* (pp. 115-142). IGI Global Scientific Publishing.

Sanfelice, R. G. (2015). Analysis and design of cyber-physical systems: A hybrid control systems approach. In Cyber-Physical Systems: From Theory to Practice (pp. 3–31). CRC Press. DOI: 10.1201/b19290-3

Sarker, I. H. (2023). Multi-aspects AI-based modeling and adversarial learning for cybersecurity intelligence and robustness: A comprehensive overview. *Security and Privacy*, *6*(5), e295. DOI: 10.1002/spy2.295

Sasikala, B., & Sachan, S. (2024). Decoding decision-making: embracing explainable AI for trust and transparency. *Exploring the frontiers of artificial intelligence and machine learning technologies, 42.*

Saurabh, B., Utkrisht, S., Sandeep, S., Kumar, D. P., & Rajkumar, U. (2024, October). Generative AI Enabled Actionable Decision Support in Cyber Security Operations for Enterprise Security. In *2024 ITU Kaleidoscope: Innovation and Digital Transformation for a Sustainable World (ITU K)* (pp. 1-8). IEEE. DOI: 10.23919/ITUK62727.2024.10772892

Saxena, A., Goebel, K., Simon, D., & Eklund, N. (2022). Damage propagation modeling for aircraft engine run-to-failure simulation. *2008 International Conference on Prognostics and Health Management*, 1–9.

Schmitt, M. (2023). Securing the digital world: Protecting smart infrastructures and digital industries with artificial intelligence (AI)-enabled malware and intrusion detection. *Journal of Industrial Information Integration, 36*, 100520. DOI: 10.1016/j.jii.2023.100520

Selcuk, S. (2017). Predictive maintenance, its implementation and latest trends. *Proceedings of the Institution of Mechanical Engineers. Part B, Journal of Engineering Manufacture*, *231*(9), 1670–1679. DOI: 10.1177/0954405415601640

Sen, P. (2024). Balancing Act: Navigating Artificial Intelligence, Data Privacy, and Legal Challenges in the Digital Age. Issue 2 Int'l JL Mgmt. &. *Human.*, *7*, 3062.

Serpanos, D., & Wolf, T. (2018). *Industrial Internet of Things: Cybermanufacturing systems*. Springer., DOI: 10.1007/978-3-319-56222-3

Shafik, W. (2024). Artificial intelligence and machine learning with cyber ethics for the future world. In *Future communication systems using artificial intelligence, internet of things and data science* (pp. 110–130). CRC Press. DOI: 10.1201/9781032648309-9

Shafto, M., Conroy, M., Doyle, R., Glaessgen, E., Kemp, C., LeMoigne, J., & Wang, L. (2010). Modeling, simulation, information technology & processing roadmap. *NASA Technology Roadmaps, 32*.

Shamim, N., Asim, M., Baker, T., & Awad, A. I. (2023). Efficient approach for anomaly detection in IoT using system calls. *Sensors (Basel)*, *23*(2), 652. DOI: 10.3390/s23020652 PMID: 36679447

Shamshirband, S., Anuar, N. B., Kiah, M. L. M., & Patel, A. (2013). An appraisal and design of a multi-agent system based cooperative wireless intrusion detection computational intelligence technique. *Engineering Applications of Artificial Intelligence*, *26*(9), 2105–2127. DOI: 10.1016/j.engappai.2013.04.010

Sharma, B., Sharma, L., Lal, C., & Roy, S. (2023). Anomaly based network intrusion detection for IoT attacks using deep learning technique. *Computers & Electrical Engineering*, *107*, 108626. DOI: 10.1016/j.compeleceng.2023.108626

Sharma, V., You, I., Andersson, K., Palmieri, F., Rehmani, M. H., & Lim, J. (2020). Security, privacy and trust for smart mobile-Internet of Things (M-IoT): A survey. *IEEE Access : Practical Innovations, Open Solutions, 8*, 167123–167163. DOI: 10.1109/ACCESS.2020.3022661

Shehzadi, T. (2024). Reinforcement Learning-Based Autonomous Systems for Cyber Threat Detection and Response. *Eastern European Journal for Multidisciplinary Research*, *1*(1), 123–137.

Shi, J., Wan, J., Yan, H., & Suo, H. (2011). A survey of cyber-physical systems. *2011 International Conference on Wireless Communications and Signal Processing (WCSP)*, 1–6. DOI: 10.1109/WCSP.2011.6096958

Shinde, N. K., Seth, A., & Kadam, P. (2023). Exploring the synergies: a comprehensive survey of blockchain integration with artificial intelligence, machine learning, and IoT for diverse applications. *Machine Learning and Optimization for Engineering Design,* 85-119.

Silvestri, S., Islam, S., Amelin, D., Weiler, G., Papastergiou, S., & Ciampi, M. (2024). Cyber threat assessment and management for securing healthcare ecosystems using natural language processing. *International Journal of Information Security*, *23*(1), 31–50. DOI: 10.1007/s10207-023-00769-w

Sindiramutty, S. R. (2023). Autonomous threat hunting: A future paradigm for AI-driven threat intelligence. *arXiv preprint arXiv:2401.00286*. Habib, K., & Leister, W. (2015, July). Threats identification for the smart internet of things in ehealth and adaptive security countermeasures. In *2015 7th International Conference on New Technologies, Mobility and Security (NTMS)* (pp. 1-5). IEEE.

Sindiramutty, S. R., Tan, C. E., Lau, S. P., Thangaveloo, R., Gharib, A. H., Manchuri, A. R., & Muniandy, L. (2024). Explainable AI for cybersecurity. In *Advances in Explainable AI Applications for Smart Cities* (pp. 31–97). IGI Global Scientific Publishing. DOI: 10.4018/978-1-6684-6361-1.ch002

Singh, B., & Kaunert, C. (2025). Fortifying the Digital World and Shielding Smart Infrastructures: Artificial Intelligence (AI)-Enabled Malware and Threat. In *Utilizing AI in Network and Mobile Security for Threat Detection and Prevention* (pp. 1-22). IGI Global Scientific Publishing.

Singh, A., Chatterjee, K., & Satapathy, S. C. (2022). An edge based hybrid intrusion detection framework for mobile edge computing. *Complex & Intelligent Systems*, *8*(5), 3719–3746. DOI: 10.1007/s40747-021-00498-4

Siniosoglou, I., Sarigiannidis, P., Argyriou, V., Lagkas, T., Goudos, S. K., & Poveda, M. (2021, June). Federated intrusion detection in NG-IoT healthcare systems: An adversarial approach. In ICC 2021-IEEE International Conference on Communications (pp. 1-6). IEEE.

Sisinni, E., Saifullah, A., Han, S., Jennehag, U., & Gidlund, M. (2018). Industrial Internet of Things: Challenges, opportunities, and directions. *IEEE Transactions on Industrial Informatics*, *14*(11), 4724–4734. DOI: 10.1109/TII.2018.2852491

Sodhro, A. H., Sangaiah, A. K., Sodhro, G. H., Lohano, S., & Pirbhulal, S. (2018). An energy-efficient algorithm for wearable electrocardiogram signal processing in ubiquitous healthcare applications. *Sensors (Basel), 18*(3), 923. DOI: 10.3390/s18030923 PMID: 29558433

Somasundaram, R., & Thirugnanam, M. (2021). Review of security challenges in healthcare internet of things. *Wireless Networks, 27*(8), 5503–5509. DOI: 10.1007/s11276-020-02340-0

Song, Z., Hackl, C. M., Anand, A., Thommessen, A., Petzschmann, J., Kamel, O., Braunbehrens, R., Kaifel, A., Roos, C., & Hauptmann, S. (2023). Digital twins for the future power system: An overview and a future perspective. *Sustainability (Basel), 15*(6), 5259. DOI: 10.3390/su15065259

Soundariya, A., Behera, N. K., Chandel, P. S., Gupta, S., & Manjunath, T. C. (2025). AI and Environmental Ethics: The Role of AI in Addressing Climate Change Ethical Considerations in AI-Driven Environmental Solutions. In Chakraborty, S. (Ed.), *Human Values, Ethics, and Dignity in the Age of Artificial Intelligence* (pp. 321–346). IGI Global Scientific Publishing. DOI: 10.4018/979-8-3693-9035-1.ch013

Sreekanthaswamy, N., Anitha, S., Singh, A., Jayadeva, S. M., Gupta, S., & Manjunath, T. C. (2025). Digital Tools and Methods. In Çela, E., Paliktzoglou, V., Sengar, S., Eappen, P., & Vajjhala, N. (Eds.), *Enhancing School Counseling With Technology and Case Studies* (pp. 25–48). IGI Global Scientific Publishing. DOI: 10.4018/979-8-3693-8392-6.ch002

Srinivasan, M., & Senthilkumar, N. (2025). Intrusion Detection and Prevention System (IDPS) model for IIoT Environments Using Hybridized Framework. *IEEE Access : Practical Innovations, Open Solutions, 13*, 26608–26621. DOI: 10.1109/ACCESS.2025.3538461

Srivastava, G., Jhaveri, R. H., Bhattacharya, S., Pandya, S., Maddikunta, P. K. R., Yenduri, G., . . . Gadekallu, T. R. (2022). XAI for cybersecurity: state of the art, challenges, open issues and future directions. *arXiv preprint arXiv:2206.03585.*

Stark, R., Fresemann, C., & Lindow, K. (2021). Development and operation of digital twins for technical systems and services. *CIRP Annals, 68*(1), 129–132. DOI: 10.1016/j.cirp.2019.04.024

Stouffer, K., Falco, J., & Scarfone, K. (2011). Guide to industrial control systems (ICS) security. *NIST special publication, 800*(82), 16-16.

Stouffer, K., Pillitteri, V., Lightman, S., Abrams, M., & Hahn, A. (2015). Guide to industrial control systems (ICS) security (NIST Special Publication 800-82, Revision 2). National Institute of Standards and Technology. DOI: 10.6028/NIST.SP.800-82r2

Subasi, A., Algebsani, S., Alghamdi, W., Kremic, E., Almaasrani, J., & Abdulaziz, N. (2021, April). Intrusion detection in smart healthcare using bagging ensemble classifier. In *International Conference on Medical and Biological Engineering* (pp. 164-171). Cham: Springer International Publishing. DOI: 10.1007/978-3-030-73909-6_18

Sundaramurthy, S. K., Ravichandran, N., Inaganti, A. C., & Muppalaneni, R. (2022). The future of enterprise automation: Integrating AI in cybersecurity, cloud operations, and workforce analytics. *Artificial Intelligence and Machine Learning Review*, *3*(2), 1–15.

Sun, Y., Lo, F. P.-W., & Lo, B. (2019). Security and privacy for the internet of medical things enabled healthcare systems: A survey. *IEEE Access : Practical Innovations, Open Solutions*, *7*, 183339–183355. DOI: 10.1109/ACCESS.2019.2960617

Surianarayanan, C., Lawrence, J. J., Chelliah, P. R., Prakash, E., & Hewage, C. (2023). A survey on optimization techniques for edge artificial intelligence (AI). *Sensors (Basel)*, *23*(3), 1279. DOI: 10.3390/s23031279

Sutton, R. S., & Barto, A. G. (2018). *Reinforcement learning: An introduction* (2nd ed.). MIT Press., https://web.stanford.edu/class/psych209/Readings/SuttonBartoIPRLBook2ndEd.pdf

Sztipanovits, J., Ying, S., & Cohen, I. (2012). Cyber-physical systems: A model-based approach. *2012 IEEE/ACM Third International Conference on Cyber-Physical Systems*, 1–2. DOI: 10.1109/ICCPS.2012.35

Tan, K. Y., Tan, S. C., & Chuah, T. C. (2025). A Multi-Phase DRL-Driven SDN Migration Framework Addressing Budget, Legacy Service Compatibility, and Dynamic Traffic. *IEEE Access : Practical Innovations, Open Solutions*.

Tao, F., Qi, Q., Liu, A., & Kusiak, A. (2018). Data-driven smart manufacturing. *Journal of Manufacturing Systems*, *48*(Part C), 157–169. DOI: 10.1016/j.jmsy.2018.01.006

Tao, F., Zhang, M., Liu, Y., & Nee, A. Y. C. (2018). Digital twin in industry: State-of-the-art. *IEEE Transactions on Industrial Informatics*, *15*(4), 2405–2415. DOI: 10.1109/TII.2018.2873186

Tariq, S., Baruwal Chhetri, M., Nepal, S., & Paris, C. (2025). Alert fatigue in security operations centres: Research challenges and opportunities. *ACM Computing Surveys*, *57*(9), 1–38. DOI: 10.1145/3723158

Ten, C. W., Manimaran, G., & Liu, C. C. (2010). Cybersecurity for critical infrastructures: Attack and defense modeling. *IEEE Transactions on Systems, Man, and Cybernetics. Part A, Systems and Humans*, *40*(4), 853–865. DOI: 10.1109/TSMCA.2010.2048028

Thamilarasu, G., Odesile, A., & Hoang, A. (2020). An intrusion detection system for internet of medical things. *IEEE Access : Practical Innovations, Open Solutions*, *8*, 181560–181576. DOI: 10.1109/ACCESS.2020.3026260

Tiwari, D., Bhatele, K. R., Jha, A., & Chaudhary, K. (2025). Electrical digital twins–enabled smart grid. In *Digital Twins for Smart Cities and Villages* (pp. 489–512). Elsevier. DOI: 10.1016/B978-0-443-28884-5.00021-X

Tiwari, S., Sresth, V., & Srivastava, A. (2020). The Role of Explainable AI in Cybersecurity: Addressing Transparency Challenges in Autonomous Defense Systems. *International Journal of Innovative Research in Science, Engineering and Technology*, *9*(3), 718–733. DOI: 10.15680/IJIRSET.2020.0903165

Tripathi, A., Upadhyay, P., & Goel, P. K. (2025b). Industrial Control Systems (ICS) Security: AI-Based Threat Detection and Prevention. In *AI-Enhanced Cybersecurity for Industrial Automation* (pp. 149-172). IGI Global Scientific Publishing.

Tripathi, A., Yadav, V., & Kumar, S. (2025e). Leveraging Artificial Intelligence for Rural Education: A Systematic Review of Transforming Learning Opportunities and Bridging the Urban-Rural Divide.

Tripathi, A., Upadhyay, P., & Goel, P. K. (2025d). Geospatial Data Analysis for Mapping Carbon Sequestration Hotspots. In *Advanced Systems for Monitoring Carbon Sequestration* (pp. 193–218). IGI Global Scientific Publishing. DOI: 10.4018/979-8-3373-2091-5.ch009

Tschider, C. A. (2018). Regulating the internet of things: Discrimination, privacy, and cybersecurity in the artificial intelligence age. *Denv. L. Rev.*, *96*, 87.

Tsiknas, K., Taketzis, D., Demertzis, K., & Skianis, C. (2021). Cyber threats to industrial IoT: A survey on attacks and countermeasures. *IoT*, *2*(1), 163–186. DOI: 10.3390/iot2010009

Tuor, A., Kaplan, S., Hutchinson, B., Nichols, N., & Robinson, S. (2017, February). Deep Learning for Unsupervised Insider Threat Detection in Structured Cybersecurity Data Streams. In *AAAI Workshops* (pp. 224-231).

Tyagi, P., & Bargavi, S. M. (2023). Using federated artificial intelligence system of intrusion detection for IOT healthcare system based on Blockchain. *International Journal of Data Informatics and Intelligent Computing*, *2*(1), 1–10. DOI: 10.59461/ijdiic.v2i1.42

Uddin, M., & Syed-Abdul, S. (2020). Data analytics and applications of the wearable sensors in healthcare: An overview. *Sensors (Basel)*, *20*(5), 1379. DOI: 10.3390/s20051379 PMID: 32138291

Uhlemann, T. H. J., Lehmann, C., & Steinhilper, R. (2017). The digital twin: Realizing the cyber-physical production system for Industry 4.0. *Procedia CIRP*, *61*, 335–340. DOI: 10.1016/j.procir.2016.11.152

Upadhyay, P. (2025). Analyzing Soil Organic Carbon Storage. *Advanced Systems for Monitoring Carbon Sequestration*, 455.

Vajpayee, P., & Hossain, G. (2024, March). Reduction of Cyber Value at Risk (CVaR) Through AI Enabled Anomaly Detection. In *SoutheastCon 2024* (pp. 623–629). IEEE. DOI: 10.1109/SoutheastCon52093.2024.10500040

Varshney, N., Madan, P., Shrivastava, A., & Srivastava, A. P., KUMAR, C. P., & Khan, K. (2023, December). Real-time anomaly detection in IoT healthcare devices with LSTM. In *2023 International Conference on Artificial Intelligence for Innovations in Healthcare Industries (ICAIIHI)* (Vol. 1, pp. 1-6). IEEE. DOI: 10.1109/ICAIIHI57871.2023.10489823

Verma, P., Newe, T., O'Mahony, G. D., Brennan, D., & O'Shea, D. (2025). Towards a Unified Understanding of Cyber Resilience: A Comprehensive Review of Concepts, Strategies, and Future Directions. *IEEE Access : Practical Innovations, Open Solutions*. Advance online publication. DOI: 10.1109/ACCESS.2025.3551887

Vinayakumar, R., Alazab, M., Soman, K. P., Poornachandran, P., Al-Nemrat, A., & Venkatraman, S. (2019). Deep learning approach for intelligent intrusion detection system. *IEEE Access : Practical Innovations, Open Solutions*, *7*, 41525–41550. DOI: 10.1109/ACCESS.2019.2895334

Vogel-Heuser, B., Diedrich, C., Pantförder, D., & Göhner, P. (2015). Coupling heterogeneous production systems by a multi-agent based cyber-physical production system. *2015 IEEE International Conference on Industrial Informatics (INDIN)*, 713–719. DOI: 10.1109/INDIN.2015.7281837

Wahab, F., Zhao, Y., Javeed, D., Al-Adhaileh, M. H., Almaaytah, S. A., Khan, W., Saeed, M. S., & Kumar Shah, R. (2022). An AI-driven hybrid framework for intrusion detection in IoT-enabled E-health. *Computational Intelligence and Neuroscience*, *2022*, 2022. DOI: 10.1155/2022/6096289 PMID: 36045979

Wang, S., Qureshi, M. A., Miralles-Pechuan, L., Huynh-The, T., Gadekallu, T. R., & Liyanage, M. (2021). Applications of explainable AI for 6G: Technical aspects, use cases, and research challenges. *arXiv preprint arXiv:2112.04698.*

Wang, S., Wan, J., Li, D., & Zhang, C. (2016). Implementing smart factory of Industrie 4.0: An outlook. *International Journal of Distributed Sensor Networks*, *12*(1), 3159805. DOI: 10.1155/2016/3159805

Wang, Y., Nazir, S., & Shafiq, M. (2021). An overview on analyzing deep learning and transfer learning approaches for health monitoring. *Computational and Mathematical Methods in Medicine*, *2021*(1), 5552743. DOI: 10.1155/2021/5552743

Wan, J., Tang, S., Shu, Z., Li, D., Wang, S., Imran, M., & Vasilakos, A. V. (2019). Software-defined industrial internet of things in the context of Industry 4.0. *IEEE Sensors Journal*, *16*(20), 7373–7380.

Wazid, M., Das, A. K., Rodrigues, J. J., Shetty, S., & Park, Y. (2019). Iomt malware detection approaches: Analysis and research challenges. *IEEE Access : Practical Innovations, Open Solutions*, *7*, 182459–182476. DOI: 10.1109/ACCESS.2019.2960412

Wiboonrat, M. (2022, October). Cybersecurity in Industrial Control Systems: An integration of information technology and operational technology. In *IECON 2022–48th Annual Conference of the IEEE Industrial Electronics Society* (pp. 1-6). IEEE.

Willems, C., Bode, S., & Schürmann, B. (2015). Security in cyber-physical systems: Challenges and solutions. *2015 IEEE International Conference on Industrial Informatics (INDIN)*, 1–6. https://doi.org/DOI: 10.1109/INDIN.2015.7281744

Wolf, W. (2009). Cyber-physical systems. *Computer*, *42*(3), 88–89. DOI: 10.1109/MC.2009.81

Wu, P., & Mei, X. (2024). Microgrids energy management considering net-zero energy concept: The role of renewable energy landscaping design and IoT modeling in digital twin realistic simulator. *Sustainable Energy Technologies and Assessments*, *63*, 103621. DOI: 10.1016/j.seta.2024.103621

Xue, C., Lin, L., Huang, Y., & Wang, X. (2024). Graph neural network-based anomaly detection for human cyber physical systems. *Zhongguo Gongcheng Xuekan*, *47*(8), 977–984. DOI: 10.1080/02533839.2024.2407294

Xu, L. D., He, W., & Li, S. (2014). Internet of Things in industries: A survey. *IEEE Transactions on Industrial Informatics*, *10*(4), 2233–2243. DOI: 10.1109/TII.2014.2300753

Yan, W., & Yu, L. (2015). On accurate and reliable anomaly detection for industrial control systems. *2015 IEEE International Conference on Systems, Man, and Cybernetics (SMC)*, 138–143. https://doi.org/DOI: 10.1109/SMC.2015.37

Yao, K., & Zheng, Y. (2023). Fundamentals of machine learning. In *Nanophotonics and machine learning: Concepts, fundamentals, and applications* (pp. 77–112). Springer International Publishing. DOI: 10.1007/978-3-031-20473-9_3

Yaqoob, T., Abbas, H., & Atiquzzaman, M. (2019). Security vulnerabilities, attacks, countermeasures, and regulations of networked medical devices—A review. *IEEE Communications Surveys and Tutorials*, *21*(4), 3723–3768. DOI: 10.1109/COMST.2019.2914094

Yayla, A., Haghnegahdar, L., & Dincelli, E. (2022). Explainable artificial intelligence for smart grid intrusion detection systems. *IT Professional*, *24*(5), 18–24. DOI: 10.1109/MITP.2022.3163731

Yousef Alshunaifi, S., Mishra, S., & Alshehri, M. (2022). Cyber-Attack Detection and Mitigation Using SVM for 5G Network. *Intelligent Automation & Soft Computing*, *31*(1), 13–28. DOI: 10.32604/iasc.2022.019121

Yu, J., Shvetsov, A. V., & Alsamhi, S. H. (2024). Leveraging machine learning for cybersecurity resilience in industry 4.0: Challenges and future directions. *IEEE Access : Practical Innovations, Open Solutions*, *12*, 159579–159596. DOI: 10.1109/ACCESS.2024.3482987

Zachos, G., Essop, I., Mantas, G., Porfyrakis, K., Ribeiro, J. C., & Rodriguez, J. (2021). An anomaly-based intrusion detection system for internet of medical things networks. *Electronics (Basel)*, *10*(21), 2562. DOI: 10.3390/electronics10212562

Zhang, Z., Al Hamadi, H., Damiani, E., Yeun, C. Y., & Taher, F. (2022). Explainable artificial intelligence applications in cyber security: State-of-the-art in research. *IEEE Access : Practical Innovations, Open Solutions*, *10*, 93104–93139. DOI: 10.1109/ACCESS.2022.3204051

Zhang, Z., Kumar, V., Pfahringer, B., & Bifet, A. (2025). Ai-enabled automated common vulnerability scoring from common vulnerabilities and exposures descriptions. *International Journal of Information Security*, *24*(1), 1–20. DOI: 10.1007/s10207-024-00922-z

Zhou, Z. H. (2021). *Machine learning*. Springer nature.

Zubair, M., Ghubaish, A., Unal, D., Al-Ali, A., Reimann, T., Alinier, G., Hammoudeh, M., & Qadir, J. (2022). Secure Bluetooth Communication in Smart Healthcare Systems: A Novel Community Dataset and Intrusion Detection System. *Sensors (Basel)*, *22*(21), 8280. DOI: 10.3390/s22218280 PMID: 36365978

About the Contributors

Chin-Shiuh Shieh is a distinguished academic and researcher in the field of electronic engineering and computer science, currently serving as a Professor in the Department of Electronic Engineering at National Kaohsiung University of Science and Technology (NKUST), Taiwan. He received his Ph.D. in Computer Science and Engineering from the National Sun Yat-sen University, Taiwan, and has since dedicated his career to pioneering research and teaching in areas including computer networking, wireless communication, information security, computational intelligence, embedded systems, and medical informatics. With a career spanning several decades, Professor Shieh has made significant contributions to both academia and industry. In the past five years alone, he has authored or co-authored 28 journal papers, of which 24 are indexed in SCI (Science Citation Index), and 80 conference papers, encompassing 26 international and 54 domestic conferences. His editorial acumen is evident in his role as editor for two international academic conference proceedings. Professor Shieh has been actively engaged in various research initiatives, participating in 10 Ministry of Science and Technology (MOST) projects, leading five of them. He has also been involved in three Ministry of Education projects, one of which he led, and a campus research project. Furthermore, his strong industry collaboration is reflected in 10 industry-academia cooperation projects, eight of which he led. He has also contributed to one technology transfer authorization. As a recognized figure in the global research community, Professor Shieh is affiliated with four professional societies, and serves as a reviewer for 106 academic journals. He has participated as a committee member for 21 journals and 175 international conferences, underscoring his influence and expertise in his fields of specialization. Among his recent notable publications is the 2024 SCI-indexed paper titled "Open-set recognition in unknown DDoS attacks detection with reciprocal points learning" published in IEEE Access, which highlights his innovative work in cybersecurity and artificial intelligence. He has also played key editorial roles in conferences such as the International Conference on Genetic and Evolutionary Computing (ICGEC) and Intelligent Information Hiding and Multimedia Signal Processing (IIHMSP). His work has earned multiple accolades including Best Paper Awards and Excellent Paper Awards in international conferences. He has co-developed cutting-edge methods in machine learning, optimization algorithms, and adversarial defense mechanisms, particularly in the domain of cybersecurity threats such as DDoS attacks. His academic journey, prolific publication record, leadership in research projects, and commitment to interdisciplinary collaboration have established him as a leading voice in advancing electronic engineering and computing sciences in Taiwan and beyond.

Pawan Kumar Goel is a seasoned academician, researcher, and institutional leader with over two decades of rich experience in the field of Computer Science and Engineering. Presently serving as an Associate Professor in the Department of Computer Science & Engineering at Raj Kumar Goel Institute of Technology, Ghaziabad (affiliated to Dr. A.P.J. Abdul Kalam Technical University, Lucknow), Dr. Goel has made significant contributions to teaching, research, innovation, and academic administration. His academic journey is marked by a relentless pursuit of excellence, supported by strong educational credentials that include a Ph.D. in Computer Science Engineering, M.Tech in Computer Science & Engineering, and an MBA in Human Resource Management. He is also UGC-NET qualified in Computer Science and Applications and has cleared GATE multiple times. He earned his B.Tech in Information Technology with distinction. His impressive academic qualifications are complemented by numerous certifications from premier institutes in cutting-edge fields like AI, Blockchain, Cloud Computing, Cybersecurity, Quantum Computing, and more. Over his professional career, Dr. Goel has held several key academic and administrative positions. Throughout his journey, he has consistently demonstrated leadership in institutional development, curriculum innovation, accreditation processes (NAAC and NBA), and faculty mentoring. Dr. Goel is a prolific writer and editor, having authored and edited numerous books with globally reputed academic publishers such as IGI Global, Bentham Science, and Scientific International Publishing House. Some of his notable titles include Strategies for E-Commerce Data Security, Cloud Computing and IoT Strategies for Industry 5.0 Innovation, and Improving Security, Privacy, and Trust in Cloud Computing. He has authored over 50 book chapters in diverse areas such as AI for mental health, blockchain for social media, AI-based security for communication networks, and ethical considerations in cybersecurity and artificial emotional intelligence. His scholarly work is widely published in Scopus and UGC-indexed journals, and he has presented at leading IEEE international conferences such as IC3SE, ICDT, ICCSP, and AECE. Dr. Goel's research interests are interdisciplinary, encompassing cloud and edge computing, AI and machine learning, cybersecurity,

IoT, wireless sensor networks, and blockchain technology. He has also filed several patents, including designs and systems for smart agricultural drones, IoT health monitoring devices, and blockchain-integrated IoT data management systems. His technological innovations reflect his commitment to solving real-world problems through applied research. Dr. Goel has received multiple awards and accolades for his academic and professional excellence. He was honored with the International Achiever Award 2023 for Distinguished Teaching by Gyan Uday Foundation and the Educator of the Year Award 2022 by Namaste India Council of Educators. He has also been recognized for his role in quality assurance and curriculum development by institutions like Quantum University and IIMT Greater Noida. In addition, he has received appreciation for his contributions as a reviewer and advisor at various international conferences and journals. An active contributor to professional and academic communities, Dr. Goel holds memberships in a wide range of reputed organizations including IEEE, ACM, CSI, IAENG, IACSIT, IFERP, CSTA, and SCIEI. He serves as an editorial and review board member for several international journals such as IJRAR, IJCSIS, JITE, and IJSCE. He is also the Institutional Ambassador for IFERP and serves as the Single Point of Contact (SPOC) for Infosys Campus Connect Program, further strengthening academia-industry collaboration. As a committed educator and academic facilitator, Dr. Goel has organized and coordinated several faculty development programs (FDPs), seminars, and workshops. He has played key roles in AICTE-sponsored FDPs, including being the Co-Coordinator of the ATAL FDP on Quantum Machine Learning in January 2025. He also serves as the Local Coordinator for the Remote Center of NITTTR Chandigarh, enabling the conduction of numerous FDPs and STCs through ICT mode. His organizational acumen and passion for innovation have enabled the successful execution of national-level events and knowledge dissemination platforms. Dr. Goel continues to actively participate in continuous learning and professional development, having completed numerous AICTE-ATAL FDPs in areas such as Cybersecurity in AI, Deep Learning, Quantum Computing, and Ethical AI. He has also successfully completed various NPTEL MOOCs on subjects including Blockchain Architecture, Data Science, Privacy and Security in Online Social Media, and NBA Accreditation processes. An enthusiastic academic with a strong foundation in pedagogy and research, Dr. Goel teaches core computer science courses such as Programming in C, Data Structures, Computer Networks, Database Management Systems, Cloud Computing, and Cybersecurity. His teaching philosophy emphasizes conceptual clarity, problem-solving, and the integration of emerging technologies into the curriculum. Dr. Goel's personal qualities—leadership, optimism, perseverance, and hard work—have earned him admiration among his peers and students alike. His multifaceted contributions to academia, research, and innovation position him as a thought leader and change-maker in the Indian higher education landscape. He continues to inspire generations of learners and researchers, contributing significantly to the digital and technological transformation of the education ecosystem.

Mong-Fong Horng received his B.S., Ms. and Ph.D degrees from National Chiao Tung University and National Cheng Kung University, Taiwan in 1989, 1991 and 2003, respectively. He now is a jointly-appointed professor with the department of Electronics Engineering at National Kaohsiung University of Science and Technology, and Kaohsiung Medical University, Taiwan. He served as the president of Taiwanese Association of Consumer Electronics (TACE), Chair of Tainan Chapter, IEEE Signal Processing Society. His research interest includes Internet of Things, machine learning, computer networks and medical informatics and related industrial cooperation.

***

Shibsankar Bala has been working as an Assistant Professor in Asansol Engineering College, Asansol, West Bengal, India. He has 22 years of experience in teaching. He received M.Tech in Computer Science from Birla Institute of Technology (BIT), Mesra, Ranchi Jharkhand, India in the year 2002 and is currently pursuing PhD in Engineering. He has published 09 research papers in Conference and reputed Journals. He has research interest in Elastic Optical Networks and Optimization Techniques. Orcid ID:0000-0002-1978-9182

Sujoy Kumar Basu has been working as an Assistant Professor in Asansol Engineering College, Asansol, West Bengal, India. He has 20 years of experience in teaching. He received M.E in Software Engineering from Jadavpur University, West Bengal, India in the year 2009 and is currently pursuing PhD in Engineering. He has published 03 research papers in Conference and reputed Journals. Till date, he has 7 patents against his name. He has research interest in Internet of Things.

Rajesh G is a passionate educator and researcher with over 20 years of experience in higher education, academic administration, and research. He is currently serving as a faculty member in the Department of Electronics and Communication Engineering at New Horizon College of Engineering, Bengaluru. He holds a B.Tech in Electronics and Instrumentation Engineering, an M.E in Applied Electronics, and a Ph.D. in ECE with a focus on Medical Image Analysis. A UGC-qualified lecturer and VTU-recognized research supervisor, he has mentored several postgraduate and doctoral scholars. His research spans image processing, biomedical RF systems, embedded systems, IoT, WSN, VLSI design, and machine learning. He has published widely in peer-reviewed journals, presented at international conferences, and holds multiple patents. Dr. Rajesh has held leadership roles including HOD, Exam Section In-Charge, and BoS/BoE committee member. He has also served as an ExeCom member of IEEE Bangalore Section and IEEE Sensors Council Chapter. As an Innovation Ambassador under MoE, he contributes to fostering innovation and entrepreneurship. Committed to bridging academic knowledge with real-world applications, he is actively involved in technical program coordination, quality assurance, and continuous professional development.

Md. Iqbal is a distinguished academician and researcher currently serving as a Professor in the Department of Computer Science & Engineering at Quantum University, Roorkee, Uttarakhand. With a robust academic background and extensive experience in both teaching and research, Dr. Iqbal has made significant contributions to the fields of Data Mining, Machine Learning, and Blockchain Technology.

Soumen Prakash Kabi has been working as an Assistant Professor in Asansol Engineering College, Asansol, West Bengal, India. He has 19 years of experience in teaching. He received MCA from NIT, Durgapur West Bengal, India in the year 2006. He has published 02 research papers in Conference and reputed Journals. Till date, he has 6 patents against his name. He has research interest in Machine Learning.

Ashwani Kumar received the B.Tech degree in Computer Sciences & Engineering from Uttar Pradesh Technical University (U.P.T.U) Lucknow U.P India in 2009. He has done his M.Tech & Ph.d degree from Jaypee University of Information Technology, Solan H.P India in 2011 and 2017 respectively. He is a Life time member of Indian Society for Technical Education (ISTE) the leading National Professional non-profit making Society for the Technical Education System in India. He has published more than 10 scientific papers and books in the field of image security and watermarking technique. He is currently an Associate Professor at Vardhaman College of Engineering, Hyderabad Telangana, India. His research interests cover the Image Security, Watermarking Technique Multimedia Application, Network Security & Cryptography.

Pravin Kumar is an experienced academic with over a decade of teaching Marketing Management and related subjects at reputed institutions across India. He currently serves as Assistant Professor at Brainware University, Kolkata, and has previously taught at different Management Institutions. He holds a Ph.D. in Management from T.M. Bhagalpur University, focusing on visual merchandising on consumer behavior in branded apparel. He also holds an MBA in Marketing and an M.A. in English, reflecting his interdisciplinary background. Dr. Kumar has published widely in Scopus, UGC-CARE, and peer-reviewed journals on topics including consumer behavior, brand personality, and AI in sales. He has presented at numerous national and international seminars and FDPs on subjects like cross-cultural marketing and leadership. His industry experience in the automobile and pharmaceutical sectors adds practical value to his teaching. Known for his engaging teaching style and commitment to Universal Design for Learning.

T.C. Manjunath was born on 6th February 1967. He did his B.E. from RV College of Engg. in 1989 (B'lore Univ), M.E. in Robotics & Automation from Govt.'s LD College of Engg., (Gujarat Univ., Ahmedabad) in 1992 with FCD-First Rank & PhD in Systems & Control Engg. from IIT Bombay in the year 2007, got best research scholar award for the entire IITB. He is currently working as the Dean Research (R & D) and as Professor in Dept. of Computer Science & Engg. with specialization in IoT, Cyber Security, Blockchain Technology in Rajarajeswari College of Engineering, Bengaluru, Karnataka. He has got a teaching (academic), research & administrative experience of more than 35+ years (10 years as Principal & 8 years as HoD, 1 year as Dean Research & rest as faculty) and has published more than 1500+ research papers in various national & international journals & conferences, with 175+ patents, 100+ book-chapters, 25 awards, 100s of Keynote talks and also published 25 text books in various field of science, engineering & technology, completed projects worth Rs. 9 Crores till date & guided 10 PhD scholars in VTU. He is a member of 30 Professional Society Chapters and is a fellow of IE, IETE, AMIEE, Sr. Member of IEEE and a chartered engineer.

Rampelli Manojkumar received his Ph.D. in Power Engineering from the Indian Institute of Technology Guwahati in 2023. He obtained his Master of Technology in Power and Energy Systems from the National Institute of Technology Karnataka, Surathkal, India, in 2015. He is currently an Assistant Professor in the Department of Electrical and Electronics Engineering at BVRIT Hyderabad College of Engineering for Women. He is currently the Early Career Editor for the International Journal of Ambient Energy and the Guest Editor for PLOS ONE. He has been a speaker at the IEEE Smart Grid webinar series and has contributed to multiple funded research projects on smart transformer-based microgrid systems and distributed generation management. He has published 9 SCI journal papers, including articles in IEEE Transactions on Power Systems, IEEE Transactions on Industrial Informatics, and Sustainable Cities and Society. His research expertise spans energy management, hybrid AC/DC distribution systems, energy storage, and power electronics applications in modern distribution systems. Additionally, he is an active reviewer for around 20 SCI journals, including IEEE Transactions on Industrial Informatics, IEEE Systems Journal, Journal of Energy Storage, Applied Energy, etc.

Raj Kumar Mishra is an Assistant Professor at the Institute of Management Sciences, University of Lucknow, with 14 years of teaching experience. He has also gained valuable experience working at prestigious institutions like PSIT Kanpur and BBD University. He has authored one book, holds one patent, and has published 21 research papers in esteemed national and international journals. With a Ph.D. in Management specializing in Marketing, his current research focuses on the influence of emerging technologies such as AI and Big Data on consumer behaviour and brand engagement. He also explores the effectiveness of personalized and healthcare marketing, as well as the role of ethical advertising in fostering consumer trust.

Keerthana N V is an Assistant Professor with 8 Years of experience in teaching and 1-year experience in research (IUCAA LIGO Data Centre, Pune). Her area of interest is Network Security, Blockchain Security, and Machine Learning Algorithms. She is pursuing PhD at Anna University in Security in Blockchain. She has a working experience in High-Performance Computing (HTCondor) in LIGO INDIA Project. She has written many research articles in Network Security and assisted Scientists in analyzing Datasets in HTCondor.

SelvakumarP. is currently an Associate Professor in the Department of Science and Humanities at Nehru Institute of Technology, Coimbatore, Tamil Nadu, India. Prior to joining Nehru Institute of Technology, he held positions as an Assistant Professor in the Department of Science and Humanities various engineering colleges in Coimbatore, Tamil Nadu, India, spanning from 2011 to 2023. Dr.P. Selvakumar's academic and research interests lie primarily in the field of phytochemistry. He has made significant contributions to his field, with an impressive record that includes 30 journal publications, 12 patents, and 20 conference papers. Additionally, he has organized 5 seminars and conferences, further demonstrating his commitment to academic and scientific exchange. Throughout his career, Dr. P.Selvakumar has been recognized for his dedication and excellence in teaching, having been honored with several awards, including the Best Teacher Awards. He holds a prominent position in the academic community, contributing actively to research.

AnandhiR J did her BE in Computer Science, M.Tech in Computer Science and Ph.D in Computer Science with a specialization in SpatialData Mining. She is associated with New Horizon college of Engineering, Bengaluru since 2018. She has a rich experience of 26 years in teaching and industry. A recognized PhD guide under VTU, she has numerous publications under her name and has attended many conferences, workshops and symposiums. She has been awarded for the best publication in the International conference held at Singapore. Under her guidance various project proposals have been approved by the Secretary,

Karnataka State Council for Science and Technology (KSCST) under the "Student Project Programme-38th, 39th and 40th Series". She has chaired many international conferences as resource person. She was the coordinator and member, of Board of Examination, VTU and External Examiner for Ph.D at VTU and Anna University.

Rimmy is an Assistant Professor in the Department of Computer Science and Engineering at Quantum University, Roorkee, Uttarakhand, India. With over 12 years of experience in academia and research, she holds a B.Tech and M.Tech in Computer Science and Engineering, specializing in machine learning and data science. Her research interests encompass machine learning, natural language processing, and cybersecurity, with numerous publications in peer-reviewed journals and presentations at international conferences. Ms. Rimmy is dedicated to mentoring students and advancing innovative solutions in computer science, contributing significantly to curriculum development and industry-academia collaboration at her institution.

Shalini S. N is a dedicated educator in the MBA Department at New Horizon College of Engineering and research scholar at Christ University Bangalore. Known for her energetic teaching style and commitment to student success, she actively engages in research, curriculum development, and mentoring, helping learners build strong managerial, analytical, and ethical decision-making skills.

Ajay Kumar Sharma is an Associate Professor in the Department of Sciences at Quantum University, Roorkee, India. He is also working as the Head of the Department (HOD) of Sciences at the university. Dr. Sharma has been actively involved in academic and administrative roles, including serving on the Proctorial Board and participating in university events such as the Sustainable Innovation for Energy and Sustainable Development (SIESD) conference.

Avinash Kumar Sharma currently working as Associate Professor, Department of Computer Science & Engineering, Sharda School of Computing Science & Engineering (SSCSE), Sharda University, Greater Noida. Dr. Avinash Kumar Sharma has completed Ph.D from Uttarakhand Technical University, Dehradun (A State Govt. University) in Cloud Computing. His research areas are Cloud Computing, Machine Learning, Smart Agriculture, Artificial Intelligence. He has more than 18 years of teaching experience. He has published about 30 research articles in national / international conferences, journals, and book chapters. Dr. Avinash Kumar Sharma edited 07 books with IGI Global. He has also published 05 patents including 01 design patent.

Ajeet Sharma holds a Ph.D. in Computer Science and Engineering and has over 10 years of academic experience in teaching and research. His expertise includes advanced computing technologies, cybersecurity, AIML,Data Engineering and emerging areas of computer science, with a strong focus on scholarly publications and academic mentoring.

Charanjit Singh has been working as an Assistant Professor in Asansol Engineering College, Asansol, West Bengal, India. He has 1 years of experience in teaching. He received MCA in Computer Applications from Asansol Engineering College, West Bengal, India in the year 2023.He has research interest in Cyber Security. Orcid ID:https:https://orcid.org/0009-0006-9302-167X

Prateek Srivastava is an accomplished academician and researcher currently serving as an Assistant Professor in the Department of Information Technology at the University Institute of Engineering and Technology, CSJM University, located in Kanpur, Uttar Pradesh, India. He is dedicated to advancing knowledge in the field of Information Technology and contributing to the academic development of students through innovative teaching and research-oriented learning. With a strong passion for education and technological advancement, Prateek Srivastava has been actively involved in teaching undergraduate and postgraduate students in various areas of Information Technology. His teaching approach emphasizes conceptual clarity, practical application, and the development of analytical and problem-solving skills among students. He continuously strives to integrate modern technological tools and contemporary industry practices into the classroom to enhance students' learning experiences. Throughout his academic career, he has shown a keen interest in emerging areas of Information Technology such as Artificial Intelligence, Machine Learning, Data Science, and Cloud Computing. His research interests focus on exploring innovative technological solutions to real-world problems and contributing to the rapidly evolving digital ecosystem. He has been involved in academic research activities, scholarly publications, and participation in conferences, workshops, and seminars related to his field. As a faculty member at the University Institute of Engineering and Technology, he actively contributes to curriculum development, student mentoring, and academic administration. He encourages students to engage in project-based learning, research activities, and technical competitions to enhance their practical understanding of Information Technology concepts.

GopikhaS. is an Assistant Professor in the Department of Information Technology at St. Joseph's College of Engineering, India. She holds B.E. and M.E. degrees in Computer Science and Engineering. Her research centres on artificial intelligence (AI), machine learning (ML), deep learning (DL), and natural language processing (NLP), with applications in medical image analysis.

Arunadevi Thirumalraj, did ME Computer Science Engineering in K.Ramakrishnan College of Technology, (KRCT), Tiruchirappalli. She is actively involved in the field of innovative teaching and Learning. She has publishing a good number of papers in indexed journals.

Himanshu Tyagi is currently an Assistant Professor in the Department of Computer Science & Engineering at Quantum University, Roorkee. With a strong academic and research background, Dr. Tyagi has been actively contributing to the field of Machine Learning,Computer Vision.

Prashant Upadhyay is an Assistant Professor at, the Department of CSE, School of Engineering and Technology, Sharda University Greater Noida, Uttar Pradesh, India. He is currently pursuing his postdoctoral research at National Kaohsiung University of Science and Technology. He received his doctorate of philosophy (PhD) in Computer Science and Engineering, from Gautam Buddha University, U.P. He received his M.Tech (CSE) from ABES Engineering College, U.P. He has done B.E. from Vindhya Institute of Technology and Science, M.P. He has more than 7 years of teaching and research experience. He published more than 45 research papers in internationally reputed journals indexed in Web of Science, SCOPUS & SCIE and top-rank conferences as author or co-author. His research findings are published in Archives of Computational Methods in Engineering Springer, Neural Computing and Application Springer, IGI Global USA, IEEE Xplore. He served as a TPC and reviewer in Various International Conferences. He is the Editor of Books: Enhancing Medical Imaging with Emerging Technologies, Future of AI in Medical Imaging, Digital Deception: Uncover the Dark Side of AI in Social Networking. He served as session chair in several international conferences- ICDT-2024, ICDETGT-2023, and ICDT-2023. He has authored a book for Wiley Publication- Introduction to Python, ISBN: 978-93-5746-219-8. He has published three Indian patents in the years 2022 and 23. His research area includes Computer Vision, NLP.

Index

A

B

C

D

E

F

H

T

W

www.ingramcontent.com/pod-product-compliance
Lightning Source LLC
LaVergne TN
LVHW060006031026
849161LV00025B/1491